# "The THREE MUSKETEERS of the ARMY AIR FORCES"

# "The THREE MUSKETEERS of the ARMY AIR FORCES"

## FROM HITLER'S FORTRESS EUROPA TO HIROSHIMA AND NAGASAKI

ROBERT O. HARDER

Naval Institute Press
Annapolis, Maryland

Naval Institute Press
291 Wood Road
Annapolis, MD 21402



First Naval Institute Press paperback edition published in 2022.
ISBN: 978-1-68247-835-6 (paperback)
ISBN: 978-1-61251-903-6 (eBook)

**The Library of Congress has cataloged the hardcover edition as follows:**
Harder, Robert O.
"The three musketeers of the Army Air Forces" : from Hitler's Fortress Europa to Hiroshima and Nagasaki / Robert O. Harder.
pages cm
Includes bibliographical references and index.
ISBN 978-1-61251-902-9 (alk. paper) — ISBN 978-1-61251-903-6 (ebook)
1. Hiroshima-shi (Japan)—History—Bombardment, 1945. 2. Nagasaki-shi (Japan)—History—Bombardment, 1945. 3. Tibbets, Paul W. (Paul Warfield), 1915–2007. 4. Ferebee, Thomas, 1918–2000. 5. Van Kirk, Theodore Jerome, 1921–2014. 6. Bomber pilots—United States—Biography. 7. Bombardiers—United States—Biography. 8. Flight navigators—United States—Biography. 9. United States. Army Air Forces—Officers—Biography. 10. World War, 1939-1945—Aerial operations, American. I. Title. II. Title: From Hitler's Fortress Europa to Hiroshima and Nagasaki.
D767.25.H6H338 2015
940.54'49730922—dc23

2015020274

♾ Print editions meet the requirements of ANSI/NISO z39.48-1992 (Permanence of Paper).
Printed in the United States of America.

30 29 28 27 26 25 24 23 22     9 8 7 6 5 4 3 2 1
First printing

For **Paul, Tom, Dutch,**
and their **families**

Two names kept popping up when talking with Paul Tibbets. . . .
I remarked that they must have been good friends of his.

"Friends?" said Tibbets. "We were the three musketeers.
Tom Ferebee, Dutch Van Kirk, and I were the Three Musketeers."

—from D. M. Giangreco's foreword to
*My True Course*, Suzanne Simon Dietz's
biography of Theodore "Dutch" Van Kirk

# Contents

# Preface

This book probably had its genesis on a Sunday evening in May 1968 at McCoy Air Force Base, Orlando, Florida. A newly rated first lieutenant B-52D navigator-bombardier had just arrived at his first operational duty station, filled with all the eagerness and trepidation one might expect on such an occasion. After checking into the BOQ (Bachelor Officer Quarters) and preparing to report to his new squadron commander the next morning, he walked the two blocks to the Officer's Club for dinner, followed by a much-anticipated stop at the bar.

"What'll you have, lieutenant?" the bartender asked, almost certainly a moonlighting noncommissioned officer. The club room was dark and appeared half-closed; the young man assumed he was the only customer that quiet Sunday evening.

"Scotch and water—and make it a stiff one!"

The drink came quickly. The junior officer had no more than gotten the glass up to his lips when from the other end of the bar a glass slammed down hard on the counter.

"Hit me one more time!" came a booming, authoritative voice hidden behind the large draft beer taps. Before the young man knew it, the fellow had moved to the stool next to him.

"Hi ya, lieutenant," the older man said not unkindly, ostentatiously checking out the junior officer's slick navigator wings. The young man's eyebrows shot up when he saw the eagles on the fellow's blue uniform coat.

"Tanker or bomber nav?" the colonel asked.

"Bomber, sir," the lieutenant said, his heart sinking. All he had wanted to do was down a drink or two and hit the sack. Instead, on his first night, he had to worry about saying something stupid to a high-ranking wing officer. Ye gods! He had never before even spoken *mano y mano* to a bird colonel.

After taking another look at the lieutenant's name tag, the colonel nodded knowledgeably. "You'll be on a newly formed crew. We need to get several additional combat crews qualified over the summer before the wing rotates back to Vietnam."

The young man voiced another respectful "yessir" while surreptitiously checking out the colonel's Master Navigator/Bombardier Wings and ribbon rows. The old boy had really been around.

"They're still cross-training you fellows, right? Gotta be a nav before bomb school?" The colonel knew the answer of course; the questions were only presented to keep the conversation alive.

The lieutenant nodded, preparing to blather on about how well he had been trained and how excited he was to become a part of America's vaunted Strategic Air Command when the colonel mercifully intervened.

"So tell me. What do you think of the Air Force so far?"

Without giving any consideration as to how odd such a question was, coming as it did from a senior wing officer he had just met, the silver bar lieutenant reflexively spit out an answer. "I have a Regular commission, sir," he said proudly. "I plan to make the service my career."

The colonel swirled the ice cubes in his drink before responding. "Well," he said carefully, "I hope it works out for you."

A clumsy pause in the conversation ensued; while the younger man desperately sought an escape route from the increasingly uncomfortable encounter, the colonel continued to shake the ice in his glass. At length, the latter gave into his thoughts, his thick North Carolina accent even more pronounced than earlier.

"Look lieutenant, a word to the wise. You'd best get out of this aircrew business as soon as you can. Transfer into a service or support organization and make your mark there. That is, if you have any idea of rising to serious rank in this man's Air Force."

"Sir?" the young officer said. He was puzzled, if not a little shocked by the remark. What could be better for a prosperous and lengthy career than being a rated flying officer? Why should he get into, say, personnel or supply or maintenance or whatever, when the cockpit was where all the action was? And why was this senior officer planting such ideas into the head of a lowly first lieutenant he had only just met?

"Well, maybe I've said too much," the colonel said, seemingly reading the young man's mind. "But the fact is I'm hanging it up soon and am done with all this Mother, God, and Country stuff." He suddenly spun on his stool and looked the junior officer directly in the eye.

"Look, kid. This is a pilot's Air Force. Only they get the good operational jobs, all the commands. The ugly truth is the career nonpilot-rated crewdogs—the navigators, bombardiers, electronic warfare officers—get diddley-squat." The colonel touched the lieutenant's arm, looking almost sorrowful. "I can tell you right now what's going to happen—unless a miracle occurs, you will never get out of SAC. After a few years seasoning as a navigator, they'll upgrade you to radar navigator/bombardier, where you will stay for at least another ten years and probably longer. If you are clever or lucky, you might find a way to unstrap the beast from your ass and finish with a command post job or a staff bomb/nav slot. For sure," he tapped the eagle on his left shoulder with a forefinger, "you can forget about wearing one of these."

With that, the colonel drained his glass and thunked it down on the bar in a gesture of finality. "If I were you, lieutenant, I'd just chuck the whole thing—get the hell out of the service at the first opportunity." He stood to depart, leaving the rookie navigator stunned in his wake.

The lieutenant had wanted desperately to ask him a host of questions: *I don't understand, sir. What about you? You're a navigator and a bombardier, just like me, and judging from the badges and salad on your chest, you've had a great career and made full colonel. It all worked for you, didn't it? How come I don't have the same chances?* The lieutenant wanted to ask him those things and much more but never got the opportunity. The colonel was already striding out the door, tossing a farewell finger wave at the bartender.

The young man took the balance of his liquor in one large gulp and signaled for another round. The sergeant came over with a refill. He had heard every word of the exchange.

"Lieutenant, you got any idea who that was?"

"No, I do not," this writer said that warm Florida evening nearly a half century ago. "And what's more, I don't think I want to know!"

The sergeant thought differently. He leaned into me, both elbows on the bar, his face strangely serious. "He's Col. Tom Ferebee, bombardier of the *Enola Gay* and the man who, on August 6, 1945, dropped the atomic bomb on Hiroshima."

Satisfied with the shocked look on my face, the sergeant dragged his bar rag through the scotch puddle I had just created and, without another word, disappeared into the back room. I stared at what was left of my drink for a full minute before finally pushing it away and departing for the BOQ. Sleep came hard that night.

Two and a half years later, as I strode into my squadron commander's office to resign my commission, I remembered that encounter with Colonel Ferebee. His prediction as to my situation had by that time matched my own conclusions, and I had decided to act on the result. Yet, for all of that, Ferebee had also infected me with a lifelong fascination with the Manhattan Project, the B-29 Superfortress, Hiroshima, and the men of the *Enola Gay*. During most of my working life, that interest was confined to reading books and magazine articles on the subject and attending War Bird airshows, occasionally collecting related memorabilia.

Circumstances began to change, however, after I retired from the business world. Thinking there was still time to indulge a lifelong ambition, I decided to write about a subject long neglected in military historiography—rated, nonpilot U.S. Air Force flying officers. From that determination came *Flying from the Black Hole: The B-52 Navigator-Bombardiers of Vietnam* (Naval Institute Press, 2009). While pondering a follow-up work to that book, I realized that little had been written about two of the most notable men in the nonpilot flying officer professions—Thomas Ferebee and Theodore "Dutch" Van Kirk, distinguished World War II combat veterans and deliverers of the first air-released atomic bomb. It further occurred to me that I might be among the last of a generation of navigator/bombardiers who could still write a technically competent history of Ferebee, an optical / Norden bomb aimer, and Van Kirk, an "old-fashioned" World War II lead navigator—both of whom had been trained in much the same way as I had been. Also, as a commercial pilot and certificated flight instructor with a multiengine rating (piston-propeller), I thought I could hold my own regarding representations of their leader and lifelong friend, Paul Tibbets. Along the way I was rewarded with many delightful surprises, including a new appreciation of how very close the three men were, the very real impact they had on the outcome of World War II, and the influence they and their 509th Composite Group had on the policies and procedures of the future Strategic Air Command.

It is important to stress what this book is *not* about. It is not a history of World War II strategic warfare, the U.S. Army Air Corps/Air Forces, the Manhattan Project, the Los Alamos laboratories, atomic weapons, or a treatise on the morality of nuclear warfare. For further reading on these topics, the books listed in the bibliography are a reasonable starting point. In this narrative, the focus is on the personal and professional lives of Tibbets, Ferebee, and Van Kirk—showing how in just a few short years they went from ordinary American young men to a consummate air warrior team entrusted with the first delivery of the most powerful weapon ever conceived by humankind.

While a number of books and magazine articles have appeared about Paul Tibbets's life (see bibliography), little had been published about the other two fellows and next to nothing about the three's relationship with one another until the spring of 2012, when historian and author Suzanne Simon Dietz, with Dutch Van Kirk, released his biography, entitled *My True Course* (see bibliography). This charming book has given us many new insights into Van Kirk's life and relationship with his two lifelong pals. (It also made Dutch the butt of some good-natured ribbing—he was the last man still alive from the two atomic bomber crews, and his friends accused him of waiting until everyone else was dead so he could have the final word.) I am very grateful to Sue Dietz for generously allowing me to quote liberally from her work.

Until the effort in front of you, however, and except for a handful of newspaper interviews, written history has been largely silent on the life of Thomas Ferebee—which is ironic, for in some ways he was the most interesting of the trio. Tom chose to be anonymous, studiously avoiding writing his own memoirs. A very private person and gifted baseball player once in the St. Louis Cardinal system, he told interviewers late in life, "I would much rather have won a World Series than been known for Hiroshima."

One might legitimately ask why the life stories of these three airmen are relevant to today's readers of aviation/military history. To begin with, few today know what fascinating and sometimes extremely dangerous experiences they shared. Their combat adventures alone could carry most World War II story lines. But there is much more to it than that; the three's narrative also has major historical implications. Tibbets, Ferebee, and Van Kirk literally opened American strategic warfare in 1942 Europe by leading the first daylight bombing raids against Hitler's *Festung Europa* and they literally closed it out three years later with the dropping of "Little Boy" on Hiroshima. Prepatory to and during Operation Torch, the invasion of North Africa, Tibbets and company were selected to fly extremely dangerous ferry flights carrying generals such as Mark Clark, Jimmy Doolittle, Carl Spaatz, and Dwight Eisenhower in their treasured B-17F, the *Red Gremlin*. In 1944 they created the 509th Composite Group, the world's first atomic bomber attack force (the term "nuclear" was not used until the hydrogen, or thermonuclear, bomb became a reality in 1953). Col. Paul Tibbets became the group's commander, with Ferebee serving as group bombardier and Van Kirk the group navigator.

I will also draw the reader's attention to any number of inaccuracies that have occurred in the many-score books, magazine articles, and newspaper stories published on this subject over the past seventy years. The great majority of those works were written by journalists or others not intimate with the details of piloting, navigation, and bombing, leading to mistakes and much that has either been left out or misunderstood. In the case of published personal stories by 509th aircrew members (of which there are several, see bibliography), occasional memory lapses, certain embellishments, and perhaps even a bit of rear-end covering has sometimes occurred. In all these cases, I have made every effort to root out the truth and set the record straight.

It further occurred to me that questions or a wish for a more detailed explanation on a certain point might arise in the reader's mind. I have tried to anticipate and respond to those silent queries either in the text or in the notes section.

Regarding the many published narratives of the *Enola Gay* (Hiroshima) and *Bockscar* (Nagasaki) flights themselves, I have discovered that all previous accounts contain at least some misrepresentations, errors, or omissions along with occasional comments stemming from overactive imaginations. In this book, I have taken special pains to render the most accurate reconstruction of those two sorties yet attempted.

And with that, let the story begin.

# 1

# TIBBETS

It was late afternoon Sunday, August 5, 1945, on Tinian Island in the Marianas, in the western Pacific Ocean. Scores of men, both military and civilian, were streaming into a small briefing hut and jockeying for a spot on one of the benches. In front, momentarily alone, sat a tight-faced colonel solemnly smoking his pipe.[1] For nearly a year Col. Paul Tibbets had enjoyed almost omnipotent powers commanding what was arguably the most important individual combat unit of World War II. Two decades later he would tell writer Joseph Marx, "I am certain no officer, particularly as junior in rank [as myself], ever had or will have such authority [again] vested in him."[2] Not only was he one of the most experienced bomber commanders in the U.S. Army Air Forces, having previously led forty-three combat missions in Europe and North Africa, he was also the nation's most highly qualified pilot of the B-29 Superfortress—the only American weapon system capable of dropping an atomic bomb.

While the colonel was highly respected by the men for his rock-like stability and inspiring leadership, woe be to anyone in the 509th Composite Group who failed in his duties. For Tibbets was also feared, capable of unleashing his fiery temper on both subordinates and superiors alike if he felt his perfectionist mission standards were being compromised. Indeed, early on, some thought him too demanding, too confident, perhaps even a little cocky, and felt he had a tendency to throw his weight around. By early August 1945, however, the final objective was in sight, and nearly all of that was now water under the bridge. No other American unit commander was more important to the nation's war effort—his name hung heavy even in the mind of President Harry Truman, then on board the heavy cruiser USS *Augusta* en route home from the Potsdam Conference. The most senior, gray-haired American generals and admirals from the Pentagon to Okinawa were under strict orders to support and supply him with virtually anything he asked.

Colonel Tibbets had not achieved such heights without personal cost. Many considered him a cold fish, perhaps even borderline heartless. It was not true, of course; those he did not intimately know usually misread his deep need for control as not caring about others. He had always cared; he simply was incapable of showing it. To betray deep feelings, to shed tears, to be tender, to understand the emotional needs of even wife and children, was simply beyond his ken. In his mind, emotional display was the equivalent of breaking discipline, which meant showing weakness, and that was something he absolutely could not do.

Oddly enough, that iron will did not mean he was a spit and polish soldier—far from it, almost to a fault. As a former aviation cadet without a college degree, an officer who had come up through the ranks the hard way and was still looked down upon by many who had walked the Hudson River's Long Gray Line, he could be unusually tolerant of a man's appearance, lack of formal education, or personal peccadilloes as long as the fellow was professional in his work and never let the group down. This characteristic often put him at odds with some West Pointers who were convinced that poor military bearing was incompatible with good operational results. They believed in the absolute necessity of formal protocols and tight discipline—especially when in unforgiving (combat) environments. Long afterward, the colonel must have grudgingly conceded to himself he might have profited by listening to some of that advice. He misjudged a few of his key aircrew, especially regarding being overly tolerant of certain character issues, and they did let him down. It is important to emphasize, however, that such mistakes were few, countable perhaps on one hand. The vast majority of the 1,800 men Tibbets commanded that August were top troops—well trained and highly professional—certainly one of the finest B-29 groups in the Army Air Forces.

While some thought the commander hard to work for and with, most believed he was fair and evenhanded to both officers and enlisted men alike. Many a lowly soldier unexpectedly found Tibbets handing him a pass or issuing a leave to travel home to visit an ill mother, marry the hometown girl, or even, when spontaneous opportunities presented themselves, an extra R&R (rest and recreation) night on the town. By showing loyalty to his men, he demanded (and almost always received) the same in return.

Personally courageous, Tibbets expected no less from every one of his combat crew and was absolutely unwilling to suffer fools or cowards. A natural loner, he appeared to deal easily with the hoary "loneliness of command" chestnut often attributed to leaders who must send men to their deaths. It was only in old age that he admitted under persistent questioning by writer/reporter Bob Greene that he had put on a brave front, that he indeed was very lonely during his combat commands but could not bring himself to share those feelings with others.[3] No matter what happened, he always kept his poise and determined persona—he was never seen to break character. He was one of those rare combat commanders whom his men thought of as invincible—over Europe and North Africa, his aircrew believed that if anybody could get them through the flak and fighters, put the bombs on the target, and get them back home, it was him. Not surprisingly, then, the airmen of the *Enola Gay* approached that August day in 1945 with complete certainty he would pull it off one more time.

Col. Paul Warfield Tibbets Jr. was just thirty years old. A solidly built, good-looking fellow of medium height and curly black hair, he had always carried himself with authority and confidence. Even as a youngster he had been in charge—he just assumed the role; "it never occurred to me *not* to be the leader."[4] He was the boy that organized the ball team, decided where the treehouse would be built, and outlined how the after-dark raid on the neighbor's apple orchard would be conducted. He also discovered early on that he was attractive to girls, though his life-long inability to share his emotions likely mitigated much of what a more openly warm man might have enjoyed.

Tibbets was born into a moderately well-to-do midwestern family at the beginning of what was already being called the Great or World War.[5] His Welsh-Irish father, Paul Sr., came from a long line of merchants, bankers, and physicians in the northern Illinois–Iowa border region. His mother, Enola Gay Haggard, was a prominent farmer's daughter from Glidden, Iowa, whose folks had emigrated from Holland.[6] The two had met when Paul Sr. traveled to Glidden on a sales trip for the Tibbets-Warfield family's wholesale grocery business. The couple married in 1913; their first child, Paul Jr., arrived on February 23, 1915 (a sister, Barbara, came along five years later).

The Tibbets family moved around a great deal, with Paul Jr. spending the bulk of his growing up years in Quincy, Davenport, and Des Moines, Iowa. Over the years, they prospered, enjoying the use of an automobile and most of the other modern conveniences that were rapidly transforming American life. In his autobiography, Paul Jr. tells with great fondness that exciting day when a new addition to the living room appeared: "A Zenith Superheterodyne radio with four dials for tuning." Unlike many, if not most, boys of that era, he had access to much of the better life—a multidialed cabinet radio was thought to be the province of the wealthy.

In 1923 the Tibbets family underwent a major, albeit self-inflicted, upheaval. Paul Sr. decided to visit his mother, who was then living in Miami, Florida. After departing by train from Des Moines in the midst of a fierce winter blizzard, he arrived two days later in warm, palm tree–filled Miami, then a sleepy southern city of some 40,000 souls. Thoroughly captivated by the climate, Paul Sr. impulsively (and uncharacteristically) moved his family to the Sunshine State—lock, stock, and barrel, as a saying of the day went. Fortunately the move agreed with everyone; although senior did join in the highly speculative Florida land boom, he was a conservative real estate investor and was not badly hurt when the bubble burst. Always a good businessman, he soon cofounded Tibbets & Smith, a wholesale candy confectioners.

That business flourished from the first—Paul Sr. would a few years later prove it was no fluke when he was forced to return to the upper Midwest and rescue the Tibbets-Warfield family grocery chain. After four years of unrelenting sacrifice and toil—he and Enola Gay took a small Chicago South Side apartment for the duration—he was able to restore the business to profitability, eventually selling the stores to the National Tea Company (one of the first of the grocery "chain" stores). With the family's fortune restored, Paul Sr. and Enola Gay eagerly returned to Miami, ready for new adventures, having sold the confectionery business in 1930 prior to the Chicago grocery store rescue.

For Paul Jr., the Florida years were a golden time. The Miami of the middle and late 1920s did not have the problems that plagued most of the larger cities of that day. With few paved roads and little crime, its character was more rural than urban. Even better for young Paul, he had few responsibilities and there was always enough money to indulge in such youthful pastimes as cowboy movies (silent pictures until "talkies" arrived in 1928), soda fountain treats at the local drugstore or five and dime, and playground fun with his many friends. Best of all, his father sold candy for a living!

This latter circumstance led to Paul Jr.'s first experience with airplanes.[7] It was January 1927—what was to become the most heralded year in aviation history—and the Curtiss Candy Company had decided to include Miami as one of the cities where they would introduce what became their fabulously successful new candy bar, the Baby Ruth (the gods had smiled—that summer baseball star player Babe Ruth set the long-standing home run record of sixty round-trippers). Curtiss Co. hired famed barnstormer pilot Doug Davis to drop courtesy Baby Ruth bars to the thousands attending Miami's Hialeah Horse Racing Track. Paul Sr. was the resident wholesaler for the candy company, and pilot Davis reported to and worked through him. As it happened, an almost twelve-year-old Paul Jr. was in the office when Davis mentioned he would need a "bombardier" to throw out the candy.

"I can do that," the boy blurted. Paul Sr. shook his head; he did not think that was a good idea. He had long remarked that airplanes were notoriously unreliable and often downright dangerous. Much later, Tibbets speculated that what actually may have been behind the reluctance was his father's own fear of fast-moving vehicles, particularly motorcycles and flying machines—both of which had frightened him terribly during his World War service.[8] Fortunately for young Paul, pilot Davis sensed how badly he wanted to go up and said, "He looks like a bright boy. He won't have any trouble."

The youngster never forgot a minute of that day's experience—helping to tie all the tiny parachutes on the bars; the thrilling takeoff in the open-cockpit Waco 9 airplane, his first airplane ride; the rushing air sweeping over the top of the fuselage, almost taking his breath away; the thrill of thousands below rushing for the Baby Ruth bars; and, after landing, the satisfaction of knowing he had performed his duties to complete satisfaction. Tibbets later wrote it was on this flight that he first had the idea of flying airplanes for a living.

Aviation was the last thing Paul and Enola Gay Tibbets had in mind for their only son. Since before Paul Jr. could remember, everyone in the family had assumed he would follow the Tibbets family professional tradition and become either a doctor or a dentist. At the time, the boy was agreeable to the idea. "On my grandfather's farm . . . I had been fascinated by . . . the birth of animals and the castration of pigs. The sight of blood gave me no squeamish moments."[9] Nevertheless, it could not have escaped the boy's notice that his father had already broken the doctor/dentist link by becoming a merchant and that doing something else with his own life could be an option.

But before medical school or anything else could happen, there was the matter of a secondary education. For Paul Jr., this was to mean a dramatic change in his life at the age of only thirteen. Paul Sr. had served as a U.S. Army captain in the 33rd Infantry Division during World War I and had always believed he had been better prepared for that and his subsequent business career because of having gone to Blees Military Academy in Mexico, Missouri.[10] The father determined his son should have the same advantages. Apparently this course of action was not discussed with the boy because it came as a thorough shock when he was informed he would be attending the Western Military Academy in North Alton, Illinois, near St. Louis.[11]

Not surprisingly, a regimented military school did not agree with the footloose and free lifestyle Junior had previously enjoyed. After just two weeks, he was homesick and distraught, certain he had been abandoned, as he later put it, to the life of a convict. Appeals to his father for a pardon fell on deaf ears—he must serve the full five-year sentence. Eventually young Tibbets settled down and came to terms with his fate, though it was never easy. Western Academy had patterned itself after the service academies, mostly West Point, using nearly the same U.S. Army cadet uniforms. Discipline was rigid in every aspect of cadet life, and the teenaged boys were expected to carry themselves as adults during work, study, physical training, and private time. In spite of his frustrations, Tibbets would later admit that the school had been very useful to him in coping with all the problems he faced during his long military and business careers.

In the fall of 1933, high school diploma in hand, he entered the University of Florida at Gainesville as a premed student.[12] After five years of rigid discipline at Western (he had immediately made Florida's varsity wrestling team), it was almost inevitable Paul Jr. would succumb to the easygoing atmosphere of a regular college campus, especially with regard to gratifying those pleasures of the flesh earlier denied.[13] Although the school was not then co-ed, the local girls were much attracted to highly eligible young college men, especially if the fellow was good-looking and driving a late-model two-door Chevrolet Roadster with a rag top. As if that was not enough, Tibbets joined Sigma Nu fraternity, which offered even more social opportunities. It may have been about this time that he got drunk on moonshine and became so ill he never again could tolerate the smell of strong liquor.[14] In any event, the Great Depression then raging throughout the land had little effect on the young man—at least not until that fateful day when Junior found himself on the verge of flunking out. Medical school was suddenly very far away.

Paul Sr. was livid when he learned of his son's low marks. He made it abundantly clear to the boy that he was old enough to be responsible for himself and to grasp the fundamentals of self-discipline, not just the enforced regimentation he had been subjected to at Western, and that if his scholastic standing did not improve immediately, funding for his college education would terminate.

To his credit, Tibbets understood just how terribly he had let his family down. He grimly determined to settle down and concentrate on his studies—finally grasping how essential personal responsibility was to success. His grades improved substantially during his second year at Gainesville, "mostly Bs with an occasional C," with chemistry and physics his favorite subjects. It had been yet one more watershed moment in his young life.

During this same traumatic period, Paul Jr. felt compelled to take additional flying lessons at the local Gainesville airport, picking up where he had left off the summer before at Miami's Opa Locka airport. It had been at the latter airfield in the summer of 1933 that Paul Warfield Tibbets Jr. had taken his first flying lesson. His instructor, future Eastern Air Lines captain Rusty Heard, had soloed him in a Taylor Cub after logging just six or seven hours of dual instruction ("eight hours to solo" was the mantra of that age). He had discovered not only that he loved flying but that perhaps he could even be good at it.

So the internal questioning intensified. Should he persevere with his medical studies, thereby upholding the family honor? Or follow what his heart and all his instincts were telling him—become an airplane pilot! It took another year of advanced medical study at the University of Cincinnati for the matter to resolve itself. A day came during a friendly card game with a number of doctors who had taken the young man under their wing. His mentor and family friend Dr. Alfred Harry Crum sensed he was wrestling with something. Crum told Tibbets, "I'm not so sure you want to become a doctor." Paul Jr. reluctantly agreed. The doctor asked why he did not act on it. "Frankly, I'm afraid of what my old man would say."[15] Dr. Crum did not hesitate, giving what Tibbets always regarded as some of the most salient advice he had ever received. "To hell with the old man. He's lived his own life and didn't ask you what he should do."[16]

When Tibbets finally worked up enough nerve to tell his folks that he wanted to be a pilot and not a doctor, his father did not attempt to hide his disappointment. His mother, however, understood and strongly supported his decision, a gesture that deeply moved Paul Jr. and stayed with him for the rest of his life.

With that, the die was cast. Now it became not *what* to do but *how* it could be accomplished. Anyone wishing to become an airplane pilot in 1936 faced more than training issues; there was still a strong feeling among the public that flying was a daredevil's business and that serious, responsible young men did not get involved. Indeed, for a time the situation looked hopeless for Paul Jr. There was no way his father, who was still angry about the boy dropping out of college, would underwrite the necessary funds for his son's pilot training. Paul Jr. realized he had but one hope—he wrote to the Army Air Corps.

Over the winter of 1936–37 the young man became increasingly impatient waiting to learn if his application, physical exam, and personal interviews had met the entrance standards and that he had been accepted. So great was Paul Jr.'s confidence in himself and his own abilities that he was oblivious to the fact that thousands of young applicants during that same cycle had already been rejected. Finally the good news came—he was ordered to report to Randolph Field at San Antonio, Texas, and enroll in Class 38-A (i.e., the first class to graduate in 1938). During his initial three months he would be a "dodo," roughly the equivalent of a West Point plebe.[17]

U.S. Army Air Corps pilot training was an extremely rigorous program in 1937; few were able to stay the course from first day to winning their wings. Often a little luck helped even the most promising candidate. A friend of Tibbets' father, a Navy blimp pilot named Roland Blair, counseled the young man prior to his departure for Randolph to "not let anybody down there know you've ever been in an airplane. Just listen to [the instructors]."[18] The Air Corps wanted their students to learn flying the Army way and would actually hold it against those fellows who insisted on flying the way they had previously been taught. Tibbets was always grateful for Blair's sound advice.

Perhaps a third to a half of the candidates in Class 38-A were West Point graduates and already second lieutenants. For them, the dodo phase was familiar territory; basic preflight training, close-order drill, eating at attention, white-glove inspections, and so on, was old hat. So it was also for Paul Tibbets; after five years at Western Academy, he knew the score and also flourished.

Flight training itself started off in the open-cockpit Consolidated PT-3 (primary trainer #3), what was even then considered an ancient aircraft. First produced in 1927, it was a two-place biplane powered by a single 220 HP Wright Whirlwind (the same engine Lindbergh used in the *Spirit of St. Louis*). The student sat in the front seat, the instructor in the rear; communications were one-way—the instructor shouted through the gosport speaking tube and the student listened.[19] Instrumentation was very rudimentary, with gauges only for altimeter, tachometer, engine oil pressure, and cylinder head temperatures. Turn and slip indications (coordinated rudder and aileron) were provided by how much wind resistance one's left or right cheek received from off the narrow windshield.

Despite a good start and previous flight experience, Tibbets did hit a snag during his primary stage (the first three months). For whatever reason, he developed a nagging fear he would damage the fragile PT-3 while attempting to satisfy the so-called three-point landing requirements of the day (two main wheels and small tail wheel or skid meet the runway simultaneously, the nose remaining high throughout). The result was a series of botched landings attempts.

Tibbets' instructor, Lt. George Slater, an officer who carried himself as one might imagine a dashing airman of that day would—Clark Gable moustache, Sam Browne belt strapped diagonally across his uniformed chest, swagger stick, jodhpurs, and riding boots—yelled at Tibbets through the gosport: "I'll show you that you can't hurt this goddamned thing!"[20]

Slater proceeded to fly the seemingly delicate trainer right into the ground, whereupon it bounced back up into the air perhaps a hundred feet or more, the landing gear still intact. Having made his point, Slater added full power at the top of the ricochet and climbed back into the pattern. The demonstration sunk in. Tibbets' next two landings were good enough for the instructor to crawl out of the cockpit and nod at his student to "go kill yourself"—the young man's first military solo. On later reflection, Tibbets came to understand this had been the kind of moment when many other student pilots were simply left to their own devices and subsequently washed out. As gruff as Slater was, he had guided Tibbets through his worst flight training experience.

After finishing the primary stage, he was off to basic (another three months), also at Randolph Field. Here he was introduced to the North American BT-9, a higher performance, more powerfully engined, low-winged monoplane that was also, unfortunately, very unforgiving on the controls and burdened with terrible stall characteristics. Tibbets continued to progress through the program with above-average evaluations. Another bad time came, however, when his best friend and roommate, Frank Fisch, was killed in the treacherous BT-9. As it happened, that event became another defining moment for Paul Tibbets, one that would later reap great dividends when he was leading large bomber formations over Nazi Europe. In his autobiography he stated that Fisch's death steeled him with a certain fatalism about flying that helped him get through the worst of his combat flying. Sometimes good men must be sacrificed for the greater good, never mind they might be close friends.

It was during basic training that Tibbets discovered he had a particular affinity for instrument flying, a difficult-to-learn skill even many of the most famous early flyers never mastered. Even as late as the mid-1930s, "blind flying" skills were not as highly developed in the Army Air Corps as they should have been (to their chagrin, many Air Corps pilots of that day discovered that U.S. civilian airline captains usually had better instrument flying capabilities). Tibbets' proficiency improved at a rapid rate, and at the end of basic he found himself holding the highest overall flying rating in his class.

After six months at Randolph Field, San Antonio, it was time to move cross-town and become a "Kelly Field Mister." Once a flyer got to Kelly, "the

West Point of the Air," it was assumed he could capably fly an Army airplane, and it was at Kelly that he would get specialized training in a particular category of military flying machine. In Tibbets' time, only two advanced courses were available—Pursuit (fighters) and Observation (everything else).[21] Being a top-rated student, he could easily have gone into Pursuit, what everyone expected he would do. But after listening to a friend who was also a Randolph tactical officer, Paul decided on a different agenda.

"If you go into fighters," the fellow advised, "you'll [be] going into General Headquarters Air Force. . . . All your flying will be in formation with someone else deciding where you go and how you get there."[22] On the other hand, the friend explained, in Observation he would be able to make his own decisions. This reasoning had great appeal for Paul Tibbets; he had joined the Air Corps not to be a soldier but as the most expedient means for him to learn to be a professional flyer. Observation meant flying different and mostly larger, multiengine airplanes, which would open the door to what the young man felt—long range—were the kind of aircraft that held the most promise for his own future.

The final three-plus months of Advanced Stage in Observation at Kelly Field went swiftly and smoothly. Paul Tibbets Sr. was in attendance the day in February 1938 when his son was awarded the silver wings of an Army Air Corps pilot and commissioned a second lieutenant. After learning from a senior officer that his son had graduated at the top of his class, he told Paul Jr. that "I feel a hell of a lot better about this thing. . . . I can see why you like it and I think it's going to be great for you."[23] Tibbets made clear in his autobiography that his father's comments lifted a great burden from his shoulders.

With his formal flight schooling concluded in the spring of 1938, it was off to active duty, beginning at Fort Benning, Georgia. Whereas but a few short years earlier the idea of a major war involving the entire planet would have been unthinkable, the rise of the dictator Benito Mussolini in Italy, a newly militant Germany under Adolf Hitler, and Imperial Japan's increasing aggression and recent savaging of China the scales had now tipped in the opposite direction. Paul Tibbets instinctively grasped that his earlier hopes for a civil aviation career were almost certainly not to be—at least in the short run. He therefore concluded to immerse himself in flying, determined to become the Air Corps' most capable multiengine pilot.

As so often happened during his career, Paul Tibbets found himself in the right place at the right time. While most of the rest of the Air Corps was still struggling with limited budgets and pilots were begging for flying time, he had three things going for him at Fort Benning. First, his commanding officer was very accommodating and allowed Paul to fly whenever and whatever he could lay hands on. Second, that same commander was friendly with his counterparts at nearby Maxwell Air Field, Alabama, a major training center with several types of aircraft that were often made available to Tibbets. Third, Maxwell also had the newest and most modern bomber in the Air Corps—the all-metal two-engine monoplane Martin B-10B.[24] For some reason, there was a pilot shortage at Maxwell that summer of 1938, which opened up a golden opportunity for Tibbets. In just a few months, he and one or two other pilots racked up a terrific number of hours towing targets off the Gulf of Mexico for the Army coast artillery. Such fortuitous circumstances allowed Paul Tibbets to quickly become one of the Army's highest-time multiengine pilots. By December 1941, he had accumulated over two thousand flying hours and would be poised for a leadership role in the initial buildup of the first American strategic bombing forces sent to England in the summer of 1942.

At one point during Tibbets' prewar 1938–39 Fort Benning tour of duty, in one of those unlikely turns of events that sometimes made his life story read like a novel, he met Lt. Col. George Patton, the same officer who went on to lasting fame as one of the country's ablest fighting generals. It seems that Patton was an avid skeet shooter and 2nd Lieutenant Tibbets, who had been taught to shoot by his father when he was twelve years old, was himself a crack shot. As a result of Tibbets' skill, he had been given the additional job of assisting in the operation of the fort's skeet range. Patton thrived on good competition, and soon Tibbets became the very junior member of a foursome. He got to know the future general well, commenting in his autobiography that Patton was almost desperate to win every round, though noting that the senior officer always treated the young Tibbets well, once he had cooled down after a competition had ended. A nearby Columbus, Georgia, businessman was apparently the best shooter in the group, with Tibbets claiming second place, though conceding that Patton "carried off his share of quarters."

During this same period, the increasingly dashing Paul Tibbets Jr. found himself enmeshed in a serious romance with a lovely "Georgia peach" named Lucy Wingate. After a whirlwind courtship of just two months, with Lucy a good Catholic girl and Paul Jr. a self-described nominal Protestant, they were married on June 19, 1938, at a Catholic seminary in the nearby town of Holy Trinity, Alabama. When Tibbets took his new bride to Miami to meet his parents, he rather abruptly introduced her as "Mrs. Tibbets."[25] After shaking their heads once again at their unpredictable only son, both Paul Sr. and Enola Gay quickly recovered, graciously welcoming Lucy into the family. The newlyweds were joined by a son on November 19, 1940, whom they named Paul Tibbets III.

After another half year of towing targets and the like out of Fort Benning, Paul, Lucy, and baby reported to nearby Savannah, Georgia. Tibbets had received orders to train in the new and very advanced A-20 Havoc medium-attack bomber.[26] It was likely during this period that Lucy Wingate Tibbets got her first inkling that her husband had no intention of giving up his first and most powerful mistress—the airplane. As he did throughout his life, he threw himself into his work and ignored whatever collateral damage might be happening on the domestic front.

While the A-20's sleek look and promising allure very much appealed to Paul Tibbets, he discovered it had an unpredictable side. As is so often the case with just-rolled-out production aircraft, the Havoc had early engine problems, which Tibbets, as he later did with the B-29 Superfortress, helped iron out. More critical to his personal development was the A-20's mission itself. The Americans had learned from the then-at-war British about their new radio detection and ranging system (dubbed RADAR), which among other things could detect high-flying aircraft. The bad news, according to the Brits, was that the Germans were building their own high-altitude radar air defenses. The U.S. Army Air Corps had therefore decided to develop a low-level medium-attack bomber to counter the Nazi capability, with the A-20 the result.

Flying the Havoc gave Tibbets his first introduction to high-speed formation flying. (He would later credit the A-20 assignment with teaching him what it really meant to be a precision pilot.) There was no room for error with the low flying that he and his mates began practicing in the summer of 1941; one false move on the controls and there would either be a midair collision with another A-20 or a prompt auguring in. Indeed, Tibbets tells us there were instances when Havocs actually bumped into each other or a propeller would chew off part of another fellow's elevator.[27] The British had relayed intelligence that German flak towers were one hundred feet off the ground, which meant the A-20 brief had the American pilots flying those ships at an absolute altitude the same or lower! Anyone who has flown a heavy machine at or above 200 mph indicated airspeed just off the deck can attest to how rough a ride it almost always is, making a precise touch on the flight controls even more difficult.[28] It is never far from the aviator's mind, with stress and fatigue accumulating accordingly, that not only does one have to control his own aircraft, he must trust that the other fellow just off either wing can also control his. Certainly, there could have been no better training for the young pilot to enhance his "stick and rudder" skills, and Tibbets thoroughly enjoyed the challenge. As it happened, he was on one of those formation A-20 sorties above Georgia when over his radio he heard the Japanese had attacked the American fleet at Pearl Harbor.

That winter of 1941–42 was a confusing time for military flyers, with sometimes conflicting orders that often batted pilots and aircrews from one end of the continent to the other like ping-pong balls. American political and military leaders were filled with indecision as to how they should best deploy American defenses against what was now a worldwide conflict—Germany and Italy having joined Japan in declaring war on the United States. Despite having substantially beefed up its armed forces since the European war started in 1939, the

United States remained woefully deficient in all areas of war-fighting matériel. Additionally, there was the Germany versus Japan priority argument—which do we take on first? This was no easy call; while reason suggested the greatest threat came from Hitler, should he defeat England, what about those treacherous Japanese—they who had just killed our boys at Pearl? And then there was Douglas MacArthur's army trying to hold out against seemingly hopeless odds on Bataan in the Philippines. How could we abandon them? (The Japanese finally settled that matter when MacArthur was evacuated to Australia and the last Philippine bastion, the Corregidor Island fortress, surrendered in late spring 1942.) Also, and perhaps most worrisome, there were the Nazi submarines sinking Allied shipping directly off the U.S. coast.

This latter circumstance had a direct effect on Paul Tibbets' duties. As early as January of 1942, Martin B-10Bs and the slightly more advanced Douglas B-18 Bolos were being bombed up and sent out to patrol all three coasts (Pacific, Atlantic, Gulf of Mexico) against enemy submarines. Tibbets, by then a captain, found himself the squadron commander of thirty-three B-18s based in North Carolina with orders to guard the waters off Cape Hatteras.[29] Unfortunately, the B-18s were mostly bluff. With only a 130-mph cruise speed, a measly payload of just four 500-lb. bombs, and a service ceiling of but 12,000 feet, the Bolos' only advantage was a long loiter time over the water—a huge fuel capacity and relatively low two-engine burn rate enabled them to stay aloft for up to seventeen hours. Tibbets' crews were as inexperienced as their airplanes were inadequate, and even at that time he doubted his men could hit anything, should they have seen an enemy target (which they never did).

After several weeks of fruitless patrolling, the newly designated Army Air Forces (AAF) realized it was wasting time, money, and men.[30] It began transitioning the bulk of its bomber aircrews into the new four-engine B-17s coming off the production lines. In the spring of 1942, Tibbets and family were on the move again, ordered to MacDill Air Field near Tampa to help organize the new 97th Bomb Group (Heavy). He was promptly given command of a new squadron. Tibbets certainly had his work cut out. The new Flying Fortress pilots were second lieutenants fresh out of flying school, their only preparation prior to MacDill a brief multiengine course performed in aircraft like the Cessna UC-78.[31] A basic wood-and-fabric twin that was the military version of Cessna's T-50 light commercial transport, the UC-78 was not at all sufficient to prepare pilots for a B-17 cockpit. Tibbets therefore decided to first rush the newly arriving pilots through three six-hour sorties in the B-18 Bolo medium bomber before attempting to transition them into his B-17D models. The AAF could not afford to wash any pilots out at this stage, so squadron commanders like Tibbets worked with each individual flyer until he was at least competent in the aircraft. Once the transition work was complete, Tibbets and his pilots (and copilots) would move on to nearby Sarasota, where they would be joined together with the other men in their Flying Fortress crews.

Until the Martin B-10 came along in the mid-1930s, and with the exception of the occasional "observer," there had been only pilot crew positions in Air Corps combat aircraft. Starting with production B-10Bs, however, dedicated navigator, bombardier, and gunner positions were installed in the aircraft, though the pilots themselves continued to fill those stations when not actually operating the aircraft, taking turns at each.[32] While this arrangement—training pilots ad hoc in other crew positions under supervision of their local commanders—had worked "OK" in a peacetime, two-engine bomber Air Corps, there was no way such nonstandardized, high-volume training could be sustained with the coming of the much more complex B-17 Flying Fortress. By 1940 nonpilot aircrew—bombardiers, navigators, flight engineers, radio operators, and gunners—were being trained in scores of formal, specialized schools scattered throughout the American South and West. Once they graduated, they were sent to individual bomber squadrons where they were joined by the pilot teams and melded into complete flight crews. The burden of ensuring this process was successful fell on the respective squadron commanders.

Men like Paul Tibbets embraced the challenge. In what had already become a pattern, he worked killer hours at MacDill and neglected his family.[33] Lucy and the baby were living in nearby Tampa while Paul worked day and night with his pilots. There were many occasions when he simply never bothered to go home, sleeping in his clothes in an office cot. An increasingly bewildered Lucy must have more and more wondered what she had gotten herself into. It was perhaps around this time that the first signs of regret appeared at yielding so quickly to the rush and thrill of their hurricane-like courtship. In all likelihood, neither Paul nor Lucy ever grasped what enormous personal sacrifices would be asked of military spouses, especially in times of war.[34]

In April 1942 the pilots and copilots of the four squadrons of the 97th Bomb Group were moved to Sarasota. Most of the nonpilot officers and enlisted airmen had already arrived from their training schools, and the crew-melding process began immediately. It was at this point the senior pilot of each B-17 was also designated the aircraft commander (AC) and made responsible for a (then) crew of eight other men. As the 340th Bomb Squadron's commander within the 97th Group, Capt. Paul Tibbets was responsible for fifteen planes and crews. He directed his staff to immediately begin matching up the other aircrew with each AC and copilot pair, a process that was, in the hurly-burly of a recently declared war, more random than scientific.

One day in the middle of April 1942 Tibbets was reviewing the rosters of each of his aircrews, pausing at the name of one of the ACs. Already the officers on this particular crew had developed a reputation as rowdies and hard to handle. He determined to keep a close eye on them, making a mental note of their names:

> B-17E Airplane No. 41–9174
> (Pilot/AC) 2nd Lt. James D. Rockett, Serial # O-436538
> (Copilot) 2nd Lt. Eugene M. Lockhart Jr., O-437973
> (Bombardier) 2nd Lt. Thomas W. Ferebee, O-443490
> (Navigator) 2nd Lt. Theodore J. Van Kirk, O-659024[35]

2

# FEREBEE

Thomas Wilson Ferebee entered this world at Cana, North Carolina, on November 9, 1918, two days before the Armistice that ended World War I. He was the third child of what would be eleven offspring (four boys and seven girls) born to William Flavius "Flav" Ferebee and Zella Ward Ferebee, both lifelong residents of rural Davie County.[1] Zella's family were mostly Dutch; Flav's founding ancestor was John Ferebee, a French/Celt born in England who immigrated to the Colony of Virginia about 1660.[2] By the early 1700s, the Ferebees were living in the part of southern Virginia that later became North Carolina.

Although "old colonial" in their American lineage, the family was neither landed nor wealthy; like the vast majority of unskilled New World immigrants, the early Ferebees scraped out a living however they could. Reading between the lines of the rather skimpy family histories, it appears succeeding generations going well into the twentieth century never fared much better regarding "getting ahead." While Tom was still very young, Flav and Zella moved to yet another tenant farm, a 112-acre place four miles south of Cana, just off the Statesville Highway.[3] The nearest town was Mocksville, the Davie County seat, about twenty-five miles southwest of Winston-Salem.

With but fifteen hundred souls within the city limits, post–World War I Mocksville was not unlike a thousand other small southern towns of that era. Most farmers still tilled the soil with teams of mule and oxen.[4] Automobile motorists endured the dusty dirt roads when the weather was dry and kept the Tin Lizzie in a shed when rain turned the surfaces into axle-deep red gumbo. Town folk took the evening air sitting on porches built under umbrellas of maple and oak trees while enjoying a bowl of persimmon pudding and nodding at the neighbors strolling by on after-supper constitutionals. Every backyard and farm grove had berry and grape vine arbors, peach and plum orchards, and all manner of huge shade trees to ward off the brutal summer sun.

Although the local area contributed many sons to the "cause" during the "War between the States," as it was known in the South, Davie County was never a hotbed of southern grievances and had also been spared the worst excesses of General Sherman's 1865 Carolinas invasion.[5] As a consequence, a more balanced political climate prevailed as compared to most of the old Confederacy. During the 1920s—Tom's formative years in Mocksville—Republicans were strong in the rural areas while the Democrats held sway in town, with most citizens' concerns centered on local issues. In short, the community and surrounding area reflected mainstream rural America of that time.

While Paul Tibbets Jr. of Miami, Florida, had enjoyed an upper-middle-class growing up, young Tom Ferebee experienced the Depression in all its dimensions. Which is to say Flav Ferebee, like nearly every other southern tenant farmer of that era, was dirt poor. While he and his family were members of the Mocksville Methodist Church, religion and the hereafter did not appear to be an especially important part of their day-to-day—the emphasis was on earning an honorable living in this life.[6] Flav's children saw little of conventional entertainment; like most of their playmates, they made their own fun at the swimming hole, used scraps of plasterer's lath to make pirate swords, erected scavenged-lumber tree houses, organized baseball games in a local cow pasture (part of the fun was dodging cow pies), and so on. Such activities had a common denominator—they required no cash outlays. Fortunately, a quality primary and secondary education was by then offered in nearly every corner of America; the Ferebee youngsters reaped enormous benefits from the free public schools.

Except for sports—which were as mandatory for Tom as was attending school—there was rarely time for extracurricular activities, though once in a while a too-good-to-pass opportunity presented itself. In the fall of 1936, the *Mocksville Enterprise Record* ran a story about thirty Mocksville High School senior boys, referred to as "agricultural students," who had visited the nation's capital.[7] The fellows rode up to Washington, D.C., on an open flatbed truck, with some having to stand the entire way. Long afterward, Tom Ferebee recalled he had been told to bring along five dollars, but he was never able to raise the money. The paper published a photo of the young men posed in front of Capitol Hill. Eighteen-year-old Thomas Ferebee is standing in the middle of the group, arms folded over his bibbed overalls.

Most of the time when not at school, Tom worked on the farm. All that physical labor developed an unusually muscular body on Tom, one that would serve him well for the rest of his life. The family's main cash crops were tobacco, cotton, and wheat, with one-third of the meager earnings going to pay the landlord. The balance of their livelihood revolved around what agriculturist's today call subsistence farming, which is to say the Ferebees grew and raised as much of their own food as they possibly could. For resourceful, hard-working American farm families like theirs—even during the Depression—such conditions did not mean starvation. Indeed, during the 1930s many cash-poor farm families ate better than the average urban resident.

As Ferebee entered his teenage years, he gained a little more independence and discovered new diversions. Girls became much less annoying; he liked being around them, and they enjoyed being around him. Like another Davie County boy, famed frontiersman Daniel Boone, Ferebee loved to hunt—rabbits and raccoons being the favored game. When he was not busy at the farm, school, or playing ball, he was out hunting. Some years later, he would regale his fellow Air Corps aviation cadets about the joys of North Carolina hunting at such great length and in so profound a countrified accent that they dubbed him "Coon" Ferebee.[8]

Tom was a fine natural athlete with powerful forearms and huge hands. At Mocksville High School he became a standout in track and basketball and was the fullback on the football squad and the top pitcher on the baseball team.[9] Although he excelled at and enjoyed all sports, it would be baseball that he loved the best and that seemed to offer the most personal promise. As it happened, a college football injury would eventually put into jeopardy not only that promising baseball career but his military aviation hopes as well.

Tom had been fascinated with flying from a young age. Once, when he was nearly ten years old and around the time Lindbergh flew the Atlantic (which Tom had read about in a neighbor's newspaper, his family too poor to subscribe), his mother put the boy to bed with a combined case of measles and mumps only to catch him a short time later outside watching an airplane fly overhead.[10] While in his teens, she was mortified to learn he had paid some very hard-to-come-by cash to an itinerant barnstorming pilot for an airplane joyride.

After high school graduation in the spring of 1938, Tom Ferebee received an athletic scholarship to Lees-McRae College, a (then) private two-year school located in Banner Elk, North Carolina. That scholarship was not just important; it was essential if young Ferebee were to have any advanced schooling. As he put the matter later in life in his typically understated way, "Very few people had money in those days. We had less than the average, I guess."[11]

Tom became Lees-McRae's first three-letter athlete, starring in football (a halfback and captain of the team), basketball, and track (javelin and broad jump). To his deep disappointment, the college did not have a baseball team. That matter finally came to a head during winter and spring of 1940, when the team motored back to Banner Elk following a basketball tournament. Tom asked his coach, "How about baseball? Are we going to have a team?" The coach shook his head. "We just don't have the money."[12]

"Teed off," Ferebee took a leave of absence from the college and arranged a baseball tryout with the St. Louis Cardinals' farm club at Albany, Georgia. The fellow he reported to was none other than Frank Rickey, brother of Cardinals owner, Branch Rickey. Tom thought his chances were good that he would be called up to the team. While Ferebee was skilled at pitching and playing outfield, his best position was catcher, and his great dream was to someday be the Cardinals' man behind the plate. He threw right-handed and was a switch hitter, though most thought he was more effective batting right. Tom had played the game for many years and had good baseball "sense." He had one serious personal flaw, however, which he finally revealed many years later: "I drank beer before games and even one would throw off my timing." As for the Cardinal tryout, his basic baseball skills had become rusty since he had been playing mostly other sports since entering Lees-McRae. Bottom line: Tom did not make the cut. Years later, he told newspaper interviewers his tryout results had been "disappointing" because "I wasn't ready."[13]

Despite the setback, Ferebee took to heart Frank Rickey's advice not to give up and to both finish his schooling and keep playing. On June 3, 1940, he completed two years at Lees-McRae with sixty-three semester hours and a general degree. His intention for the fall was to enter Davidson College near Charlotte, which did have a baseball team. During the summer he worked at and played ball for the nearby Reynolds Tobacco Company, well known nationally for manufacturing Winston, Salem, and Camel cigarettes as well as Prince Albert pipe tobacco.[14]

Meanwhile, the newspapers were filled with stories about Hitler's blitzkrieg invasion of western Europe. Tom became increasingly concerned about his own future, convinced America would eventually be swept into the conflict. Aware that Congress was about to pass a new draft law (the Selective Service Act of September 1940) and that he was single, exactly the right age, and in good physical condition, Ferebee understood he might soon be a foot soldier if he did not watch his step. Having retained his early interest in aviation and likely captivated by all the glamour associated with it, he decided against Davidson and applied for Army Air Corps pilot training. While probably a prudent move in light of the fact that within the next eighteen months he almost certainly would have been drafted into the Army, not going on to Davidson was something Tom always regretted. Late in life, he wistfully told the *Winston-Salem Journal*: "If I'd gone on to a four-year school and gotten a couple of years more experience, I think I could have made it [to the baseball major leagues]."[15]

Unlike most who took the Air Corps aptitude profiles and physical examinations, Tom Ferebee sailed through the tests. He was a splendid candidate—possessing two years of college, great physical condition, excellent coordination, and perfect eyesight. Promptly accepted for pilot training under the Aviation Cadet program, he reported to Hicks Field near Fort Worth, Texas. As it had been with Paul Tibbets some years earlier, his first three months consisted of the primary stage. Prior to any flying, of course, the Army insisted that cadets receive several weeks of the basic training every soldier endures, including close-order drill and rigorous physical conditioning. Concurrent preflight preparation involved schooling in the principles of flight, the effects of altitude on the body, and an introduction to personal flying equipment, aviation nomenclature, cockpit familiarization, and so on. After several weeks, Ferebee was ready for his first flight lesson in one of Flying Training Command's standard-colored blue-and-yellow trainers. Tom drew the Fairchild PT-19 "Cornell," a much more appropriate "starter" airplane than Paul Tibbets' by-then retired PT-3.[16]

All went well during the primary stage, and he advanced to basic stage, another three-month course that included a move during the winter of 1941 to Randolph Field in San Antonio, Texas. Tom's basic trainer was the North American BT-14, a rugged 450-hp single-engine monoplane that was being used by several Allied nations to train their pilots. For the first few weeks, he progressed normally. However, about a third of the way through basic, Ferebee hit a couple of major snags. One was physical, or so he wrote his family at any rate—an old college football knee injury was making it difficult to handle the rudder pedals in the more advanced BT-14, especially in an open cockpit at higher altitudes.[17] Another issue was the more serious, which he did not write home about. His instructor wrote him up as a "hot-dogger," saying he was "trying maneuvers the airplane couldn't perform."[18] This apparently festered into an attitude problem, made all the worse by Ferebee's growing internal conflict about what he really wanted to do with his life. Should he continue his present course and become an Army pilot? Or return to college baseball (chancing the Army draft) and make a serious run at the major leagues? Technically he was not yet a sworn member of the Armed Forces and could voluntarily walk away from Aviation Cadets and return to civilian life. He may even have harbored a naïve hope that he could somehow win his wings but not be required to go on active duty, allowing him to continue pursuing his baseball dream.

The matter resolved itself on February 3, 1941, when, after accumulating 108 flying hours, he washed out of pilot school. Unfortunately, Ferebee had also been burning bridges, having unwittingly left behind an unsavory paper trail in his pilot training files. Those records would come back to haunt him several months later.

After returning to Mocksville, Ferebee arranged another "job" playing baseball for a local cotton mill (town and company baseball teams were very big during that era). Despite doing what he enjoyed most, Tom became increasingly restless as the summer wore on.[19] Although it was never mentioned in his papers, there must also have been increasing concern about receiving a draft board "Greetings" letter. Due to his several months of exposure to military matters, he was much more realistic than most young men about the probability of war. Ferebee knew that one way or the other he was going to be an active participant, and he had become absolutely certain he did not want to be an Army infantryman.

Before the summer was out Tom made formal application to a newly announced program—Army Air Forces (AAF) Bombardier Training. He was promptly rejected, his first inkling of how serious his mistakes had been during pilot training. Fortunately the young man was persistent; after writing several impassioned letters to Washington and sweating it out for many weeks, he was finally accepted. On October 16, 1941, Ferebee reported to Maxwell Air Field, Alabama, for a ten-week basic training/preflight course (much of it a repeat of his earlier stint at Hicks Field) followed by a transfer to Kirtland Field at Albuquerque, New Mexico, where he began a three-month optical bombardier course. (By early 1944 the course length had expanded to a much more appropriate six months.)

Kirtland was among the initial group of many new formal bombardier schools that were teaching the Army's now-standardized course curriculum.[20] Prior to 1940, as mentioned earlier, the bombardier position had been a part-time job for the pilots, who took turns at the station in the Martin B-10Bs and B-18 Bolos.[21] The curriculum in those earlier days was set by each local airfield commander with no Air Corps–wide standard protocols. With the advent of the new, multicrewed, and relatively complex B-17 Flying Fortress, however, it became clear that such informal programs were completely inadequate. The decision was made to set up dedicated bombardier schools; by March 1941 Lowry Field near Denver had graduated the first three classes of 125 optical bombardiers. Using those first graduates as instructors, a school at Barksdale Field near Shreveport, Louisiana, also opened, followed by another at Kirtland. Before war's end, seventeen training schools graduated more than 48,000 optical and radar bombardiers.

Cadet Tom Ferebee, of course, was blissfully unaware of the U.S. Army's near-desperate need to quickly gin up a very large bomber crew force and, despite the constant fatigue, never really questioned why so much was being thrown at him in such a short amount of time. He would log 325 ground school hours on subjects that included bombing theory, the use of the air navigation/dead-reckoning E6-B circular slide rule, the characteristics of the Sperry and Norden bombsights, interpreting complex bombing tables and graphs, bombsight/autopilot linkage, trouble-shooting, safety procedures (ditching, bailing out), and bomb scoring.[22] During the flying phase he was credited with seventy-five hours in the B-18 Bolo (the same aircraft Tibbets was then flying on coast patrol off Cape Hatteras) and the specially modified two-engine Beechcraft AT-11 Kansan trainer. While airborne, Ferebee learned equipment familiarization, instrument calibration, search operations, bombardier and pilot coordination, and, most importantly, practice bombing (in clear skies, bad weather, day and night). Up to two hundred practice bombs were dropped by each cadet, with strong emphasis given to small circular error (CE) hits. (It is worth noting the contemporary catchphrase "putting it in a pickle barrel from 20,000 feet" was pure propaganda.)

Later on, in January 1943, the AAF would formalize the various CE standards for bombardier cadets, using as a final grade an average of all the drops made from 12,000 feet (the standard training altitude used at that time) under eight separate classification conditions.[23] (One example classification was titled "Standard, horizontal, low speed, 120 seconds [length of bomb run].") During this phase a cadet could earn one of three skill ratings. To qualify for a rating of bombardier, his CE must average 185 feet or less; to qualify for master, 136 feet or less; to qualify for distinguished, 106 feet or less. Unfortunately, even at that relatively late date, the Army's grading criteria continued to raise false expectations. What was still not being accounted for in the bombardier schools was that the actual bombing altitudes used in European combat would be *double* the training altitudes, with those resulting actual CEs exponentially much greater—drops from 25,000 feet under highly stressful combat conditions, with the usual bad weather thrown in, typically resulted in thousands of feet of error. All this led to great frustration once in England—both to the combat bombardier ("why am I having trouble hitting my mark?") and to Eighth Air Force leaders (puzzled by even their best bombardiers' inability to accurately hit targets).

As we now know, Eighth Air Force strategic bomb aiming deficiencies—so serious they materially hindered the war effort—were the result of two major factors: substandard stateside bombardier training and inherent errors in the Norden optical bombsight coupled with irreconcilable issues with all gravity-propelled weapons.[24] Both directly affected Tom Ferebee's combat experiences.

The substandard training was the result of three critical issues that lasted well into 1943. First, due to acute shortages of Norden sights, Flying Training Command received the poorest quality, sometimes even operationally rejected, units. What is more, the stateside training aircraft were not equipped with the revolutionary new Honeywell C-1 autopilot.[25] (Contrary to popular belief, the aircraft autopilot was not invented in order to relieve pilot workload—though that benefit was quickly perceived—but as an integral component of the Norden bombing system.) Bombers not equipped with an autopilot invariably had poorer results. Unfortunately, Tom Ferebee would not fly a single sortie using a C-1 autopilot-equipped aircraft until he got to England.

Second, the Bolo and Kansan twin-engine trainers were obsolete aircraft that could not fly practice sorties above 15,000 feet. As mentioned earlier, the CE of gravity-dropped bombs deteriorates at an increasingly higher rate with every 1,000 feet of altitude. Tom Ferebee would fly his initial combat missions between 20,000 and 25,000 feet without ever having been higher in an airplane than 15,000 feet. Third, there was a critical shortage of bombardier instructors, with the first training school at Lowry having opened only a year and half earlier.[26] The urgent need for both instructors and operational bombardiers would not begin to ease until mid-1943.

The second major bombing deficiency the Eighth Air Force had to contend with revolved around the Norden optical bombsight itself. It was inherently inaccurate, burdened by so many complex trigonometric realities and engineering difficulties that some problems were never completely overcome. It was also an extremely difficult bombsight to manufacture, with machining tolerances so extraordinarily fine that they averaged to the nearest ten-thousandth of an inch.[27] With some of the most delicate parts, even closer tolerances were necessary. To make matters worse, there were never enough qualified technicians at the Norden plants to monitor the manufacturing work.

If that was not enough, gravity bombing accuracy was further complicated by uncontrollable external factors. For example, it was almost impossible to predict the varying wind shears that inevitably occurred between the bombing altitude and the earth's surface, even if the winds were known at both the drop and impact points. To say it another way—a bomb dropped from 25,000 or 30,000 feet can easily pass through two or three directional changes in air movement, substantially affecting the ballistic trajectory of any gravity-powered object. And improperly manufactured or defective bomb casings, especially regarding the tail fins (sometimes causing what were called "flyers"), could cause additional unanticipated downward trajectories. These difficulties proved so severe they defied a satisfactory solution all the way through the Korean and Vietnam Wars and would only finally be solved (or negated) by modern laser-guided or GPS-directed so-called smart bombs.

Despite Norden having invented the first truly effective gyroscopically stabilized optical bombsight in 1933—the transforming Mark XV—World War II began with more Sperry sights in the Army inventory than Nordens. The reasons for this rather puzzling anomaly went back a long way, the result of a long-term incestuous relationship between the two competing firms.

In 1904, Dutchman Carl Norden immigrated to the United States and went to work for Elmer Sperry, whose company was already engaged in making gyrostabilizers for ocean liner navigation and control. During World War I, as the airplane matured, Sperry directed Norden to perfect an accurate aerial bombsight, a vexing mathematical challenge that had so far defied even a partial solution by either the Allied or Central Powers. Thanks mainly to Norden's brilliance, the Sperry Corporation achieved a number of breakthroughs and was granted patents on a "vertically stabilized bombsight that relied on a gyro assembly driven with DC power."[28] Shortly thereafter, Carl Norden left Sperry to start his own firm perfecting aerial torpedoes, although he continued research into optical bombsights. By the early 1930s he had made sufficient progress to unveil his revolutionary Mark XV; by 1934 it had become the American military's gold standard.

The Sperry Corporation, which had made improvements on its own bombsights during the 1920s, was not about to take this intrusion into their bailiwick lying down. While grudgingly recognizing Norden's technical advances, but with the knowledge and legal standing that they had with their own bombsight patents, the company promptly came up with the "Sperry S-1"—what we would today call a "knockoff" of Norden's Mark XV.

It was at this point that 1930s procurement politics entered the picture—in Sperry's favor.[29] In an odd marketing twist, Norden had been designated a so-called dedicated U.S. Navy source, and the only way the Army Air Corps could get the XV was to order them through the Navy. Not only that, because the XV had been specially designed for the lower operating altitudes and slower speeds of Navy flying boats (their primary bombing platforms at that time), the XV would require modification in order to accommodate the large, higher flying four-engine land bombers the Army had on the drawing boards. To complicate the matter even further, Norden developed manufacturing problems (due to the technical problems discussed earlier) and could not deliver the Navy's orders in a timely fashion. As a result, in January 1936 the Navy suspended all Army orders for Norden bombsights until their own requirements could be met. The door was therefore kicked wide open for the Sperry Corporation's S-1. It was several years before Norden finally ironed out its quality control and production issues and was able to gain control of both Navy and Army bombsight orders. In the end, Sperry and Norden each delivered about 50,000 units during World War II.

While both bombsights were serviceable and in operation when Tom Ferebee went through Kirtland, most considered the Sperry inferior to the Norden (despite many bombardiers who later proclaimed their loyalty to the S-1).[30] The truth was the Sperry *did* have a lot going against it. Its sighthead weighed seventy-five pounds, versus thirty-five pounds for the Norden, no small matter from a handling standpoint. More importantly, official tests conducted from 1940 to 1942 indicated the Norden was "superior in ease of operation, accuracy, and maintenance." By late 1944 nearly all the Sperrys were gone from Army inventories. The Norden was the only bombsight ever used by Tom Ferebee.[31]

Early in the war, the Norden bombsight was considered "top-secret"—even period Hollywood movies reinforced the idea that it was an almost magical super weapon. After each training sortie or combat mission, bombardiers were required to remove the highly classified Norden sighthead from the airplane (the lower stabilizer portion was permanently bolted to the fuselage) and either keep it in their personal possession or commit it to a guarded safe. Ferebee's class (like many other early ones) was obliged to give a solemn oath that they would give up their lives before allowing the enemy to come into possession of the Norden bombsight.[32] By 1943 technical advances by both sides had rendered that pledge moot and security was greatly relaxed. By 1944 Nordens were no longer specially controlled; both sighthead and stabilizers were left in planes after combat sorties.

All this, of course, was far in the future for the early-1942 bombardier candidate Tom Ferebee. His only concern was to get through the course successfully—no easy matter. Operating the Norden was very nearly as complex as the device's difficult birth and mixed early history. By all accounts, Cadet Ferebee excelled in bombardier school. A classmate and fellow North Carolinian, Harry Booth, told the *Charlotte Observer* on the fiftieth anniversary of the Hiroshima mission that "[Tom] was clearly among the top of the class. . . . He had the eyes and head for it. He was calm in action."[33]

Thomas W. Ferebee graduated from Kirtland Field in Class 42-4 on March 21, 1942, and was awarded his bombardier wings and commissioned an AAF second lieutenant.[34] He was immediately ordered to Sarasota Army Air Field, Florida, where he and hundreds of other aircrew were assigned to the newly created 97th Bomb Group, which was being equipped with B-17E Flying Fortresses. Ferebee was directed to the 340th Bomb Squadron, as was a second lieutenant aircraft commander (pilot), James Durwood Rockett. Strangely enough, Rockett was also a North Carolinian, raised in Conover, just forty miles southwest of Tom's own hometown of Mocksville.

Lieutenant Rockett informed his new bombardier that their squadron commander was a captain named Paul Tibbets, and no, he did not know anything about the fellow but he seemed all right. A little further along in their first conversation, Tom was nonplussed to learn Rockett himself had but thirty-five hours of flying time in the B-17. Ferebee soon discovered, however, that such low time among the squadron pilots was more the norm than the exception. With the surprise war just four months old, most pilots and copilots in the 97th were, like their airplanes, "fresh from the factory."

A large group of just graduated navigators had also recently arrived at Sarasota and were being assigned to aircrews. The day came for Rockett and his crew to fly their first training sortie together. Ferebee was in the "greenhouse" Plexiglas nose of the B-17, located ahead and below the two pilots. He was checking out his bombsight and equipment prior to takeoff when a short, baby-faced guy poked his head through the hatch.

"Hi," the fellow said. "You the bombardier?"

Tom nodded.

"I'm your navigator." He extended his hand in greeting. "Ted Van Kirk."

# 3

# VAN KIRK

Like Tom Ferebee, Theodore "Ted" Van Kirk was born into a tenant farm family. Sunday, February 27, 1921, had been just another typical Pennsylvania winter day off Route 11 between Northumberland and Danville.[1] At the time his parents, Frederick and Grace Snyder Van Kirk, were living with Grandpa and Grandma Snyder. With Ted now newly arrived, the house seemed suddenly to be filling up. Fortunately, theirs was a close-knit, extended family with common values and heritage—the Van Kirks were Holland Dutch, the Snyders Pennsylvania Dutch.[2] Ted and his yet-to-be-born younger sister, Jean, could look forward to a warm and loving upbringing. As it had been with the Ferebees in North Carolina, a lack of hard cash did not prevent them from eating well—Grandmother Snyder was an exceptionally good cook, even when makings were scarce. Long afterward, Ted Van Kirk told his biographer, Suzanne Simon Dietz, that "it seemed as if my grandmother could take a pot of water and feed us."[3]

The Snyder farm actually belonged to a wealthy local family who also owned a popular bakery, and although they apparently treated the Snyders and Van Kirks decently, every young couple wants a home of their own. Fred and Grace soon moved into Northumberland proper, setting up housekeeping at 672 Queen Street in a home owned by a Ukrainian family named Biega. Years later, Ted's sister would fondly recall "Daddy Biega" and his three sons, who would also serve in World War II.

Northumberland in the 1920s was about the same size as Ferebee's Mocksville and a typical small Pennsylvania town. Founded in 1772 at the confluence of the West and North Branches of the Susquehanna River, it had become a solidly prosperous farm community by the 1860s, growing essential food grains to help sustain the North in its struggle against the rebellion. Although just eighty miles north of Gettysburg (the farthest north Gen. Robert E. Lee's army penetrated), Ted's hometown was spared the ravages of that conflict. As with most young people, Van Kirk gave little thought to his hometown's history, no matter how much it might have impacted his own upbringing on the shores of the Susquehanna. With the river just a few blocks and a railroad switching yard away, he and his "semi-rowdy" friends were more interested in imitating Mark Twain's Tom Sawyer and Huckleberry Finn, two famous delinquents the boys considered their "fellow river rats." When her brother was small, Ted's sister Jean said, "he was a little devil." For such rambunctious young boys, the river and surrounding woodlands offered all the playground needed to blow off normal, growing-up steam.

Still, all was not fun and games. Like Tom Ferebee, when young Van Kirk was not attending school, he spent the bulk of his time helping the family earn a living. It is difficult for twenty-first-century readers to appreciate an era when there were no social safety nets—no food stamps, no social security, no unemployment insurance, no national health insurance, and, after 1929, little to no work. Folks depended on relatives, friends, neighbors, and—when in extremis—community charity to get by. Fred Van Kirk had a limited education and no marketable skills, having to earn his living with his hands. Like all responsible fathers, he did whatever he could to make enough money to support his wife and two children. In addition to a watchman job at a factory across the river at nearby Sunbury, he and Ted earned extra dollars dredging hard coal from out of the Susquehanna's North Branch.

The city of Scranton, about eighty-five miles upriver from Northumberland, was the nation's most important producer of hard, or anthracite, coal. When it was processed, the mine operators dumped the so-called fine coal (broken bits and pieces, euphemistically called "rice, barley, or peas") into the Susquehanna.[4] The discards floated downstream past Northumberland, offering entrepreneurial opportunities for wildcat dredgers like Fred Van Kirk. Apparently a good deal of fine coal did indeed appear (anthracite was widely used as a home-heating fuel) for Ted later said he and his Dad sold what they gathered to locals for two dollars a ton.

About this time Ted wangled his first airplane ride, his own story mirroring Tom Ferebee's to a remarkable degree. Somehow he convinced his father to pay for a few turns around the patch with a local pilot, John Abusio, who owned "an old biplane." John took folks up from the local Riverside Park at the rate of four to five dollars a ride. Ted said that after his turn he "was hooked. I never wanted to walk again."[5]

In June 1938 Ted graduated from Northumberland High School; that fall he entered Susquehanna University. After his first year, however, he realized he had made a mistake—Susquehanna was a liberal arts school and did not offer courses in his preferred fields of engineering or chemistry. Ted's new plan was to return to his part-time high school job at the local Weis Food Market and save enough money to start the next fall at Bucknell University in nearby Lewisburg, Pennsylvania. Meanwhile, Ted's social life had heated up. Naturally gregarious and blessed with an engaging personality, he had many friends. The previous winter he had joined a gang heading for a sledding party. While towing sleds back up the hill, he met a lovely young Northumberland girl three years his junior named Mary Jane Young. Around the same time the *Sunbury Daily Item* was reporting the startling news war had broken out in Poland, Ted Van Kirk found himself "hooked" a second time.

The years 1940 and 1941 became a bit of a slog for young Ted Van Kirk, he alternately working at the Weis Market, saving money for college, and trying to figure out a way to avoid the consequences of the Selective Service Act. Like Tom Ferebee, he did not want to be in the infantry, and he was alert enough to understand it was going to be up to him to avoid that fate. Having also been bitten by the aviation bug, Van Kirk applied for admission to the Army's Aviation Cadet program. He took the physical and entrance exams, the latter much more difficult than he had expected.[6] To his great surprise, he passed. Ted returned home thinking he would soon be notified of a class opening, but many months passed and no word came. While waiting it out, Van Kirk decided not to go back to college but to continue working at the market.

At long last, on September 29, 1941, Aviation Cadet Ted Van Kirk arrived at Harvey Parks Airport on the northeast side of Sikeston, Missouri, to begin pilot training. The Missouri Institute of Aeronautics, a fixed-based operator on Parks, was under contract to the Army Air Forces (AAF) to conduct a three-month primary training course. Three days later, Ted got his introductory ride in a Stearman PT-18 Kaydet, a trainer that performed similarly to Tom Ferebee's PT-19 Cornell. Van Kirk soloed after the usual eight hours of dual and seemed to be progressing well enough, though piloting was not coming easy to him. By the end of November he was clearly on the bubble regarding moving on to the basic training stage.

On December 8, 1941, the day after the Pearl Harbor attack and Van Kirk's ninth week in primary stage, he wrote his folks that he was in serious trouble. His daily flight instruction had been coming from civilian instructors, and they were willing to pass him, but the AAF insisted on doing their own testing at each critical stage of the training. On December 12, during a final check ride, Van Kirk sheared the airplane's gear off while landing, and the hammer finally dropped. After sixty flying hours, he was washed out.

There are few experiences that can be as devastating to a confident, prideful young man who has always before succeeded at nearly everything he attempted than to wash out of pilot school. It hits him on a visceral level; washing out was (and still is) perceived by students and instructors alike as some undefinable personal weakness, perhaps even a character flaw.[7] No matter that such a view is patently ridiculous, it is nonetheless felt most acutely by the washoutee himself. At least for a few days, he is wrapped in an almost irreconcilable despair, alternately kicking himself at one moment for failing and wondering in the next breath what in the world he should do now.

For Ted Van Kirk on December 12, 1941, there was something else in the air. An insidious poseur lurked nearby, dangling a promise that the dream could still be fulfilled. Royal Air Force (RAF) recruiters had gathered themselves at the front gates of every American pilot training school, ready to pluck up any or all disappointed American pilot washouts. The terribly vulnerable boys listened eagerly to the offer of a fresh start in an English or Canadian flying school, which would culminate in earning the wings of an RAF pilot. Of course, what those recruiters neglected to mention was England's desperate need for large numbers of warm bodies to pilot their aircraft, along with the very slim likelihood the average American washout could survive for any length of time against skilled Luftwaffe combat veterans.

For several days Van Kirk wrestled with himself as to whether to sign up with the RAF or take up what his superiors were recommending—AAF navigator training. His academic standing at Parks had been high, the AAF told him, and he fit nicely into the ideal navigator profile. An exit interview with the Sikeston post commander along with his own intuitive judgment that the RAF option was likely foolhardy finally convinced him to stay in the U.S. Army. On Christmas Day 1941 Van Kirk boarded a train for navigation school at Kelly Field, San Antonio, Texas.

On December 29 he started ground school classes; on the thirtieth he had his first flight. Like the country itself, frantically preparing for war, everything at Kelly had been speeded up. Demand for bomber and transport aircrews was so intense that the AAF had recently reduced the navigator training curriculum to fifteen weeks, which included basic military training and physical conditioning. As with bombardier training, there were no dedicated U.S. Army navigator schools before 1940; indeed the official titles of navigator and bombardier, along with their respective flying badges (wings), had only recently been created. Before the war, whenever the Air Corps needed specialized navigator training, they would select certain pilots to be cross-trained at the Pan American Airways civilian navigation school at Coral Gables, Florida.[8] (As late as 1939, the U.S. Army Air Corps had only five hundred officers trained in the navigator classification.) Flying commercial Sikorsky, Martin, and Boeing flying boats over both the Pacific and the Atlantic, Pan Am operated the world's premier overwater navigation training school.

As World War II heated up and with the new four-engine transports and bombers coming into production, the military services realized they were facing an enormous shortage of navigators capable of guiding their aircraft when flying outside the United States. While North America had a good system of low-frequency radio navigation aids (the "A-N" four-course radio range navigation system), no such thing was available over the oceans or in other parts of the world, to say nothing of the lack of any sextant-trained air navigation officers. In response, in November 1940, the Air Corps set up its first formal navigation school at Barksdale Field near Shreveport, Louisiana. More schools quickly followed as soon as an original core of instructors could be trained. By war's end, over two dozen navigation training facilities had been established throughout the climate-friendly American West and South.

The official objective of 1942 AAF navigation training was to "qualify students as precision dead-reckoning navigators with basic proficiency in pilotage, radio, and celestial navigation." Dead-reckoning navigation (a corruption of the phrase "deduced [ded] navigation") can be defined as a pencil and plot method of determining an airplane's current position by advancing a previously known position using only heading, estimated wind/drift, airspeed, and time elapsed. Pilotage meant holding a certain desired course by looking out the cockpit window and using known cultural and topographic features as checkpoints. (Pilotage combined with dead reckoning were the methods used by Charles Lindbergh on his 1927 solo Atlantic flight.) Radio navigation meant identifying Morse code signals transmitted from ground stations and then either mentally or physically plotting bearings to and from each. Celestial navigation, the most challenging of all navigation disciplines, required taking sextant observations off the sun, Jupiter, Venus, the moon and up to forty selected stars, then mathematically computing lines of position from those observations and resolving them on a chart into a "fix," a known location.

In his first weeks at Kelly, Van Kirk was introduced to these basic principles and issued his personal dead-reckoning kit, which included a second-setting (hack) watch, Weems plotter, dividers, and the same E6-B circular slide rule issued to Tom Ferebee, universally known as the "whiz wheel." With those tools Van Kirk learned basic navigation procedures—drawing up a sortie on a chart with turn and action points; plotting and measuring courses for each leg; using the dividers (to mark off distances); and maintaining a navigator's log. The log was central to preplanning the mission, determining estimated time of arrival to each action point, in-flight course corrections, and recording what actually happened during a flight.

Next came introductions to the navigator's panel instruments—primarily the indicated airspeed meter, pressure altimeter, outside air temperature gauge, and the fluxgate compass (a directionally stabilized, electrically operated modification of a magnetic compass). The cadets also discovered the absolutely critical importance of getting a precise "time hack" on their second-setting watches prior to each takeoff. The watch had to be set as close as possible to the nearest second Zulu (Greenwich Mean Time) if one expected any kind of accuracy in his navigation work, especially regarding star fixes and sun lines. Instruction was also given on how to take bearings and establish lines of position using the aforementioned low-frequency radio range stations located around the country.

Once a solid foundation had been established, the training curriculum called for an alternating mix of ground school and flying—for every hour of flight, Van Kirk spent about five hours in the classroom. As the cadets gained confidence in being able to track the path of the airplane and compute estimated times for arrival and alter headings, the subject load broadened. Soon the cadets were learning about basic meteorology (weather), reconnaissance, bailout procedures, ditching, and so on. The training curriculum continually doubled back to reemphasize basic dead-reckoning techniques, pilotage skills, the use of the driftmeter for measuring wind and ground speed, practice in taking radio bearings from multiple stations and plotting their intersection, and as much celestial navigation instruction that could be imparted in so short a time.

Van Kirk trained in another of the many variants of the famed civilian Beechcraft Model 18, this one known as the AT-7 Navigator, a twin-engine monoplane similar to the bombardier's Kansan. The AT-7 carried a pilot, an instructor navigator sitting in the copilot seat, and three students. The students would rotate as lead navigator, with the other two monitoring lead and logging their own fix positions. At the end of the flight, the logs were compared to see who had been the most accurate, with grades apportioned accordingly.

The day (sun, moon) and night (stars, planets, moon) celestial training flights were arduous and fatiguing, especially the night missions. Every sortie was filled with anxiety: *How can I possibly find the assigned stars on such a cloudy night? Can I do the mathematical calculations fast enough to "stay ahead" of the airplane? Is there always this much turbulence while I'm trying to line up a body in my sextant eyepiece?* And most importantly, *Do I have what it takes to get through this stage and on to graduation?*

Humorous moments during training often eased the heavy tension, little things that years later were among those memories the trainees recalled the clearest. For instance, every student who flew the lead navigator position had at least once gotten disoriented and given the pilot a reciprocal heading at a turning point (180 degrees in the opposite direction). The instructor invariably let it go long enough to be embarrassing (and unforgettable, which was the point). Then there were those inevitable days when a fellow became so hopelessly lost he gave himself up for dead, only to be reborn when a water tower with the town's name emblazoned on it suddenly flashed by. Ditto seeing an airport moniker plastered in big letters on the roof of a large hanger. Another memorable example of head-shaking training experiences a student navigator takes to his grave, one that may well have originated during Van Kirk's time at Kelly Field, carried over into my own era. It was commonplace for Texas navigation cadets to fly a triangular course beginning at San Antonio, then to Houston, followed by a turn toward Austin, and then back home to San Antonio. It has also been forever common to have a celestial student "back in" lines of position if he becomes lost. On those occasions when it was clear a fellow flying the standard Texas triangle course had bungled his night celestial shots but still managed to come up with a final position that was amazingly close to the desired result, the instructor would dryly remark, "Ah yes, another Dubhe, Deneb, and Dallas three-star fix." The temptation to look out the window before charting one's final plot was sometimes irresistible.

For Van Kirk, the weeks passed by in a blur, though he sensed he had found his niche. A natural perfectionist—a dominant characteristic of every outstanding navigator—he was doing very well in the air, and his classroom work was excellent. The deep disappointment he had felt after washing out of pilot school was slowly being replaced by a growing sense of pride in becoming a skilled "Magellan" and taking his place among the top students in the class. Van Kirk discovered he had a particular knack for celestial work—it became his favorite navigation discipline. In 1942 he would be one of the few Army Air Force navigators truly good at it.

In mid-March Van Kirk and 29 other cadets ("the 30 best men" out of 140) were abruptly informed they had been put on a fast track and were to finish training by the end of the month (three weeks would be lopped off their program).[9] A new group of B-17s was being formed, the first American bombers to be deployed to England, and navigators were desperately needed to fill out the aircrews. The chosen thirty cadets were put on a killer, hurry-up, eighteen-hour-a-day ground school and flying schedule that left the men exhausted. Tough as it was, they all stayed the course.

On April 1, 1942, in a formal ceremony at Kelly Field, Cadet Theodore Van Kirk (Class 42-05) was awarded his Certificate of Aeronautical Rating—Aircraft Observer (Aerial Navigator) and took the oath of office as a second lieutenant in the AAF. Filled with enthusiasm and pride, every man embraced the navigator's new motto: "Get 'em there—Get 'em back!" All thirty fellows were ordered to active duty effective that same date, reporting without delay to the 97th Bomb Group at Sarasota, Florida. There was no time for a leave home; everything had become rush-rush.

On April 9 Van Kirk arrived at Sarasota Army Air Field, Florida. Recently leased to the AAF, the former Sarasota-Bradenton Airport was a pretty poor excuse for a military facility. The field had in fact been located in what could only be described as a swamp-filled palmetto patch, complete with alligators and snakes. When it rained the ground was so soft the runways often could not support the weight of the planes. Even more discouraging as far as crew comfort went, the quarters were pitiful. When Van Kirk arrived, enlisted men in particular were being housed in a temporary "tent city." At first glance, the situation did not look good for newly arriving flying officers.

Fortunately for Van Kirk, he was "ordered" to live in an off-base house on Laurel Street with a number of other bachelor officers. Even more amazing—in another indication of how much his luck had suddenly changed—nearby was the all-female Ringling School of Art.[10] The student body warmly welcomed the exciting young flyers, the girls especially lonely after having already lost most of their local boys to the recruiters and draft boards. Van Kirk remembered that, while there was a lot of socializing, it was mostly communal fun with little pairing off. Over the next few weeks, Van Kirk and his roommates were hard-pressed to balance this unexpected social windfall with their heavy eleven-hour-a-day training schedule. Eventually, the workload and commute proved too much and the fellows were forced to move into Sarasota Field's rude tents and tar-papered shacks.

When Van Kirk arrived at the 340th Bomb Squadron, his commander, Capt. Paul Tibbets, had assigned him to 2nd Lt. James Rockett's crew. Van Kirk tracked down Rockett on the day of their first flight together and introduced himself. After the obligatory formalities, the pilot pointed him at their B-17E Flying Fortress, where the crew's bombardier, Tom Ferebee, was already pre-flighting his equipment.

# 4

# SARASOTA

After the initial "howdy-dos" and "where-you-froms," the two second lieutenants silently sized each other up. Tom Ferebee remembered his first impression of Ted Van Kirk: "He looked like a Cub Scout. He didn't [even] have a beard."[1] Van Kirk did not recall his thoughts those first minutes; certainly he grasped the fact Tom was the older man and had been in the service longer. It is always an unsettling moment when you first meet a fellow you are going to be intimately teamed with for who knows how long and intuitively understanding that this fellow may one day hold your own life in his hands. Van Kirk and Ferebee were playing out a scene that had happened many times before and has happened many times since.

Other factors were in play as well. The United States of 1942 was a much different place than it is today. The modern age is a time when individuals from one end of the nation to the other are instantly linked, with accents and outlooks much more homogenized. That was not at all the case three-quarters of a century ago; young men suddenly thrown together from different parts of the country had absolutely no idea of the other fellow's abilities, interests, or even values. What little they might have in common came largely from the daily newspapers and local movie theaters, the latter via biweekly Pathé newsreel shorts and the current feature starring one or more stars from a galaxy of universally known Hollywood personalities. The one thing a soldier/airman/sailor of that time would be sure of—at least in his own mind—was that nearly everyone else had an accent.

As Tom and Ted began running down their checklists items, donning parachute harnesses, and arranging their stations in the bomber's nose—so close they could almost touch—they continued chatting. Despite Ted's youth, he was an innately articulate fellow, blessed with a rich, sonorous voice that belied his baby-faced countenance. Although he would not have recognized it at the time, he too bore an accent, the flatter midwestern inflections of a central Pennsylvania native. While not naïve, he was barely twenty-one years old with little life experience outside Northumberland, still feeling his way along in the sometimes baffling American military. Tom Ferebee, on the other hand, was a bit of an operator and had two years of college and about a year's more military service. To Ted, his bombardier's profoundly rural North Carolina drawl seemed to accentuate the contrasts between them even more. Hailing as they did from such different regions, it was not in the least surprising that the two found themselves stumbling through the conversation. "Hey," Tom suddenly piped up, after not quite understanding what Ted had just said, though clearly remembering his last name. "I can't understand what you're saying, you must be speaking Dutch." Ted Van Kirk batted the ball right back. "Yeah? Well, I think *you're* talking like you have a mouthful of grits."[2]

About this time their pilot, 2nd Lt. James Rockett, and his copilot, 2nd Lt. Gene Lockhart, and the flight engineer climbed through the forward entry hatch and scrambled up to their cockpit perches. Behind them the radio operator, along with the waist and tail gunners were doing same through the aft fuselage hatch. Rockett and Lockhart ran through the prestart checks and made ready to crank up the B-17's engines. Ferebee and Van Kirk, who were sitting forward of the pilots in the nose section and not able to observe the drivers, waited for the tell-tale cough and rumble of the Wrights. Minutes went by and nothing happened. At length, in their headsets, the two men heard a lively exchange break out between the crusty crew chief, Sgt. Pancho Kendall, and Lieutenant Rockett. After a couple of more tries at starting number one, an exasperated Sergeant Kendall exploded: "For Chrissakes lieutenant, if you can't start it, you can't fly it!"[3]

Eventually the pilots did get the engines going and the flight itself was completed without incident, but the experience did little to build the crew's confidence in their aircraft commander. Once finished with the postflight critique and debriefing, Van Kirk and Ferebee likely adjourned to the Officer's Club, where they probably had a hearty laugh at Rockett's stumbling attempt to bring his flying machine to life. It is probable they also began the first of their many discussions extolling the virtues of Northumberland and Davie County, respectively, though neither ever convinced the other his hometown was the better place to live. Nor did they have an inkling that first day would mark not only the birth of Ted's nickname but also marked the day they would be almost inseparable for the next year.

Training for the fifteen crews of the 340th Bombing Squadron had begun immediately and did not let up for the entire six weeks they were at Sarasota. The work days were lengthy and demanding; it did not take long for the crews to learn their commanding officer was a stern taskmaster. Captain Tibbets had discovered that Rockett could not control his men and made a mental note to wait for the right moment to strike.[4] Long afterward, Tibbets would tell a reporter he remembered thinking at the time that Rockett and his crew were "my kind of meat."[5]

An opportunity came soon enough. Deciding to instill more discipline into his airmen by making temporary infantrymen out of them, Tibbets ordered all fifteen crews to participate in a training bivouac (a temporary encampment with no provided shelter). Taking a page from his Western Military Academy days, he ordered the men to pack up tents, cooking gear, bedrolls, and so on; hike over to a field near the airport; and pitch camp. Rockett apparently thought the hike was too much work and had his crew drive their gear over in a car. An angry Tibbets came down hard, meting out a classic military punishment. The crew was ordered to break out their shovels and dig a very large hole. When it was finished hours later, he told them to fill it back up.

When Tom Ferebee related this anecdote to the *Winston-Salem Journal* in 1987, he added an amusing postscript. In fact, the punishment did not quite go the way Tibbets had intended. The four officers contrived to assume "supervisory" roles, making the enlisted men do all the spadework—upholding another long and hoary military tradition in which the least guilty suffer the greatest penalty. As the day wore on, however, Rockett and his officers were puzzled as to why the men seemed to be almost enjoying their "hard labor." It was later learned the fellows had stashed a liberal supply of whiskey at the bottom of the hole. Ferebee laughed when he told the reporter, "They were drinking the entire time they were digging!"[6]

Mulling over the bivouac caper, Van Kirk and Ferebee huddled on what it meant for their immediate future. They concluded that their squadron commander had "a hot temper" and they would have to "really watch him." Even if Tibbets had overheard their remarks, he would not have cared a whit. Understanding much better than his men how badly undertrained they were, his instruction program became even more intense. Pilots were ordered to practice touch-and-goes so relentlessly, it was said the Sarasota Field runways were left with permanent dents. Navigators and bombardiers worked continually on difficult navigation and bombing problems, both on the ground and in the air. As if the grueling training regimen was not enough, the crews were constantly frustrated by matériel shortages. Even such rudimentary supplies as proper navigational charts were hard to come by, and improvisation became the order of the day.[7] The crews were reduced to scraping up and dropping empty gasoline drums into the ocean as practice targets for their gunners. The work went on seven days a week, the pace never slackening.

The Sarasota training ended abruptly after six weeks when Tibbets received middle-of-the-night orders to take his squadron to Fresno, California, presumably to be sent into the Pacific theater of operations. He was told to first stop at the Air Depot at Duncan Field, San Antonio, Texas, for critical defensive modifications on their B-17E models.[8] The Royal Air Force's pre–Pearl Harbor experience with the B-17C model had uncovered a serious problem regarding fighter attacks directed at the bomber's unprotected underbelly. Newly designed ventral ball turrets, each equipped with twin .50-caliber machine guns, were therefore being retrofitted on all B-17 fuselages. Here it was that each of the B-17 crews picked up another aircrew member—the ball turret gunner. Also installed at Duncan Field was a single .30-caliber machine gun with optional right and left side-mounting ports in the forward bombardier/navigator compartment.

While the airplanes were being modified (one or two at a time), Tibbets kept the aircrews' noses to the grindstone; he was far from satisfied with their overall proficiency. Well aware that most of the men had only been in the military a few months and did not fully grasp that their lives were going to depend on how well they knew and did their jobs, the squadron commander insisted on holding each man to the highest standards possible. While at Duncan and on his own initiative, Tibbets arranged for additional formation flying, cross-country triangular navigation legs, practice bombing, and gunnery drills. His crews began to grumble about spending nights as well as most days in the air, with many openly resenting Tibbets' perceived "chicken shit" training approach. Later, in England, when they saw that their own losses were fewer and bombing efficiency greater than other squadrons, they came to understand and deeply appreciate what the boss had done for them. After the war, 340th Bomb Squadron members affectionately remembered this period as the "Battle of San Antonio."[9]

During that Texas stay most crews managed to get themselves quartered at the storied Gunter Hotel in downtown San Antonio. According to Van Kirk, when Tibbets did give the fellows a little time off, gambling and carousing were the usual pursuits. Ferebee had already gained a reputation as a first-class poker player and unnaturally lucky at craps; it was probably about this time that he began giving his friend Van Kirk some finer points on those games. Later, in North Africa, it would become hazardous to one's pocketbook to gamble with either man, but especially Tom Ferebee. It was also at the Gunter that Aircraft Commander Rockett got into his first serious jam, along with his bombardier and navigator.

It seems that one evening Ferebee and Van Kirk decided to go to a movie. When they returned, they discovered a huge party had broken out in Rockett's hotel room, both officers and enlisted men (which was against the Army's no-fraternization policy). Everybody was already half in the bag, with Rockett particularly rambunctious. According to Van Kirk, Rockett was naturally hotheaded, which would explain what happened when the hotel detective knocked on the door to put a lid on things.[10] Rockett grabbed his regulation .45 automatic and headed for the door, muttering he was going to shoot the guy. Ferebee and Van Kirk immediately jumped up to defuse the situation; Ferebee walked Rockett down the hall and Van Kirk took the house detective in arm and headed the other way. That partially calmed things down, but the room party continued and very soon thereafter the military police arrived, promptly hauling everyone down to their headquarters station. Somehow it all blew over; only later in

England did Van Kirk and Ferebee discover they had been completely exonerated because the military police credited them with breaking up the initial fight. What Tibbets thought about this incident has gone unrecorded, but apparently he ignored it (squadron commanders simply could not afford to lose an entire crew over a brawl), for even Rockett escaped any serious punishment. Tibbets may also have noticed about that time that two of the "troublemakers" had also been getting very good training marks—plus the records showed that both Ferebee and Van Kirk had graduated near the top of their bombardier and navigator cadet classes.

Meanwhile the intense flying training continued, especially for air navigation. Tibbets had discovered to his horror that the majority of his navigators were so undertrained that they were virtually incompetent. When he first arrived at San Antonio and began sending out cross-country navigation training flights he "had airplanes landing all over the state of Texas."[11] There had been nothing to do but keep the pressure on.

After two weeks at the San Antonio Air Depot, the Fortress modifications had been completed and the fifteen B-17s of the 340th (along with the other three squadrons of the 97th Bomb Group) continued on to Fresno, California. Upon his arrival, Tibbets was dumbfounded to be handed orders to turn his airplanes 180 degrees in the other direction and proceed eastward to Bangor, Maine.[12] What was not known until later was that their initial movement had been precipitated by secret intercepts that the Japanese were going to attack Midway Island at the northern tip of the Hawaiian archipelago.[13] Army Air Forces commanding general Hap Arnold had ordered immediate reinforcements in that direction. However, by the time the 97th Bomb Group arrived in Fresno, the battle had already been decided in America's favor.

The additional navigation training was finally beginning to pay dividends; the long cross-country to Bangor went smoothly, with all the aircraft arriving in good order.[14] Nevertheless, newly promoted major Paul Tibbets remained concerned that his crews were still not ready for what would come next—Operation Bolero.[15] The four squadrons of the 97th Bomb Group had been ordered to attempt what few airmen outside of British and American ferry crews had done before them—cross the North Atlantic Great Circle Route from North America to England. Almost none of the navigators had ever flown even a single one-way leg across the open ocean. Now the rookies would have to find their way over thousands of miles of trackless tundra, ice packs, and open sea, crossing one of the most rugged, least-inhabited regions in the world.

The Flying Fortresses of the 97th Bomb Group began the movement in mid-June with Lieutenant Rockett's crew among the last to leave on June 27, 1942. Departing Bangor's Dow Army Airfield in small groups as weather allowed, the group was also tasked with escorting eighty single-seat P-38 Lightning pursuit/fighters, which lacked the navigation capability to find their way alone from

Bangor to Prestwick, Scotland. The first leg of about 770 miles ended at Goose Bay, Labrador, and was the least difficult, flown mostly via pilotage and dead reckoning over the northern forests and coastlines of eastern Canada.[16] It was at Goose Bay, however, that the heavy lifting began. The weather was fearsome in the Far North; planes were often delayed several days or more because of poor conditions either at Goose Bay or ahead at their next stop.

This second and most hazardous leg ended at Greenland, a mountainous island giant with an up-to-two-mile-thick icecap. A part of Denmark, the Danish government-in-exile had granted the United States permission to build airfields there and provide for the island's security. The first two strips were located about 225 miles apart and given the names Bluie West One (BW-1) and Bluie West Eight (BW-8).[17] BW-1 was on the southern tip of Greenland about 775 miles from Goose Bay; BW-8, farther up the western coast, was roughly 1,000 miles away and 60 miles north of the Arctic Circle, too far for the short-legged P-38 fighters the 97th Bomb Group was escorting. As a result, most of the B-17s were instructed to land at BW-1. For those bombers not escorting fighters, having two airfields available did offer an extra margin of safety; if one was socked in, the aircrews could divert to the other. Nevertheless, during the early war years there were still more than a few fuel starvation incidents and crashes.[18]

Of the two Greenland fields, BW-1 on the southern tip was the most challenging. Three narrow fjords lay close together as one approached from the sea, all of which looked essentially alike though only one led to the airfield. Once a pilot started his ship into any one of the three steep-sided canyons, it was doubtful he would have enough room to pull the bomber up and out if he had picked the wrong fjord. As a result, in addition to careful map reading before entering, it was essential that the pilots and navigators cross-checked their pilotage with radio direction-finding bearings from nearby Semitak Island.

BW-1 was located sixty miles inside the correct fjord. Even if the crew felt reasonably certain they had chosen the right entrance, the usual low visibility often left aircrew apprehensive until they passed a wrecked ocean freighter at the halfway point. After that, the only remaining worry was whether the weather at the field had changed since the earlier voice radio report. The single runway at the end of the fjord was situated on the side of a mountain and laid out on a steep slope atop a glacial moraine, and there was no other flat land for hundreds of miles in any direction. This meant pilots always landed uphill on Runway 07 (070 degrees magnetic or to the east northeast) and took off downhill on Runway 25 (250 degrees magnetic, or west southwest), no matter which way the wind was blowing. Such flying was dangerous and not for the faint-hearted, challenging the green, low-time pilots every bit as much as their Magellans were being tested by the over-ocean navigation.

As it turned out, elements of the 97th would be forced to use both Greenland airfields. Major Tibbets' flight of B-17s and his complement of P-38 "chicks" landed in good weather and without incident at BW-1, able to push on immediately. Second Lieutenant Rockett and company were not as fortunate when their turn came. When approaching the fjord, a weather radio message reported that BW-1 was socked in. They and their four P-38s were forced to turn around and fly all the way back to Labrador. Some days later, in mid-July of 1942, conditions had improved somewhat and Rockett's B-17E finally landed safely at the more northerly BW-8 (sans P-38s). Along with a number of other crews, they were grounded for five days at BW-8 until the weather cleared enough to move on to Iceland. Not surprisingly, the men chaffed at the delay. The fellows were hard put to find things to do—the isolated station's facilities were extremely primitive and there was insufficient space to accommodate large groups of layover crews. Some, including Van Kirk, tried to relieve the boredom with a little hiking in and around the nearby glaciers. Rockett's crew was also interviewed at BW-8 by a Hearst newspaper correspondent looking for stories about the first American bomber crews sent to England. The piece was published around the United States—Ted Van Kirk and Tom Ferebee's first exposure to getting their name in the paper.[19]

It was about 850 air miles to the next landfall at Reykjavík, Iceland. Every airman making his first North Atlantic crossing could not help but notice a certain irony in that, from the air, Iceland's broad grass expanses appeared quite green while the surface of Greenland's nearly 800-mile length was almost entirely covered with ice and snow. After the very tough stretch between Labrador and Greenland, the Iceland leg promised something of a breather. As before, the bombers settled into a cruising altitude between 8,000 and 10,000 feet using leaned-out fuel mixture settings that yielded roughly a 150-mph indicated airspeed, the winds and temperature dictating actual ground speed. The B-17 Flying Fortress had to stay at relatively low levels because its yellow oxygen tanks carried an insufficient supply to sustain a bomber crew flying above 12,000 feet for long periods, to say nothing about the discomfort of continually breathing through an oxygen mask during a half a day aloft. Additionally, there were no useful navigation charts of the large midsection of Greenland—Van Kirk's map showed only a large blank "Unexplored" notation along their route. All that the airborne observers could see were glaciers with huge brown and black mountain peaks poking up through the white crust. During this leg, Van Kirk mostly used dead reckoning, supplemented by his B-5 Driftmeter. Essentially an upside-down telescopic periscope, the instrument measured drift by tracking a ground object using its vertical reticles, with the ground speed determined by stop-watch timing the object's passage between its horizontal reticles. After roughly a 375-mile crossing over the most inhospitable terrain any of the crew had ever seen, the crew reached the eastern coast of Greenland. Van Kirk and the pilots studied the available topographic and cultural features and took a departure fix via pilotage (i.e., identifying unique peninsulas and the two or three small settlements near the coast) before heading out into the Denmark Strait.

For the remaining 475-mile overwater leg to Iceland, the navigation would rely on dead reckoning and the sextant. In the summer there was almost no night along the Arctic Circle, and the only celestial body available for observation was the sun. Still, that single line of position could be incorporated into a refined dead-reckoning position that gave a fairly reliable indication of the airplane's actual location. The most vexing polar navigation issue the bomber crews faced was the erratic nature of their compasses caused by the huge magnetic variation—the difference in degrees between the geographic North Pole and the magnetic North Pole (located hundreds of miles away in northeastern Canada).[20]

Operational orders had specified skeletal transoceanic aircrews, which meant sending most of the gunners over by ship. The radio operator was needed to make regular position reports and assist the navigator in taking direction-finding bearings from ground stations, and usually two gunners rode as engine scanners. The bombardiers were brought along so as to not break up the officer crew, but they were just along for the ride. While the two pilots and Van Kirk were almost literally lashed to the yoke for the entire flight, Tom Ferebee found a comfortable spot in the forward navigator/bombardier compartment and sacked out for the duration. In early 1942 bombardiers received no navigation training; later, after the crews had been combat-baptized, the error was realized in not cross-training the bomb aimers in case of emergencies. By 1943 several weeks of dead reckoning and pilotage instruction were being included in the bombardier school curriculum. Of course, those future developments were of no help to Rockett's crew. While Van Kirk never expressed resentment, it is true there is nothing more annoying to a deeply fatigued, working navigator than having a fellow nonpilot flying officer, a man equal in rank and pay to oneself, engaged in blissful slumber just a few feet away and of absolutely no use.

The approach and landing at Keflavík Field on the extreme southwest corner of Iceland was uneventful. Located thirty miles from the country's largest city, Reykjavík, its new runways had only recently been rebuilt and were now capable of handling the largest Allied bombers, fighters, and transports en route to England. Prior to 1939 and the start of the war, Iceland had been a "sovereign kingdom in personal union" with Denmark, though with strong diplomatic and economic ties to Nazi Germany. Then, in the spring of 1940, Germany seized Denmark. Iceland did declare technical neutrality but remained sympathetic to Germany, even allowing Nazi soldiers to establish a presence on their soil. Deeply worried about the possibility of an aggressive German base so close to vital shipping lanes between the United Kingdom and America, the British invaded in May 1940, sweeping aside the weak resistance and taking control of the island nation. In early July 1941 the United Kingdom transferred the defense of Iceland to the United States. Shortly after Pearl Harbor and Germany's declaration of war against America, the United States allocated funds to beef up the main Icelandic commercial airport near the community of Keflavík, which also serviced the capital city, Reykjavík. By May 1943 further airport improvements and the development of longer-range four-engine transports allowed Greenland to be bypassed and enabled Keflavík to become the first stopover point for ferrying combat and the newly designated Air Transport Command aircraft departing from North America.

Finding mostly clear skies at Keflavík and after taking on a full load of fuel, Rockett's crew was quickly bound for Prestwick, Scotland, an 840-mile leg. It was now late July, and they were among the last of the 97th Bomb Group to make the crossing; Tibbets had been in the leading formation and missed the bad Arctic weather, arriving in Great Britain some three weeks earlier. At Prestwick, located on the western coast of Scotland on the Firth of Clyde coast, the B-17s picked up a British navigator to guide them to their new home—RAF Polebrook Airfield in Northamptonshire, England, about sixty-five miles north of London. By July 27, 1942, the Operation Bolero movement was declared complete, with a total of five B-17s and six P-38s lost.[21] The 97th Bomb Group/VIII Bomber Command and the 1st Fighter Group/VIII Fighter Command of the Eighth Air Force had become the first large American air group to reach Great Britain during World War II.[22]

5

# FORTRESS EUROPA

The selection of Polebrook as the group's base had not been random.[1] Through President Franklin Roosevelt's Lend-Lease program, a squadron of American B-17C models had been sent to the airfield in the summer of 1941, before the United States had entered the war. The Royal Air Force (RAF) had used them in a number of daylight attacks, though with disappointing results. As a matter of fact, the U.S. Army Air Forces (USAAF) had declared the C model not combat-worthy, but the RAF had been so desperate they took the airplanes anyway.[2] And while later in 1941 the English withdrew the Cs from battle (to be used as trainers), positive developments did come from their early use. The first Flying Fortresses, despite their name, were in fact undergunned. More stingers were needed (including the ball turret previously mentioned) and their punch increased from the .30-caliber range to the more formidable .50 caliber (half-inch diameter bullet). Further, the airplane's rear fuselage had to be enlarged in order to strengthen the airframe and provide for a tail gunner position to ward off the Luftwaffe's increasingly effective stern attacks. Those and other improvements were manifested in the B-17E models the 97th Bomb Group had brought to England. An additional benefit of that early Fortress association with RAF Polebrook had been a commitment by the British to upgrade their aerodromes (as they called airfields) to accommodate the American B-17. Polebrook's main runway had been lengthened to 5,850 feet; the two secondary runways extended to 4,200 feet. Other English airfields had been similarly improved.

Strangely, after the frantic rush to get the bombers to England, the 97th Bomb Group's leadership fell victim to a peculiar lethargy.[3] It was almost as if the commanders had deemed their mission objectives accomplished once they had arrived, rather than a starting point toward prosecuting the air war against Germany. As Paul Tibbets described it in his autobiography, they "yielded to the temptations . . . in the neighborhood." It had all been very jolly in the beginning—the Americans were warmly welcomed by the English people, who were so very glad to have at last a familiar ally. The Russian resistance on the eastern front had certainly been welcome and appreciated, but the Americans were helping to defend their homeland and, even better, spoke (mostly) the same language.

The most gracious and well-meaning hospitality that the Army Air Forces (AAF) enjoyed came from the Rothschilds, upon whose property the Polebrook airfield had been built. The wealthy banking family's Ashton Estate became party central, with their thatched-roof Chequered Skipper pub (named after a rare butterfly) opening in the early afternoon and the booze and good times flowing until well into the wee hours.[4] Tibbets said that only one other squadron commander (Maj. John Knox) stayed away from "riding the hounds and high tea," those two officers sticking to business by way of intense maintenance and flight training schedules.[5] Overall, however, according to writer James Parton, the 97th Bomb Group remained not only undertrained it was a "lackadaisical [unit], loose-jointed, fun-loving and in no sense ready for combat."[6] Roughly a week after Rockett and his crew arrived, the situation was recognized as out of control.

On August 2, 1942, Maj. Gen. Carl "Tooey" Spaatz, Commander Eighth Air Force, and Brig. Gen. Ira Eaker, Commander VIII Bomber Command, sacked the 97th Group commander and installed in his place Col. Frank A. Armstrong Jr.[7] An erect West Pointer and widely respected, Armstrong purged several other officers and realigned his command structure, appointing Maj. Paul Tibbets group executive officer. A clear message had been sent all the way down to the lowliest private.

As it happened, Colonel Armstrong fell ill almost immediately. With the commander's concurrence, Major Tibbets stepped in as his surrogate and immediately laid down the law on discipline while demonstrating he was also a hands-on leader—a prime example being his work with the group's gunners. Drawing on his firearms training at the Western Military Academy, Tibbets taught them to wash their guns down in gasoline after every training sortie in order to prevent grease and other foreign materials from jamming the delicate mechanisms at high, freezing altitudes. While many of the gunners grumbled at the exec's intense, even hard-ass approach, they later admitted he had been right—while newly arriving groups' guns constantly jammed, those of the 97th functioned reliably. Tibbets also intensified both ground and flight training throughout the group, earning a reputation as a commander who would patiently explain the correct way to do things but expecting to only need to do it once. Those who were slow or sloppy were confronted by a steely eyed, temper-prone impatience. In the end, it all paid off. Within just a few weeks, Paul Tibbets and Frank Armstrong had turned the 97th Bomb Group around.[8]

Meanwhile, down in the junior officer ranks and when not under Tibbets' training lash, Van Kirk and Ferebee (the two did not like Rockett personally and saw little of him outside of duty hours) spent the bulk of their nonduty day like other newly arrived second lieutenant flying officers—discovering where the daily training schedule was posted, updating pay and personnel records, figuring out where to do the laundry and where to take chow, locating the barber, and so on. Always they were on the alert for a little fun, which most of the time took the form of poker playing and swapping scuttlebutt with the local RAF types over scotch and sodas at the Polebrook Officer's Club (the Chequered Skipper having fallen on hard times). It was during those early days at Polebrook that Dutch and Tom began to pal around with another 97th bombardier they had first met at Sarasota—Lt. Kermit K. Beahan, a man who became a great friend and would share much of their own destiny.

The American newcomers soon discovered what was meant by the well-known saying that described England and the United States as "two nations separated by a common language." A truck became a lorry, vehicle hoods were bonnets, airplane radios were the wireless, wrenches were spanners, flashlights were torches, and one went to the cinema instead of the movies. Some fellows had brought over electric radios and razors only to discover none of that stuff worked in England; the United States had a 120-volt system while the United Kingdom used 240 volts. The chief mode of personal transportation became the bicycle since few vehicles were available. If one was fortunate enough to have motorized travel available, "petrol" was always desperately short. The nation-wide blackout, something completely foreign to the Americans, also made it dangerous to travel at night. Headlamps were kept turned off and it was not uncommon for one person to sit on the front bumper and shout directions to the driver.[9]

Generally during those early weeks the fellows stuck close to Polebrook Field. Van Kirk wanted to familiarize himself with the geographical features of the English countryside and western Europe, along with learning RAF navigation protocols and chart usages. Ferebee needed to become more intimate with the bombing procedures they would be using, especially at higher altitudes. Most critically, the pilots had to be trained from scratch on mass assembly formation flying—how to get scores and later hundreds of airplanes all properly clustered together before departing English airspace.[10] There was also the weather problem. U.S. aviators had been trained in the flying-friendly American South and West and were shocked at the terrible conditions they encountered over Great Britain and coastal Europe, particularly with respect to fog and widespread overcasts. The Americans had also to learn about and use the unfamiliar English VHF (very high frequency) ship-to-ground and ship-to-ship wireless, a skill crucial to mass bomber launches and assemblies.

On August 7, Van Kirk wrote his folks that Lieutenant Rockett was ill and had been grounded for an undetermined time. He, Tom Ferebee, and the balance of the crew were now flying with Major Tibbets, who Van Kirk said "had been flying for a long time and is really good."[11] Tibbets did not have a crew of his own prior to the change; he had been flying as the supernumerary first pilot with another fully manned crew. Serendipitously, Rockett's illness afforded Tibbets an opportunity to have his own crew without further disruptions within the 340th Squadron. We can be reasonably certain the major would have made other arrangements if he had not believed Rockett's bunch was at least competent. Both Ferebee and Van Kirk, manning the two most critical positions on a bomber besides the aircraft commander, had been performing well. Still, there might have been something else—Van Kirk once asked Tibbets how it had all happened. Paul responded somewhat enigmatically: "You guys were so damn screwed up, I wanted to find out if anybody could straighten you out!"[12] Van Kirk was never quite sure if he was kidding or not. Likely the primary factor had been the immediate availability of Rockett's crew; Tibbets could slip into the left seat and that was that. If it did not work out, he could always get another crew.

All the while General Spaatz and General Eaker had been chafing at the bit to get into the fight against Hitler's Fortress Europa. Under great pressure from the Pentagon, they finally decided they were ready enough. Orders were cut to prepare for VIII Bomber Command's first combat mission, to be launched on Monday, August 17.[13] It had been decided that twelve 97th Bomb Group B-17Es would attack the railroad marshaling yards at Rouen, located in northern France on the English Channel coast. Six other Fortresses would launch at the same time, making a feint away from the primary target. RAF Spitfires were tasked to protect the heavies.

Two of the group's four squadrons had been disbursed to RAF Grafton Underwood, fifteen miles west of Polebrook. From there Major Tibbets was to pilot the lead plane with group commander Col. Frank Armstrong flying as his copilot. Tibbets had made arrangements to have his own B-17 and crew brought to Grafton, but somehow the order was bungled and the wrong plane was sent. At the last minute Tibbets was forced to cobble together an emergency crew and switch to another plane. Tom Ferebee, Dutch Van Kirk, and the rest of the men were left at Polebrook scratching their heads.

Taking off in the *Butcher Shop*, Tibbets and Armstrong assumed the wave lead in the first flight of six bombers; Brig. Gen. Ira Eaker was on board *Yankee Doodle*, the lead bomber in the second flight of six.[14] General Spaatz was on hand for the takeoff. It was an important event, watched carefully by both British and American brass alike. The Brits were quite skeptical about the U.S. plan to bomb by daylight; they had already tried it and had come up wanting. The Americans insisted they could do it. In a nutshell, a lot was riding on the mission.

It was a very short run across the Channel, and the Americans caught the Germans by surprise. While the railroad assembly yard targets were relatively minor targets in the overall scheme of things, they nevertheless were mostly destroyed. The B-17s unloaded successfully, and though two were damaged by flak, all ships returned safely to England. The AAF was jubilant, believing their strategic plan of daylight bombing using the "invincible" Flying Fortress had been vindicated. The British were genuinely happy for the Americans and said it aloud, though it would soon be made apparent to everyone that a very great deal was left to be learned about daylight strategic bombing. Still, it was an important moment for the Allies. The Americans had finally dipped their feet in the war waters, and the beginning of the beginning was finally behind them.

Well after the war, the events surrounding the early American strikes against Occupied Europe would be immortalized in the award-winning 1949 movie, *Twelve O'Clock High*. The screenplay had been adapted from a novel of the same name, written by Beirne Lay Jr. and Sy Bartlett. During this earlier period of the war, Lay—a rated bomber pilot himself (he would later see heavy combat as a B-24 group commander)—was a captain on Brig. Gen. Ira Eaker's staff; Major Bartlett was working for General Spaatz. Both had been in a position to observe how Armstrong and Tibbets had turned the 97th around in August of 1942. Armstrong later conducted another turnaround with the troubled 306th Bomb Group during the winter of 1943. The movie is a dramatic composite of actual events and real personalities from both groups.[15] In the film, the fictional character Brig. Gen. Frank Savage (Gregory Peck) was based partially on then-colonel Frank Armstrong; the fictional Major General Pritchard (Millard Mitchell) was based on a composite of then–major general Spaatz and then-brigadier general Ira Eaker. The group's crusty executive officer, the fictional Maj. Joe Cobb (John Kellogg) was largely patterned after Maj. Paul Tibbets. Interestingly, most aircrew of the Eighth Air Force considered this film to be the most accurate movie Hollywood ever produced about their war. Lay and Bartlett have been quoted as saying that Gen. Curtis LeMay, one of the great combat leaders in the airfight against the Luftwaffe, once told them he "couldn't find anything wrong with it."

VIII Bomber Command's second mission came just two days after the Rouen raid.[16] Twenty-four B-17s were scheduled to strike the German Abbeville-Drucat airfield located about 110 miles north of Paris. The primary objective was the destruction of the aircraft and support facilities of Jagdgeschwader (JG) 26, which literally translates as "Hunting Squadron #26."[17] The unit was the equivalent of three U.S. air groups, what the Americans would later call a "wing." First winning fame during the Battle of Britain under the leadership of then-major Adolf Galland, JG 26's yellowed-nosed Messerschmitt (ME) Bf-109s and Focke-Wulf FW-190s were especially feared by Allied bomber crews, who nicknamed them "the Abbeville Boys."[18] The two fighters could approach speeds of 400 mph and were armed with 13-mm (.51-caliber) machine guns and 20-mm cannon; along with the dreaded, remorseless flak that appeared over every worthwhile target, they represented the greatest threats to the Allied strategic bombing campaign.[19]

After returning from the Rouen mission, Maj. Paul Tibbets returned to Polebrook and found he had already been designated leader of the 97th Bomb

Group's next attack. This second mission—with Tibbets, Ferebee, and Van Kirk flying in the lead bomber position—set a pattern that endured for nearly all the combat missions the three men flew together. They were the first to take off, the first to meet flak or fighters, the first over the target, and the first to take heat when things went wrong—bearing all the burdens those responsibilities suggested.

For Ferebee and Van Kirk, both of whom were just beginning to understand how terribly undertrained they really were for the very important jobs they had been given, those early missions were especially difficult. First, they had to demonstrate to Tibbets their competence to fly lead—no small thing. Second, lives and results would depend on their ability to absorb some extremely accelerated on-the-job training. As incredible as it might seem to twenty-first-century readers, Tibbets' navigator had never flown above 10,000 feet and his bombardier had never dropped a bomb from above 12,000 feet. The attack on August 19, 1942, against Abbeville was to be from 20,000 feet. As Van Kirk related in *My True Course*, "I looked down and thought, 'Christ that looks different!' "[20] He also admitted that he was terribly frightened on that first mission and was always grateful they did not get shot at—his chief worry, like that of every other individual who first goes into combat, was whether he could take it and not let down his buddies.

There was a great deal to learn about four- to five-mile-high bombing in a nonpressurized Flying Fortress. Never before had the crews of the 97th Bomb Group experienced such excruciating cold and discomfort. Wrapped in cumbersome flying suits, fur-lined jackets and caps, and thick gloves and encumbered by an extremely irritating oxygen mask and dangling hoses, even the smallest of tasks could be performed only with great difficulty. For navigator Van Kirk, it was a little warmer up in the nose but still difficult to use plotter and dividers and to provide Tibbets with accurate headings and ETAs. Perhaps the most serious nonhostile hazard at 25,000 feet was oxygen deprivation. Hypoxia, which can quickly lead to anoxia—permanent physical damage or death—seemed to most often come when the aircrew's attention was elsewhere, such as on a bomb run, or when under attack. Several times while busy at a task or scrambling from one machine gun to another Van Kirk and Ferebee rescued the other man from a loose oxygen mask. "Dutch, do you know where you are at?" Tom shouted on one frenetic mission.[21] After getting a dull stare for an answer, Ferebee giant-stepped over to Van Kirk and rearranged his oxygen mask, it having unknowingly slipped off to one side. A minute later, Van Kirk had thrown off the hypoxia and was back to work.

Only later would Tibbets, Ferebee, and Van Kirk learn their Abbeville-Drucat strike had been of special significance, a diversion intended to support Operation Jubilee, a so-called reconnaissance-in-force by six thousand Canadian troops landing near the French coastal city of Dieppe.[22] The objectives of the raid were to learn more about how to conduct a cross-channel invasion by seizing and holding an occupied port for a short period, gathering intelligence, and destroying as much of the enemy's coastal defenses as possible. In so doing, it was expected the raid would help take pressure off the Russians on the eastern front and boost morale in the United Kingdom. Unfortunately, none of the objectives were met. After less than half a day, the operation was in shambles. Sixty percent of the Canadians had been killed, wounded, or captured; the RAF gave up ninety-six aircraft to the Luftwaffe's forty-eight; and the Royal Navy lost one destroyer and thirty-three landing craft. Clearly, it was going to be a long time before the Allies could mount an effective ground offensive against Fortress Europe.

Tibbets and his bombers did better on that second mission, though in the overall scheme of things it was not very meaningful. While twenty-two B-17s inflicted substantial damage on the Abbeville-Drucat airfield (two turned back due to mechanical problems), the raid did nothing to affect the outcome at Dieppe. The very next day, August 20, Tibbets and company led a twelve-plane raid on the railroad marshaling yards at Amiens, with eleven ships reaching their target. With each subsequent mission, VIII Bomber Command's thinking was rapidly maturing. Tactics were jelling and increasing flexibility was being given to target selection. Major Tibbets and lieutenants Ferebee and Van Kirk continued to lead most of the group's missions, the latter two functioning as group bombardier and group navigator. Van Kirk, in particular, had been given major responsibility for planning and charting the strikes.

Some things did not change, however. Prior to one of the early sorties, Ferebee and Van Kirk once again reverted to their juvenile delinquent tendencies. If it had happened with any commander other than Tibbets, there would have been hell to pay. It seems the two young devil-may-care lieutenants had wangled a pass to London for some rest and recreation. As sometimes can happen when a couple of fellows are having too much fun, they overstayed their time. To avoid a run-in with the main gate Polebrook military police, they got back on post by climbing a fence. Surprise! The group was at that very moment in the middle of aircraft preflights, preparing for a combat mission, and Tibbets had been forced to hunt up another navigator and bombardier.

"Where the hell have you guys been?" the major demanded.[23] The thoroughly chastised duo had no response. Tibbets dismissed the replacements and said little else except to tell his two miscreants to take up where the others had left off, making them fly the mission while still dressed in their Class A uniforms. A relieved Ferebee and Van Kirk instantly grasped that this was the lightest punishment they could possibly have gotten. That was the moment, Van Kirk later stated, that the three's relationship began to change. Tibbets could have crucified them but instead had protected them from possible dereliction of duty charges, the second time he had looked the other way when they ran afoul of the authorities. Then and there, the two silently vowed never to let Paul Tibbets down on a mission. And they never did.

On August 21, Tibbets' crew led an attack on a Rotterdam shipyard. It was on this trip—Tibbets' fourth mission and Ferebee's and Van Kirk's third—that the boys had their first real scrape with the Luftwaffe. Due to a communications foul-up, the twelve B-17s were late rendezvousing with the fighter escorts.[24] Low on gas, the RAF Spitfires had to return to base just as the bombers headed out over the English Channel. Tibbets' wave had no more than arrived at the Holland coast when senior commanders realized the risk was too great and issued a recall order. It was almost too late—after the Americans turned around they were jumped by a couple of squadrons of Me-109s and FW-190s and had to run a gauntlet to get back across the Channel. Somehow all the Forts returned to England with only a few casualties, though several B-17s were holed. The mission had brought a couple things into clearer focus—the B-17 was indeed a tough airplane, but the enemy was no pushover either.

So far no B-17s had been lost, and the Americans had begun to think their "fortresses" were exactly that.[25] Unfortunately, the actual reason the bombers had been spared was more prosaic.[26] Not only were there fewer B-17s involved in the American daylight raids compared to the large-formation British night attacks, but the design of the Fortress itself restricted it to only relatively small bomb payloads. As a result, the Americans had not yet done enough damage to warrant sending up large numbers of fighters to thwart them—in a sense, VIII Bomber Command's own weak punch had lulled it into a false sense of security. This institutional complacence began to end on August 24, 1942, when VIII Bomber Command lost the first of what would become a great many B-17s to enemy fire. It was also a day when the Luftwaffe nearly caught up with Tibbets and his men over the Le Trait shipping yards near Le Havre on the French coast. Paul Tibbets would later say this was "the most frightening brush with death I was to experience [during the war]."[27]

By that time—the fifth strike by the 97th Bomb Group—a certain launch protocol had been sorted out, one that Eighth Air Force in England would essentially follow for the balance of the war. Once a target was selected, assets committed, and a date and time for launch assigned, the air, ground, maintenance, and munitions crews would reverse schedule their own planning requirements in order to meet takeoff times. Prelaunch specialized and general briefings were held to include fuel and bomb loads, aircraft weight and balance data, mission routing, escort fighters required, altitudes and airspeeds, weather conditions, available electronic navigation aids (e.g., radio station frequencies for bearings), target study, enemy fighter and flak-battery locations, alternate airfields, sea rescue assets, ditching reminders, and so on—a thousand details. Once the briefs were completed, watches synchronized to the exact same "tic," and the so-called last meal consumed, the crews were transported to the hardstands and the individual preflights begun.

On that morning of the Le Trait mission, Paul Tibbets and his copilot, 2nd Lt. Gene Lockhart, performed their usual aircraft walk-around inspection to ensure the wings were indeed attached to the fuselage; landing gear and tires were in proper condition; aileron/elevator control lock pins (for gusting winds) removed; propellers and lifting surfaces free of damage; no oil or hydraulic fluid leaks; and, together with the crew chief, all previous write-ups on the Maintenance Form 1A had been repaired or accounted for. Meanwhile Tom Ferebee inspected the bomb-bay doors and weapons load, removing the red-flagged bomb-fusing safety pins. After entering the airplane through the nose hatch, he worked his way forward into the greenhouse to arrange his station, crosschecking panel switches and instruments and carefully loading in the precomputed altitude, airspeed, and bomb ballistics data into the B-17E's Norden bombing system (sighthead, stabilizer, and C-1 autopilot).

Immediately to Ferebee's left rear and facing the left side of the fuselage, Van Kirk arranged charts, dead reckoning kit, and mission folders on his navigation desk before checking out his panel instruments, master compass, and driftmeter, giving the latter an especially careful going over. On these relatively short missions there would be no time or opportunity for sextant observations. Navigation on nearly all European Theater of Operation (ETO) missions would be conducted via combinations of radio bearings from ground stations, pilotage, dead reckoning, and driftmeter readings (aided later in the war by mapping radar).[28] After finishing with the specialized equipment at their individual stations, the two men checked out the nose compartment's machine gun, oxygen system, radio headsets and throat mikes, survival kits, flare pistols, and parachutes.[29]

By this time Tibbets and Lockhart had finished their external walk-around and they and the flight engineer/top turret gunner, Sgt. Warren "Blackie" Hughes, were running the pre-engine start checklists.[30] On the other side of the bomb-bay catwalk the radio operator, Sgt. Orville Splitt, was checking out his direction-finding equipment and long-range Morse code transmitter/receiver. When airborne radio navigation was being used, the radio operator and navigator worked together closely—Splitt would tune in and identify the station, then read off the bearing over the ship's intercom to Van Kirk, who plotted it on his chart. At the same time the waist and ball turret gunners, Sergeant Fitzgerald and Sergeant Rich, were inspecting their Browning M2 .50-caliber machine guns and ammunition belts, with Sgt. John T. "Willie" Tittsworth doing the same with his own twin-50-cals in the tail. Following these external and internal preflights, the entire crew assembled at the nose of the airplane where Aircraft Commander Tibbets inspected, then signed off each man as ready for launch.

When the proper moment came for engine start, Tibbets waved a single finger (indicating the number one screw was about to turn) out his left side window at the crew chief standing on the tarmac and instructed copilot Lockhart to hit the starter switch on number one. (All four-engine aircraft power plants are numbered in the same fashion—left wing outboard engine is #1; left inboard, #2; right inboard, #3; and right outboard, #4.) The chief and his assistants were standing by with fire extinguishers as number one turned, coughed, then came to life. A few minutes later all four were up and running. Tibbets idled the throttles at 1,000 rpm while he and Lockhart checked for their normal operation and ensured the electrical and hydraulic systems were functioning properly. With the bombers operating in radio silence so as not to alert the Germans that a launch was imminent, Van Kirk monitored taxi time (every bomber navigator functioned as a "traffic cop," notifying the crew of action points, turns, and airspeed and altitude changes). At the proper moment, Tibbets advanced the throttles and the twelve B-17s rolled into takeoff position.

Some minutes later and after the ignition/engine run-up checks had been completed, Polebrook tower fired the launch flare. Pressing down hard on his toe brakes, Tibbets ran the four Wright Cyclone engine throttles up to 2,500 rpm and set the turbosupercharger controls at 46 inches Hg (engine manifold pressure measured in inches of mercury)—maximum takeoff power.[31] With engines howling and the aircraft pawing at the runway as if it were as anxious as the men to get going, the flight deck crew performed a last instrument scan to ensure all four sets of tachometer, manifold pressure, engine head temperature, and oil pressure gauges were reading normally. Satisfied, Tibbets released the brakes.

The Fortress lurched forward, beginning the always agonizingly slow build-up to flying speed. Using throttle adjustments on the two outboard engines to maintain directional control, Tibbets kept the bomber rolling down the middle of the runway. At around 60–70 mph, the increased airflow racing past the lifting surfaces began to take hold and Tibbets switched to his heels (engaging the rudder) for runway alignment. At about 100 mph, the pilot eased back on the yoke. Twenty-six tons of bomber, fuel, and payload slowly rose into the air, with Tibbets tapping his toe brakes one last time to stop the main wheels from spinning. He signaled Lockhart to raise the landing gear while Van Kirk checked his watch and logged the takeoff time. The five remaining bombers in Tibbets flight of six followed every thirty seconds, with the second flight of six quickly on their heels.

After passing 200 feet above ground level and in order to lessen the enormous strain on the engines, Tibbets reduced the four throttles to a climb setting of 2,300 rpm on the tachometer and pulled the manifold pressure back to 42 inches Hg. Reaching down with his right hand, he twirled the manual elevator trim wheel on the control pedestal to neutralize fore and aft control pressures, stabilizing the ship at the proscribed climb indicated air speed of 135 mph. After passing 400 feet above ground level and ninety seconds had elapsed, he made a gentle 180 degree half-needle-width turn. The number two aircraft repeated that same sequence ten seconds later, then number three and so on until the other five ships had tucked into position behind Tibbets.[32] The B-17 pilot training manual called for clearances between aircraft of 50 feet from nose to tail and wingtip to wingtip, but for the still-green pilots of the 97th, that would have been too much to ask, and a much looser formation was used for the Le Trait mission. The airplanes continued their climb, with the crews going on oxygen after passing 10,000 feet. After the two six-plane flights had assembled and leveled off at their cruise altitudes, the pilots manipulated the throttles to between 1,800 and 2,000 rpm and manifold pressure to around 34 inches, settings that would yield roughly 150 mph indicated airspeed at 25,000 feet (about 225 mph true airspeed at that altitude).[33] Lead navigator Van Kirk fingered his throat mike and told Tibbets to take up a southerly heading of 180 degrees magnetic for the short run across the English Channel to Le Trait, France.[34]

The formation assemblies over England were hairy enough in the early days when there were only twelve or fifteen planes per mission; one can only imagine how complicated—indeed, *dangerous*—such maneuvers became later in the war when many hundred plane raids became commonplace. Putting together very large formations into what became known as the mutually supporting, stacked "combat boxes" was made even more difficult by the treacherous English weather, especially the persistent low clouds and infernal fog. Except for those terrible minutes when under direct fire by enemy flak or fighters, most Eighth Air Force aircrew came to consider the assembly maneuvers the most hazardous part of a combat mission.

The bombing run itself on the Le Trait port went well enough, but the results were poor, with only a quarter of the weapons striking the targets. Even Ferebee, the lead bombardier, was still having difficulty adjusting to visual bombing from twice the altitude he had been trained at. The real trouble came on the return home near the French–Belgian border when Tibbets' wave was attacked by the yellow-nosed Abbeville Boys. There was a terrific air battle, with Me-109s darting helter-skelter in and out of the Fortresses, cannon and machine-gun fire raking the bombers from all directions. Several B-17s were hit, though all managed to stay in formation. After several minutes of intense fighting, the Americans burst into the clear, and it seemed the worst was over.

Suddenly, from the twelve o'clock "in-your-face" position, a yellow-nose streaked head-on at Tibbets' lead bomber.[35] He instinctively began evasive action but still the enemy pilot's tracers kept homing in on the Fort. All at once a 20-mm shell slammed into the right side of the cockpit and exploded. Tibbets felt the sting of metal fragments and glass hitting his right side while observing blood spraying over the forward instrument panel. He glanced to his right and saw most of it was coming from copilot Lockhart, who had part of his left hand shot off.

Down in the nose compartment, Ferebee and Van Kirk (physically separated from the others by the pilots' forward instrument panel bulkhead) could only wonder what the hell had happened. All the two knew for sure was that they had gotten the bejesus shot out of them—the shell had impacted just above their heads.

"Tom, come up and help us!" Tibbets shouted over intercom, at least solving a portion of the mystery. Van Kirk looked over his shoulder and saw a red-colored liquid dripping down the bulkhead from below the pilot's feet. "Jesus, Tom," he yelled wide-eyed. "Is that blood?" Ferebee, who was racing through the hatch door that led up to the flight deck, paused a moment to swipe a finger through the fluid and take a quick look. "Naw," he shouted over a shoulder as he kept moving, "it's only leaking hydraulic fluid."[36]

The Fort began shuddering in protest over the onslaught and Tibbets' attention was drawn away from Lockhart and back to the controls as he instinctively remembered the most fundamental tenet drilled into every pilot: No matter what else is happening, always fly the airplane!

It was at this moment that panic came, though from an entirely unexpected quarter.[37] Col. Newton Longfellow, a senior commander on his first combat mission, had asked Tibbets to take him along for the ride. Longfellow was a long-serving officer with a tough-guy reputation who had become friendly with Tibbets while playing handball at the RAF's facilities on Polebrook. The group exec had said "sure" without giving it another thought. Actually, there was no choice—Longfellow's "request" had only been a courtesy. In any event, the last thing the major would have expected was the very highly experienced colonel's reaction to the emergency.

Longfellow had been standing between the pilot and copilot stations when the 20-mm shell tore through the forward instrument panel. Tibbets had kept his left hand clamped firmly on the yoke while grabbing Lockhart's mangled left hand with his right, holding it high in the air to reduce the heavy blood loss. Ferebee had no more than got up to the cockpit when Colonel Longfellow suddenly reached out to the center control pedestal and, for reasons even he would never understand, retarded all four turbo controls and engine throttles.[38] Tibbets' lead bomber slowed dramatically and began dropping out of the tight formation. Had that movement continued for any length of time, he and his crew would likely have collided with another B-17 or quickly dropped out of the protective formation, becoming easy prey for enemy fighters.

Tibbets yelled at Longfellow to stop messing with the controls, but the man would not back off. Long seconds passed with the situation at a complete impasse. The aircraft commander realized desperate measures would have to be taken if they were not all to be killed. With Longfellow still leaning in over the center pedestal only inches away, Tibbets released Lockhart's bleeding left hand, cocked his own right arm, and let fly with a vicious elbow into the colonel's chin, knocking him senseless. Ferebee caught Longfellow on the fly and laid him out on the flight deck, then hustled up to Lockhart and tied a handkerchief—all Ferebee had—around the injured hand. The bombardier then pulled the copilot out of his seat and half-dragged him back to the radio operator's station behind the bomb bay. At that point Ferebee (grudgingly) passed out from hypoxia—he had raced upstairs without a portable yellow oxygen bottle. Meanwhile, Sergeant Rich in the nearby ball turret position was screaming at the top of his lungs, "I'm dying! I'm dying!"[39] He had been shot in the foot and was bleeding badly, having confusingly smeared blood all over himself in the chaos. Someone slapped an $O_2$ mask on Ferebee and the bombardier quickly came around; he and Sergeant Splitt then tended to the wounded ball turret gunner, who had been hurt bad but not mortally.

While all this was going on, another enemy fighter had attacked the ship.[40] A bullet creased the top of Sergeant Hughes skull, the flight engineer who was now manning the top gun turret. Hughes fell unconscious, landing on top of Longfellow. The impact of Hughes, plus the terrifically cold air blasting into the cockpit through the holes in the fuselage left by the earlier cannon fire, brought the colonel back to full consciousness. Tibbets tells us Longfellow's earlier panic appeared to dissolve as quickly as it had appeared, and he got into Lockhart's seat to take over copilot duties. By then the aircraft commander had regained full control of the ship and was working his way back into the lead position. Within minutes, the B-17s were well out into the channel and nearly back over England. Tibbets tells us Longfellow performed well for the balance of the mission, including firing without being prompted the Very pistol's "wounded on board" flare on final approach to Polebrook. When they were back on the ground, a mortified Colonel Longfellow apologized for his actions, telling Tibbets he had done the right thing. Tibbets later said he was relieved to learn their friendship had survived intact. In the end, probably thanks to Tibbets' silence on the incident, Col. Newton Longfellow did not suffer professionally from the experience—he was promoted to brigadier general, later serving as the commanding general of VIII Bomber Command, though with decidedly mixed results.[41]

It was touch and go with Lieutenant Lockhart for a few days due to so much blood loss and his left hand almost gone, but he did eventually recover. Interestingly, the encounter itself offered VIII Bomber Command a public relations coup. A couple of weeks after the mission Major General Spaatz invited the press to observe him decorating a number of VIII aircrew, including the Purple Heart for Hughes, Rich, Lockhart, and Tibbets. Tibbets was embarrassed to be included because his injuries had been minor. He complained to Capt. Beirne Lay, who was then serving as General Eaker's public information officer, saying he had a job to do and did not have time for this nonsense.[42] Lay, who was himself a "Kelly Field Mister," told Tibbets in no uncertain terms that he too had a job to do and that he, Tibbets, had better be at the ceremony with bells on. Many U.S. newspapers published stories and photos of the presentation; *Life* magazine dedicated an entire page including a photo featuring Tibbets and Lockhart, whose left hand and arm had been spectacularly bandaged.

Promotions also began coming through. Both Tom and Dutch made first lieutenant effective September 1, 1942; Ferebee's silver bar was somewhat belated considering he had several months more service than Van Kirk. Notwithstanding his duties as group exec, Major Tibbets had also to deal with a major reorganization of his own crew.[43] Lt. William "Junior" Ryan replaced Gene Lockhart as copilot. While radio operator Orville Splitt remained on the team, the injured Blackie Hughes was replaced by Herman "Horizontal" Hague, an infamous sack rat who had been on the first American B-17 shot down. New sergeant gunners Peach and Quate joined Fitzgerald and Tittsworth, with Sgt. Zach Gowen replacing Sergeant Rich in the dangerous rotating ball turret station located in the Fortress's tender underbelly.

The B-17E originally assigned to Lieutenant Rockett had to be scrapped after the Le Trait mission, and Tibbets was given another E model. There would be no time for the guys to lick their wounds; the missions were coming one after the other, with Tibbets and his crew continuing out in front leading the group. It was about this time that it began to dawn on Van Kirk and Ferebee that their chances of completing the required twenty-five combat missions were not promising. They also had been closely observing their pilot and aircraft commander, Paul Tibbets. He must be, they reasoned, as frightened deep down as they were when things got hot, but he never let it show. Nor did his performance as a pilot or commander ever waver—he was as steady as they came. The major had, they sensed, somehow given himself up to providence and was therefore able to get on with his job without dwelling on the matter. After contemplating Tibbets' fatalistic approach to the war and discussing the odds of their own survival, Dutch and Tom came to the conclusion there was no chance they could live through a full tour, and as a result they might just as well stop worrying about it. Following Tibbets' lead, a certain calm resignation fell over the two fellows, which helped them immeasurably in dealing with their remaining time in combat.

Nevertheless and despite the philosophy, one can be sure that as the missions continued and the flak and fighters once again began swarming around them, the sweat poured just as freely as it had before. On one sortie while under attack, Van Kirk had arbitrarily moved from one machine gun to another, discovering a few minutes later four bullet holes next to where his head would have been, had he stayed at the old spot. On another mission Van Kirk took some shrapnel in his butt from a flak burst that was sufficient to need bandaging but not enough for either hospital or Purple Heart. At that point, the two fellows took it upon themselves to lay armor plating on the aircraft's nose compartment deck floor for a little extra insurance—flak suits were not yet in use. (Van Kirk told me he never wore a flak suit during the war.)

They were going to need all the protection they could get on the two missions following Le Trait. The first was once again against the shipyards at Rotterdam, where Tibbets' men claimed they saw the worst antiaircraft fire of the war. According to Van Kirk, "The Germans shot the hell out of us."[44] When the crew landed back at Polebrook, a war correspondent interviewed Tibbets' crew. It seems that Van Kirk had been a mighty busy fellow both navigating the lead bomber and manning the nose .30-caliber machine gun, moving it to either the left or right side insertion port depending on the direction of the threat. The tail of their B-17 had been severely damaged by cannon fire, and Tibbets was barely able to get the airplane back to England. The correspondent's report reached Van Kirk's hometown newspaper back in what the U.S. military was now calling the "ZI," or Zone of the Interior. The *Sunbury Daily Item* had titled the story, "North'd Aviator Shines in Raid on Rotterdam." The very next day, on August 28, the fellows took on the Avions Potez airplane factory at Méaulte, France. The opposition was nearly as bad as at Rotterdam, with Van Kirk and Ferebee firing madly away to no avail at the German fighters. Again their B-17 suffered more hits, though no one was injured.

September brought additional strikes on the strong German fortifications at Rouen, Méaulte, and Rotterdam. Raids were also conducted on the German airfields located on the French airfields at Morlaix-Ploujean and Saint-Omer, with VIII Bomber Command taking ever-increasing casualties in men and airplanes. Groups of the new B-17F models along with the other American heavy, the B-24 Liberator, were flowing into the ETO almost weekly. More bombers meant larger raids could be mounted, with Tibbets' bunch leading most of them.[45] On September 27, Col. Hampton "Hamp" Atkinson became Tibbets' boss when he relieved Col. Frank Armstrong, who was returned to VIII Bomber Command's Headquarters staff.

As the weeks went by, Tibbets found himself becoming more and more pleased with his crew. The boyish-looking new copilot, Junior Ryan, was working out well and the enlisted crew—all of whom were sergeants—had been handling themselves first-rate. He was particularly pleased with the performance and unflappability of Ferebee and Van Kirk. Van Kirk had been consistently reliable as the wave lead navigator, maintaining his courses and hitting his ETAs consistently on every mission. Ferebee's aim as the lead bombardier had become extraordinary; he possessed an almost uncanny ability to put his bombs on the target mission after mission. His reputation for steadiness and accuracy under fire soon spread beyond the group.[46]

By the first week of October, Tibbets' second E model had also been used up, and he needed another airplane. He picked out a shiny new B-17F bearing the serial number 41-24444.[47] Tom Ferebee and Dutch Van Kirk, both of whom had already gained reputations as card sharks, took one look at it and declared the airplane had "a winning poker hand." Sgt. Orville Splitt, the crew's pipe-smoking radio operator and resident intellectual, had an inspiration. He had uncovered an anonymous 1920s poem written by someone in the RAF, which was subsequently adopted by its World War II No. 1 Photographic Reconnaissance Unit (PRU). "The tale of the Gremlins, Told by the PRU" was a rhyme invoking the role of gremlins in aviation. Even today, many airmen claim they at least half-believe such mythical creatures inhabit every flying machine and that from time to time are wont to suddenly appear and wreak mischief, especially when the crew is distracted by other problems or threats. Splitt modified the verse to fit Tibbets' crew and in the process sealed the deal on a name for their new bomber. Here is a portion of the sergeant's version of the PRU poem (brackets show the original RAF recon unit's wording; the last two stanzas are apparently original to Splitt), which he titled "In Tribute to the *Red Gremlin*":

When you're five [seven] miles up in the heavens
(That's a Hell of a lonely spot),
And it's fifty degrees below zero,
Which isn't exactly hot;

When you're frozen blue like your Fortress [Spitfire],
And scared a mosquito pink;
When you're a thousand miles from nowhere,
And there's nothing below but the drink;

It's then you will see the Gremlins,
Green and purple [gamboge] and gold,
Male and female and neuter,
Gremlins both young and old.

White ones will wiggle your wingtips,
Orange [Male] ones will muddle your maps,
Grey [Green] ones will guzzle your glycol,
Green [Female] ones will flutter your flaps.

BUT
Don't be too quick to condemn them,
Don't cuss every Gremlin you see,
For the little RED GREMLINS will help you,
If ever in trouble you be.

And so as sort of a tribute,
To the Little Known Guys on Our Crew,
We've named our fortress "RED GREMLIN,"
We thought that's the least we could do.[48]

The F model B-17 was much improved over the E, so much so that many aviation historians deem it the first really battle-worthy Fortress.[49] Nearly identical externally to the E model, the F incorporated over four hundred changes. Among the most important was improved aircraft performance via slightly longer and wider so-called paddle blade Hamilton Standard propellers. The addition of a second machine gun in the nose provided for additional frontal attack protection, with both of those weapons becoming fixed and upgraded to the larger .50 caliber. There were also significant improvements to the bomb racks, ball turret guns, landing gear, brakes, and crew oxygen system. Of particular interest to Ferebee and Van Kirk had been the greatly increased firepower at their nose stations. Instead of just one .30-caliber "squirt gun," as Van Kirk called it, now each man had his own dedicated, powerful machine gun.

At least in the Red Gremlin's case, there is not much evidence that better nose armament appreciably improved the ship's overall defense. As mentioned in an earlier chapter, in the rush to get the early bomber groups to England, there was no time to give navigators and bombardiers formal gunnery training. In fact, the first time Ferebee and Van Kirk shot their machine guns was in anger. Van Kirk told me that, prior to their first combat mission, neither he nor Ferebee had ever once fired the standard military sidearm, the M1911 Colt/Browning .45 semiautomatic pistol. As witnessed by their combat performance, this lack of training clearly showed—by their own admission the two never hit anything, always shooting behind the enemy fighters. There was irony here. In 1995 Van Kirk told the *Charlotte Observer* what he had been thinking the first time they went up against the feared German "yellow-noses": "How lucky can I be? I've got this [great hunter from Davie County] and hot shot marksman with me here in the nose of this B-17! As it turned out, we were probably the [one] navigator and bombardier [team] who shot the most ammunition in the war without hitting anything."[50]

At the time the two consoled themselves with the thought that at least they could vent their fury by firing and cursing at the slashing Messerschmitts and Focke-Wulfs, maybe once in a while scaring one a little. Van Kirk, always a man to find sardonic humor in any situation, said the RAF Spitfire pilots told him the most dangerous part of their escort work was meeting the bombers when they returned to England because the Americans would shoot at anything that moved. Fortunately, as Van Kirk and Ferebee had already ruefully learned, they told him "you could never hit anything."

Inevitably, Tibbets, Ferebee, and Van Kirk began to talk about what their bombing was doing not just to Germans soldiers but also to the civilians below, who were also getting injured and killed. The twentieth century had brought a new dimension to warfare; it was no longer only the combatants that were involved. The respective home fronts had become crucial to their own side's successful prosecution of the conflict, which in most minds made them legitimate targets as well. After a lot of back and forth, the three men finally decided the entire matter was irreconcilable. Aside from clear-cut, individual instances of needless brutality, one had simply to accept that there was no morality to begin with in any war. As soldier and officers sworn to do their duty and who believed in the national cause, they could only do their jobs and hope for the best.

The 97th Bomb Group continued to hammer at German military fortifications in Holland and France throughout October. With the continuing influx of new bomber groups, other units began leading some of the missions, giving Tibbets and his crew a breather. While group exec Tibbets was required to keep his nose to the grindstone, junior lieutenants Ferebee and Van Kirk took advantage of every opportunity to sample the night life in London and Cambridge, the latter much nearer to Polebrook.[51] There was the usual entertainment enjoyed by GIs everywhere, of course, including sponsored dances put on by British and American support services. While Van Kirk went out a few times, he remained very much dedicated to his Northumberland sweetheart, Mary Jane Young. Ferebee, on the other hand, had no romantic interests in the ZI and was free to play the field. He had been dating a young lady in Peterborough about six miles north of Polebrook and one night got caught there during a German air raid, giving him quite an adventure getting back to the field in the near-pitch-dark blackout. When not pursuing the fair sex, there was local sightseeing and going to the movies; the boys were greatly amused by the local theaters playing the British national anthem, *God Save the King*, before and after each picture.[52]

It was also around this time that ordinary British citizens began to feel the full impact of having so many young, healthy American boys descend upon their small island nation. The Rothschild "my house is your house" feelings of only a few months earlier was rapidly being replaced by a certain resentment. The situation had become somewhat akin to having an exotic cousin who comes for a visit and then not only overstays his welcome but wants to move into the household. As the Brits saw it, the Yanks were "over paid, over sexed, and over here."

On October 9, 1942, recently promoted Lt. Col. Paul Tibbets led the first American raid of one-hundred-plus bombers against Lille, France, the capital of the Nord-Pas-de-Calais region located about fifty miles inland from the English Channel. The specific targets at Lille included a massive complex of steel and engineering works along with the adjacent railroad marshaling yards. The size of the attacking force—a mix of eighty-four B-17s and twenty-four

B-24s from the newly arrived 93rd Bomb Group, all escorted by hundreds of British Spitfires—underscored both to their English ally and to the German foe that the American VIII Bomber Command was at last to be taken as a serious armed force.[53]

Unfortunately the raid turned out poorly. Roughly 30 percent of the bombers did not even reach the primary target—thirty-three airplanes either aborted or were shot down. The B-24s in particular took a real drubbing, the Germans having discovered that those first-arriving Liberators were much more vulnerable to a belly attack than the B-17s. Fourteen of the twenty-four B-24s turned back or were shot down.[54] Tibbets' own 97th Bomb Group fared well; only one of its twenty-two bombers failed to reach the target. While American bomber crews initially claimed fifty-six fighters shot down, it was soon realized kills were being double and triple counted by gunners from different airplanes, and the official number was later downgraded to only twenty-one. In spite of the brave front VIII Bomber Command put on to the press, it was not at all an auspicious beginning to America's first large-scale daylight bombing raid. The results were especially sobering when one reflects that the targets were literally just across the English Channel. The warnings the RAF had given the Americans about the terrible risks that daylight bombing would run were back to center stage in the minds of AAF leadership. What would happen when the bombers began deeper penetrations into Germany?

As it turned out for Tibbets, Ferebee, and Van Kirk, those questions were rendered moot within days of their return to Polebrook. Unbeknownst to everyone but the top brass, something very big on the political front was brewing. Joseph Stalin's complaints about the absence of a second front had reached a fevered pitch; Churchill and Roosevelt found themselves compelled to respond. Only weeks earlier, friends and foes alike had assumed that the Americans would throw all their might into a direct invasion of France at the earliest practicable date. Now a combination of Soviet pressure, the Dieppe fiasco, and a full realization of the tremendous logistical challenges involved in supporting a cross-channel invasion had triggered a major change in strategy. There was to be a second front all right, but from a direction no one would have predicted.

6

# THE GENERALS AND NORTH AFRICA

Lt. Col. Paul Tibbets smiled at Junior Ryan as the *Red Gremlin* broke out of the heavy overcast and into sunshine. It was midday on October 18, 1942, and they were well out into the Atlantic flying on a sweeping southerly arc around the German-patrolled Bay of Biscay and the nominally neutral countries of Spain and Portugal.[1] Since leaving RAF Hurn at Bournemouth, England, it had been several hours of nothing but heavy overcast, requiring mostly instrument flying; the suddenly clear weather had perked both pilots up.

After Dutch Van Kirk finished resolving a rather shaky driftmeter observation, he decided to crosscheck those findings with a wave reading technique he had picked up from an old Bournemouth sea captain.[2] Always the inquisitive man, Van Kirk was not the sort to let any kind of valuable tip slip away, especially in the midst of a war when such knowledge might have a bearing on his own personal survival. The driftmeter was a reliable instrument over land, but at sea sometimes the white caps tended to break up or not stay stable long enough for accurate wind and ground speed observations. If there was another way to judge the wind and drift over water, Van Kirk was all ears.

To get a better perspective, the navigator edged his way up next to Tom Ferebee and peered down through the bottom of the nose greenhouse. The old sea captain had told Van Kirk that the wind is always perpendicular to the white caps—if they are regular in size, the wind is twelve miles per hour; breaking and foaming caps meant eighteen miles per hour. Van Kirk studied the eastern Atlantic for a few minutes, noted the observed values in the navigator's log, then spun them out on the wind side of his E6-B circular computer. Little did he know that while this new technique would serve as an interesting crosscheck on the way to Gibraltar, it was to become extraordinarily important on the flight back to England.

Van Kirk finished calculating what he knew Tibbets was waiting for and, fingering his intercom throat mike, radioed it up to him. The pilot rogered an acknowledgment and turned to speak to the man in a makeshift seat between him and Junior. The tall, distinguished-looking officer wearing a lieutenant colonel's uniform leaned forward to better hear what the pilot was shouting over the engine noise. "Navigator tells me we're one hour out of Gibraltar!"

Maj. Gen. Mark Clark nodded slightly and returned his attention to the documents in his lap. It was imperative that he learn more about the man he was on his way to secretly meet, the top Vichy French commander in Morocco and Algeria—Gen. Charles Mast. Clark was deputy to Lt. Gen. Dwight Eisenhower, commander of the upcoming Operation Torch, the Allied invasion of North Africa.

Thirty-six hours earlier, Tibbets had received a surprise telephone call from Gen. Tooey Spaatz. The general tersely informed the colonel he was to fly General Clark to Gibraltar on a clandestine top-secret mission. Two B-17s would be required, with Tibbets transporting Clark and his group in the *Red Gremlin* and another VIII Bomber Command pilot, Wayne Connors, flying the alternate group headed by Brig. Gen. Lyman Lemnitzer in *Boomerang.* Earlier General Mast had sent a highly confidential message to the U.S. State Department stating that he would welcome the opportunity to talk with a high-ranking American general about French military dispositions in North Africa. That had been enough to set the wheels in motion—within days a plan had been drawn up whereby Mast and Eisenhower's designee, General Clark, would meet in a remote location on the Vichy-held Algerian coast. The U.S. objective: arrange for the peaceful surrender of French troops who might otherwise oppose the American landings at Oran, Algiers, and Casablanca, scheduled in just a few weeks.[3]

The plan Clark was to execute had been hatched at Eisenhower's headquarters in England and was so fantastic it would have had difficulty getting sold as the plot for a novel. Clark, along with key staff and French interpreters, was to fly to Gibraltar where he and his entourage would be met by the British submarine *Seraph* and transported to Cherchell, Algeria, a remote coastal location about forty miles southwest of Algiers.[4] There they would hurriedly meet with the French general staff, secure an agreement, and return within hours via the same way they had come. Time was of the essence due to the very short time between the Mark Clark mission and the upcoming invasion; Clark had a great deal of difficulty getting all the diplomatic and technical issues resolved in time. On the evening of October 17, the general had been smuggled into RAF Hurn dressed in a lieutenant colonel's uniform so as not to be recognized. After spending an anonymous evening in something like an American bachelor officer's quarters, Clark and party boarded the two B-17s early the next morning.

Lieutenant Van Kirk and Lieutenant Colonel Tibbets had spent most of the prior day planning and charting the long overwater flight. This was especially challenging because neither officer had been in that part of the world before. It was necessary to be sure of course lines, altitudes on each leg where enemy threats might appear, to become familiar with the different magnetic variations that could affect compass headings, to study unusual weather patterns, and to learn the Gibraltar approach, frequencies, and runways—an almost endless menu of hurried flight planning details that only aircrew could fully appreciate. They got it done, and the flight from England was routine.

At the expected time the Strait of Gibraltar hoved into view and Tibbets throttled back and began his descent. After entering the pattern to the airfield at the foot of "the Rock" (Tibbets thought it looked just like the pictures in the Prudential Insurance ads), he landed uneventfully just behind Wayne Connors in *Boomerang*. The aircrews had been briefed to use caution; they would almost certainly be under constant observation by German Abwehr agents positioned just a few thousand feet away—Fascist Spain and Gibraltar, a British Overseas Territory, shared a 1.2-km land border at the extreme southwest tip of Europe on the Iberian Peninsula.[5] Tibbets was made to understand he was facing no hypothetical threat—since the war began, Germany and Italy had already committed scores of sabotage acts against the Gibraltar fortress. With that in mind, General Clark and General Lemnitzer were immediately driven to the governor's house, where they would remain in seclusion until nightfall. The aircrews and other ground personnel were tasked with moving Clark's equipment and baggage to a covered location near the *Seraph*'s berth. Lieutenant Van Kirk led a detail specifically charged with unloading and transporting a large number of very heavy six-inch square boxes, filled with what he later learned was $2 million in gold coins. The money was to be used to quite literally bribe the French high command not to oppose the upcoming invasion.

Later in the evening and under cover of darkness, Clark and his small group loaded themselves into the sub and sailed the 450 miles to Cherchell, a frustratingly slow trip (the *Seraph* was an old English boat) for the impatient Clark. Due to a late arrival at their scheduled rendezvous, they had to remain submerged for an entire day. On the night of October 21, successful contact via flashlight was at last made with Mast's shore party. Clark and his team embarked from the submarine in tippy, collapsible boats (one capsized) and rowed to the beach. Guided by French soldiers, Clark was conducted to a nearby farmhouse where the meeting with General Mast was held. It went off well, with Mast agreeing not to oppose the landings and, one presumes, deftly accepting the gold coins.

Suddenly, a shout went up that Vichy gendarmes had arrived; local Arabs had apparently tipped them off. Cutting the meeting short, Clark and his men successfully evaded capture by locking themselves in a storeroom. It was not until four o'clock in the morning on October 22 that the Americans were able to get back to the beach. The surf was high and roiling, and in the scramble to get in his boat, General Clark somehow lost his trousers.[6] Despite that peculiar embarrassment, everyone got back to the *Seraph* safely and she got under way immediately. Later that morning, the submarine radioed Gibraltar that the mission had been a success; Clark and his men were in turn notified that a PBY Catalina flying boat would shortly rendezvous with the sub and fly the Americans back to the Rock. Tibbets and his men could only shake their heads that somehow the bizarre mission had actually succeeded. The *Red Gremlin* was ready to depart for England the moment General Clark arrived at the airplane.

But there was a new problem. While glad to be done with several days of living in what was a very confining and extremely security conscious British military complex dug into the side of a mountain, Tibbets, Ferebee, Van Kirk, and the rest of the crew were becoming increasingly concerned about the return trip's weather. After finishing his flight plan and getting a detailed meteorological forecast, Van Kirk went to Tibbets.

"Colonel," he said, speaking the form of address to Tibbets he and Ferebee would use in public for the remainder of the war, "I do not want to take off."[7] Tibbets did not like the weather conditions either, but he was sure they would have no choice; it would have been impossible to hold General Clark back. Clark absolutely had to personally deliver the news of the agreement to General Eisenhower as quickly as possible—from a security standpoint, it would have been out of the question to use the radio, especially with regard to General Mast's diplomatically sensitive pledge that he would order his men to "not oppose but assist the American landings."[8] And so it was, and without further discussion the *Red Gremlin* took off from Gibraltar near midnight on October 22 and pointed its nose west by northwest, flying in reverse the same sweeping arc out over the Atlantic as on the trip down.

It was a flight no one on board the airplane would ever forget.[9] Van Kirk told me that from the standpoint of navigation, it was his most difficult sortie of the war. As predicted, the weather was just awful; Van Kirk would remember flying through at least six fronts, the constant turbulence making even the smallest task nearly impossible to accomplish. As good a pilot as Tibbets was, Van Kirk was satisfied if the man could hold the assigned heading within ten degrees (navigators are very fussy about their pilots holding the proper heading; even one or two degrees off will generate an admonishment). As far as navigation aids went, Van Kirk was down to the bottom of the barrel. Sextant work was out of the question; he never saw the stars. Pilotage was not possible over the ocean even in clear weather. The heavy overcast and moderate to severe turbulence, to say nothing of the difficulty of finding a relatively motionless spot on the ocean at night, rendered the driftmeter useless. While radio operator Orville Splitt was able to pull in a few bearings from stations along the Spanish and Portuguese coasts during the first hour or two, they were not first class. During those several hours before sunrise, Van Kirk was down to a single aid—dead reckoning (DR).

It was because of just such occasions that from day one every navigator had drummed into him the importance of precise chart and log work. Van Kirk had learned those lessons as well as any man, and now for the first time he would be forced to rely upon them. On what could only be described as a weak departure fix based on a DR course line and a speed line bearing from one of the Iberian radio stations, he advanced that position on his chart from one leg to the next (using plotter and dividers) with time elapsed, compass heading, and guesstimated drift and ground speed as his only inputs. This would have been difficult enough to do in calm air; in the *Red Gremlin* early Friday morning on October 23, 1942, it became a Herculean task.

At daybreak, Van Kirk continued to have nothing else going for him except DR, the ship still enveloped in heavy cloud. Tibbets had been keeping the airplane in the 8,000- to 10,000-foot range in order to maintain at least the hope of contact with the earth's surface, to avoid using supplemental oxygen, and to keep the cabin temperature more comfortable. As the sun continued to rise, however, the crew began noticing breaks in the lower clouds. It was at this point that the navigator remembered the old sea captain's trick of estimating wind direction and velocity by studying the ocean white caps. Once again Van Kirk made his way up to Tom Ferebee's greenhouse, eventually catching enough breaks in the clouds to make a wind drift and speed estimate from off the waves. He hustled back to his working table and using those observations recalculated a new DR position.

By this time, Tibbets was becoming more and more apprehensive about their location and began to second-guess Van Kirk, a not uncommon occurrence between "drivers" and "bubble chasers" when things get sticky.[10] And well the pilot should get involved, for they had been flying blind for hours over the ocean without a solid fix, and it had become an "all hands on deck" moment. Most particularly, Tibbets was concerned that the heavy weather may have caused the *Red Gremlin* to be closer to the enemy-held continent than Van Kirk's DR had them. The winds over the Atlantic are westerly prevailing, which can cause airplanes to drift farther to the east than sometimes anticipated, especially when flying through violent lows and highs where wind and velocity changes can occur quite abruptly.

"Navigator, do you know where we're at?" No, he did not, but any Magellan worth his salt will never admit he is lost; on occasion he may perhaps acknowledge a certain "temporary disorientation."

"Roger, pilot," Dutch responded. "I think my DR position is pretty solid." Tibbets was not really buying it. "We can see some islands, just ahead," Tibbets said. "Those aren't the Channel Islands, are they?" The colonel was referring to the British Crown dependency island group, the largest of which were the Jersey and Guernsey Islands, just thirty miles west of France's Cotentin/Cherbourg peninsula. The islands had been occupied by the Germans since June 1940.

Van Kirk gripped his throat mike again. "Negative, pilot. They can't be the Channel Islands." Tibbets was still not convinced. He turned to General Clark and shouted over the howling engine and slipstream noise, "Navigator says those aren't the Channels. Let's find out for sure. I'll drop down and circle them. If they are German they'll start shooting at us, then we'll know." One can only imagine General Clark's patrician eyebrows arching over Tibbets' nonchalant though eminently practical solution to their dilemma. In the end, the maneuver was completed and no fire was received.

Meanwhile, Van Kirk had walked off the time/course/distance from his last DR position using his plotter and dividers, checked his watch, and then made an estimate of where the ship was at that moment. Dutch cleared his throat and went for broke.

"Navigator to pilot. Those islands have to be the Isles of Scilly. That would make us about forty or fifty miles southwest of Land's End, England." As if on cue, Sgt. Orville Splitt called over the intercom. "Radio operator to navigator. I have received a QDM bearing of 240 degrees to RAF Hurn at Bournemouth. They say we are going the wrong way."[11]

Splitt had been in Morse code contact with Hurn and had gotten the bearing via a "Q" signal. Q signals were a three-letter shorthand method used to send many words briefly in Morse.[12] For example, QRJ meant: "I cannot receive you. Your signals are weak." QRS meant: "Send more slowly." In this case, the *Red Gremlin* had received a QDM translated as: "Your magnetic bearing to our station under no wind conditions is 240 degrees." The low-frequency radio-bearing navigation technique, though rudimentary, usually gave fairly accurate bearings, although it did not have a distance-measuring capability. Distance-measuring equipment would not become available until the 1950s.

The *Red Gremlin* pilots, both of whom had extensive radio direction-finding training, quietly blanched. If Hurn was correct, they were far to the east of Bournemouth and over Europe, having already flown the entire north–south length of both Vichy and Occupied France! Van Kirk could almost hear the wheels clicking in their heads. Indeed, his own thoughts were moving at light speed. Could Hurn possibly be right? Yet, if the *Red Gremlin* had been over German-held territory that long, then surely the enemy would have been shooting at them. But there was no one shooting, and the crew had just observed an ocean and islands, not a great land mass. Nevertheless, everyone on the ship remained agitated, for Splitt had tapped out a request for confirmation of the bearing to Hurn and the QDM operators were insisting that the bearing they had given to their station—240 degrees—was correct.

And then it dawned on Van Kirk what was happening; he had seen the same mistake made in navigator training. The Hurn operators were reading off a reciprocal bearing.[13] That is to say, they had misinterpreted their equipment—the correct bearing to Hurn was actually 060 degrees, or 180 degrees in the opposite direction. Because of the nature of 1940s direction-finding equipment, it was easy to pick off the opposite number if one did not maintain what is called situational awareness—mentally visualizing the airplane's approximate position in space relative to where one wants to go. Van Kirk picked up his plotter and dividers, lined them up on the chart, and ran a course from his current DR position to Hurn/Bournemouth, reading a number close to 060 degrees. Confirmed.

However, the pilots—and now General Clark—remained thoroughly alarmed, believing the QDM to be correct. Van Kirk got on the horn and took them through his entire thought process, explaining in detail his conclusions. He told them that if they did turn to 240 degrees, as the QDM operators kept demanding, there was no doubt in his mind they would run out of gas and crash in the middle of the Atlantic. He would later credit his serendipitous conversation with the old sea captain about reading the waves with "saving me on that particular day."[14]

Tibbets elected to trust his navigator, and the *Red Gremlin* landed safely at Hurn. He and Van Kirk confronted the RAF officers about the grievous QDM error that had nearly cost them their lives. To their credit, the Englishmen were contrite and apologized profusely. Still, it left a lasting impression on Van Kirk about the quality of RAF navigation training (at that time—later RAF pathfinders proved excellent navigators), he believing it inherently inferior to the Americans' training due to their more confined, mostly over land, theater of war.

The sortie also left a lasting impression on Tibbets—previously Ferebee had proved himself an exceptional lead bombardier; now Van Kirk had convinced Tibbets he was one of the best navigators in VIII Bomber Command. It went even further—in 1987, in an article in the *Winston-Salem* [N.C.] *Journal*, Paul Tibbets paid tribute to his two friends' resourcefulness and courage. "Tom was damn near fearless. And so was Van Kirk. Tom functioned under stress like no one else. We were one hell of a good team."[15] The feelings were mutual. In a 1995 article in the *Charlotte Observer*, Ferebee told the reporter that from the start back in 1942 at Sarasota he saw in Tibbets "a decisive leader who treated his men like brothers. And man, could he work the controls. He was accurate [meaning he held very steady headings and altitudes during bomb runs], hard to rattle."[16]

On top of this mutual respect, the men were discovering that they were also becoming fast friends. They had a lot in common—all three were intelligent and quick to pick up a useful new technique or lay a sly gibe on a comrade. They found they enjoyed playing cards together and had compatible, robust senses of humor.[17] Oddly enough, Tibbets, seemingly as strait-laced as one can be, would also turn out to be a bit of a practical joker, something that came naturally to Ferebee and Van Kirk.

Less than a week after returning from the Clark mission, the *Red Gremlin* was given another critical assignment. Tibbets was to lead a top-secret flight of six B-17s back to Gibraltar carrying the Operation Torch general staff, from where, on November 8, 1942, they would launch the invasion of North Africa. The supreme commander, Lt. Gen. Dwight Eisenhower, would fly in the *Red*

*Gremlin*; his deputy, General Clark, would head up a headquarters delegation in the number two Fortress. The balance of Eisenhower's forward staff was to follow, with recently promoted Brig. Gen. Jimmy Doolittle, commander of the invasion's U.S. bomber forces, and Brig. Gen. Lyman Lemnitzer, Eisenhower's chief of staff, in the last B-17, piloted by Lt. John Summers and Lt. Thomas Lohr.[18]

Tibbets and his crews received an extensive briefing on their planned route—low-level flying hazards, weather, air and sea threats along the Iberian Peninsula, and a lot of other technical information.[19] The ships would be gassed up to accommodate an eight-hour, 1,200-mile flight. Oh, yes, Tibbets was told, there was one more thing. His six B-17s would not be returning to England. After twelve combat missions over Europe for the pilot and eleven each for Ferebee and Van Kirk, they were to stay in North Africa—the 97th and 301st Bomb Groups were being transferred out of VIII Bomber Command to form the nucleus of a newly organized Twelfth Air Force to be based in North Africa.[20]

The next morning the *Red Gremlin* flew from Polebrook to Hurn, once again the jumping-off point. Tibbets was fielding his usual crew except copilot Junior Ryan had come down with a debilitating case of dysentery and was replaced by Lt. Charles R. "Dick" Wiley. Preparations went smoothly; the earlier Clark mission had knocked away most of the unknowns, and Tibbets briefed the crews accordingly.

In the foggy and rainy early morning hours of November 5, Eisenhower, Clark, Doolittle, and others arrived on the Hurn flight line in several buses and hurriedly loaded their gear into the bombers.[21] Minutes later, the generals and several pilots were in deep conversation, huddled under the *Red Gremlin*'s wings to avoid the downpour. The weather conditions were beyond terrible; by the rulebook, conditions were completely unacceptable for a takeoff—one could barely see beyond the man standing next to him. The increasingly worried top brass, still in raincoats and shivering, kept looking imploringly at flight leader Tibbets. Pilots Wayne Connors and Maj. John Knox—the same Polebrook squadron commander who had, like Tibbets, resisted the "call of the Rothschilds" the previous summer—had come over and joined the group to help with the hoping—nay, *praying*—for a break in the overcast.[22]

Tibbets related in his autobiography that General Eisenhower kept looking at his watch. The supreme commander was falling further and further behind his timetable. At one point, Eisenhower turned to Doolittle and asked him what they should do. Doolittle deferred to Tibbets, saying it was his show. Eisenhower turned to Tibbets, who had heard the exchange. "If it was just the crew and me, I'd go," Tibbets said. "But I've got to think about you and your staff."

"Well, son," the general said. "I've got a war about to begin down there and that's where I have to be." Tibbets replied, "OK, sir. Let's go."[23] With that, everyone scrambled on board their planes, started engines, and began taxiing to Hurn's active runway. Although Tibbets had to strain to see the "Follow Me" truck just a few yards in front of him, everything was progressing satisfactorily until Lieutenant Summers, in the number six Fortress, suddenly lost his brakes. The B-17 was unable to stop, hurtling head-first toward the tail of the bomber just ahead of it. Summers yelled at copilot Lohr to crank the emergency hydraulic pump. Nothing. Just as it seemed a collision was inevitable, with Summers shouting "Pump! Pump!" and jamming the left toe brake, at the last second Lohr finally got up enough pressure for the ship to veer away and go into the mud. The other bombers, completely absorbed by the difficult takeoff and unable to see anything beyond their own noses, were unaware of the accident behind them until after takeoff. Doolittle, who was on board Summers' plane, later said it was a very close call; an impact could have caused a chain reaction on the bunched up Fortresses that might have changed the course of the war. It took all the next day to repair the hydraulic system, and Summers did not get off until the morning of November 6.[24]

Meanwhile Tibbets had just been able to find the white centerline of the runway and get lined up. With General Eisenhower ensconced at Orville Splitt's radio operator station behind the bomb bay—perhaps the most "comfortable" position in a B-17—Tibbets and Wiley did their run-up checks. The colonel and Van Kirk had a brief discussion. "Navigator to pilot, be damn careful right after takeoff of that tall church steeple just fifteen degrees off to portside, you do not want to turn to the left." He paused, adding, "I can't even see the end of the left wing out my window."

"Roger, navigator. I have reset my directional gyro to the runway magnetic heading and will steer that all the way through the takeoff." It was to be a completely blind launch.[25] The colonel poured the cob to the *Red Gremlin*'s four Wright 1,200-hp radials and the ship leaped forward. While everyone on board held their breath, Tibbets calmly showed why he had been selected to fly the supreme commander.[26] The arguably best bomber pilot in VIII Bomber Command skillfully put the Flying Fortress through its paces; the departure would have been viewed by nonfliers who did not understand the situation as having gone fairly routinely. Within minutes they were out over the ocean on what was to be a very low-level flight. Tibbets flew the first legs completely on instruments and at two hundred feet, which kept him under the German radar positioned along the French coast. The earlier enemy, fog, was now their friend. When they were well out to sea, the *Red Gremlin* broke out into the clear and the colonel climbed to eight thousand feet.[27]

With the hairy takeoff and departure behind them and the sun shining through the cockpit windows, everyone's spirits were lifted. General Eisenhower came forward and flashed the cockpit crew his famous smile. The ground crews had fashioned a two-by-four into a kind of chair he could sit on between the pilot and copilot, which encouraged an agreeable conversation. Eisenhower made a point of chatting with everyone, mostly small talk, even crawling down the hatch and forward to the nav/bombardier compartment. Ferebee was his usual laid-back, taciturn self and avoided initiating a conversation, not wishing to draw attention to himself. Van Kirk spoke to the general while sitting at his navigation station but later could not recall what they talked about. Tibbets remembered sharing a cup of coffee from Eisenhower's personal thermos. None of the men would forget their brief time with the general, impressed that the supreme commander conducted himself like a regular guy and gave every indication that he would be comfortable chatting with even the lowliest GI.

To everyone's relief, the balance of the trip to Gibraltar was uneventful.[28] Upon landing, General Eisenhower was whisked away to his command headquarters inside the mountain; the invasion was to begin in less than forty-eight hours. Tibbets and his men found their quarters, hoping for some crew rest and getting reacquainted with a number of individuals they had met on the earlier Clark mission. Later that evening, a British officer interrupted what was probably a blackjack game to invite the boys to a high lookout point on the Rock for something "worth seeing." Van Kirk recalled standing in the moonlight and watching Eisenhower's vast armada sail through the Straits of Gibraltar, calling it one of the most memorable scenes of his life.[29]

The invasion began as scheduled in the very early morning hours of November 8, 1942. Thanks to the French generals' medieval ideas of honor, coupled with their personally conflicting ambitions, the result was as muddled an operation as any conducted during World War II. Fortunately, most of the opposing forces offered only desultory resistance. Fighting against Italian and French soldiers was heavy only in a few locations, and all three landings—Oran and Algiers on the southern Mediterranean coast; Casablanca on the Atlantic side—were declared successful after the first day.

One of the important early objectives had been the capture of the Maison Blanche airfield near Algiers.[30] The Allied air forces had decided it was to be their initial North African operating base; Gen. Mark Clark was to set up a forward operating headquarters at that location. He sent word to Tibbets that he would need two airplanes to transport himself and his staff to Algiers first thing in the morning.[31] Tibbets made arrangements with Wayne Connors and the *Boomerang* to assist him. The two ships flew low out of Gibraltar along the North African coastline, accompanied by thirteen Spitfires that were tagging along for both navigation purposes and to protect the two bombers from marauding German fighters. The RAF pilots became quite restive after flying over water for several hours and in an environment they could not track. Van Kirk later recalled a radio exchange that took place when the formation was only minutes out of Maison Blanche: "Where the hell *is* that Yank taking us?" said one Spit pilot to his mates. "There's nothing but water down there."

Van Kirk was infuriated. "Pilot, would you tell those fellows off?"

Tibbets had become irritated with the bitching as well but did not want to get into an argument. "If you want to tell them something," he said to his nav, "you make the call."

Dutch got on the ship-to-ship radio. "To all you Limey pilots wondering where to go. Fly fifteen miles straight ahead, drop down through the clouds and you will find an airfield there. Land on it. I hope it is captured."[32]

Tibbets and Connors landed their valuable human cargo on the airfield shortly thereafter, just in time for a Ju 88 counterattack. Only minutes after General Clark had been unloaded and hustled away in a Bren gun carrier, several bombs exploded within one hundred feet of the *Red Gremlin*. Although the Three Musketeers did not know it at that moment, they were pretty much finished with chauffeuring the brass and back in a shooting war. Furthermore, with Clark delivered, they were now on their own with no orders past delivering him to Algiers. On his own initiative and as the 97th Bomb Group executive officer, Tibbets radioed the other four B-17s that he had brought down on the Eisenhower ferry to leave Gibraltar and join himself and Connors at Maison Blanche. The tiny squadron had no more than gotten settled in a hangar dormitory when the Americans were subjected to one of their most terrifying experiences of the war.[33] For once *they* would be on the receiving end of an air attack.

Van Kirk later remembered that he and Ferebee had been frying eggs on the second floor of the hangar when it began. Tibbets was apparently in another hangar, perhaps with the enlisted men. Along came what was believed to be "Five O'clock Charlie," a solo, harassing Junkers so named for his unfailing punctuality. Except this time Charlie had a surprise. It was a full-scale attack. With bombs raining down, plaster falling off the ceilings, and general chaos everywhere, Van Kirk instinctively ducked under a bed. Fortunately for him, Tom Ferebee came running in, shouting, "Dutch, come on! We got to get out of here!" At that moment, another string of bombs struck, the concussion waves almost literally knocking the air out of the two men. Van Kirk immediately saw the wisdom in Ferebee's advice and they got the hell down the stairs and out into the open as fast as their legs would carry them. Meanwhile, Tibbets took charge of his people, blowing a whistle and instructing the men to clear the dormitories and head for shelter.[34]

Dutch and Tom were desperately running for who knew where and undoubtedly hyperventilating when Dutch ran out of gas. "God, Tom," he gasped. "I can't go any farther." They jumped in a ditch just as two strings of bombs straddled their position. Realizing their extreme vulnerability, they scrambled back on the macadam road and joined a host of other fleeing GIs. As if things were not already bad enough, several Stuka dive bombers started lobbing ordnance on the road.

By that time Van Kirk and Ferebee had reached Maison Blanche's surrounding vineyards. Knowing they had to get off the road, they bolted into the fields. Ferebee was the better athlete and was soon far ahead of his short-legged navigator. In the confusion they lost track of each other. Van Kirk huddled in the vineyards until the attack was over, then went back to the hangar.[35] Ferebee showed up the next day; he had spent the night with some antiaircraft gunners. All of Tibbets' airmen were pretty shook up, coming away with a profoundly deeper understanding of the kind of medicine they had been dishing out. And now more than ever, after the Luftwaffe's rude treatment, that was precisely what they wanted to get back doing.

Fuming over the air raid, anxious for some payback, and without any orders for his small force—at a minimum it was going to take several days to get the forward elements of the 97th to Maison Blanche—Tibbets got an idea. He went to Air Marshal Sir William Welsh, commander of the North African RAF and the man responsible for covering the Allied Eastern Assault Force, and offered him his men and the six Flying Fortresses. Welsh pulled out a map and pointed at Sidi Ahmed aerodrome at Bizerte on the Tunisian coast about 375 miles east, remarking in a classical British upper-class accent: "If you chaps would go up there and harass them with a few bombs, it would be of inestimable service to us." When should he go, Tibbets asked? Whenever you can get ready. Tibbets realized he had been given carte blanche, in charge of his own little air force.[36]

Air Marshal Welsh gave the Americans what they needed to get started from British stores, most importantly bombs, .50-caliber ammunition, and fuel. Most of the work would have to be done by Tibbets' airmen because his little squadron had outrun its own ground crews. The fueling was especially onerous; the men had to stand in bucket-brigade fashion and transfer about 500 five-gallon gas cans per each bomber from out of lorries and up ladders to the fuselage and wing fueling ports.[37] Fortunately, the American B-17 bomb bay shackles were roughly compatible with the connecting lugs on the British bombs, though that was still difficult and unfamiliar work. Once the servicing, munitions, and maintenance side of the operation had been completed, the actual mission planning could begin.

Tibbets turned mission planning over to his navigator, who had no charts for anything east of Maison Blanche. After scratching his head for a time, Van Kirk tracked down an RAF group captain operations officer and, in his own inimitable American way, asked, "Where the hell is Bizerte?"[38] An aide was finally able to come up with a prewar Standard Oil road map, and that is what lead navigator Van Kirk used to open up American strategic bomber warfare in North Africa. Fortunately, geography came to his aid; all one really needed to do was follow the coast to the east, interpreting the topographic and cultural features along the way. On those occasions when he needed something extra to get a fix, Van Kirk adopted the Paul Tibbets "special navigation technique" whereby he would point the *Red Gremlin* at a city or port and note if the maneuver generated any enemy antiaircraft fire.

At last all was ready in the morning hours of Monday, November 16, and the six-ship American air force was off to Bizerte.[39] Coming in at a very low 6,500 feet, three of the B-17s attacked the port; the other three hit Sidi Ahmed aerodrome. There was a lot of heavy ground tracer fire, but all the planes bombed their targets and returned safely home. In fact, the Germans were reeling so badly that there was time to return to Maison Blanche, quickly bomb and gas up, and make a second strike.[40] Air Marshal Welsh was extremely pleased with the damage to both the port and airfield, having gotten something more than "harass them with a few bombs," although the full extent of Luftwaffe losses that day would not be known until well after the war, when Colonel Tibbets was assigned to a NATO base in Europe. He discovered in conversation with German officers that one of the bombs from the two sorties scored a direct hit on an officer's mess hall. It had killed nearly an entire squadron of Me-109 pilots, severely crippling the German fighter response for some time.[41]

On November 19, Tibbets led his six Fortresses on another raid on the El Aouina aerodrome in Tunisia, pounding the field's facilities and parked enemy aircraft. A new *Red Gremlin* gunner, Sgt. Russell Ofala, and Sgt. Orville Splitt were credited with one of the three Me-109s shot down. On November 21 Tibbets' crews struck El Aouina again, with equally excellent results.

Meanwhile, the balance of the 97th and 301st Bomb Groups were getting up to strength in North Africa—with the recently promoted Major General Doolittle commanding—and were soon conducting regular, full-force raids behind German lines and in support of Allied ground forces. At the same time, the U.S. Army was making excellent progress pushing the Germans and Italians back east. All of this was creating very crowded conditions on Maison Blanche, which was unable to accommodate the many fighters, bombers, and transports pouring into the theater. On November 22 General Spaatz and Major General Doolittle decided to open up another Twelfth Air Force forward operating base, selecting Tafaraoui Airfield near Oran, Algeria. Tibbets and the *Red Gremlin* were among the first to arrive, with the crew setting up pup tents under the airplane's wing. Unfortunately, the rainy season had just begun, and while the runways were paved, nothing else was. The crews very quickly dubbed it "Goo-ey Tah-fahr-ah-wee," a truly miserable place to operate an air force.[42] Aside from the misery of having to live in the mud and rain next to the airplane (Van Kirk and Ferebee assuaged their woes with cheap champagne), it was very difficult to launch Flying Fortresses in the foot-deep sludge. The ground crews had to somehow drag the airplanes up onto the hard-surface runways, clean off the clods and muck, and then get them ready for combat.

Still, Tibbets and the 97th Bomb Group commander, recently promoted brigadier general Hamp Atkinson, managed to get missions launched. Atkinson was ill during this time, and as he had done months earlier under similar circumstances for Col. Frank Armstrong, Tibbets assumed most of the commander's duties.[43] On November 23 the group struck the Elmas aerodrome in Sardinia; on the twenty-fourth it was the Bizerte docks; the twenty-seventh, the Sidi Ahmed aerodrome; the twenty-ninth and thirtieth, the Bizerte docks again; on December 1, El Aouina airfield; December 5, the Tunis docks and enemy shipping; then back to Bizerte, and then Bizerte again.[44]

On one mission an antiaircraft 88-millimeter shell (a flak projectile about three and a half inches in diameter) hit a bomber just off Tibbets' left wing and the ship was virtually vaporized—the pilot was a good friend, and Tibbets had a "but for the grace of God" moment. On another mission the musketeers had an even closer call. An 88 went directly through a wing spar, but for some reason it missed the control cables and fuel lines and did not explode.[45] Once again, the *Red Gremlin* crew had been spared, they attributing their good fortune to the bomber's quadruple-four serial number—the "winning hand." As Van Kirk later put the matter of surviving 1942–43 ETO/North African air combat: "It was better to be lucky than good."[46]

It was during those very difficult weeks in North Africa that the three men really became close. The lieutenant colonel and the two junior first lieutenants (an unlikely combination in its own right) were not just together in the air. At Tafaraoui they were tenting (it blew down one night during a driving rain), shaving, sleeping, and messing together, with Tibbets often the cook. While still always calling him "sir" or "colonel" when among others, privately Dutch and Tom would sometimes use "Paul." As Van Kirk told me, "You can't eat a guy's fried chicken without getting close to him."[47] For the three, it was the beginnings of a deep and permanent bond, one that would eventually bring the type of brotherly intimacy that can only be forged in the red-hot cauldron of war. Van Kirk and Ferebee depended on Tibbets to get them home after each mission; Tibbets depended on Van Kirk to be flawless in his navigation, and on Ferebee to be the best and steadiest bombardier in his command. This lifelong trust in one another can perhaps be best expressed by remarks they made when old men. Speaking for himself and Ferebee, Van Kirk said: "[We] always thought Paul Tibbets was an invincible pilot."[48] Tibbets would tell interviewers: "I trust those two guys with my back turned."[49]

In any forward operating war theater, everyday routines quickly become informal, especially in observing the military conventions. Clothing selections become optional, unauthorized headwear appears, ties are long gone, haircuts take a little longer to happen, saluting becomes lax, and so on. In particular, when opportunities for entertainment, female companionship, food, and liquid refreshment arise, they are almost always seized upon with an alacrity that would not be tolerated on a peacetime post. World War II North Africa was no different, although "fun" of any type was still hard to come by. The one bit of recreation the boys were always able to indulge in, however, was gambling—specifically poker, craps, and blackjack. And much of that was high stakes.

Invariably, a cigar would be clamped in Ferebee's mouth as he rolled the die or dealt the cards. Van Kirk tells of a craps game in North Africa that came down to Ferebee and a general, with $20,000 riding on the outcome.[50] According to Van Kirk, Ferebee said, "One of us is going to leave here broke and it won't be me."[51] Ferebee did win but apparently never collected all the IOUs. Tibbets was too smart to play against Ferebee in dice or poker, only challenging him at blackjack. Van Kirk seems to have been the sage opportunist, jumping into the "money games" only when he sensed he might have an edge or could ride on Ferebee's coattails. They both sent money home regularly, with Tom leading in that department as well.

The matter of decent rations remained a continual problem, and there was no end of scrounging and even outright conniving. At one point Van Kirk had to steal food to feed the crew. The airmen at "Gooey" remained largely out in the open, which made them miserable twenty-four hours a day—either living in the mud or flying very hazardous combat missions against an increasingly desperate enemy. At the same time, neither the ground war nor the air war in North Africa were going well for the Axis, which was making *their* soldiers and airmen that much more tenacious in a fight.

At last it was realized Tafaraoui was untenable, and General Doolittle moved the main bomber base to Biskra, Algeria, a much drier climate deeper into the Sahara about four hundred air miles east southeast of Oran. Biskra had three hard-surfaced runways, allowing aircraft to takeoff three abreast, an infinitely more efficient airfield to conduct bomber and fighter operations. The *Red Gremlin* arrived in mid-December, and the crew was greatly relieved to be put up in a hotel and have access to much better chow, including coffee, dates, oranges, and wine. The flight line, however, offered no relief. The *Red Gremlin* and its operators continued to fly two or three days out of every four well into January 1943, nearly always in the lead position. Targets included harbors, shipping docks, bridges, and airfields all the way up and down the Tunisian coast—anything that would hinder Rommel's supply line, his Achilles' heel.[52]

The heavy combat flying was extremely fatiguing, and the necessary recreation needed to blow off steam was becoming even harder to come by. Little things took on exaggerated importance. Tom Ferebee's response had been to grow what was known by the men who cultivated the look as a Clark Gable–type "overseas moustache," giving him what the ladies thought was a dashing look. Ferebee also did his part to keep up the other men's spirits, usually through some prank. Perhaps his best stunt, as related by Van Kirk, involved an aging, apparently well-to-do local Arab merchant. It seems that, in a truly inspired move, the bombardier cozied up to the old gentleman and, after some negotiations, exchanged one thousand fresh eggs for the *Red Gremlin*.[53] After each mission, the crafty Arab bargainer would stand proudly nearby and watch "his" airplane taxi back to the hardstand. Then, one day in late January 1943, #24444 took off and never came back. The outfit had been moved to Chateaudun-du-Rhumel, Algeria, about one hundred miles north of Biskra. One can only imagine the expression on the old trader's face when he realized he was out both eggs *and* B-17.

From time to time during that January, Tibbets and the *Red Gremlin* had been called upon by General Eisenhower to ferry him to forward operating headquarters for consultations with the British and American ground commanders, then returning Eisenhower to his own headquarters in Algiers.[54] The *Gremlin* also hosted General Doolittle once or twice; Doolittle could not stay out of the cockpits of his air force, never mind that he had already gotten into trouble with Eisenhower for spending too much time flying (the general had told him: "You can either be a major and fly Spitfires or a Major General and be my senior air officer!"[55]).

Also during this period the first of many decorations began flowing in—Tibbets, Ferebee, and Van Kirk each received a Distinguished Flying Cross and several Air Medals each.[56] Rumor soon had it that Lt. Col. Paul W. Tibbets Jr., with forty-three combat missions to his credit, was headed upstairs to staff. Sure enough, orders came down from Doolittle assigning him to Twelfth Air Force headquarters in Algiers, reporting to Col. Lauris Norstad, the general's operations chief, where Tibbets would serve as the bombardment expert. Concurrently, 1st Lt. Thomas W. Ferebee was reassigned to the North African 5th Bomb Wing as assistant wing bombardier.[57] 1st Lt. Theodore "Dutch" Van Kirk would remain as the *Red Gremlin*'s navigator, with a new aircraft commander and bombardier. Just like that, the Three Musketeers were broken up; as far as the fellows knew there was little likelihood they would ever crew together again.

Unbeknownst to all, at what appeared to be an assignment that would serve as the springboard to a general's flag, Paul Tibbets was about to get blindsided in a way almost unimaginable. The episode would have the most profound effect, both bad and good, on the rest of his life.

# 7

# INTERREGNUM

Despite the implicit recognition that the job offered, Tibbets was not happy with the assignment to Doolittle's staff. He had been the executive officer for two different group commanders and was very successful with each. Brig. Gen. "Hamp" Atkinson had only a week earlier promoted him to full colonel in recognition of his outstanding combat leadership. Getting kicked up to headquarters' staff was a bitter pill. In Tibbets' mind, his place was out on the line, preferably commander of his own group. Still, he enjoyed an excellent relationship with General Doolittle and had determined to make the best of the situation.

Tibbets had no more than gotten settled behind a desk when he learned that his immediate supervisor, Col. Lauris Norstad, had blocked his field promotion to bird colonel by refusing to sign off on the published order. According to Tibbets, Norstad was a man of fierce ego who reportedly said, "There is only going to be one [full] colonel in operations, and I'm it." Tibbets was not a man to take that kind of snub lying down and immediately went to Doolittle to protest. An astounded Paul Tibbets listened while Doolittle explained that, despite being the famous Jimmy Doolittle, he could do nothing about the injustice—Norstad was not only well thought of by senior Army brass, he was also bound at the hip with Col. Hoyt Vandenberg, Doolittle's chief of staff and the nephew of Arthur Vandenberg, the long-serving and powerful Republican senator from Michigan. What is more, Norstad and Vandenberg were West Pointers—both Tibbets and Doolittle had been aviation cadets, very much an inferior species in the Army officer corps of that day. Further, Doolittle had been a civilian reserve officer for many years prior to World War II and had rescued his military career only because of a long friendship with U.S. Army Air Forces commanding general, Hap Arnold. The fact was, at that time in his military career Doolittle had little to no behind-the-scenes influence in Pentagon circles.

According to Tibbets, Norstad and Vandenberg were very close—so much so that they "push-pulled" (Tibbets' phrase) their way up the promotion ladder. Each man did what he could to get the other promoted either from above or below. To make matters even worse for Tibbets, both Vandenberg and Norstad were extremely capable, every inch the professional soldiers and worthy of the four-star rank each eventually attained. Both were also enormously ambitious, and God help any man that got in their way.

Tibbets swallowed the castor oil and returned to work, but it was clear his relationship with Norstad going forward would be tenuous at best. Unfortunately—and almost predictably, given the nature of the two men—it did not take long for a second act to follow. The port of Bizerte had once again become troublesome, and another large bomber strike was needed to neutralize German shipping. As an important aside, it had recently been noted by staff that the enemy's antiaircraft defenses there had been upgraded substantially. Norstad, who seems to have had an infinite amount of confidence in his own abilities, planned the mission himself without regard to those new defenses, then presented it to his own Twelfth Air Forces operations staff for what he expected to be a rubber stamp. Tibbets immediately grasped the implications and was horrified. Perhaps if Tibbets had not been so "shot in the ass" with his own self-confidence, a direct collision with Norstad might have been avoided.[1]

"You can't send those B-17s in at 6,000 feet," Tibbets blurted, without thinking things through. "We just can't do it."

Norstad was aghast at such impudence, especially by a more junior officer and in front of his entire operations staff. "What do you mean we can't," he said icily.

"I've been there," Tibbets replied. "If we send them in at 6,000 feet, they'll be wiped out."

At that point, a furious Norstad decided to cut the upstart down to size. If what transpired was as Tibbets related it, then Colonel Norstad was way out of bounds—he who had not flown even one combat mission. The very reason Doolittle had brought Paul Tibbets to Algiers in the first place was for precisely the kind of advice he had just given. To have B-17s fly so low in the face of murderously accurate flak would seem pure folly even to armchair strategists; perhaps if Tibbets had chosen a less confrontational approach and tone, he might have made his point without so much collateral damage. But, as it was, his hot-headed manner thoroughly provoked Norstad, and to save face the senior officer struck back hard. "Gentlemen," the operations chief said imperiously. "It appears that Colonel Tibbets has been flying too much. He may be suffering from combat fatigue."

Norstad might as well have waved a red cape in front of an angry bull. One can almost hear Tibbets' jaw grinding and visualize the blue veins popping from his temples. As far as Paul Tibbets was concerned—an old-fashioned man who valued personal honor above all else—he had just been called a coward. With "fists clenched" and throwing caution to the winds, Tibbets unloaded with both barrels. "I'll tell you what I'm prepared to do, colonel," he said, his voice dripping with rancor, "I'll lead that raid myself at 6,000 feet if you will come along as my copilot."

A seething Norstad had the good sense to remain silent over what was clearly an insolent remark from a subordinate officer. Tibbets partially recovered his own composure during the lull and laid out a solid rationale as to why a low-altitude mission was not only too risky for the crews, it was also unnecessary. Equivalent results could be had at 20,000 feet with many fewer casualties. An intelligent man, Norstad apparently realized he had nothing to gain and much to lose by not hearing out his senior bombardment expert; after all, that really was the man's job. Further, Norstad must have grudgingly admitted to himself that Tibbets probably was right, which could only have made the man even more furious.[2]

The immediate winners of the clash were the American aircrews and the Allies' cause. The Bizerte strike was conducted at 20,000 feet, and results were excellent despite heavy opposition by flak batteries that concentrated their fire, as Tibbets had predicted, on the lower altitudes. Everyone was at least outwardly pleased there were no losses. It was only a couple of weeks later, in mid-February 1943, with the operations section focused on new objectives, that just-promoted brigadier general Lauris Norstad got his revenge. Lieutenant Colonel Tibbets was working at his desk when Doolittle abruptly called him into his office.

"Larry Norstad wants to court-martial you," the general said, "and I can't stop him."[3] Doolittle was candid; his hands, he said, were tied. Paul Tibbets was staggered. He could not understand how a man like Doolittle—a legendary air racer, an Army Air Force major general, and winner of the Congressional Medal of Honor for leading the 1942 Tokyo Raid—could be intimidated by a couple of officers junior to him. But there it was. If the accounts are as Tibbets described them—Doolittle does not mention this incident in his autobiography—the episode does not reflect well on any of the parties. One can only imagine the near-despair that must have come over the just-fired and now up-on-charges Twelfth Air Force bombardment expert.

Fortunately, a fragment of the old Paul Tibbets luck held—perhaps one of Sgt. Orville Splitt's good red gremlins had followed him to Algiers. What Doolittle earlier in the day believed would be the loss of one of his key combat leaders because of an unrelated order foisted on him by his friend and mentor, Gen. Hap Arnold, now appeared a gift. The general realized he could solve both problems in one stroke.

"Paul," Doolittle continued, "I've just received a message from Hap Arnold. He wants an experienced bombardment pilot to come back to the States and help with the development of a big new bomber. I'm naming you for the job. Get your bags back, you are leaving right now!"[4] Doolittle was not kidding; a staff car was waiting for Tibbets to take him back to his apartment for his luggage and then directly to the airport where he was immediately spirited out of Algiers, avoiding any military jurisprudence proceedings. Nevertheless, and while he had escaped being dragged away in irons, the enemies he had made in North Africa would haunt him for the rest of his military career. Still reeling from events, Tibbets returned home the long way via the Azores and across the South Atlantic, through Central America, and then northward to the Zone of the Interior (ZI).

Meanwhile 1st Lt. Tom Ferebee (he would make captain on March 23, 1943) had settled in at the group bombardier shop at the newly formed Fifth Wing of the Northwest African Air Forces, where he was informed he could expect the occasional combat mission. 1st Lt. Theodore Van Kirk continued to fly *Red Gremlin* missions out of Chateaudun-du-Rhumel airfield, while Tibbets' copilot, Lt. Dick Wiley, was moved over to the airplane's left seat. And, after nearly succumbing to his dysentery attack, a scarecrow-thin Junior Ryan miraculously appeared to rejoin the crew as Wiley's copilot.[5] Van Kirk and Ferebee had collected Junior's clothes and gear before leaving England, expecting to send them to his nearest of kin. Ryan had misunderstood their motives and was angry at first all his stuff had been taken, but once stories were compared, the men quickly reconciled.

The newly constituted *Red Gremlin* crew participated in the American debacle at Kasserine Pass in late February 1943, the first time Van Kirk had seen B-17 Flying Fortresses operating in ground support. A following mission took them to the island of Sardinia, their first venture out of North Africa. Then it was back to Kasserine, Bizerte yet again, and something new on February 26—a German sea convoy en route to Palermo, Sicily. The next day Dutch Van Kirk celebrated his twenty-second birthday.

March, April, and May brought more of the same to Lt. Dick Wiley and his crew. The missions they were now flying concentrated on interdicting supplies and shipping to what was left of Rommel's Deutsches Afrikakorps, the strikes ranging from the North African coast to across the Mediterranean and the enemy's island bases on Sardinia and Sicily, then later into the Italian peninsula itself. By late spring, the Axis was on the ropes in North Africa, and on May 13 they surrendered—netting the Allies over 275,000 prisoners of war.

For Van Kirk, the missions of that period ranged from milk runs to truly hairy. Fortunately, the *Red Gremlin*'s crew were by then veterans and knew not only how to get the job done but how best to preserve their own hides as well. While the terror of a combat mission never left, as the weeks went by the men's downtime was spent less dwelling on the risks of war and more on milking every ounce of living out of each off-duty moment. Van Kirk seldom missed an opportunity to head for Algiers and get together with his old buddy, Ferebee. Their visits were not demonstrably different from those conducted by thousands of other recuperating airmen—except Van Kirk and Ferebee seemed always to feel the need for a little extra adventure. Van Kirk spoke of one occasion when the two headed for Algiers' bawdy house district (best place for a drink, so Dutch said). Here they witnessed what both considered the finest bar fight they saw during the war. Certain stalwarts of the British First and Eighth Armies had found themselves in serious disagreement, the nature of which of course no one ever remembered.

Van Kirk: "Do we want to get mixed up this?"

Ferebee: "Hell, no!"[6]

In the best tradition of western movie saloon brawls, the two men crouched behind the bar with heavy whiskey bottles in each hand. When one of the "Limeys" stuck his head in too close, they "conked him." Already experts in timing such encounters, they sneaked away as the party began to wind down and just before the military police arrived. The escapade would join the scores of other anecdotes and war stories the Three Musketeers would tell themselves and others for the rest of their lives.

On May 29, 1943, Van Kirk received orders relieving him of duty with the 97th Bomb Group and directing him to return to the ZI at the earliest opportunity for reassignment.[7] He had flown his fifty-eighth and final combat mission in the European and North African theaters. In typical military fashion, the Air Forces left him to his own devices as to how to get back to the States—"I had to hitchhike home from North Africa!" Ever resourceful, he did not take long to find a C-47 (two-engine Douglas transport) bound for Casablanca on the continent's northeast coast. Not keen on an ocean voyage (the U-boat threat was still very real) and with a generous allotment of forty-five days' travel time, Van Kirk spent a chunk of time in Casablanca "having a ball," waiting for an airplane to Prestwick, Scotland, the jumping off airfield for westbound transatlantic flights. In early June 1943 Van Kirk boarded an air transport command C-54, one of the new four-engine transports, this one technically belonging to TWA (Trans World Airlines). A half-day later he landed at LaGuardia Field, New York. Very shortly thereafter, he was back in Northumberland, Pennsylvania, with his family and Mary Jane Young. He spent the next several weeks resting, getting reacquainted with loved ones, and eating copious quantities of real ice cream and German home cooking.

Not so fortunate was Capt. Thomas Ferebee, notwithstanding the partial compensation he was receiving from having acquired a girlfriend in Algiers. While both Van Kirk and Tibbets were back home enjoying the "good life," the bombardier found himself deep into Fifth Bomb Wing staff work and flying combat missions into southern Europe.[8] Although, like Van Kirk, he had been eligible to return home after having fulfilled his aircrew total mission requirements, Ferebee had been promised another promotion if he would volunteer to extend his combat tour and lead "especially difficult" missions. The 97th Bomb Group was heavily engaged in air attacks on enemy targets in and around the Mediterranean—pounding bridges, railroad marshaling yards, docks, harbors, and shipping. On one raid against a bridge in Italy, flak shattered the bombardier's greenhouse and Ferebee got glass slivers in his eyes. He managed to get his bombs off and they got home OK but it took three days for him to recover. "It was pretty scary, because I thought I was [going to be] blind. The one thing [during the war] I always worried about was not getting killed but [getting hurt real bad]."[9]

On a mission to Sicily shortly before his good friend Van Kirk shipped back home, Ferebee was personally tested as he had never been before. Excerpts from his citation for a second Distinguished Flying Cross tell the story:

> For extraordinary achievement while participating in aerial flight. . . . Throughout [Capt. Ferebee's] long period of service as lead bombardier [he] has distinguished himself through outstanding professional skill and eagerness to take part in all missions. His self-denial in volunteering . . . beyond the customary number of sorties has been of high inspiration to his comrades. On 19 May 1943 he led his squadron over the heavily-defended aerodrome at Milo, Sicily. Fifty enemy fighters attacked his formation at the start of the bombing run, and a 20mm shell exploded in the nose of his B-17, wounding the navigator and tearing off his oxygen mask. Leaving his bombsight, Captain Ferebee removed his own mask and adjusted it on his wounded comrade. Swiftly administering first aid to the navigator, he then returned to his sight and, although near collapse from anoxia [lack of oxygen], led his squadron in a highly accurate bombing of the target, starting many fires and heavily damaging [enemy installations]. Displaying exceptional stamina, Captain Ferebee manned the nose guns, warding off repeated frontal attacks until his aircraft was out of danger. His proficiency and resolute courage reflect great credit upon himself and the Armed Forces of the United States.[10]

In June 1943 Ferebee led air raids in the battle for the Pantelleria/Pelagie island group midway between Tunisia and Sicily. In July he struck airfields and railroad marshaling yards in Sicily in support of Operation Husky, the Allied invasion of that large island. In September it was on to the Italian mainland, with Ferebee leading longer-range missions that struck deep into southern Europe. On at least one occasion in the fall of 1943 he led a force of B-17s on one of several follow-up strikes against the critically important Ploesti oil fields in Axis-held Rumania.[11] Since the surrender of Fascist Italy in September 1943, the foe was now solely Germany and her Balkan allies, with Allied air targets shifting more and more to such strategic objectives as oil refineries and aircraft factories.

On November 9 Captain Ferebee moved up to 97th assistant group operations officer. On December 22 he was promoted to group bombardier. Ferebee had found his niche; his performance rating sheets during 1943 showed remarkable growth.[12] As the *Red Gremlin*'s bombardier, he had been getting "very satisfactory" marks. As assistant group bombardier, he saw his marks improve to "excellent." As group bombardier, he received "superior" ratings. By January 28, 1944, however, after sixty-four combat missions in Northern Europe, North Africa, the Mediterranean, and the Balkans, even the seemingly indefatigable Tom Ferebee was done. He asked to be relieved of his combat assignment and returned to the States.

Ever since washing out of pilot school, Ferebee had been nursing a hope he would get another chance. Suddenly a window of opportunity appeared; his commanding officer and old friend of the *Red Gremlin*'s crew, Brig. Gen. Hamp Atkinson, now the Fifth Bomb Wing commander, wrote a "To-whom-it-may-concern" endorsement letter recommending him for pilot training.[13] Ferebee was also pleasantly surprised to learn that after just ten months as a captain, he had been promoted to major effective February 2, 1944. With these positive developments and the growing realization that he had, after all, survived combat, he shipped out to the ZI looking forward to the future. By March 1944 Ferebee had made his way to Washington, D.C., where, oddly enough, he found himself delivering Hamp Atkinson's recommendation letter to none other than just-promoted major general Hoyt Vandenberg (who by August would be back in the European Theater as Ninth Air Force commander).

The general was not so sure. "You've washed out [of pilot school] once, and it will take some time. Besides your name has been mentioned for something else. But I can't tell you about it."[14] To throw Ferebee off the scent of what that mysterious assignment might be, Vandenberg gave him an order of the kind GIs only dream about. Still a bachelor, he was sent to sunny Miami for an extended period of rest and relaxation; he and a friend rented a house and settled into a month of fun and games. Years later, Ferebee told the *Charlotte Observer*: "[We had] an open house 24 hours a day . . . I was 25, a major, and had just returned from 64 missions overseas. So you can use your imagination about what kind of time we had."[15]

On May 2 he was ordered to Galveston Army Air Field, Texas. In 1944 the station was primarily an indoctrination center that trained overseas veterans as instructors. By that time Vandenberg's vague references to some exotic new assignment had faded in Ferebee's memory; he now assumed he would either go on a new crew or be a bombardier instructor for the rest of the war. After eight weeks at Galveston, he was posted to another training center at Ardmore Air Field, Oklahoma, as staff bombardier. He labored there for several weeks, now certain he was going to be assigned to a new B-17G unit and sent overseas again. And then lightning struck.

In early September 1944 Major Ferebee received a top-secret telegram "with the highest priority" from Washington relieving him of duty at Ardmore.[16] He was to tell no one of his new orders, which directed him to proceed immediately to Wendover Army Air Field, Utah, but nothing more. Strangely, only days earlier, he had received instructions to report to his old group commander, Brig. Gen. Frank Armstrong, at Grand Island, Nebraska—and as far as Ferebee was concerned, that was where he wanted to go. Despite the fact he was a "mere major," Ferebee took it upon himself to call Armstrong directly. "Keep your mouth shut," the general told him, knowing the new outfit had a top priority though no idea what its mission might be, "and go on to Wendover."[17] Major Ferebee reluctantly complied.

During the same month that Ferebee had been enjoying the good life in Miami, Dutch Van Kirk was already long settled in as an instructor navigator at Selman Field near Monroe, Louisiana. When Dutch's extended home leave had ended nearly a year earlier in late summer 1943, he had reported to Mather Field at Sacramento, California, for a four-week instructor navigator course. By mid-September he had been assigned to Selman Field and had decided that it was time he and Mary Jane Young got married. Her stepbrother and his wife drove the bride-to-be down to Monroe in Dutch's car. Southern Louisiana was still the "Bible Belt" in those years, and that circumstance caused a bit of a snag—Mary Jane was only nineteen and Dutch had a devil of a time getting a marriage license. Finally, her brother was able to sign for her and at long last the deed was done at nearby Shreveport on September 16, 1943.[18] Dutch had only a few days' leave, so they spent their "honeymoon" at home at Selman Field.

Both sets of parents had wanted them to wait a while longer before getting married; they thought Mary Jane was too young and that it sure would have been nice, sometime later, if the couple still desired it, to have a big wedding in Northumberland. What the families did not consider or appreciate was how much a world war changes those who are directly involved in it. Although Van Kirk was only twenty-two chronologically, he had gained the maturity of a peacetime thirty-year-old. And since the moment they had met, Mary Jane had never cared a whit for any other boy but her "Teedy." Charged up like young lovers were during World War II, they simply could not wait. For them, the right time was *now*.

On November 19, 1943, Van Kirk was promoted to captain.[19] His duties did not materially change; he continued to contribute to navigator training curriculums and give student check rides. His work schedule was not onerous, and there was plenty of off-duty time for him to do things with Mary Jane; the young couple settled down to a quiet life at Selman Army Air Field. On February 10, 1944, a dark cloud passed over the family when Dutch's beloved mother, Grace Snyder Van Kirk, passed away from kidney disease. Times were tough for the family; his father and eighteen-year-old sister, Jean, struggled financially during the balance of the war, something that must have weighed heavily on Van Kirk's mind.[20] Following one of his periodic visits to Northumberland to check on them, Van Kirk was driving back to Selman when he heard about the Normandy landings. He listened to the news coverage on his car radio practically the entire way back, thinking, "I'm glad I'm not in that mess. My war is over. I'll just sit here and keep my nose clean."[21]

Things changed abruptly for the Van Kirks during the second week of September 1944. Van Kirk and Mary Jane had been enjoying a leave in nearby New Orleans when the telephone rang in their room. From out of the blue came the voice of Lt. Col. Paul Tibbets. Van Kirk would later wonder how Tibbets managed to track him down to that particular hotel. Both men had been so preoccupied with their own lives, they had failed to keep in touch since separating in North Africa. Still, despite nearly a year and a half apart, the two spoke as if it had only been yesterday.[22]

"I'm forming a new outfit," Tibbets said, getting straight to the point. "I want you as my group navigator. Tom Ferebee has agreed to be my group bombardier. I can't tell you what we're going to do, but it's important enough that we are going to end or significantly shorten the war. You do not have to go, but I want you and . . . I can get the orders to transfer you."[23]

When he later thought about it, Van Kirk recalled that his response was probably too automatic: "I will be there whatever it is. If you and Tom are getting together again, I want to be in on it."[24] Van Kirk had also lost track of his pal Ferebee. A young man in love sometimes has trouble keeping up with other things.

One can only imagine Van Kirk's and Mary Jane's emotions after he hung up. Just minutes earlier they had had it made; suddenly, in the stroke of a single phone call, Van Kirk had committed them to going back into harm's way. It had been a major decision, made on the spur of the moment. Fortunately, Mary Jane was made of stern stuff and supported her husband with unarguable logic—he had already survived everything the enemy could throw at him, therefore he would live through anything else that might come in the future. Youths' belief in their own immortality can indeed be breathtaking.

The Van Kirks returned to Selman Field and got ready. The paperwork came very shortly: report without delay to Wendover Army Air Field, Utah. Van Kirk wryly noted that the date on his official orders was two days prior to Tibbets' phone call. So much, he thought, for volunteering.[25]

As a matter of fact, Lieutenant Colonel Tibbets was himself adjusting to his incredible new assignment, having only learned of it the week before. Since arriving in the States a year and a half earlier, he had been devoting himself to turning around the troubled B-29 Superfortress program. It had not been easy, especially at first. Tibbets had returned from North Africa on a hair trigger, suffering both from the humiliation he had suffered at Doolittle's headquarters and likely a touch of what we today call post-traumatic stress disorder. He had lost nearly forty pounds since crossing the North Atlantic to England six months earlier and was extremely uptight, jumping at the sound of police sirens and not sleeping well. Fortunately, Tibbets had made a wise decision in reentering the United States at Homestead Army Air Field near Miami, still the home of his devoted parents. Enola Gay and Paul Sr.—who more than most fathers knew exactly what his son had been through—rolled out the red carpet. Even better, Lucy and young Paul III, who had been living with her parents in Georgia, came down to Miami to be with their husband and father. The warm and loving presence of his family proved the best of all medicines. After several weeks of what can only be imagined as the catering to every whim a man might have—gorging on his mother's cooking, especially her chocolate and banana cream pies, he regained most of the weight he had lost—Tibbets became restless, eager to get on with his new B-29 assignment. His orders directed him to travel to Washington, D.C., and report to Brig. Gen. Eugene Eubank, USAAF director of bombardment/military requirements. The news was not good.

"I don't know," General Eubank told Tibbets, "whether we'll ever have a B-29."[26] A flabbergasted Colonel Tibbets listened to a tale of woe he had never expected—the highly classified secret B-29 project was in deep trouble. Heading the parade of issues was the matter of its newly developed giant R-3350-23 eighteen-cylinder Wright "Duplex Cyclone" turbosupercharged radials, the most powerful and complex engines ever built, each capable of generating 2,200 hp.[27] Unfortunately, that complexity had made them dangerous—they "ran too hot, swallowed valves, and used excessive oil and fuel."[28] Only weeks earlier, famed Boeing chief test pilot Eddie Allen had taken the second prototype XB-29 up at Boeing Field near Seattle and one of the engines caught fire. Before Allen could set the plane down, the white-hot magnesium fire had burned up the engine and gone through the spars, causing the wing to separate from the aircraft. The plane crashed into the Frye Meat Packing Plant near Seattle, killing the pilots, ten top Boeing technicians, and twenty civilians on the ground. The program was, so General Eubank told Tibbets, in chaos. It was even being suggested that the airplane might technologically be out of reach.

Without any B-29s to work with, Tibbets was once again out of work. Not knowing what else to do, General Eubank sent him to the USAAF School of Applied Tactics in Orlando as assistant to the commanding officer, Maj. Gen. Gordon Saville, where Tibbets marked time for most of the next several months. During that period the USAAF came to grips with the fact that it had no choice on the B-29 Superfortress—General Hap Arnold and the Pentagon made it abundantly clear to all concerned that it simply *had* to be built and it *had* to become operational as soon as possible. Boeing picked itself up off the assembly line floor and set out to do what most thought impossible.

Meanwhile, back at Orlando, and thanks to an accommodating General Saville (Tibbets seemed to have had a way with his operational commanders), Tibbets wangled temporary duty at the 19th Transport Group in Milwaukee.[29] That unit was training both military and civilian air transport command pilots to fly the new Douglas DC-4 airliner on instruments. While most military pilots had received some instrument flight training, compared to the civilian airline pilots of that era, the skills of military flyers were quite rudimentary. The four-engine Douglas airliner, what would soon become the USAAF's iconic C-54 Skymaster transport, had the very latest in radio aids, artificial horizons, directional gyros, and turn and bank indicators. While Tibbets had by this time accumulated three thousand hours and understood the basics of instrument flying, he was not as proficient as he would have liked to have been at what most pilots felt was the most demanding of air disciplines to master. His Army Air Forces instructor, a former airline pilot with nearly three times as many flying hours as Tibbets, took him through the gamut of "blind flying," as it was called in those days—instrument takeoffs, departures, engine-out procedures, partial panel, holding patterns, approaches, missed approaches, and instrument landings using the four-course "A-N" low-frequency radio range. The intensely rigorous eight-day Milwaukee course was the final piece to Tibbets' formal flight training, making him the complete pilot. Despite the fact the colonel had done a great deal of "on-the-job" instrument flying in Europe and North Africa, he had never earned an instrument ticket. Now he had the coveted card, with a strong endorsement permitting him to "fly an airplane any time under his own authority."[30] It was, he said, a proud moment.

In July 1943 word came down from Washington directing Tibbets to proceed to Boeing's new Wichita, Kansas, plant. After incorporating many design changes in the airframe and power plants following the devastating Allen crash in February, several YB-29s had been manufactured and were ready for service testing. Somewhat surprisingly, there was no one at Wichita qualified to give the colonel flight instruction in the airplane—he would have to teach himself.[31] After rounding up a flight engineer who had flown with Eddie Allen and another pilot who was willing to serve as copilot, Tibbets proceeded to check himself out in the B-29. After a thorough procedures and cockpit familiarization process, the trio started out with several high-speed taxis down the active runway, lifting the machine off the ground a few feet at intervals. After satisfying himself that it was "just another flying machine," Tibbets lined up on the active, gave it full power, and took off, completing his introductory flight a few hours later. Presumably he did not self-endorse his own log book, though the effect was the same. As far as the USAAF was concerned, Lt. Col. Paul Tibbets was qualified in the Superfortress.

The B-29 had certainly been well nicknamed, for its many innovations were so far ahead of anything else on the planet, it was a game-changer. First, it was massive, measuring 99 feet nose to tail with a wingspan of 141 feet; it could lift a gross weight in excess of 135,000 pounds—two and a half times greater than what the B-17G could lift. Its four Wright turbosupercharged radials combined to produced 8,800 hp—the B-17G could muster just 4,800 hp. The internal bomb loads reflected similar advantages; the Fortress G model held a maximum of 8,000 pounds while the Superfort could carry 20,000 pounds in two separate bomb bays. The B-29's maximum speed was roughly 50 mph faster than a Fortress—peaking at about 350 mph true airspeed. Last, it had a greater combat range. A bombed-up B-17G was good for about 2,000 miles; a B-29 about 3,250 miles.[32]

There was a lot more than standard performance improvements to set the B-29 apart. For the first time in history, a production heavy bomber would have pressurized compartments, allowing much higher cruising altitudes and increased crew comfort with less fatigue, to say nothing of an unprecedented ability to escape enemy fighters, almost none of whom could operate in the stratosphere (about 30,000 to 50,000 feet). It had a state-of-the-art fire control system (FCS), allowing remotely controlled, computerized firing of ten .50-caliber machine guns located in several turrets, plus two more Brownings separately manned in the tail. Rapid advances had been made in mapping/bombing radar technologies; most 1945-built B-29s would carry the latest version—the AN/APQ-13 navigation/bombing radar system. There was also the new sturdy tricycle landing gear, which made the airplane easier to handle on the ground and gave greater visibility on taxi and takeoff. The list went on. The machine was, in short, one helluva bomber.

For the next year, Tibbets stayed busy testing the airplane and its systems and working with Boeing on further improvements. From time to time he was detached to airfields at Salina, Kansas, and Grand Island, Nebraska, to help check out those first USAAF B-29 pilot instructors assigned to train the operational combat crews. In early March of 1944, however, the program hit a serious snag. The previous January, General Arnold had been promised that 175 Superfortresses would soon be ready to send to XX Bomber Command in the Far East. When the general learned two months later that not a single Superfortress was ready for deployment to the 58th Bombardment Wing (the only B-29 unit that would ever be sent to China), he was enraged. Arnold immediately ordered a crash program to get the airplanes ready. Overnight, an additional 1,200 civilian and military personnel were dispatched to Wichita to work around the clock on the necessary modifications. Chief among the myriad of problems that needed fixing were the fire-prone R-3350 engines, a defect caused by inadequate cooling (partially solved by improved cowl flaps), lubrication issues, and poor carburetion and mixture distribution. Also requiring immediate attention were serious problems with the sophisticated but gremlin-plagued, remote-controlled, interlocking machine gun turrets.

It was regarding this latter glitch that Paul Tibbets and his trouble-shooting crew made their most important contribution during what became known in the USAAF as the "Battle of Kansas."[33] For weeks Tibbets and his men labored alongside all the other emergency teams, with much of the work performed outside in the cold Kansas winter. 1st Lt. Bob Lewis, a talented young flyer, had become Tibbets' regular testing copilot. Sgt. Wyatt "Dooz" Duzenbury was the flight engineer, with Sgt. Abe Spitzer, radio operator. Sgt. Ray Gallagher served as scanner/gunner, and in the tail gunner position sat FCS expert Sgt. George R. "Bob" Caron. It was Caron who took the primary lead in making those early Superfortress FCS systems usable. Colonel Tibbets was very favorably impressed by Caron's performance, deciding he was as knowledgeable about the B-29's guns as anybody either at Boeing or in the USAAF.

By late April most of those first production Wichita B-29s had been modified sufficiently to allow them to depart for the Far East. By May 8, 1944, at least 130 Superfortresses were in the China theater and ready to attack Japan. Unfortunately for the Allied war effort, the tremendous logistical/operational/political issues that developed in the Orient over the following months precluded any real chance for America's XX Bomber Command to be successful. After the Marianas were captured that summer, all B-29 operations on the Asian mainland were relocated to the western Pacific.

For Tibbets and company, the B-29 testing work went on. On occasion, the program brought some interesting surprises. During one TDY (temporary duty) assignment the colonel had an experience that later would have profound implications—not only for himself but also for Gen. Curtis LeMay's future operations in the Marianas. While performing simulated combat tests at 30,000 feet with a fully armed and armor-plated near-gross-weight B-29, Tibbets became concerned about the airplane's vulnerability. He noted very disturbing flight characteristics when making evasive turns; in the very thin air the B-29's wings would stall in a steep turn, easily resulting in a loss of control. It was also apparent there would be no way to fly the airplane in a tight defensive box formation as was done with the B-17s and B-24s. Further tests against a captured Japanese Zero and a Republic P-47 fighter only reinforced his concerns. Serendipitously, one day the plane Tibbets was testing went down for maintenance, and with deadlines approaching, he borrowed another Superfortress. That plane had been partially stripped down (no guns and armor plating), weighing 7,200 pounds less than his regular test aircraft. He was amazed to find the airplane's performance was dramatically improved in all phases of high altitude flight. At 35,000 feet, an altitude 4,000 feet higher than the normally outfitted B-29 service ceiling, he could even turn inside a P-47 Thunderbolt, causing the fighter to stall and fall away every time. Although the flight tests ended abruptly, Tibbets was careful to file away those important revelations.[34]

The reason the colonel had been suddenly pulled off testing was to deal with a festering personnel issue. Many new pilots entering the Superfortress training program had come to believe it was a deathtrap and, frankly, were afraid to fly it. Because Paul Tibbets had by that time accumulated a thousand hours in the B-29 and was considered its most experienced pilot, he had been tabbed to straighten things out. A particularly serious morale problem had been identified at Clovis Air Field, New Mexico, and that was where General Arnold's office sent him. Tibbets' solution was brilliant, though highly unorthodox. He would simply show up the shrinking violets by sending them up on B-29 demonstration flights flown by . . . two girls.

Colonel Tibbets had first become aware of the Women Airforce Service Pilots (WASP) a year earlier at a Colorado airfield when a two-engine medium bomber, the Martin B-26 Marauder—then perceived as equally dangerous (it was derisively called the "Widowmaker" or "Flying Prostitute")—landed and parked next to him. At first he was puzzled that he could not see anyone in the cockpit; finally a tiny thing with "trim legs in a zoot suit" crawled out the hatch. "My God," Tibbets marveled. "It's a woman!"[35]

When his orders to Clovis came through, Tibbets was at that moment TDY at Eglin Airfield, Florida, which had a WASP detachment. After securing permission from the base commander to put the word out that he wanted to talk to them, eight women agreed to listen to his pitch. When he asked if any had multiengine experience, two raised their hands—Dora Dougherty and Dorothea "Didi" Johnson. "If you are willing to give it a try," Tibbets told them, "I'll teach you how to fly that thing [B-29]." They agreed and training began in early August. Didi had made it clear she was OK with copilot duties but was uncomfortable taking on the left seat. Fortunately, Dora was fine with training for the AC/pilot chair. Their first flight was on a terribly hot southern day; with Tibbets looking on, Didi spent most of the flight mopping the perspiration off Dora's brow and forehead so she could see to fly the airplane. Dora was a small woman, and it took real strength to fly a Superfortress with its servo and wire, nonhydraulically boosted controls.

Despite the difficult circumstances, Tibbets was immensely pleased with their progress; Dougherty was a natural flyer. You had only to tell her how to do things once and she had it mastered. In just five days of instruction, the colonel declared both WASPs ready for their check ride. When Civil Aeronautics Administration (CAA) inspector Dean Hudson arrived at the B-29, he encountered the colorful image of the WASP mascot, the girl gremlin "Fifinella," painted on the fuselage along with the airplane's new name, *Ladybird*.[36]

With Hudson, Tibbets, and flight engineer Duzenbury on board, Dora and Didi took off. The testing process began immediately—as soon as the landing gear was in the wells, Dora feathered the number three engine. By the time the flaps had been fully retracted, number four was also feathered. With only one and two producing power on the left side, Dora had to step down with all her might on the left rudder pedal to compensate for asymmetrical thrust in order to keep the airplane flying straight, holding it until she could get most of the yawing neutralized with rudder trim. Once the ship was stabilized, the two WASPs continued their departure.

After bringing back the two feathered engines and climbing to a safe maneuvering altitude, Hudson took the two women through their paces, including stalls and recoveries, which is not easy for anyone in a Superfortress—it took *both* Dora and Didi to strong arm the yoke. Once the air work was completed, it was time to shoot some landings. Dora was descending through 10,000 feet when suddenly the cockpit filled with smoke. Number three engine was on fire.

While Tibbets and Duzenbury looked at each other—as in what do we do next?—Dora was already telling Didi to feather number three, barking instructions through the intercom at Dooz and finishing from memory the "Engine Fire" emergency checklist. Without pause, she hailed the tower, declared an emergency, and requested a straight-in approach. With fire trucks and ambulance racing alongside the *Ladybird*, Dora brought the airplane to a successful full stop landing. She and Didi shut down the engines, with "Captain" Dougherty calmly but firmly instructing the crew as to how to evacuate the aircraft. Dora was the last one off the airplane. Dean Hudson was waiting for her.

Putting his arms around Dora and wearing a huge smile, the CAA inspector blurted, "Honey, give me your goddamned logbook. I want to sign it!"[37] After a hearty round of relieved laughter, Hudson also signed off Didi Johnson as a qualified B-29 copilot. Perhaps the ultimate compliment came from Tibbets' grizzled thirty-one-year-old flight engineer. Duzenbury had initially disapproved of the idea of trying to qualify the two women, but after observing how well they had performed during the training and Dora's remarkable performance in handling the engine fire, he had changed his mind. In his typically laconic manner, Dooz blandly inquired, "Colonel, where do we [meaning himself and the two WASPs] go next?"

The answer was directly back to Clovis Air Field to begin the demonstration flights with the reluctant pilots. Long story short, the men's humiliation was complete—there was no way they could tolerate being shown up by two little girls. All of a sudden B-29s that had been sitting idle were scheduled up and the training program was back on track. After just two weeks, however, the word came from Washington to stand down the WASPs. Apparently the demo flights had been *too* successful; according to Tibbets, headquarters did not want "the women to rub it in too much." By the end of August 1944 Dougherty and Johnson had been reassigned.

The colonel had little time to reflect on what would always be a very satisfying personal experience. On August 31, from out of the blue, he received an urgent phone call to report the next day to Maj. Gen. Uzal Ent, Second Air

Force commander, who was based at Colorado Springs, Colorado. Tibbets' puzzlement only increased when he was told to bring a packed B-4 bag; he was not returning to Clovis Field.[38] The surprises continued upon his arrival at General Ent's office. He was met by a Lt. Col. Jack Lansdale, who strangely enough was wearing U.S. Army Corps of Engineers insignia. It quickly became apparent that the man was operating under false colors.

"I'd like to ask you a few questions before we see General Ent." Lansdale's request was clearly one that could not be refused. A half hour later, a stunned Tibbets concluded that Colonel Lansdale, whoever he really was, might very well know more about Paul Tibbets than Tibbets did himself. The question that really got him was so obscure and deeply personal that he could hardly believe it was possible the Army had the information on file: "Have you ever been arrested?"

Indeed, Tibbets had suffered what he supposed was an "arrest" while a college student, though he was not sure that brief detention really qualified as anything serious. Still, he had been scrupulous so far in answering Lansdale's questions, and something told him he had better play it straight, no matter how embarrassing. It seemed that while he had been in college at the University of Florida a nosy policeman had caught nineteen-year-old Paul Tibbets Jr. in flagrante delicto with a young lady in the back seat of his Chevrolet Roadster. At the time, the matter had generated a small paper trail but little else. The incident, however, had still been enough for Army intelligence officers to track it down. Tibbets' forthrightness in acknowledging the matter closed the deal with Lansdale: "Now let's go see General Ent."[39]

Probably the last thing Tibbets expected to see when they walked into the inner office was a distinguished-looking civilian and a uniformed naval officer sitting next to the general. Just what in the hell *was* he getting into? Lansdale spoke first, saying he was "well satisfied with Colonel Tibbets."

"That's good," said General Ent. "I felt sure you would be." Ent knew Tibbets personally and was very familiar with his military record. When Gen. Hap Arnold had given him three names to choose from, he had responded instantly, "Paul Tibbets is the man to do it."[40]

"Paul," the general began, "you have been chosen to lead the operational phase of perhaps the most important project since hostilities began. If successful, its impact might be so great it could literally end the war. Let me very strongly emphasize at the outset that this program is so very secret only a handful of senior leaders outside of the program even know of its existence. Your first directive is to keep it so. You must not in any way reveal what you are doing to anyone, and that includes Lucy. Do you understand me, Paul?"[41]

"Yes, sir." Tibbets noted that the general had not bothered to ask if he would accept the assignment. Both he and General Ent knew it would have been unthinkable for him to decline something that was being presented in such a manner. Ent turned to his two guests. "Paul, this is Dr. Norman Ramsey, a professor in physics at Columbia University, and U.S. Navy captain Deak Parsons, deputy director of the project's Los Alamos, New Mexico laboratories."[42] Tibbets' gamely nodded his head at the two men, with Ramsey speaking for both he and Captain Parsons.

"Colonel, have you ever heard of atomic energy?" Tibbets allowed that he had studied physics in college and understood there was a possibility that one day the atom might be harnessed as an energy source. Ramsey smiled indulgently, as he might before an apt pupil, and launched into his briefing. After reiterating once again that everything said was hypersecret, he laid out the essential chain of events—the 1939 Einstein letter to President Roosevelt explaining his scientific fears that Hitler was working on an atomic bomb, the creation of the Manhattan Project charged with U.S. development of same, the 1942 Enrico Fermi self-sustaining nuclear chain-reaction experiment under the University of Chicago's Stagg Field bleachers, the creation of the Los Alamos labs to do atomic scientific research, and the very difficult task of manufacturing sufficient quantities of Uranium U-235 and the newly discovered man-made Plutonium P-238 isotope, the necessary explosive materials for a nuclear device.

"In a nutshell, Colonel Tibbets, once they are ready, it will be your job to drop these atomic bombs on our European and Japanese enemies." General Ent jumped back into the discussion. "Paul, I want you to form a brand-new outfit, a self-sufficient group with every component a large Air Force unit would have—its own airplanes, matériel, administration, maintenance, military police, housing, mess halls—everything. We can't afford security breaches of any sort, which means you cannot have any direct interaction with any other AAF units." The general grinned. "Maybe some will call it the Tibbets' Individual Air Force, but officially it'll be the 509th Composite Group. And you'll be the boss of the entire operation."[43]

Ent got down to brass tacks. "Frankly, we have all our eggs in one basket on this. The B-29 Superfortress is the only vehicle the nation has capable of delivering this new weapon. That is," he said after a pause and in a loud stage whisper while nodding his head in Professor Ramsey's direction, "if the longhairs ever get the damned thing to work."[44] Everyone chuckled politely at the gibe, though to Ramsey and Parsons (the latter both a crack scientist and decorated naval officer), it was not funny. They still harbored private doubts themselves as to whether the "gimmick," as it was being called at Los Alamos, was actually feasible. And if so, could this lieutenant colonel they had just met successfully deliver it?

General Ent continued speaking to Tibbets. "I've arranged for a freshly trained B-29 squadron to be transferred to the 509th. It's the top-rated squadron ready to go operational—and you're going to get them." Tibbets would shortly learn this was the fifteen Superfortresses and aircrews of the 393rd

Bomb Squadron (Very Heavy), at that moment assigned to the 504th Bomb Group based at Fairmont Airfield, Nebraska.

"You will be given your own air field from which to train and operate in complete secrecy. You can choose from one of three fields—Mountain Home at Boise, Idaho; Great Bend, Kansas; or Wendover, Utah. I want you to decide on one of them as quickly as possible."

"Paul," General Ent said, bringing the discussion to a close by formally handing Tibbets his orders, "you are responsible for assembling the men, planes, and organization, then developing the tactics required to deliver atomic weapons. From that point your operational charge will be to standardize techniques that will take an airplane to the target, drop the bomb precisely, and get the crew a safe distance away from the blast." Something about the way General Ent had said that last got Tibbets' attention.

"What do you consider a safe distance?" the colonel asked.[45] Capt. Deak Parsons answered for the group. "We're not sure. Our best guess is at least eight slant miles." Tibbets swallowed hard, wondering if the B-29 could run away fast enough.

Very quickly, it was off to other matters. Tibbets asked a number of questions involving such issues as size and weight of the bomb, radioactivity hazards, recruitment of personnel, availability of support units, and so on. All at once, an important point occurred to him. "How much authority do I have to get what I need to do this job?"

General Ent had anticipated the question. "Whenever you can't get what you need through normal channels, you are authorized to use the code word 'Silverplate.' That word will ensure that whoever you are talking to will provide instant and complete cooperation, even from flag officers. But listen closely, Paul, you must be very responsible using this powerful tool. Any abuse of this extraordinary privilege by you or any of your men will go hard on everyone."

Ent looked at the twenty-nine-year-old lieutenant colonel and said solemnly, "We are giving you a hell of a lot of responsibility. Frankly, you are getting more authority than I've got. If you use it wrong, or if you fail, I can see you winding up in prison. Otherwise, you might be a hero. Good luck."[46]

The several days after leaving General Ent's office were extremely hectic. The very first thing on Tibbets' priority list was a telephone call to the one man he wanted beside him as quickly as possible—his old *Red Gremlin* bombardier, Maj. Tom Ferebee.

# 8

# WENDOVER

The moment Paul Tibbets gazed down at remote Wendover Army Air Field, Utah, he knew it was the right place to locate the 509th Composite Group. Salt Lake City was at least 120 miles to the east; Elko, Nevada, some 100 miles west—with very little in between. Yes, there was the tiny community of West Wendover, Utah (population 103), adjacent to the field but it offered little in the way of distractions; there was only the State Line Casino/Hotel with Western Bar and Café and Spike's Place.[1] In addition to a dance floor and live music, Spike served a wonderful $2 steak dinner that people still remembered decades later. From a security standpoint, the place was ideal—the few strangers who might stumble into the area easily stood out in the barren, desert-like hills and plains of western Utah. While those in Tibbets' group who were outdoorsmen and hunters would come to enjoy Wendover Field, most of the servicemen, wives, and dependents were more likely to identify with the sobriquet a USO-touring Bob Hope gave it months earlier—"Leftover Field."[2]

When Tibbets landed on September 8, 1944, he was met by the lieutenant colonel in charge of the permanent party after a P-47 fighter training group had departed.[3] The officer explained what the place had to offer, saying, "I don't know what you want to do, but it's the most perfect base I've ever been on. You've got full machine shops and everybody's qualified and they know what [their doing]."[4] It did not take Tibbets long to confirm for himself that indeed the field's facilities were first-rate and that he would inherit everything there.

Among the very first of the new group to show up was Maj. Tom Ferebee. Arriving in his Buick convertible, Tom was nonplussed when he saw only a few small airplanes scattered about the field and little activity. What in the world, he wondered, had all the hurry-up fuss been about? When Ferebee reported in as a bombardier, he was told, "This is a fighter base." Both puzzled and frustrated, he asked to see the commanding officer.

"About five minutes later," Ferebee recalled, "Paul stuck his head out. I was surprised to see him. He knew I was coming, but I didn't know he was there." After an exchange of pleasantries, Tibbets got right down to business and explained

Ferebee's new job. The just-appointed group bombardier understood he was also expected to contribute on personnel issues. "We can get up to two crews by name," Tibbets told him, "anyone we want. Do you know where Dutch is?"[5]

Ferebee said the last he had heard Van Kirk was an instructor navigator at Selman Field at Monroe, Louisiana. "He got married about a year ago, the hometown girl." Tibbets nodded, making a note. More discussions followed about specific names. The next man they thought of was veteran bombardier and their old friend from the 97th Bomb Group, Capt. Kermit "Honey Bee" Beahan. Like Ferebee, the dapper Beahan had also seen a great deal of combat, the primary reason Tibbets wanted him in the new group.[6] The commander was acutely aware there would be very few combat veterans—old hands—in the outfit. Tibbets and Ferebee also tapped by name the newly promoted captain Bob Lewis, Tibbets' B-29 testing copilot; his B-29 flight engineer, Sgt. Wyatt "Dooz" Duzenbury; Sgt. Bob Caron, the Superfortress gunnery expert; 1st Lt. Charles "Don" Albury, another Eglin Field B-29 test pilot; and Capt. James Van Pelt, a well-regarded instructor navigator. Later a few more men would be handpicked, but the bulk of the 509th aircrew would come from the B-29 squadron General Ent had assigned them.

Ted and Mary Jane Van Kirk arrived at Wendover in mid-October 1944, they pretty well worn out from their automobile trip.[7] It had been nothing but two-lane roads after leaving Monroe, Louisiana—slowing down every five to ten miles to pass through another village or town. It had taken three long days just to make Denver, Colorado, where they were forced to stop at an Army hospital. Van Kirk was in a lot of pain, having somehow picked up an abscess (a felon) on the end of one finger.

After administering a local anesthetic, the surgeon lanced it, telling Dutch to "get a fifth of whiskey" because it was going to hurt like hell after the sedative wore off. The doc was right. In fact, Van Kirk became so disoriented he drove sixty miles in the wrong direction after leaving the hospital. "Some navigator you are," Mary Jane chided him.

At last the Van Kirks arrived at the desolate Utah air field. Very nearly the first thing they noticed after passing through the front gate was a large, rather ominous sign (one of many scattered throughout the post) that read:

WHAT YOU HEAR HERE —

WHAT YOU SEE HERE —

WHEN YOU LEAVE HERE —

*LET IT*

*STAY HERE!*[8]

After driving past a flight line filled with what Van Kirk called "Piper Cubs," he really began scratching his head—like Ferebee, wondering what in the hell he had gotten in to. They were going to "win the war" with threatening signs and those puny crates? His head still shaking, Van Kirk drove on to base operations where he and Mary Jane were warmly greeted by Tibbets and Ferebee. It was a truly memorable reunion—while exuberantly shaking hands, Dutch's felon burst open and everyone's hands got bloody.

Tibbets ordered a quick trip to the base hospital to get rebandaged, telling the Van Kirks to find their quarters and get settled in. Dutch became even less enamored with the base when he saw the housing. Decades later, Van Kirk would tell a newspaper reporter that Wendover was "a shanty town with plumbing."[9] The newcomers quickly discovered the housing pecking order; if a couple had children they got a one-bedroom apartment. If, like the Van Kirks at that time, they were childless, it would be just a single large dormitory room (bachelors like Tom Ferebee bunked together). Although the living spaces were primitive, few in the group seriously complained. After all, the war was still raging and everyone knew conditions overseas were much rougher.

A typical Wendover apartment was either frame or concrete measuring about five hundred to six hundred square feet. There was running water, sink, refrigerator, toilet, shower, double bed, and a table with two chairs. That was it. The pot-bellied heaters and small cook stoves burned soft bituminous coal—it took the wives some time to get used to preparing meals over the smelly fuel. The coal smoke also played havoc with the family wash, and many times it had to be done over. There was also a constant struggle with the cold desert winds and keeping the apartment at least tolerably warm. The spouses fought back as best they could, with many dressing up the place with homemade crafts and fresh-cut wild flower bouquets for the table. Like everyone else, Mary Jane and Dutch made do with what they had.[10]

During those first weeks, the three men spent a good deal of time getting reacquainted. Van Kirk and Ferebee had never met Lucy Tibbets or the boys, the colonel's family having recently joined him. Tibbets and the other senior officers lived in housing only marginally better than any married man with a family. Tom and Paul had heard about Mary Jane Young for a long time and were happy to have at last met her. During their private hours, the fellows immediately picked up where they had left off in North Africa. Card games and sporting activities resumed with vigor, especially handball—Tibbets' favorite form of exercise. Captain Beahan often joined the others to make a spirited foursome in deadly serious handball tournaments. Long afterward Tibbets told an interviewer they often bet steak dinners, and at one point he owed Ferebee and Beahan "a cow."[11]

The reuniting of the old team went just as seamlessly on duty. Indeed, Tibbets' closeness with his two war comrades became so apparent that many in the 509th began to resent their relationship. Van Kirk and Ferebee took the brunt of it; the two seemed able to get away with anything they wished. Unlike everyone else on the field, Van Kirk and Ferebee controlled their own work schedules and could come and go to places like Salt Lake City or Elko as the moment moved them. Van Kirk admitted in *My True Course* that "the guys" came to think of the organization as "Tibbets, Van Kirk, Ferebee and the rest of the 509th."[12] In all probability, the boys had developed a certain swagger.

Overall, the workload during their time at Wendover was easier on Van Kirk and Ferebee. They had their narrow spheres of responsibility and could stay within them. Tibbets, on the other hand, had to boss the entire show. He was the one man in the group who knew all the secrets and bore all the responsibility for success. One of his most difficult tasks was keeping a lid on the super-secret project's security—something few fully appreciated. "I learned to be the world's best liar," Tibbets later stated. "People were always asking what I was doing [and I] was always thinking ahead of what sounded logical. Then if I met them six months later [I had to remember what I'd told them]."[13]

By the third week of October, all fifteen of the B-29s and their crews had arrived from Fairmont Air Field and the process began of pulling the entire so-called composite group together (the term and concept was original with the 509th). Captain Van Kirk received his introductory flight in a Superfortress on October 23, logging 2:30 hours of navigation time.[14] After huddling with the highly capable 393rd squadron navigator, Capt. William Wright, Van Kirk decided to let Wright continue to function in his day-to-day role, essentially acting as Van Kirk's deputy. Ferebee followed suit in his dealings with the squadron bombardier, Capt. Bobby Chapman. From the get-go, Captain Van Kirk and Major Ferebee would function primarily in evaluation, personnel, training syllabus, bomb-testing, and planning roles.

In mid-December 1944, after many weeks of frantic activity, the 509th Composite Group was nearly at full strength and officially made operational. Designated a component of the 313th Bombardment Wing, 20th Air Force, it was structured as follows:[15]

> **Headquarters 509th Bombardment Group:** Lt. Col. Paul W. Tibbets, commanding officer; Maj. James I. Hopkins Jr., operations officer; Maj. Thomas W. Ferebee, group bombardier; and Capt. Theodore J. Van Kirk, group navigator.
>
> **393rd Bombardment Squadron:** The fifteen B-29s and their aircrews detached from the 504th Bombardment Group were the nucleus of the group. The squadron commander was the highly regarded and deeply respected Lt. Col. Thomas Classen, a combat veteran of the Pacific war who had been shot down and grievously wounded. An extremely thin man, he exuded a certain war weariness that seems to have mitigated his leadership potential in the eyes of the group commander,

despite his having put together the top B-29 outfit then training in the Zone of the Interior (the reason Gen. Uzal Ent selected the 393rd). To the chagrin of many in the squadron, and despite Tibbets' declaration that he was "my kind of airman," Classen would never play a significant role in 509th combat operations.

**320th Troop Carrier Squadron:** Initially equipped with two-engine C-46 and C-47 cargo planes, Tibbets used his "Silverplate" code word to get five of the new four-engine Douglas C-54 transports. The Skymasters (military version of the DC-4 commercial airliner) were mostly crewed by those 393rd B-29 aircrew who had not been among the fifteen crews selected to man the group's Superfortresses. Capt. Charles Sweeney, a genial pilot who had ingratiated himself to Tibbets during the earlier B-29 testing programs, was appointed 320th Troop Carrier squadron commander. In the spring of 1945, the engaging Irishman would become the 393rd Bombardment Squadron commander, replacing Lieutenant Colonel Classen, the latter having been bumped upstairs to deputy group commander. The transport unit became known as the Green Hornet Line, after their C-54s' colorful fuselage art design.[16]

The independently operating composite 509th organization also included the 390th Air Service Group (which included the Headquarters/Base Services squadron); the 603rd Engineering Squadron (aircraft maintenance and repair); 1027 Air Matériel Squadron (supplies and equipment); 1395th Military Police Company; and (later in March 1945) the 1st Ordnance Squadron, Aviation (assembly and handling of the atomic bombs).

There was another unit attached to the group, as augmentation to the Military Police Company. Reporting directly to Maj. Gen. Leslie Groves (not to Tibbets), the man who headed up the massive Manhattan Project headquartered in Washington, D.C., this shadowy detachment was led by Capt. William "Bud" Uanna, a brilliant Army military intelligence officer.[17] A mysterious fellow during and after the war, Uanna was in charge of about thirty specially trained plain-clothes agents, both men and women. Officially, their mission was to preserve the overall security of the operation; in fact, they were instructed to secretly spy on all 1,800 officers and men of the 509th Composite Group. Not surprisingly, everyone called them "the creeps." Captain Uanna was The Creep.

Tibbets did not share those negative views, finding Bud Uanna a very capable officer who consistently supported the mission with his excellent work. Their relationship got off to a robust start in mid-December when the two men concocted a plan that would demonstrate to the group just how important security was to the operation. It kicked off with Tibbets' first address to his men:

> We've looked each other over. I'm not going to get stuck with all of you, but those who stay are going to be stuck with me. You have been brought here to work on a special mission, one that could end the war. Over the next several months, you will be expected to work very hard to bring skills and performance to the highest levels. Do not ask what the job is, that is a sure way to get transferred out of here. Don't be curious—just do exactly what you are told, when you are told and you'll get along fine. Never hint about this base or talk about what you are doing to anyone, including your closest family members or even your wives. The work will not be easy but I have no doubt we will succeed by working together.

Tibbets paused before dropping a bombshell. "However, we can't live by all work and no play. So, as of right now, you are authorized a two-week furlough."[18]

No one in the group could believe their ears. After weeks of tension and an unrelenting sense of urgency, the pressure had suddenly been lifted.[19] They could go home for Christmas! While still bewildered about the nature of their mission—Tibbets had only said it was so secret that for now they would just have to trust him—no one was willing to look a gift horse in the mouth. Except for a skeleton staff, the 509th went on leave.

There were few transportation venues out of remote Wendover. With auto trips out of the question due to time constraints and gas rationing, and only a few having access to military air transportation, most men had to use public surface travel. Essentially, that was confined to train and bus depots at Salt Lake City and a bus station at Elko. Captain Uanna had sprinkled large numbers of his agents at those locations posing as friendly civilians, traveling salesmen, a waitress here, a bartender there.

"Where you stationed soldier?"

"Oh yes, Wendover Air Field, that's out there on the border, right?"

"What do you do out there in the middle of nowhere."

"A big secret, eh? I see."

"My, my. So they're getting B-29s out there now. Aren't those the big, new four-engine jobs?"

Every man who had loosened his lips received a telegram from Tibbets sternly ordering him to return to Wendover immediately. As Tibbets later said, "A considerable number of our people found their holiday leaves interrupted."[20] Those dazed individuals caught in Uanna's net—most had no idea that their seemingly innocuous responses had constituted a security breach—were promptly put under "house arrest" and confined to quarters for up to forty-eight hours. After that softening up, they were brought before Tibbets and Uanna for a Gestapo-like interrogation. Each man was told he now had one strike against him and there were only two in this game. A second offense meant immediate banishment to an isolated Alaskan outpost.[21] The exercise worked like a charm, the message coming through loud and clear. Tibbets had just put the fear of God into every one of his men. Although the telephone tapping, mail reading, and probing bar encounters did continue, subsequent security issues were few and minor. While the Manhattan Project itself would suffer devastatingly from espionage (most notably by Soviet scientist-spies Klaus Fuchs and David Greenglass), Tibbets would later note with not a little pride that his group did not have a single meaningful security leak.

That was not to say Uanna did not have issues with some of the outfit's men. He had discovered at least six escaped felons, one of whom had been convicted of murder (the man apparently was also outstanding on a machine shop lathe—a specialty Tibbets was in desperately short supply).[22] Tibbets brought each of the men in and read them the riot act—any trouble at all from you, or if you do not do your job, it is straight back to prison. All six would go on to perform well, and the colonel lived up to his promise to burn their files.

Captain Uanna was also seriously concerned about Capt. Claude "Buck" Eatherly, one of the B-29 aircraft commanders. The man was forever getting into trouble with the law, a chronic womanizer, drinker, and gambler. Tibbets interjected that he was also a very good pilot, one of his best. Uanna was not convinced, telling the colonel he should get rid of him. "The guy's a psycho!"[23] As he would later learn, Tibbets would have been better in the long run to have accepted the security man's counsel.

Interestingly, Uanna also did not care much for Capt. Bob Lewis and Maj. Tom Ferebee.[24] While Lewis was an exceptional pilot—the first second lieutenant to qualify as a B-29 aircraft commander—he was also capable of unpredictable and unprofessional behavior outside the cockpit.[25] Lewis would survive several brushes with Tibbets, the most serious of which was the borrowing of a Green Hornet C-54 transport for an unauthorized trip back home to New Jersey. A similar incident resulted in a 509th staff headquarters light colonel getting banished to the Aleutians. The difference—the colonel was easily replaced; Lewis was one of the better B-29 aircraft commanders, and to remove him would also break up Tibbets own handpicked crew. As for Ferebee, Uanna thought he was too slick. In *Fire of a Thousand Suns*, George Caron and Charlotte Meares wrote that the security captain thought Tom was a "wheeler-dealer," his escapades a constant thorn in Uanna's side. Still, according to Caron, Uanna told Tibbets that "compared to Lewis . . . he looks like Shirley Temple." The personality clashes also ran sideways. Much later Bob Lewis would tell an interviewer that he had disliked Tom Ferebee from the day they met, saying he thought the bombardier "acted superior" and talked like "a playboy in the movies."[26]

In January 1945 the 509th began training in earnest when fifteen of the first-generation specially modified Silverplate Superfortresses arrived at Wendover.[27] The men very quickly had a lot on their plate—shaking down the new B-29s, continuous ground schools, very-high-altitude training sorties, testing extremely large and different bomb casing configurations (none of the bombardiers had any experience dropping five-ton blivets), pin-point navigation legs, visual bombing practice, and many hours of what airmen call "transition"—takeoffs, touch and goes, and full-stop landings.

One of the most critical problems the flyers faced was how best to distance themselves from the expected blast of the new weapon. Tibbets had been told the bomb would likely release destructive energy equivalent to 20,000 tons of dynamite. The colonel found that number hard to wrap his mind around—as he later put it, "I'd never seen even one pound of TNT blow up."[28] He would have to take the longhairs' word as to how far away he had to get before the thing went off.

In one of Tibbets' first trips to the Manhattan Project's Weapons Laboratory at Los Alamos, New Mexico, he discussed the escape problem with the lab's technical director, Dr. J. Robert Oppenheimer. The two men agreed that after release one could not overfly the target as was the usual procedure; the bomber would be almost directly over the aiming point at detonation, a sure suicide. It was also clear that a Silverplate B-29 needed to conduct the bomb run at its maximum operating altitude (which would turn out to be slightly under 31,000 feet above sea level), so at least they would start out with nearly six miles of altitude separation. But that still left the ship much too vulnerable.

The brilliant Oppenheimer had the solution, telling Tibbets he had to rapidly maneuver the aircraft away on a tangent line to the expanding, curving shock wave racing up to meet the B-29, which, expressed in lay terms, meant making a sharp turn either left or right of precisely 155 degrees from the bomb-run heading. This, the physicist said, would yield the maximum slant distance between the ship and the target at the moment of detonation.[29] Upon his return to Wendover, Tibbets took a B-29 up to altitude and tested the idea. He confirmed that a 60-degree bank (very steep for a giant Superfortress) held through Oppenheimer's 155-degree turn gave the best results. The maneuver was quite tricky—the pilot had to avoid a too-high angle of attack or the airfoil disruption on the horizontal tail surfaces would cause a loss of control, what Tibbets described as "stalling the tail." When you feel that tail flutter through the yoke, he told his pilots, you will know the turn is steep enough. Throughout the procedure the throttles were to be kept fire-walled and the airplane put into a very shallow descent to build up ground speed, thus adding that much more separation. Tibbets discovered the maneuver could be completed in forty to forty-two seconds; the calculated interval from a drop at 30,000 feet to detonation was about forty-three to forty-five seconds. This left about three seconds of straight and level flight until the bomb exploded, with but a few additional seconds before the first shock wave arrived at what the physicists were calculating would be a distance of about eleven slant miles—a very slim margin of safety indeed. The aileron and elevator work required to conduct what in the postwar Strategic Air Command became known as the "breakaway turn" proved to be extremely challenging, and it would take a great deal of practice over the coming months for the B-29 aircraft commanders to become proficient.[30] According to Sgt. Bob Caron, Tibbets was relentless on this point; those pilots who failed to execute the turn properly were temporarily grounded.[31]

The commander was equally demanding with other aircrew performance standards—especially regarding the bombardiers and navigators. The bomb aimers were expected to hold to a circular error of within 200 feet of a 400-foot painted circle target while dropping from 30,000 feet using only visual Norden synchronous/autopilot-clutched procedures. Navigators were required to come within one-half mile of their celestial navigation leg end point as computed from the solution of their final alter-heading and ETA. Interestingly, these tolerances were as close as or closer than those mandated by the later all-jet Strategic Air Command using more sophisticated nav/bomb systems and powerful hydrogen bombs. Tibbets later said the intent was to cause competition among the crews by creating an atmosphere of "let's go out and beat the old man [and his crew]."[32]

As to the matter of precision navigation, it soon became apparent to Captain Van Kirk that his Magellans, nearly all of whom were inexperienced operationally, had nowhere near the skills necessary to meet the commander's objectives, especially with respect to day and night sextant/celestial navigation on long-range overwater legs. The problem was twofold: (a) the nearest ocean was six hundred miles to the west, and (b) continuing to fly over friendly North American soil provided too much temptation for the men to back-in those infamous "Dubhe, Deneb, and Dallas" three-star fixes. Clearly, from Wendover, there was no practical way to teach serious overwater navigation. Van Kirk shared his concerns with Tibbets, who agreed something had to be done.

Dutch got his chance to rectify the situation in early January when he accompanied Paul Tibbets to Washington for a meeting with Manhattan Project director, Maj. Gen. Leslie Groves. Van Kirk was given the opportunity to present their joint proposal to send the 393rd Bombardment Squadron, along with certain support units, to Batista Air Field at Havana, Cuba, for long-range navigation training sorties over the non-hostile mid-Atlantic.[33] Other B-29 units were already using Batista for similar training prior to combat deployments to the Far East. "Aren't you worried," General Groves queried, "you are going to lose some crews out there?" Dutch responded, "General, would you rather lose them out there or when they are flying over the Pacific?"[34]

Approval came quickly, with the first crews leaving for Cuba in mid-January 1945. They would stay for two weeks of intensive training, then rotate back to Wendover, to be replaced by another set of crews and support units. Tibbets realized that this was an opportunity to accomplish a lot more than just improving navigator skills. The thousand-mile triangular-legged over-water sorties (terminating back at the Cuban airfield) also allowed the pilots to gain trust in their navigators, build experience and understanding of the need for strict heading and airspeed discipline on celestial navigation legs, and get experience on long overwater, unescorted single-plane operations. The training further included simulated high-altitude bombing runs along with tail gunnery practice. The planners, led by group operations chief Hopkins, Ferebee, and Van Kirk, did their best to simulate combat conditions during the average three to four sorties each crew flew. A bonus for the 509th came when its fine reliability record while at Batista was formally recognized by the Army Air Forces, its ground crews and maintenance teams having outperformed those several other B-29 units undergoing overseas training at the same time. Most importantly to Dutch Van Kirk, at the end of the Cuban exercise he had fifteen *real* over-ocean navigators. Altogether, a major portion of the 509th was in Cuba for six weeks; those that made the trip would always remember their time in the exotic tropics away from cold and barren Utah.[35]

Back at Wendover, Major Ferebee had continued to labor away testing bombs and calculating their ballistics on the many casing configurations sent up from Los Alamos by U.S. Navy captain William Sterling "Deak" Parsons and his people. There were many problems—this was, after all, uncharted territory. No one had ever before built such a large, complicated bomb, and new engineering issues arose almost daily. The difficulties were fundamental—the insides of all aerial bombs must somehow be made rigid enough to withstand external influence or damage until that last instant when the explosive is detonated. The nature of an atomic bomb made that problem infinitely more complicated. Further, a gravity bomb housing must be of a standardized design and shape in order to reliably calculate what is referred to as its predicted "ballistics." By definition, that meant the bomb must have a properly stabilizing tail assembly in order to provide predictable glide paths that can be put into tables for use by the bombardier.

One might presume that, through experimentation, the answers would have been reasonably straightforward—white-shirted engineers working their slide rules, jotting down mathematical formulas while constantly referring to a wide body of data on gravity bomb ballistic testing that eventually revealed the correct solution. In the case of these new atomic devices, however, it became anything but. Because of the uncertainty over the exact nature of the bombs themselves, Captain Parsons and the Los Alamos engineers could not settle on the final size and shape of the atomic devices themselves, which made it that much more difficult for anyone to design a bomb casing around them. As

**Freshly commissioned and newly rated USAAF navigator 2nd Lt. Theodore Van Kirk**
*Courtesy of the Theodore "Dutch" Van Kirk family*

**2nd Lt. Paul W. Tibbets Jr. soon after winning his wings at Kelly Field, Texas, in February 1938**
*Courtesy of the Paul W. Tibbets Jr. family*

**Aviation cadet Thomas W. Ferebee**
*Courtesy of Florence Finnegan*

RESTRICTED MARCH, 1945 BIF 6-1-1

# NOMENCLATURE AND OPERATION

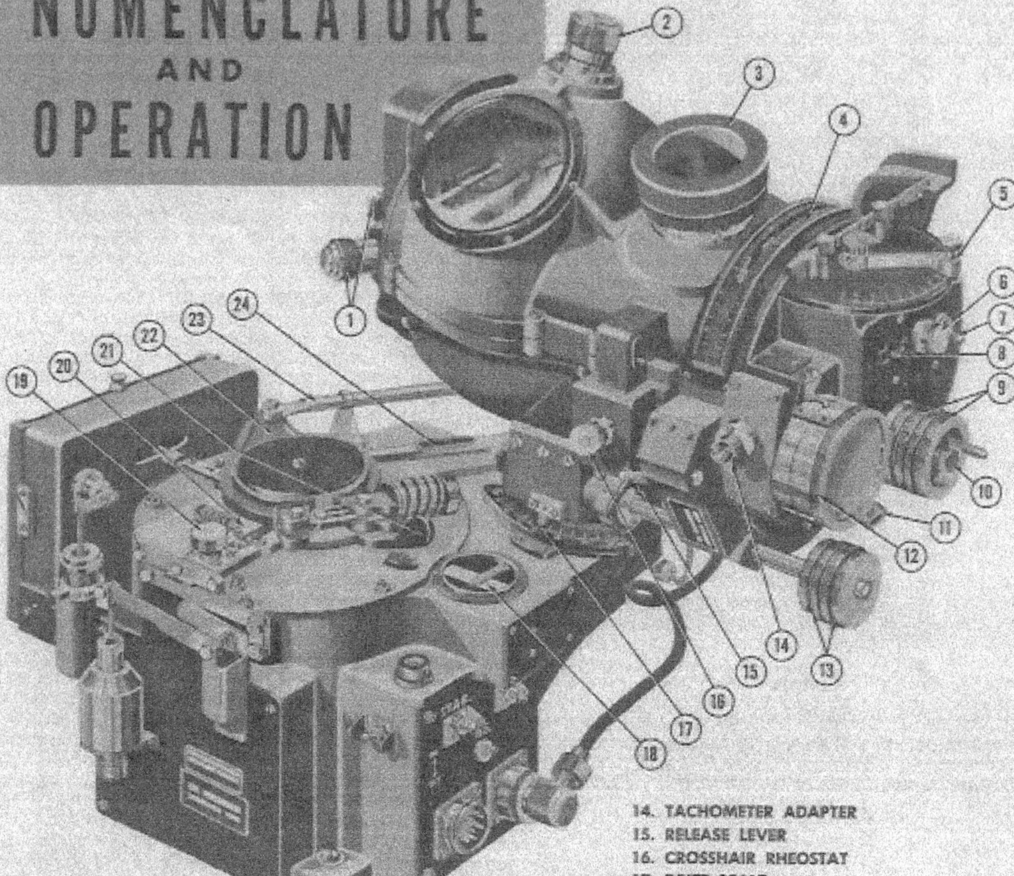

1. LEVELING KNOBS
2. CAGING KNOB
3. EYEPIECE
4. INDEX WINDOW
5. TRAIL ARM AND TRAIL PLATE
6. EXTENDED VISION KNOB
7. RATE MOTOR SWITCH
8. DISC SPEED GEAR SHIFT
9. RATE AND DISPLACEMENT KNOBS
10. MIRROR DRIVE CLUTCH
11. SEARCH KNOB
12. DISC SPEED DRUM
13. TURN AND DRIFT KNOBS
14. TACHOMETER ADAPTER
15. RELEASE LEVER
16. CROSSHAIR RHEOSTAT
17. DRIFT SCALE
18. PDI BRUSH AND COIL
19. AUTOPILOT CLUTCH ENGAGING KNOB
20. AUTOPILOT CLUTCH
21. BOMBSIGHT CLUTCH ENGAGING LEVER
22. BOMBSIGHT CLUTCH
23. BOMBSIGHT CONNECTING ROD
24. AUTOPILOT CONNECTING ROD

The bombsight has 2 main parts, **sighthead** and **stabilizer.** The sighthead pivots on the stabilizer and is locked to it by the dovetail locking pin. The sighthead is connected to the directional gyro in the stabilizer through the **bombsight connecting rod** and the **bombsight clutch.**

RESTRICTED

Norden bomb sight. The key controls were the EXTENDED VISION KNOB (6); RATE AND DISPLACEMENT KNOBS (9); TURN AND DRIFT KNOBS (13); and the BOMBSIGHT CLUTCH ENGAGING LEVER (21).

*U.S. Army Air Forces, Bombardier's Information File 6-1-1, March 1945*

Beechcraft AT-11 "Kansan" bombardier trainer over Texas. The AT-7 "Navigator" trainer was very similar—note the sextant observation dome.
*National Archives and Records Administration*

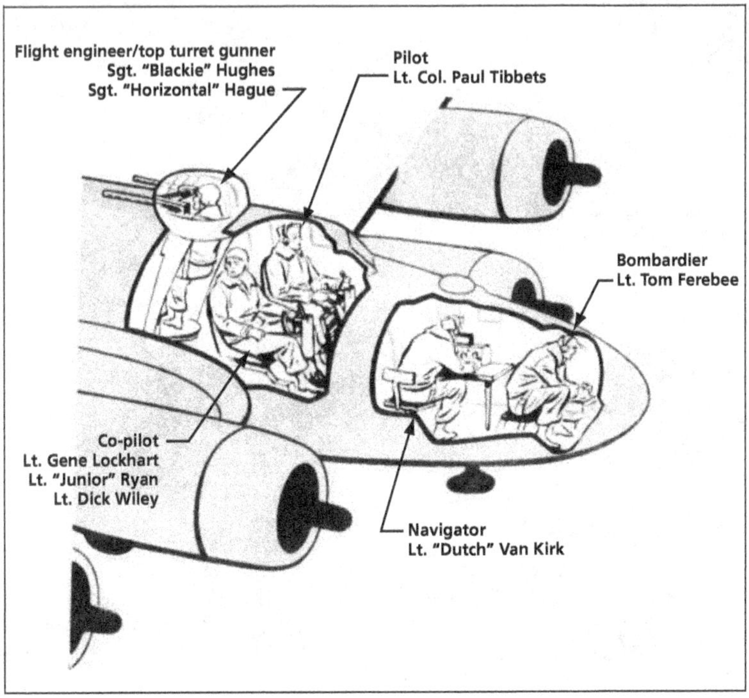


Lt. Col. Paul Tibbets' B-17E/F forward compartment aircrew—August 1942 to February 1943. *Drawing based on a USAAF B-17F Pilot Training Manual illustration via Nelson Mears*

**The *Red Gremlin*, with nose art inset**
*Courtesy of the artist, Sir Ernie Hamilton Boyette at www.aviationartstore.com*

**Left to right, WASP Dorothea "Didi" Johnson, WASP Dora Dougherty, Lieutenant Colonel Tibbets, CAA Inspector Dean Hudson. Immediately following the WASPs' action-filled check ride in the B-29 *Ladybird*, Hudson is signing the women off as qualified Superfortress pilots.**
*Courtesy Women Airforce Service Pilots Archive, Texas Woman's University*

Green Hornet Line C-54 preparing for departure from Wendover to Tinian.
*Courtesy Air Force Historical Research Agency*

North Field on Tinian Island, looking east. Runway D for Dog, to the far right, had not yet been constructed. The 509th Composite Group compound would be located in the left foreground, adjacent to Runways Able and Baker.
*U.S. Air Force*

On September 11, 1945, Dr. J. Robert Oppenheimer, head of the Los Alamos labs (left), and Project Manhattan director Maj. Gen. Leslie Groves inspected the remains of the steel tower that had housed the "Trinity" atomic bomb at Alamogordo. Note the white overshoes, intended to prevent radioactive contamination.
*National Archives and Records Administration*

The "Tinian Joint Chiefs." Left to right, Capt. Deak Parsons, USN, Rear Adm. William Parnell, USN, Brig. Gen. Thomas Farrell, USAAF.
*Courtesy Air Force Historical Research Agency*

The *Enola Gay* on North Field
*Courtesy National Museum of the U.S. Air Force*

Saturday afternoon, August 4, 1945, prebriefing to the seven crews scheduled for the Hiroshima strike. Capt. Deak Parsons (left, standing) attempted to show a movie of the New Mexico "Trinity" atomic bomb test but had to settle for slides. Colonel Tibbets stands at right.
*National Archives and Records Administration*

Early afternoon, Sunday, August 5, 1945. The *Enola Gay* is backed over pit #1 to upload "Little Boy," which can be seen in left foreground.
*National Archives and Records Administration*

North Field, 2:30 p.m., Sunday, August 5, 1945. The "Little Boy" uranium bomb is shown here in loading pit #1, resting on the hydraulic hoist. Immediately after this photo was taken, the hoist was raised and the weapon clipped into the *Enola Gay*'s forward bomb bay.
*National Archives and Records Administration*

*Enola Gay*'s ground crew, the real unsung heroes. Tibbets later said this airplane was the most "trouble-free" B-29 he ever flew. Standing (left to right): Corp. John Jackson, Sgt. Leonard Markley, SSgt. Walter McCaleb (crew chief), Pfc. Harold Olsen. Kneeling (left to right): Sgt. Jean Cooper, Pvt. John Lesniewsky.
*National Archives and Records Administration*

Aircrew of the *Enola Gay*, 1:50 a.m. on August 6, 1945, fifty-five minutes before takeoff. Standing left to right: Lt. Col. John Porter, 509th maintenance chief; Capt. Ted Van Kirk; Maj. Tom Ferebee; Col. Paul Tibbets; Capt. Bob Lewis; Lt. Jacob Beser. Kneeling left to right: SSgt. Joseph Stiborik; TSgt. Bob Caron; Corp. Richard "Junior" Nelson; Sgt. Bob Schumard; TSgt. Wyatt Duzenbury. Not shown: Capt. Deak Parsons, USN, and Lt. Morris Jeppson, USAAF
*U.S. Air Force*

Tension was heavy prior to takeoff, and there was a lot of "cheerful" chit-chat. Left to right, Lt. Col. Hazen Payette, group intelligence officer; Maj. Tom Ferebee; Sgt. Bob Schumard; Col. Paul Tibbets; Cpl. Richard "Junior" Nelson; Capt. Ted Van Kirk; TSgt. Bob Caron, looking warily at the photographer over Dutch's left shoulder.
*National Archives and Records Administration*

2:35 a.m. Monday, August 6, 1945. Tibbets had just called out "taxi!" to his ground crew. A 509th enlisted photographer, Armen Shamlian, shouted out a request to wave. When the colonel obliged, Shamlian snapped this historic image.
*National Archives and Records Administration*

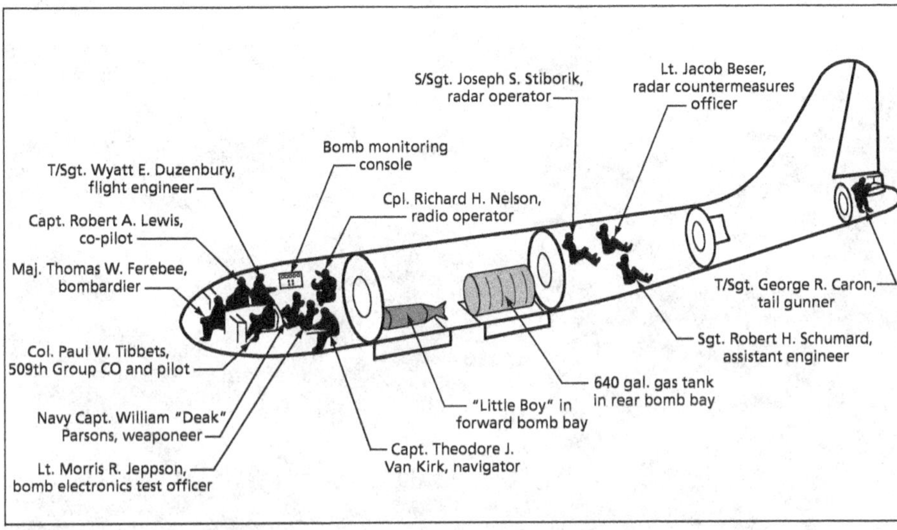


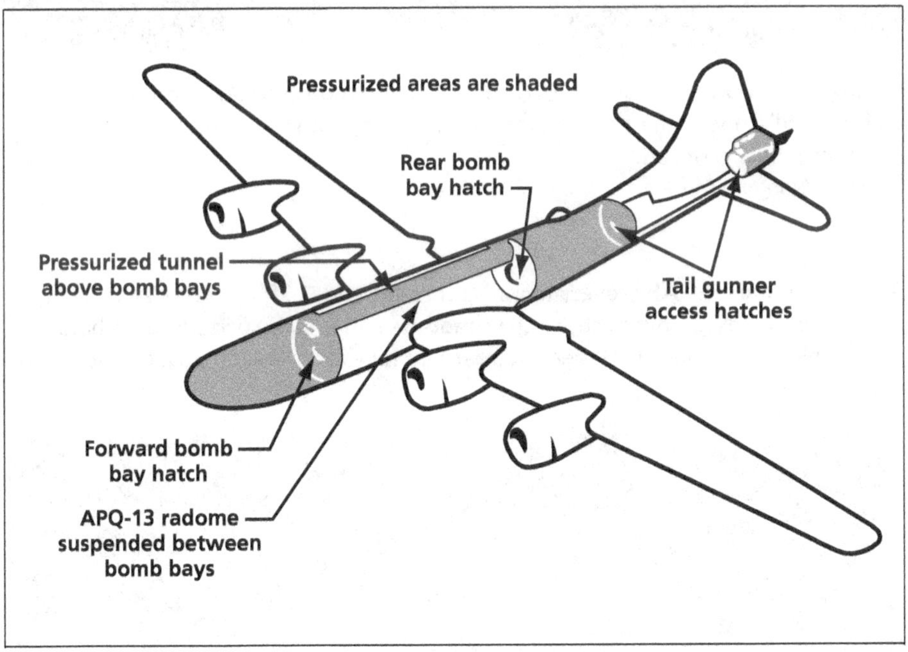


**Locations of the flight crew, "Little Boy," and other key aspects of the *Enola Gay* on August 6, 1945.**
*Illustrations derived from B-29 Plane Commander Training Manual, March 1, 1945, USAAF*

Boeing B-29 Superfortress forward cockpit. Pilot station to left, bombardier seat in middle under the greenhouse windows, copilot station to right. Norden sight is covered.
*Courtesy National Museum of the U.S. Air Force*

An unidentified USAAF crewman crawls through the B-29's pressurized tunnel, which passed over the APQ-13 radome and unpressurized bomb bays and enabled movement between the rear and forward crew compartments.
*U.S. Air Force*

Tail gunner TSgt. Bob Caron took this iconic photo just a few minutes after "Little Boy" detonated.
*U.S. Naval Institute Photo Archive*

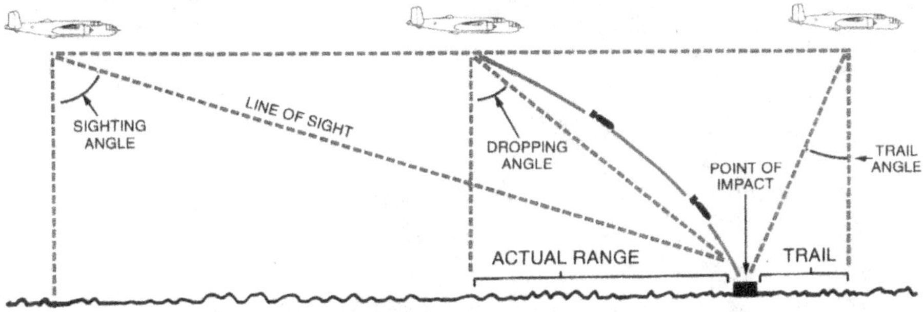


Conceptual look at how the "when" of the bomb drop was determined. When the sighting angle at last coincided with the drop angle, the bomb was released.
*Illustration courtesy of* Air Force Magazine

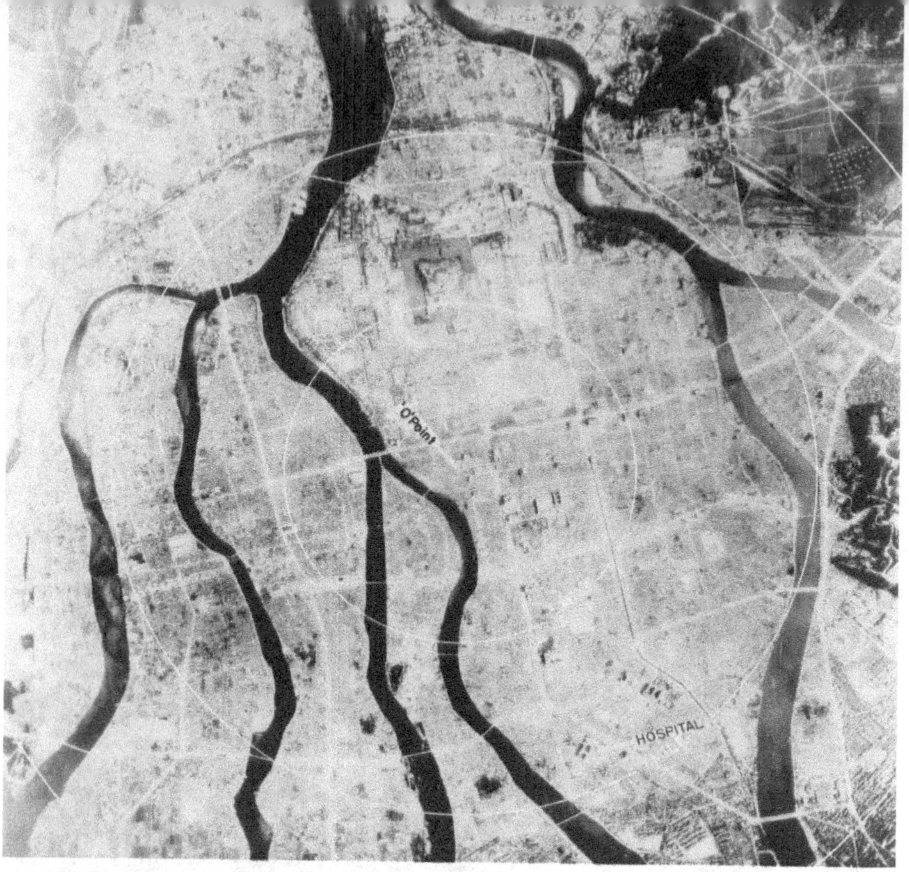


Hiroshima poststrike bomb damage assessment photo. "O" Point indicates "ground zero." The weapon detonated 1,890 feet above the ground, just 800 feet southeast of the T-shaped Aioi Bridge aiming point.
*Library of Congress*

Gen. Carl "Tooey" Spaatz presenting the Distinguished Service Cross to Col. Paul Tibbets as Brig. Gen. John Davies looks on. Note the palmed pipe in Tibbets' left hand.
*National Archives and Records Administration*

*Enola Gay* crew debriefing, late afternoon August 6, 1945. Gen. Carl "Tooey" Spaatz is at head of table, glass in hand. Clockwise around table are Capt. Deak Parsons, USN (receding hairline); Capt. Bob Lewis (hand on table next to papers); Maj. Tom Ferebee (ball cap); Sgt. Bob Caron (dark ball cap, glass in hand); Lt. Col. Hazen Payette, conducting debrief (back to camera); Capt. Dutch Van Kirk (reading from log); Col. Paul Tibbets (behind Van Kirk); Adm. William Purnell (looking at Van Kirk); LeMay's boss and Twentieth Air Force commander Gen. Nathan Twining (cigar in mouth), talking to AAF Pacific commander Gen. Barney Giles. Behind Spaatz with white T-shirt showing is Lt. Col. Tom Classen. To his left with left hand in pocket is Lt. Col. James Hopkins.

*National Archives and Records Administration*

Afternoon, Wednesday, August 8, 1945. The "Fat Man" plutonium bomb is being lowered onto its transport dolly for the trip out to loading pit #2, where it will be hydraulically raised into *Bockscar.*

*National Archives and Records Administration*

Aircrew of *Bockscar* just before takeoff early a.m. on August 9, 1945. Standing (left to right): Maj. Charles Sweeney, 1st Lt. Don Albury, 2nd Lt. Fred Olivi, Capt. Kermit Beahan, Capt. James Van Pelt, 1st Lt. Jacob Beser. Kneeling (left to right): MSgt. John Kuharek, Cpl. Abe Spitzer, Sgt. Ray Gallagher, SSgt. Edward Buckley, Sgt Albert DeHart. (Lt. Phil Barnes not shown)
*National Archives and Records Administration*

Inset: A later photo of then-commander Fred Ashworth, weaponeer
*U.S. Naval Institute Photo Archive*

a result, Ferebee and the scientists were destined to spend many frustrating months experimenting with live drops on a long series of different test bombs.

The "units," as the aircrews came to call them, were huge—some were shaped like a thin cigar nearly twenty feet long and weighing up to 10,000 pounds each; others were nearly round in shape and equally heavy.[36] Unknown to all in the group but Tibbets, the distinctively different configurations were due to the two completely dissimilar type of bombs under development at Los Alamos.[37] The cigar-shaped design finally selected to house the uranium or U-235 bomb, which early in the Manhattan Project was believed to be the only type of atomic bomb feasible, was simplicity itself. One fifty-five pound "projectile slug" of the highly refined U-235 isotope would be fired forty-two inches at a velocity of about one thousand feet per second into an eighty-five-pound "target mass" of the same material, the collision creating a runaway fission chain reaction and atomic explosion.[38]

After it was discovered how difficult and costly it was to refine U-235 from natural U-238 uranium (what a prospector finds using a Geiger counter), scientists turned to a new man-made substance called "plutonium." Plutonium-238 was first created in 1941 by a newly developed method of synthesizing U-238 first into neptunium-238, then allowing it to decay into P-238. What made P-238 so exciting was that this new radioactive uranium isotope could not only be manufactured more easily (relatively speaking) and in greater quantities than U-235, it also offered greater destructive capability. On the downside, a P-238 bomb presented greater challenges in terms of setting the thing off. A much different animal than the uranium bomb, Captain Parson's fusing team found the only way to detonate plutonium was to use a devilishly intricate implosion technique—that is, a perfectly simultaneous explosion of thirty-two finely machined wedged-shaped lenses that collapsed instantaneously into a perfect sphere thereby compressing the plutonium into a supercritical state that set off an uncontrolled chain reaction. The required degree of "squeeze" was found to be equivalent to that needed to reduce the radioactive sphere from the size of a softball to that of a billiard ball. Instead of a long, gun-barrel-type bomb, an implosion bomb needed more of a round-shaped casing, a design configuration that resulted in the construction of large numbers of dummy practice bombs that would be very similar in size and ballistic configuration to the final plutonium/implosion bomb.[39]

Although Tom Ferebee was naturally puzzled why it was necessary to test two fundamentally different bomb casings, he unquestioningly persevered with each requested drop. The many versions of each type sent up from Los Alamos were dropped over practice ranges in Utah and along the shores of California's Salton Sea. It was frustrating work, especially at first—"the first three things they gave me to drop looked like telephone poles," which, instead of obeying any kind of an acceptable aerodynamic descent configuration, simply toppled end over end.[40] By late spring, however, designs for a "thin man" uranium bomb and another for a "fat man" plutonium bomb had made dramatic progress. The final version of the "thin man" had been made a little wider and shortened, its type renamed "little boy."[41]

The word had come down from the Pentagon that these new weapons could only be dropped in daylight while using optical sighting in conjunction with the automatic Norden Bombing System—no exceptions. Even as late as mid-1945, and despite the proven success of all-weather, day or night "blind" bombing using radar, General Groves had not embraced the new technology. Entrusted by U.S. Army chief of staff Gen. George Marshall with near omnipotent powers, Groves had decreed that absolutely no chances were to be taken regarding accuracy, which in his mind meant daytime visual releases only.[42] The Wendover bombardier training proceeded accordingly.

An odd incident occurred about this time that seriously worried Colonel Tibbets, who wondered if some major glitch had developed in the bombing equipment or the newly developed ballistic tables. All of a sudden his ace bombardier, Major Ferebee, was throwing atomic test bombs all over the American Southwest, his circular error having climbed from a few hundred feet to thousands of feet. Thoroughly alarmed, Tibbets began personally piloting Ferebee's practice bombing sorties in an effort to track down the problem. On each bomb run, the colonel studied every aspect of the equipment and Ferebee's actions. While the bombardier himself was almost certainly shaken over such uncharacteristic results, he outwardly maintained his usual calm demeanor.

On perhaps the third or fourth sortie dropping a five-ton dummy plutonium bomb—what had become known as a "pumpkin" for its shape and color—over the Salton Sea range and while observing Ferebee intently, Tibbets had a eureka moment. Much like a baseball player who unconsciously changes his batting stance at the plate and goes into a slump, Tom Ferebee had adopted a different posture over the sighthead at around the sixty-seconds-to-go mark. Instead of remaining seated in the same fashion throughout the entire bomb run, as he had always done previously, he had taken to standing up in his seat in a half-crouch while continuing to synchronize the crosshairs.

"That's it!" Tibbets cried out.[43] Ferebee's new position midway through the bomb run had created a parallax, a change in the position of a viewed object when the observer changes position. What would have been an inconsequential miss in a B-17 traveling at 200 mph at 10,000 feet resulted in a dramatically magnified error when dropped from a B-29 at over 30,000 feet at 300-plus mph. The problem was fixed with a special headrest for the bombardiers, which made sure they remained fixed in the same position throughout the bomb run.[44]

As the winter of 1945 wore on, and with the group's overall training program well in hand and the prospect of an operational deployment growing ever closer, Tibbets was spending more and more time in Washington and

Los Alamos discussing actual use of the weapons and less and less time with the training at Wendover.[45] What he did not fully appreciate at the time was the serious collateral damage all this was doing to his personal life. As he later admitted, all the travel and the need to regularly lie to Lucy about what he was doing, plus his natural tendency to shy away from relationship issues rather than confront them, had further exacerbated the already existing difficulties in their marriage. Whether he fully grasped it or not, by not facing up to the problem and further throwing himself into his work, he was virtually shutting Lucy and the boys out of his life.[46]

With Ferebee busy with the bomb-testing program and with the very capable Capt. William Wright handling the bulk of the 509th navigator training, Captain Van Kirk found himself available to serve as Colonel Tibbets' personal navigator, a circumstance that brought them even closer personally. Infinitely confident in his own piloting abilities, Tibbets usually took only Van Kirk and his Skymaster crew chief, Sgt. Joseph Gagnon, along on his continent-wide shuttle flights—the former acting as both navigator and copilot. In the winter and spring of 1945, the two men spent a lot of time together in the cockpits of Green Hornet C-54s. According to Van Kirk, they mostly talked shop and played cribbage, using a pegged board that rested between the pilot and copilot seats.

One day they were blissfully flying along on autopilot and having a very lively game—complete with the usual ribbing, arms flying while slapping down cards, the hand-winner gleefully counting off his pegs. In keeping with every professional pilot's ingrained habit, Tibbets made periodic instrument panel scans. All at once he froze. "What the hell happened to number four? We don't have any oil pressure." Van Kirk looked out the right-hand cockpit window at the outboard engine. "We don't have number four," he said. "It's feathered!" In the excitement of the cribbage game, one of them had inadvertently hit the overhead feathering button.

On another occasion, the two men were in the Hollywood area and decided to take in a show featuring Carmen Miranda (a popular singer/actress known for her signature fruit hats). After the show, they joined a party. According to Van Kirk, "We were cavorting with all these women, singing the Air Force song [and so on]. I asked Tibbets, 'Do we have to go back to that war for Christ's sakes?' "

Shortly before that adventure Tibbets had finally been elevated to full colonel and the two men were returning to Wendover after another trip to the Pentagon. Van Kirk was troubled by the rough treatment Tibbets had gotten during one of the intense policy sessions from bemedaled "armchair" colonels and generals, none of whom had seen even one minute of combat and bore none of Colonel Tibbets' enormous responsibilities. Van Kirk asked, "Doesn't that piss you off every once in a while?" Tibbets gave a revealing answer. "Dutch, I will tell you. I look at them and they look at me. I know how they got theirs [decorations] and they know how I got mine, and I am happy."[47]

March of 1945 saw a great deal of new activity at both Los Alamos and Wendover. Most importantly from the standpoint of the 509th, Dr. Oppenheimer had created Project Alberta—aka the group's 1st Ordnance Squadron, Aviation—installing his deputy, Capt. Deak Parsons, as its head.[48] As leader of the Los Alamos fusing and weapons development section, Parsons had already been working with Tibbets and Ferebee on every aspect of bomb delivery issues. Now the time had come to turn theory into a practical weapon.

Eventually comprising several hundred military and civilian scientists and technicians, Parsons' Alberta folks were given the critical responsibility of transporting and assembling operational atomic bombs in a war theater. In March 1945, in order to ensure the maximum degree of interaction and cooperation, nearly all of the Alberta people were transferred to Wendover and incorporated into the 509th. So as to preclude uncomfortable questions, the civilians pretended to be military personnel and wore Army uniforms. To make clear that he would continue to retain control of the weapons, General Groves further directed that Captain Parsons would have joint responsibility with Colonel Tibbets—what business managers call a "dotted-line relationship"—to ensure the successful delivery of the bombs on enemy targets.[49] Fortunately the two men worked well together and this always-risky form of reporting relationship was never a problem, at least for them.[50] About this same time the specific leadership dynamics of the first combat drop were also worked out—Tibbets would command the B-29, the captain of the ship. But he and Parsons would share authority regarding the actual use of an atomic weapon. Parsons would have the final say as to whether the bomb would be released. It was agreed that both men would be together on the "bridge" of a Superfortress at the critical moment and jointly approve the drop.

In late spring, likely at Tibbets' request, Deak Parsons made a special trip to Wendover to inspect the group's B-29s. Both men became convinced that the first-generation Silverplate Superfortresses the 509th had received were no longer fit for further training, never mind actual combat operations. The colonel had wanted Parsons at his side on this one, to help make the case for a new set of airplanes. Deceptively mild-mannered and unassuming, Parsons was in reality a hard charger and a real power within the Manhattan Project. When Parsons talked, General Groves listened.[51]

"The Wendover B-29s must be replaced," Parsons reported on his next visit to Washington. "They not only are worn out, none of them have the additional modifications we absolutely require." Despite a Pentagon general's objection and the subsequent temporary holdup—USAAF chief Gen. Hap Arnold had to personally intervene—the order went out to the Glenn L. Martin Bomber Plant at Offutt Air Field near Omaha, Nebraska.[52] One of several U.S. airplane makers licensed by Boeing to build B-29s, the Martin plant was instructed to begin manufacturing the new Silverplate bombers. In addition to those many changes made on the first fifteen—most important of which had been an H-frame bomb bay with a single lug shackle and sway braces, plus the removal of all armor plate and gun turrets except the two tail stingers (saving 7,200 lbs. of weight)—the additional improvements included the new and near-revolutionary Curtiss Electric reversible pitch propellers, pneumatic bomb bay doors, and a "weaponeer" station with atomic bomb monitoring instruments.[53] The reversible propellers not only allowed the B-29 to back up—something no other airplane could do—it greatly improved braking power on landing. The fast-acting pneumatic doors (less than one second to open, about two seconds to close) replaced the standard hydraulic-driven and served to minimize the effects of speed-limiting aerodynamic drag, especially significant during the breakaway turn.

Most importantly, the new bombers were to get the new Wright R-3350-41 engines. By eliminating the old carburetor-equipped power plants and adding fuel injection, the Dash 41s improved Superfortress performance markedly, especially in the thinner air at high altitudes. Fuel injection coupled with improved cowl flaps also allowed for better engine cooling, which meant the bulk of the engine fires that the B-29 had been experiencing since its inception would largely disappear. According to Richard Campbell in his highly respected technical book *The Silverplate Bombers*, the new engines and reversible props alone "probably contributed more to the success of the 509th . . . than any other features of the [Silverplate] configuration."[54]

By May 1945 the first of the new bombers were ready for pick up. Crews were sent to Omaha from Wendover on a scheduled basis when their plane was ready. In June Colonel Tibbets, who had earlier made the trip to Offutt to select his personal machine, instructed Bob Lewis and his regular crew to pick up B-29 Superfortress Serial #44-86292.[55] The Martin facility at Omaha had long been considered the plant that made the best B-29s. "Trust me," the shop foreman had said to Tibbets while pointing at #86292 on the assembly line tour. "That's the one you want. It was built midweek, not on a Monday."[56] Tibbets would later say that airplane was the best-made, most trouble-free B-29 he ever flew.

All of a sudden things began to happen. For several weeks, Tibbets had suspected the Los Alamos scientists were dragging their feet. With the war in Europe winding down into an Allied victory against the Nazis—the longhairs had long perceived Germany as the only other nation that could produce a workable atomic weapon—zealousness toward the project had cooled markedly. While the scientific and technological problems were essentially solved, they were still hesitating about proclaiming the "gadget" ready. Before signing off, so they said, they thought it needed to be made near perfect. The work should continue until there is less than a million to one chance of a dud. Right now, they could only guarantee ten thousand to one.

"Hell," Tibbets told them, "nothing is that certain." After telling the Los Alamos people he had survived odds in Europe of much less than ten to one, he said, "I'll take ten thousand to one any day."[57] He would later tell writers Gordon Thomas and Max Morgan-Witts that he was determined to get his way, knowing that "without my planes there was no way the scientists could keep tinkering with their toy."[58]

Once back at Wendover and after thinking that encounter over, Col. Paul Tibbets decided on his own authority to pull the trigger. Without consulting anyone, he sent a coded message to Washington saying he was issuing orders for the 509th to be processed for overseas movement. A base for the atomic bombers had already been selected at Tinian Island in the Marianas in the Western Pacific and all the preliminary deployment work had been completed. All everyone needed was a "go" signal. Tibbets had just given it.

When Maj. Gen. Leslie Groves heard of Tibbets action he was furious. He immediately ordered the colonel to Washington to explain. Tibbets stood before the general in a brace more suitable to a West Point plebe. How dare you, Groves boomed, assume the authority to take such unilateral action? Why it is nothing but rank insubordination, the general continued, completely intolerable. Tibbets later said he pictured himself as the oldest second lieutenant in the Army Air Forces, ferrying worn-out transports out of war zones.

As the chewing-out session wore down, however, the colonel noticed a twinkle in Grove's eye. Having made his point that the real mistake was not advising him in advance of the move and that he hated surprises, the general finally settled down. Tibbets realized the man was actually pleased.

"Dammit," Groves said, "you've got us moving!"[59]

# 9

# TINIAN

Named after Spain's seventeenth-century Queen Consort Mariana of Austria, the Mariana Islands are located in the western Pacific Ocean about 1,600 miles east of Manila, 3,900 miles west of Honolulu, and 1,500 miles south of Tokyo. Of some fifteen ancient volcanic mountaintops spread out in a north–south line about five hundred miles long, only four are anything more than atolls—Saipan, Tinian, Rota, and Guam, the largest (220 square miles).[1] For nearly four hundred years, the Marianas have been variously claimed by Spain, Germany, Japan, and the United States. Since the end of World War II they have been a U.S. possession.

Japan seized the entire island group in December 1941 and held control until the islands were liberated by the United States in mid-1944. Construction of B-29-capable airfields was soon begun on Guam, Saipan, and Tinian (Rota was bypassed, its small Japanese Army garrison holding out until the emperor's surrender order in August 1945). At long last, America had the airplane—the Superfortress—and the air bases to make possible an effective strategic bombing campaign against the Empire's Home Islands.

In February 1945, U.S. Navy lieutenant commander Frederick Ashworth, Deak Parsons' soon-to-be-appointed Project Alberta deputy, had been dispatched to the Marianas by General Groves with two objectives: (1) hand deliver a highly classified letter to Fleet Admiral Chester Nimitz informing him that an atomic bomb would be available in the Pacific Theater by August 1945, and (2) find a suitable air base in the Marianas for the 509th Composite Group.[2]

Both goals were quickly achieved, with the base issue easier to solve than had been anticipated. Guam was sixty miles farther from Japan than any of the other airfields, and Saipan did not have the necessary facilities. Tinian, on the other hand, had two long runways at West Field and four 8,500-ft parallel runways at North Field. At that time the latter was the largest air base in the world, capable of accommodating up to 270 Superfortresses, and it neatly fit the bill. Once the Silverplate code word was invoked, the cooperative Tinian Island commander assured Ashworth that Colonel Tibbets would get whatever North Field real estate, buildings, and support he required.

On May 6, 1945, the troopship SS *Cape Victory* sailed from Seattle with twelve hundred 509th personnel and their equipment, reaching Tinian Harbor on May 29.[3] The advanced air echelon began arriving on May 18. The Superfortresses appeared in June, after their maintenance and support units were firmly into place. Maj. Tom Ferebee likely went over with Bob Lewis and crew in aircraft No. 86292.[4] That airplane now sported a two-digit nose number—82, the number that Tinian North Field tower and air traffic control would use as its operating "Victor" call sign (e.g., "Victor 82, you are cleared to land").[5] The ship had flown what would become the standard route used by the 393rd and Green Hornet Line between the Zone of the Interior (ZI) and the Marianas. On June 27, No. 82 departed on a two-hour flight from Wendover to Mather Field in Sacramento, where the usual customs and going-overseas preparations were conducted. On June 29, Lewis lifted the airplane off Mather and headed for John Rodgers Field near Honolulu, arriving 2,460 miles and ten hours later. After a stay overnight, the B-29 pointed its nose westerly toward Kwajalein Atoll in the Marshall Islands, arriving nine and a half hours later. After another night's rest, and having passed the International Date Line, the fellows were off again on what the calendar now said was July 2, landing on Tinian's North Field six and a half hours later. Captain Lewis and crew were the last of the Silverplate Superfortresses to arrive.[6]

Tibbets and Van Kirk left Wendover shortly after No. 82, departing in a Green Hornet C-54 with what little remained of the 509th. As luck would have it, later on the same day they left, Mary Jane Van Kirk gave birth to Thomas Lee, who was middle-named for a favorite uncle and first-named for his godfather and Dutch's best friend, Tom Ferebee. In those days of limited communication—letters only, usually delivered by ocean ships—Dutch did not learn the baby was a boy until three weeks later. The two men's arrival on Tinian marked the conclusion of the deployment.

After living through a long, bleak Utah winter, the Wendoverites were shocked to be suddenly dropped onto a tropical island that still harbored a few hundred enemy soldiers hiding in the low hills and jungle. The alluring sandy beaches, crystal-clear ocean waters, and lovely tropical foliage were offset by the oppressive tropical heat and a rank smell coming from the open *benjo* ditches that ran hither-thither—the Japanese sewer drainage system.[7] The Empire had occupied the island since World War I, and most of the island's Chamorro, Polynesian, and Korean inhabitants had adopted Nipponese ways. While the crude sanitation practices of the local population were allowed to stand, the island did see major improvements. The 107th Naval Construction Battalion (Seabees) reconstructed the runways, built new living quarters and administrative buildings, erected Western latrines and showers, constructed clever windmill-powered washing machines for laundry, and created a brand-new island road system. Additionally, General Groves had sent a trusted and well-regarded

Army engineer, Col. Elmer E. Kirkpatrick, to supervise the construction of the special facilities required by the 509th.

Tinian, about six miles wide and twelve miles long, is roughly the same size as Manhattan Island.[8] Using the latter as a template, the new roads the Seabees laid out used borough street names in so faithful a manner that native New Yorkers could navigate Tinian in the dark. Coursing down the middle of the island was Broadway. A short distance west and south of North Field was Eighth Avenue. Riverside Drive followed the western coastline. As in New York, Tinian's Broadway and 42nd Street was one of the busiest intersections. The 509th headquarters took up digs in what became known as the "Columbia University district" off Riverside Drive near 8th Avenue and 125th Street.[9]

Unlike most units already on the island who had to make do with olive-drab canvas shelters, the 509th compound consisted of elevated-floor, wood-framed tents and the even more comfortable Quonset huts.[10] Commander Ashworth's use of the magical "Silverplate" code word had worked wonders in this case; Tibbets had some of the best housing on Tinian. In the process, however, they had evicted another B-29 group who had been in-theater for some time, making them very angry. Due partly to this housing debacle and the purposeful standoffishness of 509th personnel, friction developed between Tibbets' outfit and North Field's already established B-29 cadre unit—the 313th Air Division, to which the 509th was nominally attached.[11]

Its commander, Brig. Gen. John Davies, did not have "a need to know" regarding the Tibbets mission and as a result could not grasp why the 509th was not subject to the usual mandatory training and indoctrination every new group underwent prior to flying combat missions. Further, he and other 313th Air Division senior staff had trouble dealing with this "composite group" business. Why, he asked Tibbets, did he need separate maintenance, armament, military police, and support units? Just what exactly was the colonel's mission? Naturally, such questions put Tibbets in a real bind—he was strictly forbidden to speak to anyone about the project or to divulge how different his B-29s were from all the others. The Silverplate bomb bays, in particular, were so closely guarded because anyone with the slightest knowledge would immediately notice that the forward bay was modified to carry just one *very large* bomb and the rear bay was filled with a welded-in 640-gallon gas tank.

At one point General Davies became so fed up with all the secrecy, Tibbets' non-answers, and the fact he had only an administrative responsibility for the 509th, he jumped into his jeep and drove out to the flight line to get answers for himself. When he approached one of the Silverplate B-29s and was unable to produce a security pass, the guard would not let him approach the aircraft. Davies insisted, demanding the sentry stand aside.

"I'm sorry, sir," the guard said grimly. "The general does not have a pass. However, I have a gun and have orders to use it."[12] The astonished Davies blustered a bit but quickly saw the fellow meant what he said. The general got back into his jeep and drove away. Later he asked Tibbets if the man would really have shot him if he went any farther. Colonel Tibbets responded with a firm, unsmiling "absolutely," explaining how very severely the guard would have been punished if he had allowed General Davies to enter the aircraft.

Tibbets' real bosses on Tinian were USAAF major general Curtis LeMay, USAAF brigadier general Thomas Farrell, and U.S. Navy rear admiral William Purnell.[13] General Farrell, a decorated World War I battalion commander, was also a member of the Pentagon's Military Policy Committee, which was charged with "formulating policy and providing overall direction for the [Manhattan] Project."[14] Admiral Purnell, who won a Navy Cross commanding a World War I destroyer, was the Navy's representative on the Military Policy Committee. He was also responsible for providing a close liaison between the Army and Captain Parsons' largely Navy-led Project Alberta team. Parsons, as Oppenheimer's Los Alamos deputy; Farrell, as General Groves' deputy; and Purnell soon became known as the "Tinian Joint Chiefs."

All the same, the group's day-to-day activities revolved completely around Tibbets, the busiest man in the Marianas. Bunking in a Quonset hut with Van Kirk, Ferebee, and 509th maintenance chief, Lt. Col. John Porter, the colonel was lucky to get four hours of sleep a night. There was always someone with a problem, always something to follow up on, always an administrative issue here, a training issue there. Along with his making sure the Project Alberta team would be able to provide an operational atomic bomb on schedule, the most important objective was to bring the aircrew's proficiency to a fever pitch.

Each Silverplate crew flew several local training flights and two to eleven sorties against Japanese-held (though lightly defended) Rota and Marcus Islands, after which the men were ready for their first credited combat mission against the Japanese Home Islands.[15] Each ship would carry a single armed pumpkin bomb—ballistically identical to the plutonium bomb but loaded with 5,500 pounds of conventional high explosive.[16] To simulate an atomic strike, the crews conducted a "breakaway" turn after each release. The stripped-down bombers (sans guns and armor) were able to fly faster and higher than other fully outfitted Superfortresses, giving them a real edge in staying above Japanese flak and fighter intercept.

These preparatory missions had a threefold purpose: (1) give the crews navigation experience in flying the 1,500 miles to the Home Islands and expose them to hostile action; (2) provide realistic training flying long, loose-formation, overwater flights; and (3) get the Japanese air defenses accustomed to seeing one, two, and three ship formations, in hopes the enemy would not waste their dwindling resources trying to repel such seemingly minor threats. While the live pumpkin bombs the crews dropped did produce a relatively large bang, the damage they caused was inconsequential compared to LeMay's devastating nighttime incendiary raids.

Beginning in mid-July and through the first week of August 1945, Tibbets' Superfortresses flew a total of fifty daylight pumpkin sorties against the Home Islands. Number 82, the Tibbets and Lewis B-29, flew four of them, with Lewis as the aircraft commander. Colonel Tibbets had been prohibited from flying combat missions over the Empire because of his knowledge of the Manhattan Project. Ferebee went on several practice flights to Marcus and Rota; Van Kirk flew a couple of practice sorties and one pumpkin mission to Japan as a last-minute replacement navigator. In hindsight, it is more than a little remarkable that the combined flight crew entrusted with delivering the first atomic bomb would fly together in the Pacific Theater just *one time* prior to August 6—a memorable episode we will address shortly.

While 509th internal operations were running satisfactorily, its public persona was not faring well at all. As far as the other B-29 units on Tinian were concerned, the group was a candy-assed outfit that had conned the brass into giving them some kind of piece-of-cake assignment. To make matters worse, after remembering what Tibbets had told them at Wendover the previous December, many in the 509th could not resist dropping broad hints about how they were there to "win the war." While the other groups were getting shot up daily by flak and fighters and either crashing or nearly crashing on takeoff, making an emergency landing on Iwo Jima, ditching in the sea, or just barely making it back home, the 509th seemed to be flying nothing but milk runs.[17] It was hard stuff for the veteran B-29 crews to swallow. The resentment turned to verbal taunts and even nighttime rock-throwing attacks on the tin roofs of the group's Quonset huts. An anonymous 313th Air Division headquarters' clerk penned a memorable piece of doggerel titled "Nobody Knows" that was mimeographed and widely circulated on the island. It aptly summed up the "prevailing contempt for the Glory Boys":

> Into the air the secret rose,
> where they're going, nobody knows.
> Tomorrow they'll return again,
> but we'll never know where they've been.
> Don't ask us about results or such,
> unless you want to get in Dutch.
> But take it from one who is sure of the score,
> the 509th is winning the war.
>
> When other groups are ready to go,
> we have a program for the whole damned show.
> And when Halsey's Fifth shells Nippon's shores,
> why shucks, we hear about it the day before.

And MacArthur and Doolittle give out in advance,
but with this new bunch we haven't a chance.
We should have been home a month or more,
for the 509th is winning the war.[18]

Once Tibbets' people had settled in and everyone's routines were firmly established, the inevitable informalities and off-duty antics present in every forward operating unit began showing up. One of the first things that appeared was a relaxation of the dress code. By unspoken agreement, adopted by many officers and most enlisted men, the daily uniform in the stifling hot and humid climate "became well-broken-in brown boondockers that barely cleared the ankle, 'Tinian shorts' [regulation fatigues cut off above the knees], and a white T-shirt."[19] During off-duty times, nearly everyone indulged in the inevitable card or poker game, went swimming at the officer's or enlisted men's beach, visited the Red Cross hut for American magazines and doughnuts, or took in a movie at the compound's outdoor theater, where the patrons sat on wood benches and only the screen and projector were protected from sun and rain. No matter how hot the sun, hard the rain, or bad the picture, few left a feature early.

As he had done throughout the war, Paul Tibbets occasionally relieved stress by yielding to his inner Puck.[20] One day the commanding officer had noticed two staff officers loading a couple of hospital nurses in a jeep, en route to a beach picnic. As sunset abruptly yielded to night (the nearer the equator, the briefer the twilight), Tibbets rounded up Ferebee, Van Kirk, and Honey Bee Beahan to help in an "investigation." Upon discovering the frolicking foursome indulging in a little old-fashioned skinny dipping and "not wishing to disturb the swimmers," the boys removed the distributor rotor on their jeep. "Les Trois Mousquetaires" and their friend d'Artagnan then surreptitiously removed the bather's uniforms from the vehicle and took them back to North Field "as a precaution against [falling] into unauthorized hands."[21]

What began as an amusing prank turned out to be pretty rough on the victims. With no swimming suits, the four were forced to make their way back in the raw and shoeless. Whenever a vehicle passed along the narrow road, they felt compelled to jump into the jungle for cover, which led to many bruises and scrapes due to the brush and coral. The two officers finally limped in about dawn. The anxious perpetrators never did find how the nurses managed to get back to the hospital—Tibbets later admitted "we were afraid to ask."

One of the more wholesome off-duty activities was baseball, something nearly every American boy of the day loved to watch and play. Soon after arrival, the 509th was fielding teams that played other units on the island. A day came when the team captained by Ferebee was playing a Twentieth Air Force headquarters team led by Col. William "Butch" Blanchard, General LeMay's chief of staff. At a tense moment during the game, Blanchard was a runner on third, Van

Kirk was the third baseman, and Ferebee was the catcher behind the plate. Ferebee had thrown the ball down to Van Kirk on a pick-off move, but he muffed the catch. In the confusion—and while Tom was yelling "get in front of that ball Dutch, goddamn it!"—Blanchard broke for home. It was a close play; Blanchard came blasting in and "knocked Tom ass over teacups." As he dusted himself off, the mighty colonel sneered at the mere major, "I guess you won't block the plate on me again." A few games later, as the gods would have it, the exact same scenario developed. On third base Van Kirk was thinking, oh boy, look out now! The batter rapped a grounder to second base and Blanchard took off for home. The second baseman picked up the ball and fired a fastball to catcher Ferebee, who had squared up astraddle the plate. The chief of staff slid in hard, intending another body slam. Ferebee stood his ground this time, jamming the ball into the colonel's nose so violently that blood squirted all over his face. After the dust settled, Ferebee looked down at the bleeding Blanchard and said, "I guess you won't try to bowl me over again." One did not trifle with Tom Ferebee when it came to baseball.[22]

Relations between Blanchard and the 509th took a more sinister turn in mid-July when Colonel Tibbets was back in the ZI attending Pentagon meetings and preparing to witness the July 16 Trinity test near Alamogordo, New Mexico—what would become the world's first atomic explosion. Colonel Blanchard, who had been brought into the Silverplate/Manhattan Project secret by General LeMay, had gotten wind of purported discussions by some of the Project Alberta scientists about Tibbets and Ferebee not having flown any B-29 sorties together since arriving at Tinian. While no one was apprehensive about Ferebee's qualifications—he had been flying successful practice missions over Rota and Marcus Islands with one of Blanchard's pilots, Maj. Stan Shields—the impression the longhairs left with Blanchard was that they did not think Tibbets was qualified to fly the first atomic mission. Apparently, and if these stories are true, the scientists were unaware of Tibbets' record as a B-29 test pilot and his reputation as one of the best bomber pilots in the AAF. They also could not have fully appreciated how intimate Tibbets and Ferebee were; in the air they were virtually welded at the hip. They had flown together for so long, it did not matter if it was an AT-11 Kansan trainer, a B-17 Flying Fortress, or a B-29 Superfortress—it was exactly the same Norden bombing system with exactly the same procedures. The two men could conduct a successful bomb run in their sleep.

One suspects that Blanchard took advantage of this supposed scientific unrest (how much was actually there is anyone's guess) to pursue his own agenda. Tibbets came to believe that Blanchard, once the man learned the true nature of his mission, had become jealous of the group. Undoubtedly the chief of staff was clever enough to realize whoever commanded the unit and flew the first atomic sortie would become prominent, perhaps even famous.[23] It is possible that, quite literally, stars were dancing before Colonel Blanchard's eyes.[24]

Whether he indeed had ulterior motives can never be proved; what is certain, however, is that with Tibbets thousands of miles away, the chief of staff made his move to absorb the 509th directly into Twentieth Air Force and assign his own pilot, Major Shields, to fly the first atomic mission. When Blanchard informed Ferebee of the plan and that he would still be the bombardier but with another aircraft commander, Ferebee said, "If Paul's not qualified, I'm not qualified."[25] An alarmed Ferebee refused to fly a special practice sortie with Shields, temporarily holding things up. The bombardier then fired off an urgent telegram to Tibbets in the States, telling him to return to Tinian at once as "things are getting all messed up."

Four days later, Colonel Tibbets landed his Green Hornet C-54 on North Field. When he received the wire from Ferebee—the man who was by now Tibbets' most trusted confidant—he knew his immediate return to the Marianas was imperative. Brusquely wiring General Groves and Captain Parsons that he would not be able to attend the Trinity test at Alamogordo and without waiting for their reply, Tibbets flew to Wendover for a very brief visit with Lucy and the boys and then departed for the long flight halfway around the world. Ferebee met him at the plane with "the bad news."

The two men confronted LeMay. The general confirmed he had approved the Blanchard plan to use more combat-experienced pilots to fly the atomic missions. Having learned from the disastrous Lauris Norstad encounter in North Africa to use greater tact when dealing with superiors and realizing that LeMay simply did not understand what was involved with dropping these new bombs, Tibbets used reason and restraint to calmly rebut one by one the Blanchard arguments. Probably the fact that Tibbets' men had to be specially trained for over six months just for this specific mission gave LeMay the most pause. After going back and forth for some time, it was agreed that Blanchard, a qualified B-29 aircraft commander, would give Tibbets and his chosen crew a check ride. LeMay told Butch to go down and fly with them, to see what they can do.[26]

Tibbets took the check very seriously, making it clear to each man on the crew that they would be doing everything precisely "by the book."[27] It would be a short flight; the purpose was not to examine everyday flight procedures or long-range navigation techniques but solely to demonstrate the ability of the pilot to handle the aircraft and for his crew to conduct a successful bomb run. Tibbets, Lewis, Ferebee, Van Kirk, and Lewis' enlisted flight crew took off from North Field precisely at the scheduled minute, with Col. Butch Blanchard positioned on the flight deck between and just behind the two pilots. After satisfactorily completing an engine-out performance check immediately after liftoff, Tibbets climbed to the 30,000-ft bombing altitude. Van Kirk gave headings to the designated initial point and worked with Tibbets on the proper indicated air speed (via throttle-jockeying) necessary to put the aircraft over the initial point at the designated time. Van Kirk hit it precisely and called for an inbound turn to the target, a Japanese installation on nearby Rota. Ferebee released the live 5,500-pound pumpkin bomb and scored a "shack." Tibbets immediately initiated a sixty-degree bank and diving turn.

Colonel Blanchard had not been in the least prepared for the violence of the breakaway turn—apparently Tibbets purposely downplayed that little item in his pretakeoff briefing. The unstrapped-in chief of staff was promptly thrown against the flight deck floor and kept pinned there by G forces during the entire forty-plus second procedure. When Tibbets rolled out straight and level, Blanchard's face was pale. He had no idea that kind of maneuver was required in an airborne atomic release. "That's enough," he said. "I'm satisfied."[28]

Tibbets insisted on including all the proscribed air work before declaring the check concluded and asking Van Kirk for a heading back to North Field, landing at the navigator's preplanned time. Blanchard scrambled from the plane in considerable relief, and that was the end of the challenge to Tibbets' qualifications.

The musketeers were happy to have the crisis behind them as well as quietly relieved everything went so well on what was essentially a dress rehearsal. On that same day General Groves sent a coded message to Colonel Tibbets informing him that the Trinity test had been a complete success. There was great relief not only just on Tinian but throughout the top American civilian and military leadership. In the beginning few had believed the atomic bomb would work. Now it was, incredibly, a reality. The invasion of the Japanese Home Islands scheduled for later in 1945, an operation that promised to be inconceivably bloody—estimates ranged as high as a million American casualties and several million Japanese—might very well not have to happen.

At about this same time there was a chilling incident within the 393rd Bombardment Squadron, one that confirmed Captain Uanna's deep concerns about Capt. Claude "Buck" Eatherly, aircraft commander of Crew C-11 and the B-29 Victor 85. On July 26 Eatherly and his crew were hauling a high-explosive-filled pumpkin to a target at Tsugawa, Japan. Heavy cloud precluded a release on the primary, and they began looking for a target of opportunity. Someone—probably Eatherly, though no one ever owned up to it—got the bright idea to go to Tokyo and bomb Emperor Hirohito's palace. They nearly succeeded; the 5,000-pound bomb landed within the royal grounds and blew up at least one building, though the Imperial family was unhurt. Tokyo Radio complained for the next several days about the Americans' odd single-ship attacks and their "strange new tactics." History can be grateful Eatherly's bombardier did not score a shack; on August 14 it was Hirohito himself who broke a deadlock within the Imperial War Council by insisting Japan accept the Potsdam Declaration. Had the emperor been killed, almost certainly the war leaders would have out-voted the doves and the conflict would have continued indefinitely.

When Eatherly's ship landed, Colonel Tibbets gave him "the most X-rated chewing-out I ever delivered."[29] As usual when he screwed up, Eatherly apologized profusely and begged for forgiveness. Due to his almost incomprehensibly winning manner and Tibbets' respect for his piloting abilities (if not his leadership), Eatherly was not relieved of duty. One must surely believe that Tibbets later regretted not taking more drastic action. After the war Eatherly was forced out of the service, drifted from one thing to another, engaged in minor swindles, burgled a post office, served a prison sentence, and was committed to a mental institution. Unfortunately for Tibbets, antinuclear protesters got hold of Eatherly in the 1950s and used him as a pawn in their efforts, convincing the lost soul to go public and say the atomic bombings had driven him crazy. Even worse, in Eatherly's desperation, his wildly inaccurate statements (he claimed on several occasions to have been the Hiroshima pilot) led many people to confuse him with Paul Tibbets. For the rest of his life, Tibbets was plagued by questions about his mental health.

By late July 1945 the world war was racing toward a climactic conclusion. The fighting in Europe was over and already dispositions were being made, transferring huge numbers of men and equipment to the Far East. President Truman was at the Potsdam, Germany, meeting with Prime Minister Churchill (replaced by Clement Atlee halfway through the conference) and Soviet leader Joseph Stalin, with the primary discussion topic the unconditional surrender of Japan. For the 509th on Tinian, the training was almost finished. The 393rd crews were flying operational missions over Japan, the 1st Ordnance Squadron was deep into special weapon assembly, and planning for the first atomic mission was well under way. On July 23 Gen. Tooey Spaatz, who had just returned from Europe, met with officials at the Pentagon to be briefed on his new job as head of all AAF strategic air forces in the Pacific. On July 25 he received a briefing on the Manhattan Project and hand-received a special order dated that same day:

> To General Carl Spaatz
> Commanding General
> U.S. Army Strategic Air Forces, Pacific
>
> 1. The 509th Composite Group . . . will deliver its first special bomb as soon as weather will permit visual bombing after about 3 August 1945 on one of the targets:
> Hiroshima, Kokura, Niigata and Nagasaki . . .
>
> 2. Additional bombs will be delivered on the above targets as soon as made ready by the project staff . . .

> 3. Dissemination of any and all information concerning the use of the weapon against Japan is reserved to the Secretary of War and the President . . .
>
> 4. The foregoing directive is issued to you by direction . . . of the Secretary of War and the Chief of Staff, USA . . .
>
> Thos. T. Handy
> General, G.S.C.
> Acting Chief of Staff[30]

On July 23 the Project Alberta team and 1st Ordnance Squadron assembled the first prototype Little Boy–type bomb (inert) and successfully test-dropped it off Tinian. On July 24–25, two Fat Man–type pumpkin-style bombs (inert) were dropped, successfully testing an airburst tactic using the ground-proximity radar fuses. On July 26 the heavy cruiser USS *Indianapolis* docked at Tinian Harbor with the main assembly components for the operational Little Boy, plus a lead-lined pot containing the priceless U-235 projectile.[31] On July 28–29, Green Hornet C-54s arrived on Tinian with the plutonium for the first implosion-type Fat Man bomb and the target mass U-235 for the gun-type Little Boy uranium bomb. Because of the enormous cost and difficulty in extracting U-235 from natural U-238, it was already understood the future of uranium bombs was going to be limited—only a couple of dozen Little Boy–type weapons were ever built. Going forward, all atomic and thermonuclear (hydrogen) bombs would be plutonium based.[32]

On July 30 the Little Boy was finally assembled in a special air-conditioned hut inside the 509th compound; on July 31 several Silverplate B-29s conducted final rehearsals. At the end of that day, Capt. Deak Parsons formally declared the Little Boy atomic bomb was ready to be unleashed on the Japanese. President Truman had given orders that the first special weapon could be dropped any time on or after August 3. He wanted to be on his way back to America from the Potsdam Conference when it happened, and he would not reboard the heavy cruiser USS *Augusta* at Antwerp until August 2.[33]

From the *Augusta* in the eastern Atlantic to North Field in the western Pacific, the green light was flashing; it was now up to the Tinian Joint Chiefs and the Three Musketeers.

10

# THE BIG ONE

On Saturday morning, August 4, 1945, the 313th Air Division's weather forecaster told Tibbets that, after a week of heavy cloud over Japan, the weather was finally clearing. Following a quick consultation with General LeMay and the Tinian Joint Chiefs, it was confirmed—Special Mission No. 13 would take off early Monday morning, August 6, at 2:45 a.m. local. Earlier the group navigator, Captain Van Kirk, had been ordered to reverse-plan the mission back from takeoff time, meet the critical action timelines, and communicate same to ordnance, maintenance, and operations.[1] The 509th came suddenly and spectacularly alive.

Late that Saturday afternoon, Colonel Tibbets and Captain Parsons conducted a prebriefing for the seven B-29s selected for the attack. Tibbets told the men that they had been training for eleven months, waiting for the "big one" to arrive, and at last it was here. "That makes you," he said with a tight grin, "the hottest crews in the Air Force!" Following the opening pep talk, Captain Parsons took over and said that the bomb they were going to drop was "something new in the history of warfare." The Los Alamos scientists, he said, expected it to destroy everything within a three-mile radius of the bomb's hypocenter. He created something of a stir among the troops when he added, "No one knows for sure what really is going to happen."[2]

Parsons then cued the projectionist, who started to run a film of the Trinity atomic bomb test conducted three weeks earlier in the New Mexico desert. Unfortunately, either the film had been improperly threaded or the projector malfunctioned because the sprockets promptly chewed several feet of film to bits. The only slightly ruffled Navy captain made a joke—"so much for the movie you are not about to see!"—and proceeded with a brief lecture about the nature of the bomb while showing a series of Trinity slides on the screen.[3] While those images did give the crews some idea of what was going to happen—a distinct mushroom cloud was clearly visible—due to the lack of any representation of scale in the pictures the men did not fully understand what they were looking at. Deak Parsons then passed out to every man what appeared to be welder's goggles equipped with special protective dark lenses. He carefully explained the necessity of wearing the goggles at detonation. Lastly, Deak warned the pilots not to fly into the mushroom cloud because it would be highly radioactive. Interestingly, and even after revealing so much, Parsons continued to adhere to the iron security discipline he had been observing for so long, making no mention of the weapon being an atomic bomb.[4]

After Parsons' special presentation, Tibbets got down to the mission nitty-gritty. Three weather aircraft would take off one hour ahead of the three-ship attack formation to scout the potential targets. While none of the Silverplate bombers had as yet been authorized to paint identifying nose art on their ships, most of the crews had nevertheless selected individual names. Capt. Buck Eatherly's crew, in their airplane *Straight Flush*, would check out the Hiroshima primary. Capt. John Wilson in *Jabit III* would look over the secondary, Kokura. Capt. Ralph Taylor, flying *Full House*, would scout the tertiary, Nagasaki.[5]

Col. Paul Tibbets was to command the drop aircraft, No. 82, the ship that he had specially selected at the Martin plant in Nebraska. His handpicked flight crew would consist of Capt. Bob Lewis, copilot; Maj. Thomas Ferebee, bombardier; Capt. Theodore "Dutch" Van Kirk, navigator; TSgt. Wyatt "Dooz" Duzenbury, flight engineer; Corp. Richard "Junior" Nelson, radio operator; Sgt. Robert Schumard, assistant flight engineer/engine scanner; SSgt. Joseph Stiborik, radar operator/engine scanner; and TSgt. George "Bob" Caron, tail gunner.[6] No. 82 would also crew three so-called weapon specialists: Navy captain William "Deak" Parsons, weaponeer; USAAF first lieutenant Morris Jeppson, bomb electronics test officer; and USAAF first lieutenant Jacob Beser, radar countermeasures officer. Beser was a scientifically oriented young man destined to become the first electronic warfare officer in an atomic bomber.

Flying in a loose formation off one side of Tibbets would be the instrument airplane (to measure heat, blast, and radiation) piloted by Maj. Charles "Chuck" Sweeney in *The Great Artiste*.[7] Capt. George Marquardt would be off the other wing in the photographic airplane, *Necessary Evil*.[8] Capt. Charles McKnight in the *Big Stink* would fly as far as Iwo Jima, where he would drop out, land, and take up his standby position as a spare to Tibbets' aircraft.[9] The idea was, if the drop bomber had a mechanical problem, it would return to Iwo, where Little Boy would be transferred to *Big Stink*. McKnight's crew would then hand the airplane off to Tibbets and the mission would continue.

Viewed in retrospect, the Iwo Jima contingency plan had enough flaws to give one serious pause.[10] Keep in mind that the mission planning, preparation, and action timing had already taken several full days to work out, to say nothing of those many hours required on Tinian just to carefully load Little Boy in the first place. To have suffered a sudden emergency and been required to hurry back to Iwo from some distance upstream would have been enormously unsettling. Notwithstanding a touchy landing on not that great a runway on Iwo, they would have had to *unload* an atomic bomb from one aircraft and dismount the crew, then successfully *reload* an atomic bomb in another aircraft and remount the crew. At the very least, such an exercise would have severely taxed both men and equipment. (A special bomb unloading/loading pit had been constructed on Iwo Jima, but support ground staff was limited.) The chances for critical errors and mistakes in this hurried transaction involving an atomic bomb would have been high, and it seems extraordinary the idea was even considered, much less adopted.

There is more. What about the other two aircraft in the flight? Would they not also have had to land and regroup/refuel/refit as well? How would that have gone? What about crew fatigue across the board? Every man would have already logged at least a half-day of preflight and flight, to say nothing of little sleep beforehand; one cannot fully perceive the effects of fatigue in such circumstances unless it has been personally experienced. And what about the little things that are not so little. What, for example, would have happened following a second launch from Iwo if Tom Ferebee found some previously undiscovered problem with *Big Stink*'s Norden bombing system? Or if Dutch Van Kirk somehow lost his dead-reckoning kit during the bag drag from the *Enola Gay*, which contained the absolutely essential E6-B circular slide rule necessary to calculate winds, headings, and ETAs? Such occurrences are neither implausible nor trivial—in combat these kinds of things happen all the time. There is a hard-learned soldier's axiom that it is always at the very worse time that Murphy's Law will rear its ugly head (as Major Sweeney and crew would ruefully discover during their agonizing mission to Nagasaki three days later—see the appendix).

The real clincher as to how poor the Iwo contingency plan was becomes clear when one considers the strike plan in toto. It had already been agreed by the Pentagon and Tinian Joint Chiefs that if the atomic bomb could not be dropped visually, the order was to jettison the bomb in the ocean and not bring it back to Tinian, as a crash might eliminate the base. Yet the Iwo contingency called for taking that very risk, a programmed landing on an important U.S. airbase (Iwo Jima) with a live bomb. No one seems to have grasped this deep contradiction in the strike plan.

It is difficult to understand how the very idea of an Iwo Jima spare contingency passed senior staff muster. The only sensible plan should the *Enola Gay* have had an emergency would have been to declare an abort and attempt to recover the airplane and weapon at the nearest friendly airfield—and start over. The U-235 in Little Boy was irreplaceable, produced at immense expense. It was in fact more valuable than the plane, the crew, perhaps even more important than an island base like Iwo Jima—Tibbets himself had previously been told essentially that very thing. Plus, with proper bomb safing precautions, chances would be reasonably good for a successful impromptu recovery on Iwo or any other emergency airfield. Parsons and Jeppson could have replaced Little Boy's circuit-completing red plugs with the green safety plugs (more on this later), cutting off the bomb's firing mechanisms. Likewise, the *Enola Gay* would have by then burned off hundreds of gallons of gasoline; there was little reason to believe the considerably lightened B-29 could not have safely landed with the bomb on board. All of this, of course, is Monday morning quarterbacking, but it does suggest the deep strain all were under and the hurried nature of the planning—President Truman had made it clear he wanted the first bomb dropped as soon as possible after August 2, and everyone had obediently popped to.

Following the general briefings, the men broke for the specialty sessions. The pilots and engineers huddled in one assembly, and the bombardiers, navigators, and the balance of the crew were in others—all were discussing the mission's minute details, aided and assisted by knowledgeable staff officers. After a very busy two hours, the men were dismissed. It was a somber bunch that finally headed for supper at the 509th mess hall, known by all as the Dog Patch Inn.

Several days earlier Tibbets' crew had begun the mission's detailed planning. It was all very well for the colonel, Parsons, Farrell, and Purnell to handle the large picture, but somebody had to get down into the dirty details, and that fell to Van Kirk, Ferebee, and Lewis. Lewis was required to do what all copilots have done since that position was created—calculate the fuel needed, compute the weight and balance of the aircraft, decide which and when each fuel tank would be used, determine the alternate airfields, and make sure all the necessary radio frequencies were in hand. At the same time Ferebee had all along been deeply involved with the Little Boy bomb itself—including its final assembly, transportation to the loading pit, and installation into No. 82's forward bomb bay.[11] Meanwhile, Van Kirk carefully plotted the planned courses on his chart and noted all the en route action points, including changes in headings, altitudes, and airspeeds.[12] All of this data had been reversed planned back from the designated time over target (8:15 a.m. local Hiroshima time).

Without warning and from out of the blue, Van Kirk came down with a bad case of hives, something he "was very prone to do in those days."[13] While stress may have gotten to Van Kirk a bit, he and the hospital maintained the primary cause was the local tomatoes, or at least something he ate. Perhaps it was a combination of both. At any rate, it was serious enough to hospitalize Van Kirk, which gave Tibbets a couple of very bad days. Van Kirk had been *his* navigator since their first combat sortie together in August 1942, and the man had never let him down. For the colonel, the idea of a Van Kirk substitute at this late date on the most important mission of his career was abhorrent in the extreme. Tibbets became so concerned he sent Ferebee over to the hospital to check on Van Kirk's condition. As the colonel said to a reporter in 1990, "There was no way that I was going to get into an airplane without [both] Ferebee and Van Kirk. They [always] did what they were supposed to do when they were supposed to do it."[14]

Ferebee probably helped heal the patient more than the doctors by remaining himself. Ferebee refused to commiserate with Van Kirk, telling him he must be faking it and the only reason he was there was to get the attention of the nurses. One can only imagine the bantering that went on between the two men. Several hours later the hives cleared up and the group navigator checked himself out of the hospital.

On Sunday morning, August 5, and before allowing himself to be completely caught up in what promised to be a two-day whirlwind, the supposedly unsentimental Paul Tibbets took care of a very personal matter. While deeply attached to both his parents, he felt particularly close to his mother. It was she who had stood by Paul Jr. during the 1936 Christmas holidays when he had told his deeply disappointed father that he did not want to be a doctor and was instead going to become a professional pilot. She had put her hand on his shoulder and said, "If you want to fly, go right ahead and do it, because I know you will be all right."[15]

A couple of days earlier the colonel had spoken to Ferebee, Van Kirk, and his trusted flight engineer, Sgt. "Dooz" Duzenbury. He told them he wanted to name No. 82 after his mother—did they have any objections? Not surprisingly, all three men were agreeable; Ferebee and Van Kirk in particular thought it a fine idea as they had met Mrs. Tibbets when she once visited Wendover and had liked her immensely. Junior Nelson, in his book *43 Seconds to Hiroshima*, said the colonel "felt the plane that dropped the first atomic bomb should have a classy name" and that "he did not want any artwork . . . just the name of his mother."[16] It is noteworthy that Tibbets did not consult anyone else on the crew. This was somewhat unusual among AAF crews. Usually when a plane was named the entire crew participated—officer and enlisted. In many cases it was submitted to a vote, with the name gathering the most yeas winning. Most significantly in this case, Capt. Bob Lewis, No. 82's pilot when Tibbets was not flying the airplane, had been cut out of the decision.[17] Although they had been together for a year and a half, Lewis had worn out his welcome with the commander. This was largely due, Tibbets later explained, to Lewis' immaturity on and off the field. Nevertheless, the colonel "chose him . . . for [the Hiroshima] mission because I [still] regarded him as competent and dependable [as my copilot]."[18] Bob had also been with the crew since it was formed, and the enlisted men all idolized "Cap," as they called him to his face. Lewis assiduously looked after their welfare and even socialized with them during off-duty hours, something that was frowned upon by the officer corps.[19]

Later on the morning of August 5, Tibbets hunted down one of the enlisted men who moonlighted as an airplane nose-art painter. "Here," the colonel said, handing him a piece of paper, "paint these words on No. 82." The fellow got out his brush and just behind the nose numbers and below the pilot's window he sketched out *Enola Gay*.[20] Shortly thereafter Captain Lewis walked by the aircraft and was startled by the strange new name on what he continued to regard as *his* aircraft.

"What the hell is that doing on my plane?" he reportedly barked at the ground crew.[21] When told that Colonel Tibbets ordered it, Lewis marched to the commander's office in a huff. Tibbets firmly explained the plane was U.S. government property and that by his prerogative as commander of the unit, he had named it after his mother. That ended the discussion, but the encounter did not serve to improve the two men's relationship.

A few hours later, the *Enola Gay* was towed to a special loading pit where the Little Boy bomb waited to be loaded. At about 2:30 p.m., with the Tinian Joint Chiefs, Ferebee, and several other Project Alberta scientists carefully observing, the hydraulic lift was engaged and the bomb was slowly raised into place.[22] After carefully positioning the weapon in the forward bomb bay (with only inches to spare), technicians attached the single huge lug that bore its weight, then connected the sway braces that would keep it from banging against the bay walls. At about 3:00 p.m., while standing next to the *Enola Gay* on the boiling hot tarmac, Deak Parsons drew General Farrell aside. The previous evening during a major launch, Parsons had witnessed four B-29s crash and burn off the end of North Field's runways—one of which was still smoking as the two men spoke. Despite General Groves' orders to fully arm Little Boy prior to takeoff, which Parsons had agreed with at the time, Deak was having second thoughts. "You know," he said to Farrell, "if we crack up at the end of the runway tomorrow morning and the plane gets on fire, there is danger of an atomic explosion and we may lose this end of the island, if not the whole of Tinian with every blessed thing on it."[23]

Parsons told Farrell he thought they ought to set aside the orders and arm the bomb in the air. By taking advantage of the arming circuit's red/green double-breech plug system, Deak thought that rather than inserting the red plugs on the ground as planned, he could replace them in the air, allowing a takeoff with a still safed atomic bomb.[24]

"Are you sure you can do it?" Farrell asked. "No," Deak responded. "But I've got the rest of the day to learn."[25] At 3:30 p.m. the Navy captain entered the steaming hot bomb bay, where it seemed there was not even the suggestion of breathable air. Over and over he practiced removing and inserting the plugs and simulating the placement of the powder charges. Despite the finely machined edges slicing at the ends of his fingers, he kept at it. An alarmed General Farrell offered him a pair of thin pig-skin gloves but Deak declined, saying that with them he could not give the work the delicate touch it required.[26] Parsons emerged from under the bomber around 5 p.m. drenched with perspiration, his blood-streaked, chafed fingers blackened from the fine lubrication oils. There would be just enough time to wash up, grab a bite, and prepare for the prelaunch crew briefing scheduled for eight o'clock that evening.

An hour earlier, a message had arrived at the 509th headquarters via a special teletype machine that allowed for teleconferencing and nearly instantaneous communication with the Pentagon in Washington, D.C. It was a response to the Tinian Joint Chiefs earlier message to General Groves, Gen. George Marshall, and Secretary of War Henry Stimson (who was in contact with President Truman, then still en route home on the USS *Augusta*) informing them that all was in readiness on Tinian—unless otherwise directed the first special weapon would be delivered against Japan on August 6. The coded teletype dispatch had just given the final go-ahead: *Use me as you wish.*[27]

Throughout the weekend, and while Tibbets and Van Kirk were planning the mission profile, Ferebee had virtually taken up residence with the Project Alberta team and the 1st Ordnance Squadron. When he was not carefully monitoring the bomb assembly, loading, and other operational details, the bombardier immersed himself in target study. He had been regularly shuttling back and forth between Tinian and Guam (Guam was headquarters for the theater's B-29 operations), conferring with LeMay's bomb/nav people. Several days prior to Deak Parsons' sweaty introduction to a B-29 bomb bay, in a meeting with LeMay and Col. Butch Blanchard, Tibbets and Ferebee had picked out their Hiroshima aiming point (AP) and selected the initial point (IP).[28] The discussion had first centered on the IP, with LeMay pointing out that "bombing from the height you intend, crosswinds can be a problem."[29] Ferebee agreed; his Norden bombsight could be reasonably expected to handle up to fifteen or twenty degrees of drift, but beyond that the errors would compound geometrically. It was noted during the conversation that the winds aloft could result in a drift double or more that number. Blanchard offered a solution. "Fly directly downwind. That would increase your speed and reduce vulnerability time over the target and cancel the effects of wind."

Tibbets and Ferebee shook their heads. Moving that fast over the target at an altitude of 30,000 feet would almost surely induce a large circular error. They thought it better to head directly into the wind. LeMay pointed out that meant more time over the target, a recipe for disaster in the B-17s of their old European Theater and North African Theater acquaintance. But Tibbets and Ferebee understood they now had the Silverplate version of the Superfortress, which meant flight in the stratosphere, where fighters and flak were rarely encountered. Tom Ferebee took the lead, speaking for both himself and the colonel. "Our primary purpose is to hit the target. Not to play it safe."[30]

LeMay grunted, agreeing that the run should be made from the east, flying into what the weather forecasters were predicting would be fairly strong westerly winds. The town of Mihara forty miles east of the target was selected as the IP. LeMay asked Ferebee what AP he wished to use. Tom had been studying the aerial photos for days. He unhesitatingly placed a finger on the T-shaped Aioi Bridge across the Ota River near the center of Hiroshima city.[31] It could be easily identified through the Norden optics from a great distance and also offered excellent land/water contrast for the ship's radar operator, Sgt. Joe Stiborik, who was to back up Ferebee's aiming. Nothing provided a better radar echo than a head-on approach to a massive bridge surrounded by water. Paul Tibbets piped up, closing the deal: "It's the most perfect AP I've seen in this whole damn war!"

At eight o'clock Sunday evening, August 5, the seven flight crews, 509th headquarters staff, Tinian Joint Chiefs, and briefing officers huddled for the formal mission briefing. Everything one would expect in preparation for a regular combat mission was covered—takeoff times, headings and routes, altitudes for each leg, en route and target weather forecasts, flak and fighter threat assessments, and special instructions. The latter included the reminder, once again, that the bomb could only be dropped visually—no radar drop.

An appreciable amount of time was taken up discussing air/sea rescue deployments, an agenda item that was of particular interest to aircrew. The USAAF and the U.S. Navy were both pulling out the stops. Placed strategically along the mission route were USAAF *Dumbos* (PBY Catalina flying boats) and *Super Dumbos* (modified B-29s capable of dropping large lifeboats to downed crews), plus the U.S. Navy had committed a certain number of rescue submarines that would be patrolling just off the Japanese coast.

Tibbets then rose to speak. *New York Times* science reporter William Laurence was at the briefing and he recorded what the colonel said: "Tonight is the night we have all been waiting for. . . . We will soon know if we have been successful or failed. . . . We are going on a mission to drop a bomb different from any you have ever seen or heard about. [It] contains a destructive force equivalent to twenty thousand tons of TNT."[32] Although the aircrew had seen the Alamogordo test bomb photos the previous evening, there had been no mention then of its stupendous yield. After the murmurs, puzzled looks (the word "atomic" had still not been uttered), and chair scraping settled down, Tibbets once again reviewed the breakaway turn. At long last the men were able to grasp why this difficult maneuver had been stressed so hard in the training. Deak Parsons again mentioned the absolute need to don the welder's goggles just before release. After the latest en route and target weather forecast was shared, Tibbets gave a final review. The three tail gunners would each carry just one thousand rounds of .50-caliber belted cartridges, which represented the entire defensive capability of the attack element.[33] For the 2,800-mile round trip, the two support ships would be loaded with 7,400 gallons of 100-octane gasoline. The *Enola Gay*, with just 7,000 gallons on board, would still be dangerously overloaded by about 10,000 pounds.[34] While the Silverplate bombers had long ago stripped out 7,200 pounds worth of guns, ammo, and armor from the B-29's published maximum takeoff weight of 135,000 pounds, the *Enola Gay* would still weigh nearly 145,000 pounds. The final piece of information was that the three-ship element call sign had been changed in yet another attempt to confuse the enemy—*Enola*

*Gay*/Victor 82 was now Dimples 82. Tibbets ended the session with a final set of admonitions: "Do your jobs. Follow your orders. Don't cut corners and don't take chances."[35]

At nine o'clock that evening, the group's popular Protestant chaplain, Pastor William Downey of Hope Lutheran Church in Minneapolis, closed the proceedings with a prayer. Announcements were made that Catholic services would be held in the chapel at ten o'clock; Protestant at ten-thirty. Nearly everyone attended. Such somber moments before a crucial combat mission were always affecting and this occasion would not have been any different—whether a man was a churchgoer or not.

After services, the musketeers and their bunkmate, maintenance chief Lieutenant Colonel Porter, returned to their Quonset hut for an hour or two. Although the fellows had gotten little rest the past two days, everyone was too keyed up to nap. As Van Kirk put it "How are you going to lay down and go to sleep when they just told you [to go out and drop 20,000 tons of TNT]!"[36] As usual when the boys found themselves in such circumstances, a blackjack game broke out. It was low-stakes poker compared to the trio's North African adventures, which seemed appropriate for the moment. Afterward no one could remember who won.

At eleven o'clock there was a separate final briefing for the three crews flying the weather planes, followed by a hearty breakfast at the Dog Patch Inn. In addition to a smorgasbord that included rolled oats, apple butter, sausage, and blueberry pancakes, Tibbets' treasured mess officer, Capt. Charlie Perry (the colonel had made sure he was transferred with the group from Wendover to Tinian), somehow got hold of *real eggs*.[37] Perry also prepared flight lunches for everyone—C-ration turkey sandwiches, apples, and oranges were remembered as the main items.[38]

At midnight, a short, final brief was held for the crews of the three strike B-29s, also followed by the same big breakfast. Tibbets ate sparingly while drinking several cups of black coffee. He pretended to be calm while making small talk in an attempt to put the men at ease. Charlie Perry came out with their water jugs and boxed flight lunches, along with Tibbets' favorite in-flight dish—a special batch of pineapple fritters the mess officer had personally fried up for the *Enola Gay* crew.[39] As Colonel Tibbets rose to leave the mess hall the group's flight surgeon, Dr. Don Young, approached his table and handed him a small pillbox. "I hope you don't have to use these," the doctor said with a hopeful smile.

Tibbets nodded. "Don't worry. The odds are in our favor." He slipped the twelve cyanide capsules—one for each man on the *Enola Gay*—into a flight suit pocket. Later the colonel would give one to Captain Parsons, but the other eleven stayed in his pocket for the duration of the flight. It was only later that crewmembers learned Tibbets had been authorized to issue the pills if the ship was going down and the men were in danger of capture. Many reports had been received about the terrific abuse of downed American airmen; even Japanese civilians were killing fliers without hesitation. It could only be imagined the kind of outrage that would follow an atomic holocaust. General Groves' thinking was that the men would be horribly tortured to reveal the weapon's secrets, and that the cyanide offered a merciful alternative.[40]

It was now 1:15 a.m. on Monday, August 6, 1945, and time to go out to the airplanes. Each crew had been assigned its own six-by-six Army vehicle (so named for its six driving wheels); Tibbets and Parsons sat in front with their driver while the other ten crewmen piled into the back.[41] All were dressed in the standard AAF one-piece tan flight suit, though each man wore individual headwear. Colonel Tibbets had on a straight-billed fatigue-colored baseball-type cap; Van Kirk wore a soft fore-and-aft overseas cap; Lewis a fatigue cap with a smartly curved bill; Dooz's cap was similar to the colonel's except for a radically up-turned bill in the style often worn by enlisted air and ground crewmen; Bob Caron had on his prized blue Brooklyn Dodgers baseball cap; Tom Ferebee stayed bareheaded; and so on, according to personal preference.[42]

After a stop at the personal equipment supply hut to pick up parachutes, flak vests, .45 automatic sidearms, life vests, and survival kits, the crew arrived at their hardstand and into a blaze of white light. The scene was almost phantasmagorical; no one there would ever forget it. Unbeknownst to Paul Tibbets, Gen. Leslie Groves had authorized an official photo shoot of the launch proceedings. Two big sets of wheeled klieg-type lights and jeep/truck headlights illuminated the *Enola Gay*, with a half dozen 509th photographers scurrying around snapping pictures and taking movies. Scores of higher-ranking officers had joined the group's headquarters staff, Project Alberta scientists, maintenance troops, and ground crews—altogether a couple of hundred men were milling around the B-29. The bustling, unprecedented scene created an atmosphere that many later said "looked like a Hollywood premiere."[43]

The *Enola Gay*'s ground crew chief, SSgt. Walter McCaleb, had already begun the ship's preflight. After he and his five-man team finished their own individual checks, they pitched in to pull through all four of the big four-bladed propellers. It was hard, physical work. It took the men twelve individual prop pulls on each engine, totaling three full revolutions to ensure that the lubricant oils had been disbursed over the pistons and the massive cylinders were free of vacuum lock.[44] At 1:37 a.m., everyone looked up when the three weather Superfortresses—*Straight Flush*, *Jabit III*, and *Full House*—simultaneously roared off North Field's Able, Baker, and Charlie runways.

After getting out of their six-by-six, Tibbets and Lewis shook off the onlookers long enough to perform an exterior walk-around inspection while Ferebee and Van Kirk entered the airplane to set up their shops.[45] Tom carefully examined his bombsight, panels, and auxiliary equipment to be certain no one had tampered with anything since his preparations earlier in the day, when he and Van Kirk had gone out to the airplane to organize their stations at each man's own pace.[46]

While Ferebee busied himself in the nose, Van Kirk was carefully laying out his charts, log, E6-B computer, Weems plotter, dividers, and several sharpened #2-leaded pencils on the navigator's work table.[47] Meanwhile, the always dour, all-business Dooz Duzenbury carefully inspected his fuel and engine instrument panels, confirming that every fuel tank contained the prescribed amount and that the latter added up to precisely seven thousand gallons. Although it was not part of his own official preflight, it was his long habit to carefully look the entire airplane over, starting from the rear fuselage crew compartment, then through the thirty-foot-long tunnel, and into the forward flight deck. He even inspected the bomb bay via the forward compartment hatch. Sergeant Duzenbury was what a later age would call "anal" about the physical condition of "his" B-29.

After the men finished their prestart checks, they exited the *Enola Gay.* The brass hats, photographers, and rubber neckers had been eagerly awaiting their reappearance. If it had not dawned on the crew earlier, then surely the scene that greeted them at that moment made it clear they were embarking on a historic mission. Forcing a smile, Tibbets scribbled his name on the Form 1A held up by Sergeant McCaleb, acknowledging that the ship was airworthy, the fuel load was correct, the weight and balance was within limits, and the bomb and crew were ready. It was 1:40 a.m., and the next action point was twenty minutes away.[48]

The well-wishers crowded around the crewmen, anxious to rub elbows with those who were going to make the trip. There were hundreds of images recorded, with camera shutters clicking continuously. A portrait of the *Enola Gay* crew became the most prized and was subsequently reproduced in countless books, magazines, and newspaper articles. Tibbets and the other officers are standing in the back row, with the enlisted men kneeling in front. Sergeant Caron remembered Capt. Van Kirk needling him in the backside with his boot as they posed, the grinning navigator doing his part to break up the heavy tension. Caron said he "liked the good-looking captain's easy laugh, his warm, relaxed, yet confident manner."[49]

The kibitzing and picture-taking would have gone on indefinitely if Tibbets had not called a firm halt to it at 2:00 a.m. and ordered the crew to board the aircraft. The diminutive tail gunner, Sgt. Bob Caron, was probably the first man in, entering through the left-side rear fuselage door. At the last moment, a 509th headquarters photographic officer thrust a bulky K-20 camera with preset focus into his hands, knowing that Caron would have the best seat in the house. "Just aim and click the shutter," were the hurried instructions, "until you run out of film."[50]

Sgt. Caron's first duty was to crank up the ship's "putt-putt," the gas-powered auxiliary power unit that supplied enough electricity to bring the instruments and systems to life and enabled the crew to start the engines. During more routine times back in the States and once he had the unit up and running, Caron would have called out a favorite ditty. The other rear compartment crewmen would have joined in, the chorus announcing to the pilots in the forward compartment via the connecting tunnel that "Putt-putt's on the line, Sir!" and "Putt-putt's mighty fine, Sir!" This night, however, such informality would have been inappropriate, and Sergeant Caron notified Tibbets with a terse intercom call.[51]

Once strapped-in, the crew listened as Lewis called out each challenge and response prestart checklist item. Flight controls (yoke and rudder) were tested for free and easy movement, propellers and turbo switches/controls positioned, radio frequencies dialed in, altimeter set to local barometric pressure (it then read the airfield's elevation above sea level), oxygen system checked, and hatches and windows closed.[52]

"Crew," Lewis said. "Interphone check."

"Pilot," Tibbets said tersely.

"Bombardier ready," Major Ferebee responded from the catbird seat in the greenhouse just ahead of the two pilots.

"Engineer," Duzenbury radioed from his backward-facing seat just behind Lewis.

"Navigator ready," said Captain Van Kirk, who was positioned a few feet behind Tibbets, facing forward.

"Radio operator ready, Sir," Junior Nelson said formally from the other side of Duzenbury's flight engineer panel bulkhead. The nineteen-year-old just-promoted corporal could still not believe he had been selected the colonel's radio operator.

Sitting on the flight deck floor on ersatz cushions between Duzenbury, Nelson, and Van Kirk were Capt. Deak Parsons and Lt. Morris Jeppson. Using portable interphone cords and throat mikes, they each acknowledged that they and their weaponeer bomb-monitoring equipment (sandwiched into a corner between Junior's radio table and Duzenbury's engine panel bulkhead) were ready to go. Next, the rear compartment crew checked in from the other side of the thirty-foot-long, almost three-foot diameter pressurized access tunnel above the two bomb bays.

"Radar operator ready." Sgt. Joe Stiborik was stationed adjacent to the rear end of the tunnel hatch on the starboard side. His state-of-the-art APQ-13 mapping radar, coupled with a repeater scope at Van Kirk's station in the forward compartment, would be a primary navigation tool (assisting Van Kirk) and a secondary bombing aid (backing up Ferebee).[53]

"Countermeasures ready," radioed the always-cocky Lt. Jacob Beser, who was sitting just aft of Stiborik. No one but Beser had any idea what all the oscilloscopes, dials, and switches on his instrument panel did or meant. With the probable exception of Deak Parsons, Beser was the most intellectual man on the crew, truly gifted in electronic matters. More longhair than airman, the lieutenant had a relationship with the rest of the flight crew, especially Ferebee and Van Kirk, that was never better than lukewarm.

"Scanner ready, sir," said Sgt. Bob Schumard, whose job was to back up Duzenbury and keep a close eye on the engines and control surfaces from his vantage point in the rear fuselage. His position was portside opposite Stiborik and Beser, next to a plethora of black boxes, radar amplifiers, vacuum tubes, yellow oxygen storage tanks, wires, control cables, and the honey bucket.

"Tail gunner ready," Bob Caron said from his separate, tiny cubicle. His would be the roughest ride of all; sitting in the tail of a big bomber even in mild chop was akin to being the end skater on a crack-the-whip line.

With the prestart check complete, flight engineer Duzenbury reported to Tibbets. "Ready to start engines." Tibbets slid open his left-side cockpit window and yelled down to Sergeant McCaleb. "Stand by to start engines!" The time was 2:27 a.m.

The crew chief had positioned four men armed with fire extinguishers next to each engine, ready to react to an emergency in an instant. McCaleb and another man stood adjacent to the fuselage, prepared to pull out the wheel chocks when Tibbets signaled he was ready to taxi. The colonel again shouted out his left-side window, "Props clear on number one!" Lewis did the same out the right window. Both pilots also held up one finger to positively confirm to the ground crew that the prop on number one was about to turn. This was a moment of extreme danger for ground crew, particularly at night, and it was crucial everyone understood exactly what was happening.

Tibbets turned to his right and signaled flight engineer Duzenbury, only feet away, to "Start number one." Duzenbury turned number one's master ignition switch and boost pump to "On." After about a dozen seconds the electrical power from the putt-putt had energized the engine's starter motor sufficiently for Dooz to move the switch to "Start." The flight engineer waited until the outboard port prop had made one full revolution, then flipped the number one ignition switch to "On" and hit the primer until the engine caught. The huge Wright radial thundered to life, spitting out clouds of white smoke.[54] Dooz manipulated the throttle until the engine smoothed out in a low rumble at about 800–1,000 rpm, then moved the fuel mixture to "Auto-rich." There would be no chances taken that the gasoline mixture was set too lean during takeoff; the overloaded *Enola Gay* would require every one of its 8,800 horses to get off the ground. "Number one operating normally," Duzenbury reported. "Ready on number two."

"Start number two," Tibbets ordered. The process was repeated, followed by engines three and four. Duzenbury quickly scanned the engine instruments on the panels in front of him and informed Tibbets that everything looked good. The scores of onlookers had instinctively stepped back and away from the four Wright Cyclones, their enormous 16.5-foot diameter, four-bladed propellers turning in perfect unison, though they were clearing the pavement by only 24 inches.

"Pilot to tail gunner, shut down the putt-putt." All electrical systems were now running on internal power. Sergeant Caron acknowledged and complied. The two pilots and flight engineer ran their "Before Taxiing" checklist, which included crosschecking the altimeter setting and adjusting the directional gyros to the correct magnetic heading as shown on their repeater compasses, the data coming from Dutch Van Kirk's master flux-gate magnetic compass.[55] Tibbets and Lewis carefully eyed their other flight instruments—the turn and bank indicator, artificial horizon, vertical velocity (feet per minute climb or descent), and indicated airspeed (mph) meter. In pilot vernacular, those half dozen critical instruments that monitored and informed the actual flying status of the aircraft were known as the "six-pack" because of the way they were aligned on the instrument panel. After Tibbets ordered the bomb bay doors closed, he and Lewis stuck their hands out their respective windows and gestured with hitchhiker thumbs to the two ground crewmen below to slide the chocks away from the left and right main wheel trucks.

Tibbets got on the command radio. "Dimples Eight-Two to North Field tower, request taxi." The tower came back instantly. "Roger, Dimples Eight-Two, taxi Runway Able." The *Enola Gay* would be taking off directly to the east.

Standing near the airplane's nose was Armen Shamlian, an enlisted photographer. With all the instincts of a veteran newspaper photog, he had been waiting for just the right moment to get a last shot or two. His chance came when Tibbets prepared to close his side window. Shouting above the engine noise, Shamlian yelled, "Colonel, please wave!"[56] Tibbets looked down and silently complied, forcing one last public relations smile as Shamlian clicked the shutter. That particular photograph would become one of the most widely reproduced of the first atomic mission. The colonel closed his window and advanced the throttles. The *Enola Gay* lumbered away from the hardstand and into the black tropical night; the takeoff hammerhead on Able was only a few hundred yards away.

The tricycle gear of a B-29 with its castored nose wheel made taxiing a lot easier than the old tail-dragging B-17, although a Superfortress pilot still had to apply left or right outside engine power and lightly toe the appropriate brake pedal to make turns (called differential braking). Despite the black night and limited visibility, Tibbets effortlessly guided the big bomber down the taxiway, stopping on Able's takeoff threshold. He set the parking brake and Lewis picked up the checklist. "Crew, stand by for Engine Run-up." Duzenbury pushed the four throttles forward until their tachometers registered 1,500 rpm, then carefully checked the oil pressures and engine-head temperatures.

"Check generators and lower the flaps." Electrical power readings were verified and flaps lowered all the way down to 30 degrees to check for proper movement, then retracted to 25 degrees—the takeoff setting. Looking out his window, portside scanner Sergeant Schumard confirmed, "Left flap down 25 degrees, sir." The radar operator, Sergeant Stiborik, acting as the starboard scanner, echoed, "Right flap down 25 degrees, sir."

With everything operating normally, Dooz advanced engine power from 1,500 to 2,000 rpm to run the magneto check. Magnetos were a critical safety element in piston engines, providing a source of ignition spark even if the generators or batteries failed. Testing was conducted by switching between the left and right magneto on each engine, with an allowable drop of not more than 100 rpm. Again, everything looked good, and Dooz reduced power on all four to 700 rpm.

Lewis continued with the challenges, Tibbets responding.

"Wing flaps?"

"Set 25 degrees."

"Trim tabs?"

"Set and checked." That would be rudder and aileron trim set to neutral and the elevator trim wheel spun to a precalculated setting relative to the airplane's takeoff weight and center of gravity.

"Autopilot off?"

Tibbets scanned the C-1 switches on the aisle stand. "Off."

"Crew, windows and hatches closed?" The crew reported all secure.

The turbo superchargers were put into the No. 8 takeoff position and the propellers set at "High RPM." Lewis told the crew to prepare for takeoff.

"North Field tower," Tibbets radioed, "Dimples Eight-Two ready for takeoff." The tower operator came right back. "Roger Eight-Two, you are cleared into position on Able."[57]

With the *Enola Gay*'s nose wheel pointed straight down the centerline of the runway, Colonel Tibbets made sure the magnetic compass, directional gyro, and runway headings all agreed—zero-nine-zero degrees. He stepped down hard on the toe brakes to keep the aircraft from creeping forward, then shoved the throttles all the way to the stop. Within a moment or two the instruments recorded full engine power on all four—forty-eight inches of manifold pressure and 2,600 rpm. Moments earlier, Lewis had adjusted the engine cowl flaps to their fully open position of fifteen degrees—the Wrights needed the maximum amount of cooling air during the initial stages of the takeoff to keep from overheating. After one last full instrument panel scan, the colonel released the brakes and the *Enola Gay* started forward.

Tibbets kept the airplane rolling down Runway Able's centerline by walking the two outboard engine throttles from one side to the other. He used this procedure until reaching fifty-five to sixty miles per hour, when the tail rudder began to take hold. In no event did he want to tap a brake for directional control as even the slightest reduction of speed would increase the amount of runway needed. Ever so slowly the *Enola Gay* accelerated, the meter registering eighty, then ninety, then one hundred—every ten miles per hour gain coming with agonizing slowness. To copilot Bob Lewis, the end of the runway appeared to be approaching at an alarming rate. In his mind's eye, he could still see the burning carcasses of those four bombers that had crashed on takeoff a couple of days earlier.

The colonel was feeling the heavy tension as well, but no one would have thought so at the time. While he might have looked like the calmest man on the island, Paul Tibbets' guts were churning. "I found myself gripping the controls with a nervous tension I hadn't experienced since that first combat mission from Polebrook in 1942." He kept telling himself it was just another takeoff, "no sweat." But he *was* sweating, and he "had the moisture in my palms to prove it."[58]

The airspeed meter needle crept past 125 mph, seeming to take forever to reach flying speed. Two miles away, Admiral Purnell and General Farrell were almost literally holding their breaths, able only to catch faint glimpses of the airplane's outline ahead of the four blue exhaust spurts emanating from the Wright Cyclone engines. A very relieved Farrell would tell his companions shortly after No. 82 was safely airborne that "I thought Tibbets was never going to pull it off [the ground]."[59]

Neither did Lewis, sitting in the copilot chair, his eyes wide as two moons. For some inexplicable reason, Colonel Tibbets had not shared his plans for an atypical takeoff procedure. Lewis did not know his commander was going to hold the airplane on the runway past the normal rotation point in order to build up all the airspeed he possibly could before lifting off. Lewis had expected the yoke-back pressure to come not later than 145 mph, and when it did not, he did not understand what was happening. This very serious breakdown in crew coordination can only be laid at Paul Tibbets' feet; it very nearly resulted in a wrestling match between the two pilots for control of the aircraft during the most critical phase of flight. Why the colonel did not brief Bob Lewis will forever be a mystery—the idea itself was excellent, the extra airspeed gave every chance the aircraft could survive should an engine fail on takeoff. But not sharing that plan with the copilot was a potentially catastrophic omission. The two men were not getting along very well at that moment, and it may have been that the colonel simply did not wish to interact with his copilot, assuming he would be in control in any event and could handle whatever came up.[60]

When the *Enola Gay* passed through 150 mph, Lewis could no longer stand it. Although the copilot never mentioned it later, he may have thought something had happened to Tibbets physically or that the commander had missed something. Whatever the reason, Lewis grabbed the yoke, as if to take control of the aircraft.

"Keep your goddamned hands off the wheel!" Tibbets yelled angrily. "I'm flying this plane!"[61] A chastened Lewis immediately complied. With no more than a hundred feet left before reaching the overrun and the airspeed meter reading 155 mph, the colonel at last eased back on the yoke. Everyone started breathing again when the *Enola Gay* rose gracefully off the pavement. Looking out the tail cone window at that instant, Sgt. Caron gulped. Whereas always before at liftoff there had still been hard surface runway beneath him, this night he saw only flashing glimpses of jungle vegetation followed almost instantly by the thirty-foot drop-off to the sea, a vertical margin of safety that "saved many overloaded B-29s laboring to takeoff."[62] Dutch Van Kirk recorded the takeoff time in his navigation log—2:45 a.m. local Tinian time.

Tibbets touched the toe brakes to stop the main wheels from spinning and called for gear up. That was immediately followed by "Power Condition 2." Lewis and Duzenbury instantly responded to both commands, making sure the gear rose and locked and the manifold pressure on all engines was eased back to twenty-five inches of mercury and the rpm reduced to 2,400 in order to take the extreme stress off the engines. Lewis set the cowl flaps to their maximum in-flight setting of ten degrees, which accommodated both sufficient engine cooling and the least amount of aerodynamic drag.

While spinning the elevator trim wheel counterclockwise to compensate for the increased airspeed and shifting center of gravity, the colonel ordered Lewis to begin raising the flaps, which were to come up in stages so as not to too suddenly disrupt the airflow over the wings. What was important now was to build airspeed; in the world of flight, airspeed and altitude are the twin gods. If you do not have one, you must have the other.

With the after-takeoff checklist cleaned up and the ship stabilized, Tibbets headed for Van Kirk's departure fix over nearby Saipan, the latter just barely separated from Tinian by the four-mile-wide Saipan Channel. Meanwhile, following the *Enola Gay* at two-minute intervals were Sweeney taking off from Runway Baker in *The Great Artiste* and Marquardt launching from Runway Charlie in *Necessary Evil* (No. 91). McKnight trailed behind them in the *Big Stink*.[63] The four ships would head for the Iwo Jima rendezvous in a very loose trail formation.

At the proscribed moment, Van Kirk got on the horn. "Navigator to pilot, turn left to a heading of 338 degrees magnetic."[64] The heavily laden *Enola Gay* crossed the very north tip of Saipan on that heading at 2:55:30 a.m. and began to slowly edge her way skyward. Dutch carefully penciled the time into his navigation log, with that point in space representing his all-important departure fix—the key starting point from which he would base his navigation all the way to Iwo Jima. Now that there was no longer serious concern that an emergency return to Tinian would be necessary, the altimeters in all three strike ships were reset from North Field's barometric readings to the standard datum plane setting of 29.92, that is, the inches of mercury necessary to equal the weight of a square inch of atmosphere at sea level—meaning the readings would now show what is called pressure altitude. This procedure was vital whenever local en route altimeter settings were unavailable (for example, over hostile territory) and a recognized separation between aircraft was more essential than knowing the ship's exact true altitude (elevation) above the ocean. The B-29s would maintain a two-niner-niner-two altimeter setting until their final penetration descent back into Tinian.

Shortly after departing northwesterly out of Saipan, the airplane was leveled off at 4,700 feet. The pilots and Duzenbury adjusted the throttles and turbos until the indicated airspeed settled in at a comfortable 213 mph, with the mixture controls reset to "Auto-Lean." The ship was then trimmed for a cruise configuration and the four engines synchronized in order to avoid excessive vibration and noise. Satisfied all was in order, Tibbets engaged the autopilot and nodded at Lewis to keep an eye on it. The colonel pulled out his Kaywoodie briar, Bond Street tobacco, and Zippo lighter.[65] After firing up the pipe, Tibbets leaned back in his seat and puffed contentedly.

It had begun.

11

# HIROSHIMA

Paul Tibbets had halted the climb to altitude early in order for Deak Parsons to arm Little Boy while the ship was still in line-of-sight, very high frequency (VHF) voice radio contact with Tinian and before the aircraft required pressurization, which would have prevented access to the forward bomb bay. The colonel had chosen 4,700 feet for the first leg due to cloud conditions and the promise of smoother air.

Parsons stepped across the flight deck to the pilot's station and informed Tibbets that he and Morris Jeppson were entering the bomb bay. The colonel radioed General Farrell back on Tinian, using Parsons' code name, saying that "Judge [was] going to work."[1] The brass listened nervously as Tibbets relayed Jeppson's periodic updates via the bomb bay interphone after each phase of the arming process was complete.

Tom Ferebee watched quietly from just outside the open bomb bay hatch door while Parsons settled precariously on the catwalk next to the bomb. Jeppson would run the eleven-step checklist and pass the tools.[2] Their objective was to insert four silk bags of cordite powder (a smokeless propellant that had largely replaced gun powder) into what was called the bomb's cannon breech. When the fuse was triggered, the cordite would explode, firing the U-235 projectile at high speed down the 6.5-inch smooth-bore cannon barrel and into the larger U-235 target mass thereby initiating uncontrolled atomic fission.

"Step One, check that the green safety plugs are installed."

"Remove rear plate."

"Insert [cordite] charge, 4 sections, red ends to breech."

"Connect firing line."

"Reinstall rear plate."

"Step Eleven, remove and secure catwalk and tools."[3]

The two men finished the procedure in about fifteen minutes. Three-quarters of the way through the arming process, Tibbets lost the line-of-sight radio transmission connection with Tinian, but by then Admiral Purnell and General Farrell had heard enough to feel confident that Parsons would successfully arm the bomb. After returning to the forward crew compartment from the bomb bay, Parsons and Jeppson spent another fifteen minutes monitoring Little Boy's complex electrical circuitry before declaring to Tibbets that the weapon's readings were normal. Just one last step remained—after departing Iwo Jima and before climbing to bombing altitude, the green safety plugs would have to be replaced with the circuit-completing red plugs.

With the weaponeer's activity concluded, tensions relaxed and the crew settled in for the three-hour journey to Iwo Jima. Tibbets marveled at the eerily beautiful clouds and the way a rising crescent moon served to gently backlight the night sky.[4] Bob Lewis was swinging the ship in and out of the towering cumulus with nothing more than effortless left-hand twists of the automatic pilot turn knob, almost as if he and the colonel were leisurely passengers on a commercial airliner.

Back in the rear crew compartment the radar countermeasures officer, Lt. Jacob Beser, whose primary job was to make certain that Japanese radar/radio signals did not purposefully or inadvertently jam the bomb's critical ground-proximity radar fuse, had fallen into a sound sleep just under the tunnel hatch opening. He had slept little for nearly two days and was exhausted.[5] Elsewhere, several of the crew decided to break into Captain Perry's lunch boxes. Ferebee had crawled past the two pilots and was quietly chatting with Van Kirk while they bit into some fruit. At last, they and Tibbets were on the way, their first combat mission together since North Africa. Unlike all that had gone on for the past eleven months—the stifling secrecy, the mission uncertainty, the constant second-guessing from above—today was like old times. Once again, they were the leaders and in complete control. The three men knew precisely what was expected of them and had absolute confidence in their ability to accomplish it.

It was also at this moment the 509th Composite Group's bombardier and navigator—who were about to drop the world's first atomic bomb in anger—reverted to nine-year-old boys. Tail gunner Bob Caron, who had crawled forward to grab a box lunch for himself, had alerted them that Beser was conked out just below the crawl-tunnel hatch opening. Light bulbs clicked on in Van Kirk's and Ferebee's heads. No doubt grinning devilishly over the prospect of having a little fun at the expense of a fellow they were not terribly fond of, the two pranksters grabbed several oranges from an extra bag that Charlie Perry had put together and lined them up at their end of the tunnel. Once all was ready, the boys launched the assault, ducking away from the hatch entrance as the fruit rolled down the tunnel. Seconds later they were rewarded by muffled but clearly surprised yelps from the rear compartment. At least two or three "cannon balls" had landed on Beser's head, rudely waking him up. It has never been recorded when, or if, the radar countermeasures officer ever discovered the culprits' identity.[6]

If Tibbets noticed the horseplay, he never mentioned it. Whenever the fellows were relaxed, he could be sure the situation was well in hand and that no action on his part was required. After briefly checking in on the VHF command radio with Sweeney, Marquardt, and McKnight—the latter trailing the others by up to a score of miles—the colonel informed copilot Lewis that he was heading back through the tunnel for a pep talk with the four crewmen isolated in the rear compartment. Stiborik, Schumard, Caron, and Beser greeted him enthusiastically. After a few pats on the back and words of encouragement all the way round, the colonel turned to his longtime tail gunner, Sergeant Caron.

"Well Bob, have you figured out what we are doing?" As Tibbets had long ago concluded, Caron was an alert, well-read, intelligent man. The colonel would never forget the critical contributions he had made on the B-29's gunnery systems during the 1944 "Battle of Kansas."

"Colonel," Bob replied, "with all the security you've had us under, I'm afraid to guess!" Caron had seen what had happened to people at Wendover who asked too many questions. Tibbets chuckled. "It's OK now. We're on our way. You can guess anything you want."

"Is it a chemist's nightmare?" Bob queried.

"No, not exactly."

At that moment, it dawned on Caron what they were carrying in the bomb bay. Before the war he had read articles about cyclotrons and atomic fission, many prepared by the *New York Times* science writer William Laurence, the very same man who had earlier in the evening been seen hanging around the prelaunch "Hollywood premiere." Caron remembered that since 1942 absolutely no mention of those topics had appeared in books and magazines.

"Is it a physicist's nightmare?" Bob asked.

Tibbets grinned wryly. "You might call it that." The colonel turned to reenter the tunnel when Bob called after him. "Colonel, are we splitting atoms today?"

"That's about it," Paul Tibbets responded.[7]

After returning to the flight deck, the colonel decided there was no longer any point in not telling the crew the full story—something he later realized came as a measure of relief. At last, he could get the great secret off his chest. According to most recollections, Tibbets got on the interphone to briefly explain the weapon and how it had all come to pass, using for the first time the term "atomic bomb." Interestingly, almost every subsequent account all the way to present day has claimed that Maj. Tom Ferebee knew all along the "unit" was a nuclear weapon. In fact, that is almost certainly not the case. In his 1995 interview with reporter Don Sider, Ferebee stated that the Project Alberta people had only told him he was dropping a so-called special charge that potentially could wipe out an entire city. According to this account, Ferebee first heard the term "atomic bomb" when General Davies questioned him after the *Enola Gay* landed back at Tinian. "That was the first I'd heard the word 'atomic' used," Ferebee maintained. As was his habit in military bombers when not working and nobody was shooting at him, he had been sound asleep in the B-29's greenhouse jump seat during Tibbets' explanation to the crew.[8]

Despite the colonel's public optimism regarding the prospects of a successful drop, all three musketeers had long-held private reservations about whether the "gimmick" would actually work. In the hectic days preceding the mission, Tibbets had worried about the bomb a great deal, and it seemed everyone in the 509th was placing bets one way or the other. Much later Van Kirk admitted he bet heavily that it would be a dud. "I lost a lot of money that day!" he ruefully told a 2012 audience at the National Museum of the Air Force in Dayton, Ohio.[9]

After returning to the flight deck from his visit to the rear compartment, Tibbets suddenly felt very tired, the lack of sleep over the past forty-eight hours finally catching up with him. Realizing he was operating on nothing but pure nervous energy, he first checked in with Parsons to ensure that the bomb's circuitry remained in the green before directing Bob Lewis to take over monitoring the cockpit instruments. The aircraft commander leaned back in his seat and nodded off. After less than an hour of "fitful but useful slumber" he was awakened by the copilot. It was time to start the climb for the Iwo Jima rendezvous.[10]

All this while navigator Van Kirk had stayed busy at his trade. Since his Saipan departure fix, he had been certain of his course line—basically all one needed to do was work his way up the Mariana and Coral Island atoll groups until they merged into the north–south Volcano Island chain that led directly to Iwo Jima. In the journal that Capt. Bob Lewis kept for reporter William Laurence, he wrote, "45 minutes out of our base everyone is at work. . . . Captain Van Kirk, navigator, and Sergeant Stiborik, radar operator, are in continuous conversation on the interphone, as they are shooting bearings on the northern Marianas and making radar wind runs."[11]

Because of the solid radar fixes Stiborik was getting off the islands, Van Kirk's real concern was not so much left or right drift as it was—in navigator speak—making sure of a good speed line. The best way to do that on this particular night and magnetic heading was to get a sextant shot off the North Star, or Polaris, since it offered a celestial line of position almost perpendicular to their course. After precomputing a shot time, Van Kirk entered the observation dome on top the fuselage, accessing it from inside the transit tunnel. He would be using an A-10 hand-held sextant, which was mounted on a hook inside the dome to stabilize the instrument and take away the full burden of its dead weight.[12] On a clear night like this Van Kirk could easily pick out the North Star by running an imaginary straight line through the two stars at the end of the Big Dipper's bowl upward through the top one and into a relatively black void where only one star shined with the correct brightness. The idea was to align together the sextant's crosshair reticle with the instrument's internal bubble (representing an artificial horizon) and superimpose both over Polaris. At the precomputed moment, the navigator triggered the two-minute timer, the long observation time necessary to compensate for certain inherent errors caused by both the instrument and airplane movement.

Van Kirk took three shots, one right after the other. Returning to his navigation table, he completed the computations using that day's entry in the Air Almanac and the Height Observed Sight Reduction Tables.[13] After averaging the results, Van Kirk plotted the line of position, compared it to his dead-reckoning position and radar bearings from Stibork, and decided on his location by making a navigation fix mark—a triangle with a dot in the middle—next to the calculated spot on his chart. The data would be reconciled to a fix time of 4:02 a.m. Tinian time.[14] Deftly spinning his E6-B circular slide rule, he quickly came up with the *Enola Gay*'s current wind, drift, and ground speed. It was one of those nights every Pacific navigator considers a blessing; notwithstanding the ocean's name, the air masses above that great body of water can be among the most treacherous and unpredictable in the world. Fortunately, in the early morning hours of August 6, the weather aloft north of the Marianas was placid with just a slight wind from the southwest. Van Kirk radioed up to Lewis a minor course correction to the left, new heading 334 degrees magnetic.[15] Ground speed at the lower fuel-saving, less-engine-punishing throttle settings that Tibbets was running showed an average of about 230 mph. A second combined celestial/radar fix would be repeated at 4:59 a.m., which also used Polaris and Stiborik's radar bearings.

Shortly after the second set of celestial observations, Lewis made another entry in his journal. "The first signs of dawn came at 5:00 a.m. Tom Ferebee [sacked out just in front of him] has been very quiet." Van Kirk long remembered that sunrise, later saying "it was a beautiful day."[16] For a time, then, the human voices quieted and all that could be heard on the flight deck was the steady drumming of the mighty Wright radials. Although the air in the cabin reeked of the heavy, greasy-metallic odor common to all bomber cockpits, Tibbets' aircrew took no notice of it. Like roofers who work with hot tar all day, they had long ago become accustomed to the smell.

At 5:15 a.m. Tinian time, two and a half hours after takeoff, the loosely spread-out flight of three attack B-29s began a climb to their rendezvous altitude of 9,300 feet pressure altitude. The *Enola Gay* arrived at "Sulphur Island" (the Japanese name for Iwo Jima) at 5:55 a.m. Tibbets, who could not remember the name of its dominant mountain (Mt. Suribachi), got on the VHF command radio and said to Chuck Sweeney and George Marquardt, "I'm going to come in and circle over that thing and make a left turn at slow cruise. [After] I make a 360 degree turn I want you to slide into position on my wings. Then we'll set a course to our target."[17] The maneuver was smoothly completed, and the flight of three departed in a V formation for the Empire with Sweeney in *The Great Artiste* tucked in off Tibbets' left wing and Marquardt in *Necessary Evil* on the right. During the rendezvous, Charles McKnight in *Big Stink* had, according to plan, landed on Iwo Jima and set up shop as the spare for *Enola Gay.* He and his crew would remain in the airplane carefully monitoring their radios in case of an emergency or until the bomb was released. From this point on, the ships were instructed to observe voice radio silence, communicating only through their radio operators using Morse code on the designated long-range band of 7310 kilocycles.

At 6:07:30 a.m. Tinian time, Van Kirk logged a departure fix out of Iwo Jima and steadied the pilots up on their new magnetic heading of 327 degrees.[18] At 7:15 a.m. Parsons signaled Tibbets that Jeppson was going to enter the bomb bay for the final time. The young, blond Mormon, who planned a career in physics after the war, had only a day earlier been tapped by Parsons to be his assistant on the first mission.[19] In just a few minutes, Jeppson removed the three green safety plugs and replaced them with the circuit-connecting red plugs. After returning to the cabin, he and Parsons monitored their black boxes for a time to determine if any continuity or electrical problems appeared inside Little Boy. At 7:30 a.m. Parsons notified Tibbets that the bomb was now "final"—that is, it was fully armed and ready to be dropped.[20]

A few minutes later and with the bomb bay bulkhead door sealed to enable cabin pressurization, the colonel told radioman Nelson to inform the other two ships that he was going to start his climb to bombing altitude at 7:40 a.m. and that they were to accommodate to his movements.[21] The *Enola Gay* was still a heavily burdened airplane, and she would not reach the stratosphere until after another full hour of laborious step-climbing.

Oddly enough, at this point in the mission, none of the humans on board were working nearly as hard. In fact, most of the men were practically idle. Van Kirk and Stiborik had all the radar bearings, driftmeter readings, and pilotage checkpoints they could use—with the visibility unlimited and the winds light and variable the navigation itself was a piece of cake. Tibbets and Lewis had nothing more to do than monitor their climb points and turn the automatic pilot knob whenever Van Kirk called for a heading correction. Ferebee's only worry was getting a cramp in his neck by not shifting around enough while napping in his greenhouse jump seat.

At 8:15 a.m., however, the tempo picked up. Tibbets got on the horn and informed the crew that a wire audio recorder was hooked up to the airplane's interphone system. "We're making this recording for history, so watch your language and everybody talk clear."[22] Minutes later, the colonel turned off the IFF (Identification Friend or Foe) transponder located on the top of his instrument panel dashboard. It would not be switched on again until they approached friendly Iwo Jima on the return.

At 8:30 a.m., forty-five minutes prior to the drop, the three weather planes checked in. Although Wilson (over the secondary, Kokura) and Taylor (over the tertiary, Nagasaki) both reported acceptable visual bombing conditions, it was Eatherly's message that the crew anxiously awaited. No one wanted to admit how badly they wanted to go after the target they had studied so hard for. At last word came; Nelson immediately recognized the hand of Pasquale Baldasaro, the radio operator on the *Straight Flush*. Junior scribbled the dahty-ditted code letters on a scrap of paper and rushed it up to the colonel.

Tibbets read "Y-3, Q-3, B-2, C-1." He had the translation sheet in front of him. "Low, middle, light cover less than three-tenths at all altitudes. Bomb primary." The colonel immediately got on interphone: "Pilot to crew, it's Hiroshima."[23]

The announcement had the effect of a racing starter gun. The men immediately sprang into action. Van Kirk checked the winds and recalculated his heading and estimated time of arrival to the initial point (IP). Ferebee was now fully awake, reviewing in his mind every detail of the bomb run from start to finish. Stiborik ran through his checklists, making sure his radar was tuned as perfectly as he could get it and studying his simulations of the target as they were predicted to look on the scope. The pilots were sitting up straight in their seats, scanning the instruments, and watching for enemy fighters or flak. Tibbets had set the throttles and turbos as wide open as he dared in order to get the ship as high as possible at the release point. At 30,000 feet plus, due to functions of physics related to atmospheric pressure and outside air temperature, the true airspeed of the ship would increase dramatically without benefit of a higher indicated airspeed. According to Van Kirk's calculations, that meant the bomb run ground speed would fall between 325 and 350 mph, nearly six miles a minute across the earth's surface.

Parsons and Jeppson continued to carefully monitor Little Boy's circuits, their fingers crossed that every indicator would stay positive and in the green. Beser was keeping a close eye on the full radio spectrum using his signal analysis equipment to ensure the Japanese were not operating on the obscure frequency chosen to energize the bomb's complex radar proximity fuse. Should it somehow be jammed, the weapon would not detonate.

At 8:50 a.m. Lewis wrote in his journal that "we are now only 25 miles from the Empire, and everyone has a hopeful look on his face."[24] The *Enola Gay* passed over the southern Home Island of Shikoku, flew across the Inland Sea, and headed for the southwestern end of the main island of Honshu. As it happened, the weather people had guessed wrong about a strong headwind on the bomb run; Van Kirk's radar calculations showed they were actually from the south at only 10 mph, a light crosswind that would not seriously affect the bomb run. At 9:10 a.m. the bomber coasted in on Honshu, just nine miles south of the IP.[25] Unbeknownst to everyone on the crew, Ferebee had reconfigured his Norden into extended vision mode and although the *Enola Gay* had not yet arrived at the IP, he had already identified his aiming point (AP), the Aioi Bridge in Hiroshima.

Extended vision (or the X-1 reflex sight) was one of the more unique features of the Norden bombing system (NBS). By engaging the bombsight's extended vision knob the forward vision angle could be raised by another twenty degrees, enabling Ferebee on this crystal clear day to see more than seventy-five miles away. Further aided by his own amazing eyesight, he had instantly picked out the prominent Ota River system that ran directly through the city of Hiroshima and emptied into the sea. He would hold the NBS in extended vision through the IP turn inbound and until the ship had settled on its bomb run heading, then switch it out of the long-range configuration. Those who made the mistake of not returning to normal viewing—and it did happen—suffered the horrifying consequence of watching their bombs fall well short of the target.[26]

At 9:12 a.m. Van Kirk suddenly realized he was directly over the city of Mihara. Somehow, with events happening so fast, he had overshot the IP. The airplane's heading coming into the IP had been 353 degrees and the bomb run heading was planned at 270 degrees, an 83-degree turn to the left. Dutch had waited nearly a minute too long to start his precision turn, which should have begun about four miles short of Mihara so as to roll out exactly on the preplanned bomb run course. Fortunately, based on years of navigation experience, Van Kirk knew intuitively how to quickly compensate.

"Navigator to pilot, over IP, turn left heading 264 degrees."[27] Dutch would put the *Enola Gay* on a convergence heading to the target, correcting the minor overshooting error by turning six degrees further left than the preplanned inbound heading. The bomb drop was less than three minutes away.

"Bomb bay doors coming open," Ferebee announced.

Earlier, Tibbets had gotten the *Enola Gay* up to 30,700 feet pressure altitude, as high as the airplane would go. Using his own E6-B circular slide rule, Ferebee had calculated they were at a true altitude (above sea level) of 31,060 feet. As the AP happened to be located at sea level, it was not necessary to subtract the target's elevation in order to get an absolute altitude above the surface. That latter value was a critical entering argument when determining the actual time of fall and trail values from the Little Boy bombing tables. Van Kirk and Ferebee had conferred prior to the IP on the wind and drift, agreeing on a three-degree correction to compensate for the southerly crosswind. Ferebee had then cranked the three degrees into the Norden, which provided a good starting point toward keeping the vertical crosshair from drifting off the AP, although throughout the run he would need to be ready to immediately resynchronize if it started to drift away. The horizontal crosshair, which continuously measured the ship's current sighting angle against the predetermined dropping angle was cross-checked to be certain it too was in the correct position.

"Crew," Tibbets said tersely, "put on your goggles." That would be the polarized welder goggles designed to protect the crew's eyes from the detonation's thousand-sun flash. "And everyone make sure you are strapped in."[28] When the breakaway turn began, anybody not belted or otherwise secured would meet the same fate as Colonel Blanchard had on the earlier "qualification" flight.

Tibbets again checked his instrument panel to ensure the needle on the NBS pilot directional indicator was centered, that he was holding the 30,700-foot pressure altitude, and that his indicated air speed remained steady at 230 mph, which at that altitude and outside air temperature yielded a true airspeed of 330 mph—due to the light crosswinds that was very close to the *Enola Gay*'s groundspeed. Meanwhile, as Lewis recorded in his inflight journal, the bombardier "had come into his own." Ferebee was continuously in motion—head bobbing up from the sight to scan his instruments and switches, then a quick visual check out the window to be sure he was still headed for the T-shaped bridge, then it was back again to the bomb sight. During those moments when he was hunkered over M9B Norden bombsight number Victor 4120, Ferebee's right hand darted back and forth between the drift knob (vertical crosshair) and the rate and displacement knob (horizontal/sighting angle crosshair), continually synchronizing.[29]

Behind the bombardier, Tibbets, Van Kirk, and Parsons were staring intently out the B-29's plexiglass greenhouse nose, acting out a formal ceremony that had been proscribed by the Manhattan Project director, Maj. Gen. Leslie Groves. After hard looks at the huge and magnificent visual tapestry unfolding below (the men on the flight deck were still ungoggled), the roll was taken. Van Kirk, Tibbets, and Parsons along with radar operator Stiborik said on interphone and into the ship's wire recorder, "I confirm that is the aiming point." Parsons then formally told Tibbets, "The release is authorized."[30]

According to Van Kirk, there had been a parallel dialogue a little less majestic going on off interphone between himself and Ferebee. Unlike the extremely noisy B-17, where off-interphone chats were practically impossible, face-to-face conversations could be conducted relatively easily in the pressurized B-29. In Van Kirk's 2012 talk at the National Museum of the Air Force, he said that he and Ferebee, who were probably less than a foot apart, had a short discussion that went something like this:

> A standing Van Kirk pointing past Ferebee sitting in his jump seat: "Do you see the target?"
>
> Ferebee, looking a bit bewildered: "I can't see a damn thing!"
>
> Van Kirk, getting a little flustered and jabbing a forefinger at Hiroshima: "It's the damn bridge right down there! A blind man could see it, for Chrissake!"
>
> Ferebee, squinting out the window, finally exclaiming: "Oh, that bridge! I see it, I see it!"

One suspects at that moment there was a serious "gotcha" grin on the bomb aimer's face. Van Kirk told his chuckling Dayton museum audience "that was Tom Ferebee you know."[31]

In the rear compartment, radar operator Stiborik had reconfigured his APQ-13 radar scope from its usual omniview full-scan setting to a pie-shaped sector scan—the radar sweep swiveling back and forth from its anchor at the point of the pie (i.e., the *Enola Gay*). With the magnifying power of the set now concentrated in the sector sweep, the land/water contrasts were even more pronounced and Stiborik easily pulled out the Aioi Bridge. If this had been a conventional attack over Japan at night or in clouds precluding an optical release, Stiborik would have fed Ferebee range calls and course corrections all the way through the run. Ferebee would then have inputted that data into his NBS and the bomb run would continue normally through an automatic release. In this case, however, because of the strict orders to only drop visually, Stiborik functioned solely as a crosscheck.[32]

At ninety seconds to go, Tibbets said, "Pilot to bombardier, it's all yours." Tibbets took his hands off the yoke and "slid back a bit in [his] seat in a not very successful effort to relax."[33] The pilot's job now was not to deviate in the slightest from his current altitude and airspeed. On Tibbets' command, Ferebee had manually "clutched in" the NBS, meaning he had taken over heading control via the C-1 autopilot, which was now slaved to the NBS. The ship would respond to any drift knob (vertical crosshair) corrections the bombardier made for the rest of the run. Again pressing an eye against the telescopic sighthead, Ferebee continued to synchronize on the AP using both the drift knob and the rate and displacement knob—the latter measuring the ever-closing gap (quantified in seconds to go) between the constantly changing sighting angle and the predetermined drop angle. The bomb would automatically go out the doors when the sighting angle finally coincided with the drop angle (about seventy degrees from the vertical at 30,000 feet), the *Enola Gay* at that point about five miles short of the AP as measured from the earth's surface directly below the airplane to the target. In effect, because of the airplane's high speed and height, Ferebee would be "throwing" the bomb forward those five miles, which actually gave the crew a head start on putting more distance between themselves and the explosion as they "ran away from the bomb." Because the wind was light and what little drift there was had already been cancelled out, the crosshairs were staying stable on the bridge. The view from above was amazing; Ferebee could see the entire city, nestled into a vast green coastal delta with several brown branches of the Ota River coursing through it to the sea "like the fingers of a hand."[34] Because of the ease of aiming and lack of enemy opposition, Ferebee later said it was one of the most undemanding bombing runs he had ever made.

At sixty seconds to go, radioman Nelson turned on an electronic tone.[35] This was a new device installed to alert the supporting B-29s that the release was imminent. When it stopped, Little Boy would be on its way. Sweeney and his bombardier, Beahan, were to simultaneously drop their parachute-mounted measuring/analysis instruments (Van Kirk called them "bang meters") from *The Great Artiste.* Concurrently, Marquardt's people were to get ready for the still and motion picture photography in *Necessary Evil.* The bomb tone, which was broadcast over the radio operator's frequency, proved a strong signal—McKnight and his *Big Stink* crew, still faithfully on duty at Iwo Jima, distinctly heard it nine hundred miles away.

Tibbets had at that same moment decided not to completely rely on the tone and broke radio silence. "One minute out," he announced to Sweeney and Marquardt over the command voice channel.[36] He followed that with thirty, twenty, and ten second calls from off his "to go" meter, then did a ten-nine-eight countdown to release.

When Tibbets announced "five seconds," Tom reached out his left hand and grabbed hold of the emergency manual release handle while with his right hand he continued to synchronize both hairs on the Aioi Bridge. The instant following the colonel saying "one second," the NBS signaled the automatic release sequence. Simultaneously, Ferebee pulled the emergency handle for all he was worth.[37] One way or the other, that bomb was leaving at the appointed moment; the bombardier would never know for sure which of the two release circuits actually dropped it. In his navigation log, Van Kirk wrote. "Bomb-Away at 0915:15" (Tinian time)—8:15:15 a.m. Hiroshima time.

The *Enola Gay* lurched instantly skyward, relieved of five tons of dead weight. Tibbets immediately took the ship back from the NBS and broke right in a steep 60-degree bank. He would hold the turn through 155 degrees—rolling out on a magnetic heading of 060 degrees (east by northeast). At the same time the colonel nudged the nose over in a very shallow dive in order to buy that much more getaway speed in addition to the already fire-walled engines, losing an inconsequential 1,700 feet in the process.[38] A precise touch had to be used on the aileron controls during the steep turn as there was a real danger of the ship tumbling over into a fatal right roll. This stick-handling was made even more difficult because of the B-29's massive control surfaces and their attendant lack of hydraulic boost. Van Kirk, who had strapped himself tightly into his seat, was also holding onto his navigation table, grateful he did not have to fend for handholds as did the deck-bound Parsons and Jeppson. All at once, something flew past the navigator. Tibbets discovered he could not see well enough to properly conduct the steep turn maneuver with his goggles on and had ripped them off and thrown them over his shoulder.[39]

After dropping the instrument package from the *The Great Artiste*, Sweeney performed the same breakaway maneuver in the opposite direction. George Marquardt, who after crossing the IP had conducted a standard rate 360-degree turn in order to put fifteen to twenty miles distance between himself and the other two attack airplanes, positioned his airplane in a relatively safe spot astern of the others though still close enough for his photographers.[40] There was no reason for *Necessary Evil* to further expose itself by approaching any closer to Hiroshima.

After Ferebee yanked the emergency release handle, nearly ripping it loose from its mounts, he unclutched the Norden (Tibbets had already taken the airplane back, overriding the NBS) and closed the bomb bay doors. Moments later, despite the difficulty in keeping his balance during the steep turn, Ferebee was back peering through the bombsight eyepiece. It had long been Ferebee's practice to follow his bombs down to monitor their trajectory and assess bomb damage. Without giving the matter any thought, he reverted to habit. The unit—ten feet long and twenty-eight inches in diameter—had come out of the bay broadside, then wobbled a bit before straightening out after the tailfins caught hold aerodynamically.[41]

In the late 1960s, then-colonel Thomas Ferebee held spellbound the young B-52 navigator-bombardiers of the 367th Bomb Squadron at McCoy Air Force Base, Florida, when he related what happened next.[42] Even during the steep turn, Tom was able to continue following the unit down by way of a certain manipulation of the bombsight telescopic controls. Unwittingly, he became mesmerized by Little Boy's descent—watching, watching. Sometime between thirty-five and forty seconds after release—Ferebee had still not torn himself away from the sighthead—Tibbets began to roll the Superfortress back left to straight and level flight. Perhaps the changing attitude of the ship rang a little bell. Ferebee suddenly recalled the stern warnings about the flash and threw his head back, it also dawning on him that it was too late to put on his protective goggles. Forty-three seconds after he had released Little Boy, a terrific beam of blinding light blasted up through the Norden's optical lenses and like a laser blazed against the greenhouse plexiglass ceiling.[43] Ferebee said if he had kept his head down on the sight for a few seconds longer, the flash—"like a camera flashbulb going off in a dark closet"—would have taken out an eye. As it was without the goggles, it still took some time for his sight to return to normal.

At precisely 9:15:58 on Van Kirk's watch, the bomb had fallen to a height of 1,890 feet above the ground and the radar proximity fuse triggered.[44] The circuits were now complete; the U-235 firing mass shot into the U-235 target mass, and in the next millisecond an uncontrolled chain reaction occurred. It would later be calculated that Ferebee's circular error was only eight hundred feet from the center of the Aioi Bridge. By any combat standard of the day—the extreme altitude, the use of analog equipment, an obsolescing optical release method, and the imperfectly understood ballistic trajectory of the clunky Little Boy bomb casing—it was a "shack."[45]

Tail gunner Bob Caron was the one man who saw it all, the bomb detonating in his face at a distance of between eleven and twelve slant range miles.

Unlike Ferebee, who had been looking the other way and partially shielded by the airplane, Caron would have been permanently blinded if he had not been wearing his variable-density, full-extinction polarized goggles, which admitted only the color purple through the lenses.[46] Even with the goggles set at maximum block, it took several seconds for Caron to recover from the indescribable bright light. To make matters worse, he had been battered hard against the sides of his compartment during the breakaway turn. It was no wonder, then, that when he had recovered enough to look out the window and saw "an unholy globe of compressed air" come racing at him, he could not fully comprehend what was happening.[47] Caron would later describe the sight as "a peep into hell."[48] In his book, Tibbets explained the malevolent-looking, tsunami-like atmospheric wave that "threatened to engulf them" was caused by "condensing moisture from heated air at the leading edge of the shock wave [that] made it visible, just as one sees shimmering air rising from the ground on a hot, humid day."[49] Caron keyed his interphone mike and tried to warn the crew but was so dumbfounded he strangled the words. A moment or two later, traveling at the speed of sound, the shock wave struck. Junior Nelson later wrote that when it collided with the airplane, "It sounded like a piece of sheet metal being hit by a strong and sudden gust of wind."[50]

Later estimated at a force of 2.5 Gs, the ship shook so violently that Paul Tibbets' combat instincts took over and he involuntarily yelled, "Flak!" In his autobiography, the colonel insisted the outburst had come from Deak Parsons, but in *My True Course* Dutch Van Kirk tells us that in the end Tibbets finally "admitted he was the one."[51] Ironically, Parsons was probably the only man on board who understood precisely what had happened. "No, no," he told Tibbets, "that's the shock wave."[52] Later, on the deadhead run back to Tinian and knowing how rough it had to have been for the tail gunner, the colonel would lightheartedly ask Caron how it went during the breakaway turn. Downplaying the beating he took, Caron got into the spirit of the moment by replying that it was "better than the Cyclone ride down at Coney Island."[53]

Not more than five seconds after the first shock wave hit, a ricochet wave that had bounced off the earth's surface also struck the *Enola Gay*. This time Caron was able to blurt out a warning: "Here comes another one!" To everyone's relief, it impacted with considerably less force.

Caron reached for the K-20 hand-operated 5 × 5 camera and began searching for something to photograph. It took a couple of heartbeats for him to realize the gunsight and window frames were blocking his view. "Colonel," he said over the interphone, dropping strict radio protocol—Tibbets knew his voice as well as Ferebee's or Van Kirk's—"could you turn the ship five or ten degrees one way or the other?"[54] Tibbets instantly complied. Moments later, Caron had a clear view of the huge mushroom column building in front of him and began taking photographs, one shutter click after the other.

A minute or two later, Paul Tibbets swung the ship around so the entire crew could have a look. He would not circle the blast but instead set up a station-keeping orbit to the southeast of Hiroshima, the better to enable a quick exit away from the Home Islands if circumstances suddenly dictated. The colonel could personally testify that something quite incredible had happened. Moments after the detonation, he experienced a distinct "tingling sensation in my mouth," what scientists later told him was electrolysis—"an interaction between the fillings in my teeth and the [bomb's] radioactive forces."[55]

A few days later, Tibbets would tell newsreel cameras that "the sight that greeted our eyes [when we turned around] was quite beyond what we'd expected."[56] After just two minutes, a gigantic, black-purplish, rather stringy-looking mushroom cloud had risen to a height above the *Enola Gay*—and it was still building. The city had completely disappeared beneath what Tibbets and several others described as a "turbulent mass . . . of bubbling hot tar."[57] The mid-base of the mushroom stem was boiling with angry, dark clouds—several crewmen remembered they kept changing colors. In and just above the boiling tar, countless red pricks from freshly started fires were continually winking in and out, and there were hurricane-like winds whipping through the cloud stem all the way from the surface to the top of the atomic cloud. During the entire time the crew remained on station, nothing was ever visible underneath the swirling maelstrom at the mushroom's base.

During those minutes of orbiting off to one side, most of the men gave vent to their thoughts by speaking into the interphone/recorder, with Tibbets giving everyone a chance to have their say for posterity. In his journal, Lewis would record (probably sometime on the way back to Tinian) that he had said, "My God, what have we done?" Interestingly, that was dramatic enough for the writers of the 1952 Hollywood film *Above and Beyond* to put those very same words into the mouth of Paul Tibbets (played by actor Robert Taylor). By all accounts, however, the phrase was a product of Capt. Bob Lewis' imagination, an attempt, perhaps, to carve out for himself some kind of moral high ground. According to several crew accounts, what he actually said was, "My God, look at the sonofabitch go!"[58] Unfortunately, his comment and all the others made by the crew are lost to history. Upon landing back at Tinian, Tibbets tells us that Beser turned the wire recording spool over to "an information officer . . . and it has never been heard of since."[59]

After a few more minutes of observation, Caron, he who had the best view of any on the ship and had not taken his eyes off the cloud even for a moment, once more sounded the alarm. "Holy Moses, colonel," he shouted into his interphone mike, "it's coming toward us . . . the head of the cloud is coming toward us!"[60] Either the wind had shifted or the pilots had allowed the ship to get in too close. The orders had been explicit; under no circumstances were they to fly through the radioactive cloud because, at a minimum, it would damage human organs and, at the worst, exposure could be fatal. Later, back on Tinian, Ferebee voiced a concern that the crew might have been near enough to be sterilized—finally, a danger serious enough to worry the bombardier! Fortunately, contamination fears proved groundless perhaps in no small part to Caron's alert warning. Tibbets did not hesitate to bank sharply away from the fast-moving radioactive cloud and the ship cleared it.

With that Tibbets realized nothing more could be accomplished over Hiroshima and to stay any longer over enemy territory, especially with that deadly cloud nearby, put the crew unnecessarily at risk. It was high time the *Enola Gay* got the hell out of the Empire. At 9:31 a.m., fifteen minutes after the explosion and with the ship cruising at 29,000-feet pressure altitude, Van Kirk gave Tibbets a southeasterly heading back toward Iwo Jima. The colonel steadied up on 140 degrees magnetic and, once they had cleared the Home Islands, began a very slow step-descent (for fuel economy) back to the Marianas. After huddling with Parsons, Tibbets wrote out a strike report and gave it to Nelson for transmission to General Farrell, who the colonel knew was sitting on pins and needles back at North Field waiting for word. Farrell was not the only one sweating it out—his boss, Major General Groves, was so concerned that he had set up a twenty-four-hour vigil on a cot in his Washington, D.C., office. It would be Groves' responsibility to immediately pass the strike report on to General of the Army, George Marshall; Marshall in turn would relay it to President Truman, who was still in mid-Atlantic on board the cruiser *Augusta* on his way home from Potsdam.

Junior tapped out in Morse the coded message: "82 V 670. Able, Line 1, Line 2, Line 6, Line 9." Translation: "Parsons/Tibbets to Farrell. Results clear cut and successful in all respects. Visual effects greater than Trinity. Hiroshima. Proceeding to Tinian with normal conditions in airplane."[61]

At 10:03 a.m., the entire crew was thoroughly rattled to hear someone excitedly transmit, "Fighter at seven o'clock level!"[62] Tail gunner Sgt. Bob Caron, the only man on board with any kind of defensive capability, instantly sprang into action. Believing the threat was real and immediate he simultaneously hit every one of his fire-control system power switches, instantly drawing eight hundred amps and overloading the *Enola Gay*'s electrical power needs.

"What the hell's going on?" yelled flight engineer Duzenbury, "Who's taking all my power?"[63] Although he knew exactly what effect his action would have, Caron had not dared to take the time to inform Dooz. If there was a fighter out there, his twin-fifties were their last line of defense and every second counted. Fortunately, the emergency was over before it really began. Another crewmen radioed that he was looking at the seven o'clock location, and all he could see was *The Great Artiste*, faithfully in position. It soon became apparent that Beser, who was inexperienced in a combat environment, had made the earlier call.[64]

In his 1988 book *Hiroshima and Nagasaki Revisited*, Beser pointed the finger at Caron, writing "the tail gunner announced there was a Japanese fighter approaching . . . The fighter pulled up alongside, dropped his wheels and flaps to slow down . . . slow rolled around us, then sped away."[65] In subsequent interviews, Tibbets and Van Kirk were angered by Beser's assertions. In *My True Course*, a spluttering Van Kirk stated that "I have to shake my head. . . . If a fighter had been spotted all hell would have broken loose."[66]

Once the *Enola Gay* had coasted away from the Empire and out into the western Pacific, Tibbets turned the ship over to Lewis. The colonel had no more than leaned back and lit up his pipe when Caron got on the interphone and made an inquiry that opened up the floodgates to all the questions everyone in the 509th had been dying to ask for nearly a year. "Colonel, how many people did it take to pull this thing off?"

Tibbets proceeded to give a brief overview of the Manhattan Project and then took questions, patiently answering each. How did the bomb work? Who dreamt it up? How much did it cost? What kind of scientists were involved? How could it be that so many were immigrants or foreigners? And so on and so forth. After a time the men's curiosity was sated, at least for the moment, and the ship quieted. The adrenaline was wearing off and they were suddenly feeling the effects of their deep fatigue. The balance of the trip back to Tinian was flown mostly in silence. At 10:52 a.m. Caron reported that he could no longer see the mushroom cloud. Van Kirk said they were 363 miles away from the impact point.[67] Next to the time, Van Kirk noted "Cloud Gone" in the remarks section of his navigation log.

Tibbets, Ferebee, and Van Kirk were as fatigued as everyone else, but mostly their emotions were of enormous *relief.* The damn thing had worked! All the effort, all the worry, all the stress, all the cost to their personal lives—had been worth it. They had done their jobs almost to perfection, and no one would ever be able to take that and the satisfaction it brought away from them. With those comforting thoughts, an exhausted Tibbets decided to take another nap. Ferebee and most of the other fellows were already sawing logs. As was usual on all long-range, over-ocean B-29 Superfortress deadheads, there was only one of the pilots (Lewis) monitoring fuel, heading, altitude, and autopilot; the flight engineer (Duzenbury) keeping a close eye on the engines; the radar operator (Stiborik) taking range and bearings off known surface features; and the navigator (Van Kirk) who had to stay awake.

By the time the *Enola Gay* approached Iwo Jima airspace, the partially revived crew had come to a general agreement that there was no way the Japanese could stand up to the atomic bomb. Lewis wrote in his journal: "I had a strong conviction that . . . by the time we landed . . . the Japs would have thrown in the sponge."[68]

12

# THE REST OF THE STORY

But the Japanese were not ready to throw in the sponge—their Bushido-indoctrinated warlords remained determined to commit national hara-kiri rather than surrender. It would take the Soviet Union's declaration of war against Japan, their massive invasion of Japanese-held Manchuria on August 8, and a second atomic bomb on August 9 to shock Emperor Hirohito into finally ending it. Although Tibbets and his crew would be disappointed there had not been a capitulation by the time they arrived back over the Marianas, they still believed it was only a matter of time. Once the word got around about the atomic bomb, everyone else in the Pacific believed it as well. Back at North Field, a very joyous reception awaited the men of the *Enola Gay.*

As the three returning B-29s approached Tinian airspace, Sweeney and Marquardt dropped back to allow the *Enola Gay* to land at the field in advance of their own arrival—both aircraft commanders knew a ceremony of some sort would be planned for Tibbets and his crew.[1] At 2:15 p.m. on the afternoon of August 6 and while cruising at 12,800 feet pressure altitude, Tibbets contacted North Field tower and requested the local altimeter setting and landing instructions. No longer was altitude separation between ships of paramount concern; Tibbets now wanted an altimeter reading that told him precisely how high he would be above the runway. With the tower formalities completed, the colonel switched off the autopilot and began his penetration descent, calling for the Before Landing checklist. Lewis began the challenge and responses.

It was time for everyone to wake up and pay attention. Aviators are taught early on that the two most critical areas of flight are takeoff and landing; one slip right at the end and what so far had been a perfect day could be instantly transformed into a disaster. The crew strapped themselves in and began their own checklists. Junior Nelson made sure to reel in his radio antenna, which was basically a long stiff wire with a weight on the end that trailed out behind the ship—absent-minded radio operators that left it dangling on landing never heard the end of it if their ship taxied in with the remains flapping between its legs. After passing through 10,000 feet, Bob Lewis depressurized the cabin.

"Copilot to tail gunner, stow your gun turret and crank up the putt-putt."

"Roger," Bob Caron responded.

Power was reduced to 2,400 rpm, the flaps lowered to fifteen degrees, and the ship trimmed for descent. At ten minutes out from the field and with the indicated airspeed dipping below 180 mph, Tibbets lowered the landing gear.

"Three down and locked," Lewis announced moments later, meaning left truck, right truck, and nose wheel.[2]

Duzenbury called the current aircraft weight and center of gravity figures over to Lewis and the copilot referred to the table mounted on his instrument panel to determine the best flare/stall speed, passing that number on to Tibbets. "Flaps 25, manifold 24 inches," Lewis called out. They were now on base leg at about 1,500 feet and still descending. Stiborik and Schumard would carefully monitor the engines and flaps from their rear compartment windows all the way through to touchdown, in particular ensuring that the called flap settings matched up with their visual observations.

Tibbets turned on to the final approach leg and told Duzenbury to rotate the turbos' selector dial on his flight engineer's panel to no. 8, the landing configuration of the engine superchargers. Visibility was unlimited—the sky a patchy mix of blue and the usual dramatic-looking tropical cumulous clouds.

"Flaps 35, manifold 22 inches." Power was continually being reduced and the flaps were now fully down. With Runway Able nearing and with the airspeed continually dropping, Tibbets kept spinning his elevator trim wheel to compensate for the rapidly changing fore/aft control pressures on the yoke. All the while, one eye stayed fixed on his airspeed meter, looking to be at a best flare speed of around 110–120 mph just as the main wheel trucks kissed the runway. Moments later Tibbets had the *Enola Gay* rolling down the centerline after what Nelson later called "one of the best landings I ever had seen."[3] The crew cleaned up the aircraft while the colonel taxied the ship to its hardstand. After one of Chief McCaleb's men hand-signaled the airplane into its chocks, Tibbets shut the engines down and set the parking brake. Dutch Van Kirk made the last entry in his log: "Base 1458."[4] The *Enola Gay* had landed at 2:58 p.m. Tinian time—total mission time was twelve hours and thirteen minutes.

Scores of fatigued and khaki-dressed soldiers, officers, and top brass surrounded the airplane, waiting to greet the crew. Tibbets exited the ship through the nose hatch ladder with his pipe already in his mouth, not realizing what was about to happen. The moment he cleared the fuselage and straightened up, division commander Brig. Gen. John Davies, who was standing at attention several feet off to one side, barked "Attention to orders!"

Suddenly aware that he was the subject of a ceremony, Tibbets palmed the Kaywoodie pipe in his left hand and stood stiffly in a brace as Davies read the citation to accompany the award of the Distinguished Service Cross to Col. Paul W. Tibbets Jr., the Army Air Force's second-highest award behind the Medal of Honor.[5] (A few days later, the rest of the *Enola Gay* crew received the Silver

Star.) At the conclusion of the reading, Gen. Tooey Spaatz—the same officer who had awarded a Purple Heart to Major Tibbets three years earlier at Polebrook, England—stepped forward and formally pinned the medal on the left breast of Tibbets' flight suit. After the two briefly exchanged congratulations and "thank you, sirs," Tibbets took a step back and smartly saluted the general, an ancient gesture of military respect that Spaatz promptly returned. And with that the ritual was concluded and the crowd melted away.

While Tibbets lingered behind for a few minutes accepting additional kudos, General Spaatz and the other flag officers—including Adm. William Purnell and Gen. Thomas Farrell—departed for the debriefing hut. After the *Enola Gay* crew submitted to a hasty physical exam to ensure they had not been exposed to radiation, they and other 509th headquarters staff joined General Spaatz around a large table. Lt. Col. Hazen Payette, Tibbets' group intelligence officer (they had served together in North Africa), moderated the debriefing question-and-answer session. Meanwhile, outside the building and within earshot, a jubilant celebration had broken out. Mess officer Charlie Perry was putting on a huge picnic for everyone in the 509th, complete with beer, hot dogs, and all the trimmings, followed by organized skits and games.

Payette started things off by garnering mission summaries from Tibbets and Parsons, followed by comments from Ferebee and Van Kirk, then individual questions directed at certain crewmen as circumstances dictated. The queries were of the standard combat debrief variety—how did it go overall? [Great.] Any mechanical problems with the ship? [Nope, just minor write-ups.] Any fighters or flak? [No fighters, Ferebee saw some flak at one point about ten to fifteen thousand below the airplane.] Can you assess the damage from the bomb? [No, everything was completely obscured by smoke, dust, and debris during the fifteen minutes we loitered near the target.] Did you see anything of military interest? [Yes, Van Kirk said, he had made a note on his log "8 large ships in harbor at Mishima."[6]] On combat missions where crews had been shot down, there would have been extensive questioning about their location—did you see any chutes, how many, and so on, but in this case that line of inquiry was unnecessary.

Although the session was rather lengthy and the crew bushed, everyone was in a very good humor—the kind that only comes after a very difficult or dangerous mission has been successfully accomplished. General Spaatz had made it clear it was perfectly OK for the boys to spike their coffee or soft drink with a liberal dose of post–combat mission "Old Methuselah" whiskey, a gesture greatly appreciated. Several lighthearted moments along the way also contributed to the expansive mood. Early on, Sergeant Caron, who was still wearing his blue Brooklyn Dodgers baseball cap, had gotten a dirty look from Tibbets. The colonel had tapped his own head with a finger, meaning we are indoors, uncover yourself mister. A chagrined Caron was caught between a rock and a hard place—a day earlier an in-his-cups Duzenbury decided to give Caron a haircut, and what the flight engineer produced was "a cross between a Blackfoot Indian and a patch of sprouting prairie."[7] Very reluctantly, Caron lifted his cap, saying, "Do you still want me to take it off, Colonel?" Spaatz himself led the prolonged laughter. After finally composing himself, the general exclaimed, "Sergeant, leave it on!" Later, Ferebee was asked if he thought he had hit the target. With a straight face and in his deepest North Carolina drawl, Ferebee allowed that he had missed the aiming point—the unit exploded thirteen and a half feet northeast of the bridge.[8] Van Kirk had his moment. After Payette stated that the scheduled bomb release time was 0915 hours—six and a half hours and 1,500 miles after takeoff—he asked the navigator what was the actual release time. Van Kirk replied, "0915 and 15 seconds." Payette gave Dutch a mock hard look and deadpanned, "Why were you late?"[9]

When the debriefing finally concluded and the crew arrived at Charlie Perry's picnic, they discovered the beer was already gone and the hot dogs and other eats nearly so.[10] Van Kirk and Ferebee, who both went away completely empty-handed, could only shake their heads. That was the way things worked in the Army Air Forces, they thought. While the ground pounders and staff never failed to get pleasantly fed and watered, it was always the combat aircrews that seemed to get screwed. Deciding they were too tired to party anyway, the musketeers hit the sack. The stress and workload during the past forty-eight hours, with only snatches of sleep, had left them thoroughly exhausted. Plus, any hopes the Japs would abruptly fold were already gone; the war was going to continue.

As it happened, because Hiroshima had been so completely cut off by the effects of the bomb, it took a day or two for Japanese leaders to learn what had actually occurred. The upshot of that silence from the enemy camp was to further convince Allied leadership that it was essential that another bomb be delivered as soon as possible. One of the great Allied fears was the enemy would conclude the United States had used its one and only atomic bomb and that the war could continue conventionally. American intelligence believed that Japan had enough of a uranium bomb program of their own to know that the U-235 isotope was extremely difficult to manufacture, and the Americans knew the enemy was unaware of the more easily produced plutonium substitute. A second bomb was necessary to convince them that an unknown number of atomic devices were still available.

While Tibbets, Ferebee, and Van Kirk would not be flying the next atomic mission, they were to be intimately involved in its planning, beginning the next morning, Tuesday, August 7. By then, the weather over the Home Islands had worsened sufficiently to cause the strike to be moved up from August 11 to August 9, leaving little time to prepare. Colonel Tibbets selected 393rd Bombardment Squadron commander, Maj. Charles "Chuck" Sweeney, to lead the second atomic attack element and carry the first plutonium bomb into combat.

Crew C-15, jointly commanded by Sweeney and 1st Lt. Don Albury (who on this mission would fly as copilot), also included such handpicked Tibbets people as Capt. Kermit "Honey Bee" Beahan (bombardier), Capt. James Van Pelt (navigator), Cpl. Abe Spitzer (radio operator), and Sgt. Ray Gallagher (assistant flight engineer and scanner). That mission, which took off in the early morning hours of August 9 and nearly ended in disaster, is covered in considerable detail in the appendix.

The day after Sweeney and his *Bockscar* crew dropped Fat Man on Nagasaki, both atomic crews were summoned to Guam by Gen. Curtis LeMay for a major press conference with Pacific theater newsmen.[11] This went relatively smoothly despite the correspondents' indignation at being "scooped"—editors back in the United States were furious that the most stupendous operation of the war had been conducted right under their correspondents' noses, and they had known nothing about it. LeMay had instructed his airmen to answer the questions truthfully but say nothing about the bomb's size, shape, or weight. The crews gave the reporters enough to satisfy them without revealing very much of a military nature, and the press conference was concluded without incident.

After dismissing the reporters and airmen from his office, LeMay instructed Tibbets and Sweeney to stay behind. Looking squarely at Sweeney, and in reference to the agonizing Nagasaki mission the day before, LeMay snarled, "You fucked up, didn't you, Chuck?" There was nothing Sweeney could or did say. Turning to Tibbets, with Sweeney still present, the general said he did not think an investigation into the August 9 strike would serve any useful purpose, and the matter was dropped. However, based on LeMay's demeanor at that moment (according to Tibbets), one can assume that if an investigation would not have put the Army Air Forces into such a bad public light or if the mission had failed, Major Sweeney would have at the very least faced a formal inquiry. LeMay made his continuing displeasure crystal clear by what he said to Tibbets next: "You got any more of those things?"[12]

"Yessir," Tibbets responded. "We have another Fat Man bomb ready back at Wendover."

"Get it out here," LeMay growled. "If we need another mission you are going to fly it."[13] The no-nonsense, take-no-prisoners general was not about to take any more chances with second-stringers—if atomic warfare had to continue, he wanted nothing less than his first team. Not surprisingly, the news that they would take the next strike did not sit well with either Ferebee or Van Kirk, who were perfectly content to rest on their laurels.

Fortunately for everyone, one of the most horrific wars in human history ended a few days later. On August 15 word was received that Hirohito had accepted the Potsdam Declaration.[14] That same day, the emperor made a nationwide radio broadcast (the Japanese had never heard his voice before) in which he told his subjects that Japan had suffered irreversible military losses from which it could not recover and the country must "endure the unendurable." The official surrender came on September 2, 1945, on board the battleship USS *Missouri* at anchor in Tokyo Bay.

Following the end of hostilities, General Groves still had two important tasks for the 509th before they would be allowed to return to the Zone of the Interior. First, they were to remain fully combat ready for a period of weeks—perhaps months—in case the "always treacherous" Japanese (nobody had forgotten Pearl Harbor or the Bataan Death March) should go back on their word and restart the war. Second, a 509th inspection team was to be immediately mounted to carefully survey the damage done by the atomic weapons at Hiroshima and Nagasaki. After quickly putting into place a flying training program for his airmen (it is essential for combat aircrews to train *regularly* to keep their edge), Tibbets led the inspection expedition to Japan. Accompanying him in two Green Hornet C-54s were Ferebee, Van Kirk, Lewis, Sweeney, Beahan, Van Pelt, Albury, and a number of scientists from Project Alberta.[15] Landing at Atsugi Air Field just southwest of the Tokyo-Kawasaki-Yokohama metropolitan area, the team proceeded by truck (charcoal-burning Japanese vehicles that constantly broke down) to Nagasaki for an on-the-ground look.[16] Surface transportation to Hiroshima was still nearly impossible, and the team made their survey there by air. After several days of hectic travel and fact gathering, the Three Musketeers and the others were back in their Quonset huts on Tinian.

Around the first of October, Tibbets received orders to transfer the 509th to Roswell Field, New Mexico, which was to be the new home of America's first atomic bomb strike group. The crew of the *Enola Gay* was to go on ahead and get things ready to receive the entire group. When they arrived at Hickam Field near Pearl Harbor, they had an interesting encounter with an old friend. "We met [General] Eisenhower going the other way," Dutch tells us. "[He] made a comment that I always appreciated. He said, 'You guys started it, and you guys ended it.'"[17]

That moment was perhaps the high-water mark of the Three Musketeers' shared military career. Unknown to them at the time, their newfound fame had created enormous jealousies within the Army Air Forces, and now that the war was over, the brand of guts and leadership the fellows had brought to the table were no longer in demand. Once the 509th Composite Group had been settled at Roswell, Col. Butch Blanchard became the new commanding officer. One of his first acts was to appoint a new group bombardier and navigator.[18] Colonel Tibbets, Major Ferebee, and Major Van Kirk, who had come up through the ranks as non-degreed aviation cadets, a caste of officers who had never been fully accepted by the West Pointers, were out in the cold.

It was all very civilized. "We were given nice offices," Van Kirk told writer Suzanne Simon Dietz, "[each of us had] a secretary and did not have a damn thing to do."[19] Plus, so their rationalized thinking went at the time, they were still getting monthly paychecks and there was plenty of time for handball. Van Kirk said he got into the best shape of his life.

Nevertheless, the fellows clearly understood their situation was not good. The months passed by. Early in 1946 senior U.S. leadership decided a new round of atomic tests were necessary, and because of their unique experience, General LeMay insisted Tibbets and his men were included in that program. The primary objective of Operation Crossroads was to learn specifically how atomic weapons affected naval warships.[20] Over seventy vessels—including the American aircraft carrier *Saratoga*, the battleship *Nevada*, the German cruiser *Prinz Eugen*, and the Japanese battleship *Nagato*—were to be target ships in the Bikini Atoll Lagoon located in the Marshall Islands.[21] U.S. Navy vice admiral William Blandy and his assistant, the musketeers' old friend and now commodore Deak Parsons, were in command of the overall operation.[22]

Three Trinity-type (plutonium) tests were scheduled. The first was to be an air drop. Six B-29 aircrews, including Tibbets and company in the *Enola Gay*, were to compete for the privilege of making the run. As it happened, it was a stacked deck. The animosity the boys had created within the USAAF had become so pronounced that Colonel Blanchard and his boss, Brig. Gen. Roger Ramey, decided to rig the results. Tibbets later related, "Tom and I averaged a 237-foot [circular] error . . . from 30,000 feet . . . a better capability than was claimed [even] for the Norden bombsight [and the best score of the six planes]. But a couple of sharp pencils reversed the outcome of the competition [using a] completely irrelevant factor called 'ballistic winds.'"[23]

Tibbets, Ferebee, and Van Kirk were technically scored into last place and another crew was chosen to make the drop. Just before the actual release on July 1, 1946, Tom Ferebee and Kermit Beahan (also in the competition) checked over the real-world ballistic calculations of the crew that was to do the flying. Both Honey Bee and Ferebee were incredulous; the crew had made some startling mathematical errors. They went to the colonel to tell him that the bomb would hit 1,600 feet short and to the left of the aiming point. Tibbets himself went to the aircraft commander to plead his men's math but was rebuffed. Arrogance can blind a man surer than the loss of his own eyes.

The bomb exploded 1,800 feet short and to the left of the aiming point. The expected damage to the ships was but a fraction of the actual destruction, largely negating the bulk of the scientific and biological experiments. There was also a problem with scale—it was difficult to grasp the enormity of the explosion with the fleet so far away and so few comparative reference markers. A Russian scientific observer who had expected something wondrous was completely unimpressed, mumbling to a nearby reporter, "Not so much."[24] In Tibbets' words, the test "was a fiasco," it having failed to make an impact on anyone. On another level, the Russian's comment should have given pause to those who subsequently argued that America was remiss in not first demonstrating the weapon to the Japanese before using it on them—the Bikini air burst was measured at 21 to 23 kilotons, a greater blast than had occurred at either Hiroshima or Nagasaki.

Once the dimension of the bomb's circular error became clear, an enraged General LeMay tracked Colonel Tibbets down. "What in the hell happened?" he asked. Tibbets explained about the miscalculated ballistic data. "Jesus Christ!" LeMay exclaimed. The general made an instantaneous political decision. He looked at Tibbets and said "I don't want you on this island when all those newspaper people start asking questions." He ordered Tibbets and his crew to crawl into their B-29 and leave immediately for Washington, D.C., to report the test results to General Spaatz. The men of the *Enola Gay* were packed and airborne for the continental United States within the hour, marking the end of an era for the Three Musketeers.[25]

For reserve officer Maj. Theodore Van Kirk, the indignity of Operation Crossroads and the full realization of his own limited career opportunities in the U.S. Army Air Forces proved too much. A few weeks later, at the end of July 1946, he resigned his commission.[26] For the first time in nearly five years he was again a civilian. Like millions of other returning veterans, Van Kirk decided to take advantage of the education benefits provided by the 1944 GI Bill and return to college.[27] Without the government's assistance and especially with a family, going back to school would have been impossible for men like Van Kirk. The far-sighted legislation that President Roosevelt had pushed hard for was a major factor in the nation's amazing postwar economic recovery.

That fall Van Kirk entered Bucknell University in Lewisburg, Pennsylvania, to pursue his long-cherished dream of a degree in chemical engineering. He received a bachelor's degree in 1949 and a master's degree in 1950. It was not easy; even with the GI Bill, it was nip and tuck financially, plus the schooling was intense. Nevertheless, and despite also teaching engineering metallurgy for a semester and working in a university laboratory, Van Kirk "got good grades." Shortly thereafter, he was hired by the DuPont chemical company, where he worked in various technical and marketing positions for thirty-five years, retiring as a vice president. He and Mary Jane would eventually have two sons and two daughters. Mary Jane passed away unexpectedly in 1975; a couple of years later, Van Kirk met and married Imogene "Jean" Guest.

Throughout the seven decades following that fateful day in August 1945, Van Kirk made many public appearances speaking about the war, his role, and the atomic bomb. In particular, he reached out to young people in an attempt to compensate for the contemporary de-emphasis of World War II history instruction and why in his view the bombs were not only necessary but merciful in the sense that they saved hundreds of thousands, if not millions, of American and Japanese lives by eliminating the need for an invasion of the Home Islands.[28] Theodore "Dutch" Van Kirk—the last man still alive from the combined crews of the *Enola Gay* and *Bockscar*—passed away on July 28, 2014, at the age of ninety-three.[29] His eldest son, Thomas Van Kirk, told reporters his father succumbed to age-related natural causes.

Understanding that he was now too old to have any chance at a baseball career, Maj. Thomas Ferebee elected to stay in the postwar Army Air Forces.[30] In late July 1946, only days prior to Dutch's mustering out, Tom was married to Ann Elizabeth Gwin of Houston, Texas, with Dutch as the best man and Paul ushering (by then both men felt quite comfortable openly calling Colonel Tibbets "Paul"). The Ferebees would have four children, all sons. In 1947 and while still at Roswell, New Mexico, serving as staff bombardier for the 393th Bomb Squadron/509th Bomb Group, Tom Ferebee exchanged his brown Army uniform for U.S. Air Force blue after it became a separate service. In 1949 Tom went through a rigorous nine-month radar navigator/bombardier course that made him qualified in the new B-47 and B-52 jet bombers under development. Interestingly, one of his classmates at that school was another cross-training officer—Lt. Gen. Curtis LeMay, the newly appointed head of the Strategic Air Command (SAC).[31]

During the early 1950s, then–lieutenant colonel Tom Ferebee was involved in B-47 Stratojet testing before being given a choice four-year tour with the North Atlantic Treaty Organization (NATO) stationed near Paris. His records indicate that he acquired at least some of the local language; one can only imagine what his NATO associates thought of a man speaking a halting French with a heavy North Carolina accent. In 1960 Ferebee was promoted to full colonel, spending the next several years as the B-47 deputy wing commander for maintenance at Hunter Air Force Base in Savannah, Georgia, and later at MacDill Air Force Base in Tampa, Florida.[32] He was at MacDill during the 1962 Cuban Missile Crisis. "It was a pretty scary situation," he told Miami reporter Don Sider in 1995. "For [one 24-hour period I was sure] we were going to launch. I had seventy-seven bombers . . . none of them had less than six megatons on board."[33] Later President John F. Kennedy came to MacDill to personally thank the senior SAC officers for their efforts during the crisis, which included a handshake for Colonel Ferebee.

In 1963 the 306th Bomb Wing at MacDill was relocated to McCoy Air Force Base at Orlando, Florida. By that time the wing was operating with B-52C and D model Stratofortresses. In 1966, during the initial build-up of Vietnam's Operation Arc Light, Colonel Ferebee rotated to Southeast Asia for a six-month temporary duty combat tour.[34] He subsequently returned to McCoy, where he finished out his career.

Ferebee retired from the U.S. Air Force in 1970, remaining in the Orlando area. He dabbled in real estate sales for some years, though more and more of his time became devoted to his flower and vegetable gardening, fishing, and golf. Postretirement, his marriage foundered and he and Ann Gwin were divorced.

Subsequently he met and married Mary Ann Conrad, whose former husband had also been in the U.S. Air Force. To the never-ending question as to whether he regretted dropping the bomb, Tom invariably answered the same way Dutch and Paul always did—"absolutely not!" In a 1985 interview with the *Orlando Sentinel*, Ferebee put the matter into even sharper focus when he said that writers and reporters consistently confused regret with remorse. The men of the *Enola Gay* were not sorry they had to drop the bomb, though they were sorry people had to get killed. But that was the way it was in war, Ferebee explained. The bomb was necessary because it would help shorten the war and stop the killing.[35] As Van Kirk often pointed out in his public talks, about five thousand people were still being killed every day that the fighting continued.

The man Tibbets called "the best bombardier who ever looked through the eyepiece of a Norden bombsight" died at home of pancreatic cancer on March 16, 2000, at the age of eighty-one.[36] His hometown of Mocksville, North Carolina, gave him a hero's good-bye (the funeral cortege was over two miles long), with both Paul and Dutch delivering eulogies.

After enduring a short period of purgatory under Colonel Blanchard at Roswell Field, Col. Paul Tibbets was able to get a fresh start.[37] Following graduation from the USAF Air Command and Staff School, he was assigned to the Air Force Requirements Division at the Pentagon. Due to his experience, he was posted to the bombardment division, where he would soon make significant contributions to American bomber development. One day in 1948 General Spaatz summoned Colonel Tibbets, World War II quadruple-ace Col. Dave Schilling, and Lt. Gen. Jimmy Doolittle to his office.[38] He said the president wanted to see all four of them at the White House immediately. After the officers were seated in the Oval Office, Truman entered the room and greeted everyone with a big smile. Contrary to normal protocol, Colonel Tibbets, the lowest-ranking man in the room, had been told to sit directly to the president's left. Spaatz, Doolittle, and Schilling, in that order, were seated to Truman's right.

The president got right to the point. First, he congratulated General Spaatz on becoming the first chief of staff of the U.S. Air Force. General Doolittle was praised for leading the famous 1942 raid against major cities in the Japanese Home Islands. Colonel Schilling was recognized for his groundbreaking work in aerial refueling. Truman than turned to Tibbets and looked at him for several long seconds.

"What do you think?" the president finally said. Tibbets replied, "Mr. President, I think I did what I was told." According to Tibbets, Truman slapped his hand on the desk and said, "You're damn right you did, and I'm the guy who sent you. If anybody gives you a hard time about it, refer them to me."[39]

The late 1940s was a pivotal moment for the USAF, and Paul Tibbets was right in the middle of it. The big question was whether future strategic bombers should continue to be propeller-driven (the huge Convair B-36 Peacemaker) or should they go all-jet (the B-47 Stratojet). For a variety of reasons, the decision was not as clear-cut then as it is today in hindsight. Tibbets cast his lot with the B-47, helping to sell the idea to the top brass that they should at least purchase a limited number of the sleek bombers. By 1950 the first production models were ready and Tibbets wangled his way into Boeing's flight testing program at their Wichita, Kansas, facility. Thus began what he always regarded as his most enjoyable flying tour of duty. Approximately the same size as the B-29, the Stratojet handled more like a fighter and flew at speeds just shy of the speed of sound. It was a wonderfully handling bird that Tibbets often said was a real pleasure to fly.

About this same time Gen. Curtis LeMay, who had been charged with molding the new SAC into an effective deterrent against the Soviet Union, was becoming increasingly concerned about bomber aircrew morale. The hours were long, families were continually separated, divorce rates were skyrocketing, and aircrew recruitment was down. Former bomber pilot and writer Beirne Lay Jr., following his successful book and movie *Twelve O'Clock High*, suggested to his old friend LeMay that he should agree to Hollywood's request to make a movie about the 509th Composite Group. The result was *Above and Beyond* starring Robert Taylor as Col. Paul Tibbets. The picture received mixed reviews but did well at the box office. Tibbets thought it turned out about as well as could be expected, considering the way things were done with biographical films in those days.

After his B-47 work, and like Ferebee, Tibbets drew a NATO assignment to France. A long separation from Lucy had by that time led to an amicable divorce, with the two boys remaining with their mother. While stationed in Europe he met Andrea Quattrehomme, who in 1956 became his second wife. After two years abroad, Tibbets returned to the United States to take command of the problem-plagued 308th Bomb Wing, a B-47 unit located at Savannah, Georgia. The assignment had not been simply the luck of the draw. The wing was part of Second Air Force, commanded by then–major general Frank Armstrong, who clearly remembered how well he and Tibbets had worked together turning around the 97th Bomb Group back in 1942. Armstrong's faith was amply justified—"within a year the Savannah wing moved from the bottom to the top of the SAC totem pole."[40] Paul Tibbets' reward was command of an air division and a general's star.

The early 1960s saw General Tibbets serving at the Pentagon (where he reported directly to General LeMay) followed by a military-diplomatic mission to India. Tibbets found himself mired in considerable controversy on the subcontinent—he was heavily criticized by the Indian press for his role in the atomic bombings. Although it was not a happy assignment, Tibbets served out his tour, returning to the Pentagon two years later. Unfortunately, his old enemies had exacted their final revenge.[41] He had been assigned to a minor dead-end job, an insult for a senior officer of his experience and ability. That tore it for the proud Tibbets. He retired from the U.S. Air Force as a brigadier general in 1966, credited with thirty years of service.

Paul Tibbets was not unemployed for long. He became president of Executive Jet Aviation, "an all-jet, air taxi company with headquarters in Columbus, Ohio."[42] Although the firm had its ups and downs—once again he was to lead another turnaround—the experience was quite fulfilling. He was able to both manage the business and fly many of the trips himself (Executive was among the first to operate the revolutionary new Learjet). By 1986 the business was on a sound enough financial footing to be profitably sold to a New York leasing and financing company. At that point Tibbets took stock of himself. He was seventy-one years old, his hearing was going (a price so many of the early pilots paid), and his reflexes were slowing. After nearly fifty years of "kicking the tires and lighting the fires," he decided it was time to hang up the headset.

After all three men had retired from their military and business careers, Paul, Tom, and Dutch began to spend more and more time together, occasions they all deeply treasured. They also committed themselves "to sharing the truth first hand [with the American public about the atomic bombings]. They were passionate about others hearing [directly] from them—not revisionists who were not there."[43] Always, there was order in the things they did together; even the gang's recreation was strictly organized by Paul. As it had been when young, so it was in his old age—Tibbets remained the unquestioned leader.

In the mid-1990s, concurrent with the marking of the fiftieth anniversary of the atomic bombings and the end of World War II, the Smithsonian Institution in Washington, D.C., announced plans for a new exhibit revolving around the *Enola Gay*. Initially pleased at the news, the musketeers were horrified when they saw preliminary scripts of "The Crossroads: The End of World War II, the Atomic Bomb, and the Cold War." What they had assumed would be a straightforward presentation of the facts surrounding the decision to use the weapons was instead a revisionist polemic that largely portrayed the Japanese as victims of American brutality. That theme was to be further reinforced by such charges as American racism and by stating that the number of expected American casualties (dead, wounded, missing, or captured) in a Home Islands invasion would have been only 63,000 soldiers—thus inferring that the atomic bombs had been unnecessary to gain a surrender. (That casualty estimate was preposterous in itself—the U.S. suffered 65,000 *actual* casualties during the Battle of Okinawa alone.[44]) Another item that infuriated the musketeers was the plan to show a disproportionately large number of atomic casualty images and only a handful of Japanese atrocity photos of the Rape of Nanking, the Pearl Harbor sneak attack, the Bataan Death March, the awful mistreatment of American prisoners of war, and so on—Van Kirk stated the ratio was planned at twenty to one.

Once the public and World War II veterans became fully aware of the content in the Crossroads exhibit (a campaign led most prominently by John T. Correll, then editor of *Air Force Magazine*, and by the American Legion), a great hue and cry arose. A stunned Smithsonian made several attempts to restructure the program to one more acceptable, but nothing they did satisfied the critics. After Congress got into the act, the pressure became too intense and the Smithsonian cancelled the exhibit. As the *Washington Post* put it on February 1, 1995: "Narrow-minded representatives of a special-interest and revisionist point of view attempted to use their inside track to appropriate and hollow out a historical event that large numbers of Americans alive at that time . . . had witnessed and understood in a very different—and authentic—way." All the same, it was painfully clear a growing number of people—both private individuals and public officials—had become either sympathetic to the revisionists or apathetic or ignorant about the matter altogether.

The Smithsonian affair was a bitter pill for the musketeers to swallow. With their advancing ages and this apparent new disconnect coming from their fellow Americans, much of the wind went out of their sails. Interviews grew fewer and public appearances became rarer. The men more and more retreated into their private lives, only allowing themselves to be present at events where they were certain they would be favorably treated.

In 1996 Tibbets was enshrined in the National Aviation Hall of Fame (NAHF). Located at Dayton, Ohio, in the National Museum of the U.S. Air Force, the NAHF is dedicated to honoring individuals (military or civilian) who have made unique contributions to aviation; it is one of the highest honors a flyer can be accorded. In a later tribute following Tibbets' passing, the NAHF released a statement that said "he pioneered the tactics of aerial warfare, enabled freedom to prevail in ending WWII, helped lead the Air Force from the piston to the jet age, and was instrumental to the development of corporate jet aviation."[45] They might also have added that, to the end, he consistently maintained his poise and dignity against a nearly lifelong assault on his personal character by hostile historians and antiwar and antinuclear activists.

In September 1999, very belatedly, the 509th Composite Group was awarded the Air Force Outstanding Unit Award (with Valor) "for exceptionally outstanding achievement in combat for the period of 1 July 1945 to 14 August 1945."[46] After many years, the Smithsonian Institution finally commissioned a long-overdue full restoration of the *Enola Gay*. The project was completed in 2003; incredibly, the airplane's various sections had been disassembled since 1960 and the parts shunted from one location to another—the ship treated like an unwanted orphan child. But thanks to a dedicated group of volunteers, the B-29 was at last beautifully rebuilt to appear exactly as it did on August 6, 1945, and is today on display at the Smithsonian's Udvar-Hazy Center at Washington Dulles Airport.

The decades following the atomic bombings were filled with yin and yang. The defining experience of the three men's lives was to simultaneously bring praise and criticism, admiration and loathing, honors and condemnation. Initially it had all been positive—the nation and its fighting men were enormously grateful the bombs had brought an end to the fighting, making a bloody invasion of the Home Islands unnecessary. Later, as time went on and the nation could afford the luxury of second-guessing, Hiroshima and Nagasaki became a double-edged sword. In one camp, the fellows would always be considered heroes; in the other, they became symbolic of a weapon believed so monstrous that it was itself inherently evil. The two opposite forces pulled at the three airmen for the remainder of their lives, with each man finding his own way to deal with the hand he was dealt. It had been as the new millennium dawned that they were tested the most severely. The vast majority of the American fighting men slated for the invasion and whose lives they had saved were either enfeebled or dead, the younger people uninformed or disinterested, and the critics now the louder voice. It became more and more difficult to maintain their personal perspective and public equitability. In Tibbets' final newspaper interviews, when he was beset by painful physical issues and almost deaf, one can sense the deep weariness from so long defending himself and his actions. It was almost as if he had come to welcome the fast-approaching long sleep.

In a 2005 interview with the *Columbus Dispatch*, a still-defiant Paul Tibbets said, "I don't fear a goddamn thing. I'm not afraid of dying." And how, the question was asked, do you want your passing to be handled? "As soon as the death certificate is signed, I wanted to be cremated. I don't want a funeral . . . [no] monuments or plaques. I want my ashes scatted over . . . the English Channel."[47] What went unsaid was clear enough—Paul Tibbets was not going to take any chances that his physical gravesite would be defiled.

The final wishes of Brig. Gen. Paul W. Tibbets Jr., who passed away at Columbus, Ohio, on November 1, 2007, at age ninety-two, were faithfully carried out to the letter by his wife, Andrea. He was further survived by his two natural sons, Paul III and Gene, and an adopted son, James (Andrea's son). Almost poetically, Paul III's own son followed in his grandfather's footsteps. "P4," as his family and Tibbets' old friends call him, graduated from the U.S. Air Force Academy and is a rated aircraft commander in the B-2 Spirit stealth bomber, B-1B Lancer, and the B-52H Stratofortress. Poignantly, he has served as commander of his grandfather's old unit, the 393rd Bomb Squadron of the 509th Bomb Wing (B-2 bombers) located at Whiteman Air Force Base, Missouri. In March 2014 Paul W. Tibbets IV was promoted to brigadier general, USAF, and as of this writing remains on active duty.[48]

For Paul, Tom, and Dutch personally, the decades following their military and civilian retirements were the sweetest. Their friendship, always robust, became even stronger. No matter how many individual gatherings, military reunions, public events, and family visits to such places as Branson, Missouri, they shared, it was never quite enough. They were always looking forward to the next get-together, not tiring for a moment in the telling and retelling of their old soldier stories. Always it had been and always it would be *one for all and all for one.*

# Appendix

## The Near-Catastrophic Nagasaki Mission

### The Men on Board *Bockscar*, August 9, 1945

#### *Flight Crew*

Aircraft Commander/Pilot—Maj. Charles W. Sweeney
Copilot—1st Lt. Charles D. Albury
Third Pilot—2nd Lt. Fred J. Olivi
Navigator—Capt. James F. Van Pelt Jr.
Bombardier—Capt. Kermit K. Beahan
Flight Engineer—MSgt. John D. Kuharek
Radio Operator—Cpl. Abe M. Spitzer
Assistant Flight Engineer/Scanner—Sgt. Raymond G. Gallagher
Radar Operator/Scanner—SSgt. Edward R. Buckley
Tail Gunner—Sgt. Albert T. DeHart

#### *Weapon Specialists*

Weaponeer—Cdr. Frederick L. Ashworth, USN
Weapons Test Officer—1st Lt. Philip M. Barnes
Radar Countermeasures Officer—1st Lt. Jacob Beser

While the Hiroshima mission was a textbook flight that went exactly as planned, the August 9 attack on Nagasaki was its evil doppelganger. Due to bad weather and poor decision making at both the staff and crew levels, it very nearly resulted in the jettisoning of the priceless Fat Man plutonium bomb into the Pacific Ocean and the loss of the entire *Bockscar* crew as well—which would have been a colossal disaster.

Early in the evening of August 6 and after flying the instrument aircraft on the Hiroshima mission, an exhausted Maj. Charles Sweeney was heading back to his quarters to hit the sack. He ran into Col. Paul Tibbets, who informed him that, if it became necessary—if Japan did not surrender within the next seventy-two hours—he, Sweeney, would command the second atomic mission scheduled for August 9. Detailed planning for the strike was already well under way, with the route and chart work spearheaded by group navigator Dutch Van Kirk. The targets selected were Kokura (primary) and Nagasaki (secondary).[1] The planners did not include the usual tertiary target on this mission, probably because only Niigata remained on the short list of approved atomic targets and it was too far to the north—well beyond B-29 range if Kokura and Nagasaki were preferred ahead of it.

It was already apparent that the weather en route and over Japan was going to be a problem. The relatively clear skies that Tibbets and company had enjoyed were rapidly disappearing as conditions in the northwest Pacific worsened. Most seriously, there was a typhoon brewing around Iwo Jima, which meant that the most direct track to the Empire was out. A roundabout route was developed to the three-plane attack element's rendezvous point over a very small island called Yakushima, just south of Kyushu. Due to the poor weather at lower altitudes, the decision was made to make an early climb to the bombing altitude of 30,000 feet, which meant fuel consumption was going to be greater than normal. Further, this new route meant a good five hours of flying to the rendezvous point, much of it on instruments and with few opportunities for good navigation fixes. The three ships would not be in visual contact all that time.

The more Van Kirk and Ferebee studied the navigation and rendezvous problems, the more worried they became. At length, the two men met with Tibbets and Sweeney, telling them they believed that the rendezvous plan was beyond the capability of the crews. The navigation and weather obstacles were so great, they said—to say nothing of the difficulty in actually being able to see one another while flying back and forth in the cloudy stratosphere—that a high-altitude, visual rendezvous would be next to impossible. "You cannot do it fellows," Dutch stated. Sweeney disagreed, saying "Yes we can." With that, the discussion ended.[2]

Meanwhile, technical issues arose regarding the three strike airplanes. Sweeney's (usually Albury's) "regular" B-29, *The Great Artiste*, had been modified as the instrument ship for the Hiroshima mission, and it made little sense to reconfigure the airplane just to keep his crew and "their" aircraft together. It was therefore decided that Sweeney would fly Fred Bock's bomber, *Bockscar*, with Captain Bock flying the instrument plane, *The Great Artiste*. The group operations officer, recently promoted Lt. Col. James Hopkins, would command Norman Ray's crew C-14 (Ray had fallen ill) in the photographic airplane, *Big Stink*. This last-minute switch between Bock and Sweeney resulted in the designated press correspondent on the mission, science reporter William Laurence, mistakenly reporting back to his paper, the *New York Times*, that the Nagasaki bomber had been *The Great Artiste*. Much more seriously, this seemingly routine change of airplanes contributed to major operational issues during the mission, something that would only become clear after it was too late.

As had been done three days earlier, staff and crews assembled in the afternoon and evening of August 8 for the various briefings. All went smoothly until just before it was time for the crews to board transport to their aircraft. In spite of the resolve he had exhibited in the meeting with Tibbets and Van Kirk, Sweeney had indeed been concerned about the Yakushima rendezvous. Because

Hopkins did not fly regularly (one has to wonder why another of Tibbets' highly trained, *intact* crews was not selected), Sweeney suggested a brief discussion regarding how the three ships were going to pull the thing off. According to Sweeney, Hopkins (a West Pointer) was dismissive toward the reserve officer, saying, "I know how to make a rendezvous, Major, you don't need to tell me how it is done." Sweeney said Hopkins' voice "conveyed aggravation at the intrusion." The rendezvous discussion with Fred Bock a few minutes later, on the other hand, went swimmingly.[3]

Everything was routine through the preflights and up to the time when the three aircrews boarded their aircraft to start engines. According to Tibbets, Sweeney had already started all four engines and then suddenly shut them down. Sweeney said, however, that he had not yet started the engines when his flight engineer, John Kuharek, told him the transfer pump in the rear bomb bay's fuel bladder was inoperative, trapping 640 gallons of gasoline.[4] Whichever way it happened, Sweeney and Kuharek crawled out of the airplane and walked over to Tibbets, who was standing with the rest of the staff and onlookers (a crowd understandably much reduced from the first mission). Sweeney explained about the unusable gas. Tibbets reminded him the bomb bay fuel was there mostly for ballast (to ensure the ship's fore/aft center of gravity stayed within the envelope) and should not be needed. Still, Sweeney was concerned; as the old saying went, "You never have too much fuel unless the aircraft is on fire." While Sweeney continued to dither, Tibbets told him he was already late taking off, and he would either have to go right now or, as the aircraft commander, call the mission an abort. Not surprisingly, that idea was abhorrent to Sweeney and he said OK, it is a go. He and Kuharek scurried up the nose hatch ladder and fired up their engines.[5]

At 4:15 a.m. local Tinian time, already one hour and fifteen minutes behind schedule, *Bockscar* took off, with *The Great Artiste* and *Big Stink* following right behind. As with the first mission, the weather planes had taken off an hour earlier. Capt. George Marquardt, flying the *Enola Gay*, would recon Kokura; Capt. Charles McKnight in *Top Secret* would check out Nagasaki. Capt. Ralph Taylor in *Full House* was designated the Iwo Jima spare, that part of the mission profile still in place despite the highly unlikely possibility that Sweeney would venture so far to the east and into an expected typhoon.

There were two other events or circumstances affecting the mission that warrant mention. The first involved the photo plane, *Big Stink*. According to several conflicting reports, the most authoritative written by Fred Bock in *509th Remembered*, Lt. Col. Hopkins, a stickler for regulations, discovered that one of his crewmen, Dr. Robert Serber, Project Alberta's photographic expert, was without a parachute, having mistaken a one-man life raft for his chute.[6] This was perfectly understandable. The scientist was a nonflying civilian who had been caught in the middle of a black-out—Tinian radar had detected airborne threats approaching the island while Serber was drawing his equipment and all the lights on North Field were extinguished. The upshot was Hopkins told Serber he could not fly without a parachute, and he was to get off the plane and get one. Inexplicably, Hopkins then promptly took off, leaving behind the only man assigned to his crew that knew how to operate the rather complicated Fastax camera system. In disbelief that such a thing could have occurred over a relatively minor matter on such a high-stakes mission, Serber immediately reported to Gen. Thomas Farrell, the Manhattan Project deputy director. An upset Farrell broke radio silence to contact Hopkins, whereupon after a strained conversation Serber relayed instructions to the pilot on how to use the camera. Hopkins radioed back that he hoped he had it all straight in his mind. According to third pilot Fred Olivi, in his book *Decision at Nagasaki*, the *Big Stink* flew to Nagasaki after they saw the mushroom cloud and did get some usable photography.[7]

The second and much more serious matter involved a controversy over *Bockscar*'s fuel transfer problem, one that continues to this day. Sweeney and Kuharek always maintained that the bomb bay fuel pump was completely inoperable.[8] In his book, Olivi diplomatically steered clear of the subject except to say the crew did not learn of the difficulty until they were well into the mission (which seems problematic considering the heavy discussion with Tibbets about the trouble prior to takeoff).[9] The mission's weaponeer for this flight, Deak Parsons' assistant, U.S. Navy commander Fred Ashworth, believed the bomb bay fuel transfer pump could have been made operable. Writing many years later in *509th Remembered*, Ashworth asserted that "Fred Bock's engineer proved later that there was no reason the fuel could not have been transferred." Ashworth said that the engineer, Sgt. Arnold, knew *Bockscar*'s fuel systems intimately and was familiar with the temperamental nature of that particular fuel pump, apparently having learned to deal with it. A naval aviator and combat veteran of the Guadalcanal campaign, Ashworth went on to say the mission had been put at risk by not allowing Fred Bock and his crew to fly their own airplane, rather than a crew unfamiliar with it.[10] However, everyone considered the Silverplate airplanes interchangeable and, except for unpredictable mechanicals and certain mission modifications, they were. Commander Ashworth, a single-seat Navy fighter pilot without multicrewed bomber experience, may have believed a little too strongly in the necessity of firmly wedding crews to airplanes.

Lt. Jacob Beser, the countermeasures officer and the only man to fly on both atomic missions, had a more specific criticism in his *509th Remembered* account. Beser contended that *Bockscar*'s crew chief, Sgt. Fred Clayton, personally told him that he, Clayton, had preflighted the transfer system in question and found it operational. According to Beser, Clayton then briefed Sweeney's engineer, Kuharek, telling him to "just turn the pumps on and leave them on" and the fuel will eventually start transferring.[11] In the end, the actual circumstances on that bomb bay fuel bladder may never be known.

After another hair-raising, overloaded takeoff that used nearly every foot of Runway Able, Sweeney and crew settled into the standard departure out of Tinian. Attention soon turned to monitoring the weapon, a routine that was somewhat different from the first mission. *Bockscar* was carrying a Fat Man plutonium device and could not be finally assembled in the air, so it was almost completely armed prior to takeoff. Aside from monitoring their cabin instruments, the only physical action required by the weaponeers prior to pressurizing the aircraft was for Commander Ashworth to crawl into the bomb bay (while Lieutenant Barnes held a flashlight) and replace the green safety plugs with red plugs, thereby completing the circuitry and fully arming the weapon. Once that chore was completed, the flight crew began the climb to altitude and concentrated on the navigation to the rendezvous point.

En route, the crew had a real scare when a red light began flashing on the Fat Man monitoring system, which meant, according to the book, that the fusing system had been activated! While everyone looked on apprehensively, Barnes opened up a "black box" and after several feverish minutes discovered that a ground technician had placed two bomb firing switches in the wrong position. Barnes calmly toggled them into the proper mode and the monitoring light returned to green. It was some time before the forward compartment crew, all of whom had been staring at the terrifying red light, regained their composure.[12]

At 9:10 a.m. Tinian time, *Bockscar* arrived at Yakushima and began its rendezvous orbit. Almost immediately *The Great Artiste* was sighted, with Fred Bock promptly tucking himself in next to one of Sweeney's wings. Hopkins, however, was nowhere to be seen. It was decided to give him the fifteen minutes allotted to show up. Tibbets stated in the third and most frank version of his autobiography that he told Sweeney to make just one 360 degree turn and if either of his two escorts were not there, to proceed to the target without them.[13] Sweeney, however, wrote in his book, *War's End*, that he had orders to wait up to fifteen minutes.[14] This is confirmed by Fred Olivi, who said that "everybody on *Bockscar* heard Tibbets say fifteen minutes—'No longer than fifteen minutes.'"[15]

But never mind which one of those timelines was the imperative; forty minutes later Sweeney was still orbiting. It was at this point that the dual-command structure that had worked so well under Tibbets and Parsons began to break down. Ostensibly, Sweeney was in command of the airplane; Ashworth in charge of Fat Man. If all had been going smoothly, there would not have been a problem, but on this night things were rapidly going south. The two men found themselves with very different opinions as to how to proceed.

It must be remembered that Commander Ashworth was not only a pilot and combat veteran, he also outranked Major Sweeney—his grade equivalent to an AAF lieutenant colonel. As John Correll, the former editor of *Air Force Magazine*, wrote in a July 2011 article: "Influence was another matter, and Ashworth exerted a powerful influence on Sweeney."[16] Fred Olivi tells us that during the long wait over Yakushima, Sweeney and Ashworth's discussion (the latter man now standing between the pilot and Albury) devolved into what amounted to a shouting match.[17]

This must have given the crew a deep sense of foreboding. Sweeney remained desperate to have a perfect mission—like Tibbets—and he was loath to leave the rendezvous point without the photo plane. Ashworth was equally concerned about the missing plane, but for a different reason. Due to the confusion, he thought the missing aircraft was Fred Bock's *Great Artiste*, which bore the much more important instruments critical to measuring the effects of the blast. As a consequence, the commander had kept the pressure on Sweeney to continuing orbiting, but now, after the long delay, both leaders understood the entire enterprise was being put at risk.

Also, Kuharek had to have been getting more and more concerned about their high rate of gasoline consumption. The premature climb to altitude had driven his normal fuel curve off the charts, to say nothing of that trapped 640 gallons in the rear bomb bay. At the very least, sometime during the orbiting, he and Sweeney must have discussed their precarious fuel status. Finally, after either forty or forty-five minutes (accounts vary) circling Yakushima, Sweeney said to copilot Albury, "That's it. Let's get the hell out of here." Van Pelt gave the heading to Kokura (the ancient city was renamed Kitakyushu in 1963) on the northern tip of Kyushu, and Sweeney swung the ship around to the new course.

It is still unclear what happened on the missed rendezvous. Sweeney claimed in his book that he later got the full story from RAF group captain Leonard Cheshire, who was the British representative to Project Alberta flying on board Hopkins' aircraft. According to Sweeney, Cheshire told him that Hopkins approached Yakushima at 39,000 feet, 9,000 feet higher than briefed, and made fifty-mile doglegs around the island, instead of circling the southwest corner of the island, which was apparently the designated point.[18] While Sweeney seems sincere in presenting this scenario, it requires us to suspend belief in the capability of the B-29 and its reciprocating (albeit supercharged) engines. The listed service ceiling for the wartime B-29 was 31,850 feet. Certainly anything up to, say, as high as 33,000 feet would have been hard to sustain for even brief periods. The idea of holding 39,000 feet in a B-29 boggles the mind. In his book, Fred Olivi said he did not buy the story of Hopkins being even as high as 35,000 feet and that he, Olivi, "tended to discount [Sweeney's] version of the 'missing third aircraft.'"[19]

It is my view that Van Kirk had his finger on the real problem when he warned both Sweeney and Tibbets of the difficulty of being able to actually see the other aircraft under less-than-ideal rendezvous conditions. The airplanes could easily pass within a few miles of each other and not make visual contact. I can personally attest to the difficulty; even on clear days and at those altitudes, Cold War B-52 pilots relied on their navigator-bombardiers to provide a radar-directed intercept to the KC-135 air refueling tankers. It is a very, *very* big sky. Such realities forces one to ask the most important question: Why did the three attack aircraft not simply fly up together in a loose formation? Some kind of contact could have been maintained along the way, and all of that complicated and needless rendezvous business could have been completely avoided.

I asked Van Kirk that very question. After all, other B-29s were flying in staggered formations out of the Marianas every day; it was not something new. Dutch could only shrug his shoulders.[20] Perhaps the formation idea simply never occurred to the staff. That was not the way the 509th was operating on Tinian—the Silverplate bombers had been flying most of their Empire pumpkin missions solo, and that appeared to be the order of the day.

At about the same time that *Bockscar* pointed its nose toward the initial point of its primary target, Kokura, confusion was also reigning on board *Big Stink* (in his book, Sweeney ruefully stated that name seemed particularly appropriate[21]). Hopkins had realized the mission was getting away from him, and he finally broke radio silence, sending a voice query back to Tinian: "Has Sweeney aborted?"

That communication was very unfortunate and could have had devastating consequences. As sometimes happens with high-frequency, long-range voice radio messages that skip off the ionosphere, the message was garbled as: "*Sweeney has aborted.*" Hopkins' transmission resulted in great consternation at Tinian; General Farrell assumed the worse—the mission had been lost and maybe the crew too. (Admiral Purnell became so upset he tossed his cookies, something that always endeared him to *Bockscar*'s crew.) That was not the worst of it; Hopkins' message resulted in the recall of all submarines and Dumbo and Super Dumbo rescue aircraft from their stations off the Japanese coastlines. If any of the three atomic mission aircraft still over the Empire went down now, there would be no hope of rescue.

At 10:20 a.m. Tinian time, *Bockscar* made the initial point inbound turn to Kokura. Capt. Kermit Beahan realized almost immediately that the bomb run was in trouble. The entire city was obscured by what appeared to be heavy cloud. Only thirty minutes earlier, the last weather report from George Marquardt had said the weather was reasonably clear over the target. What had happened? The answer started with something Major Sweeney had observed the night before—the launch of over two hundred Tinian-based, incendiary-weaponed B-29s directed against the industrial city of Yawata (the "Pittsburgh of Japan"), a short distance upwind of Kokura. In just that half hour, the smoke from the Yawata fires had arrived over Kokura, obscuring the city. The needless delay over Yakushima trying to find Lieutenant Colonel Hopkins was becoming exceedingly costly.

Sweeney started the bomb run with Beahan searching hard for the aiming point, the Kokura Arsenal. The minutes ticked by as the bombardier squirmed in his seat, head bobbing between looking out the greenhouse window and the Norden eyepiece. Finally: "I can't see the target! No drop!"

As Sweeney swung the ship around for another run, he saw flak bursts. Chuck said in his book that the flak was at their 31,000-foot altitude and fairly intense. Fred Olivi painted a different picture: "As we started the [second] run, I noticed a few puffs of black smoke . . . below our 29,000 altitude. . . . The ack-ack exploded well below us."[22]

The second bomb run against the Kokura Arsenal was a repeat of the first. "I can't see it!" Beahan yelled again. "No drop!" Sweeney announced. Around they went for a third time. Sweeney makes no mention of what happened over the next few minutes, but third pilot Olivi matter-of-factly spelled it out for us. Ashworth, Sweeney, and flight engineer Kuharek were having a very animated conversation on the flight deck. Olivi claimed he could not hear all of the conversation (possibly a diplomatic hearing malfunction), but what he did get greatly disturbed him. For it was at this moment, so he wrote, that he first learned of the trapped fuel in the aft bomb bay. Curiously, in a conflicting statement in his own book, Olivi published an account by Kermit Beahan stating that Kuharek had told the rest of the crew about the fuel problem while climbing to altitude en route to Yakushima, which would make more sense.[23] The matter remains yet another unresolved inconsistency in this tale.

Following the long wait at the rendezvous point and with the weather problems over Kokura, the dimensions of the fuel problems had now grown exponentially. No matter what happened from this point forward, the crew was in deep trouble. Earlier decisions were coming home to roost—the climb to pressurized altitudes relatively soon after takeoff had dramatically increased the fuel burn rate, they had spent three-quarters of an hour orbiting Yakushima, and two fruitless bomb runs had already been made on Kokura (the people of that area still today speak of "Kokura luck" when fortune suddenly smiles). All of a sudden a friendly airfield was very far away; the crew of *Bockscar* now very much *needed* those 640 gallons of gasoline trapped in the rear bomb bay (the B-29 burned about 400 gallons per hour). At length, Ashworth apparently convinced Sweeney to make a third and last bomb run on Kokura, coming in from a different angle (Ashworth later denied "insisting" on another try[24]). It was no more successful than the first two. Deeply disgruntled, the crew turned for the secondary, Nagasaki.

Another odd thing happened following the third Kokura run—like bananas, airplane troubles come in bunches. As Sweeney maneuvered his ship in a southwesterly direction toward Nagasaki, a city located on the western coast of Kyushu (and fortunately on the same relative heading needed to get to the closest Allied airfield on Okinawa), the abrupt turn caught Fred Bock in *The Great Artiste* off guard. When Fred dropped back to avoid a possible collision, Sweeney lost a visual on him. Chuck hit his mike button to ask "Where's Bock?" and in so doing he inadvertently bumped his intercom/command radio toggle switch with an elbow—instead of the transmission going over the airplane's intercom, it went out ship-to-ship. Seconds later, from out of the ether came the voice of the missing Lieutenant Colonel Hopkins in *Big Stink*: "Chuck? Is that you? Where the hell are you?"

A flabbergasted Sweeney was furious; Hopkins had needlessly broken radio silence and perhaps compromised one or both of their positions. Chuck made no effort to respond to Hopkins but instead settled himself down for the one-hundred-mile dash to Nagasaki, though he did turn to copilot Don Albury and wearily ask him if "any other goddamned thing could go wrong."[25] Twenty minutes later, he got his answer. Nagasaki was socked in with nine-tenths cloud cover.

On the way down to the secondary, Olivi had written in his mission log, "Reducing power to save gas—wonder if the Pacific will be cold? Our chances of ditching are—good!!! Bomb MUST be dropped for more reasons than one."[26]

The belabored commanders, Sweeney and Ashworth, had finally decided that if necessary they would set aside the "optical release only" orders and make a radar run. It would have been inconceivably humiliating for either man to not only fail to drop the nation's most rare and destructive weapon on an enemy target, but to also have to jettison it into the ocean and lose the priceless plutonium forever. Almost certainly, Commander Ashworth was aware there was only one more operational atomic bomb in the entire American inventory. The situation also presented a very real personal dimension—nobody on the flight deck could have been unaware that they had not the gas to carry around that five-ton payload any more than a few minutes longer and still survive themselves. Better at every level that they should take a chance on dropping Fat Man by radar and hope for the best. For sure, one way or the other, there would be time and fuel for just one run on Nagasaki, no more.

This decision to go with a radar release was not easy. While at that time in the war, U.S. radar mapping capability was still mostly classified, key leaders clearly understood the great promise it offered. By using mapping radar, which is to say a radar that paints ground returns, an operator trained properly in radar scope interpretation can almost literally "see" on his cathode ray tube presentation such ground images as lakes, rivers, dams, mountain tops, cities, and even large buildings—at night and in any weather. As discussed in the main narrative, the Silverplate bombers, like most B-29s then in the Pacific Theater, could use this radar to make a "blind" bomb run. Although both radar operators and the newer navigators had received extensive training in the new discipline, B-29 fleet capabilities in the middle of 1945 were still uneven—some crews were skilled at making radar bomb deliveries; others were still learning. As a result, radar technology was still not considered completely trustworthy, and that had resulted in the orders from General Groves to drop the atomic bombs "only by visual means." These were the circumstances, then, that presented Sweeney and Ashworth with the perfect conundrum. Radar was likely their only chance of successfully delivering the weapon, yet orders expressly forbade its use.

Beahan and the flight crew did depart the Nagasaki initial point intent on a radar run, but it morphed into something else. The bombardier would switch to the Norden optics at the last moments, maintaining all his life that he indeed "saw the aiming point" and "dropped visually." However, none other than Dutch Van Kirk is on record stating in public addresses, in his book, and in an interview with me that "Beahan never saw the aiming point! We know it. He knows it. But what the hell, the war is over."[27]

What are we to make of this? Both sources are extremely credible; Behan and Van Kirk were straight shooters. Plus, Beahan and Tom Ferebee were very close and what Behan knew, Ferebee knew, and therefore Van Kirk knew. There were no secrets between those men. Yet Beahan never changed his story, either in public or in private to his own family—without fail maintaining he had dropped visually. And so the military historian is left with yet another seemingly irreconcilable puzzle—what exactly did happen?

A possible explanation may lie in the wording of the questions asked and the answers given over the years. For example, Beahan may have meant he had lined up optically on his last-second *new* aiming point, the race track–stadium in the Urakami River valley. And Van Kirk may have been referring to the original aiming point, Nagasaki harbor's east-side docks. Of course there is one other explanation—Beahan may have seen just enough of Nagasaki through the clouds to inspire him to kind of make it an optical release, knowing at that point the bomb would hit a major portion of the city, both fulfilling the prime directive of an optical drop and giving himself and the crew at least a chance of surviving the mission. In the end, it all comes down to one's own interpretation of events. And rather than further belabor these inconsistencies, I will attempt to reconstruct the Nagasaki bomb run from what we do know, share a few of my own conclusions, and allow the reader to take it from there.

Beginning the account again with *Bockscar*'s crew crossing the initial point on the bomb run heading: the crew is doing everything it can to conserve fuel by reducing engine power to the most economical settings, which yielded an indicated airspeed of just 190 mph (accepting the risk of greater vulnerability to flak and fighters). Beahan had already inputted his precomputed bomb ballistic data into the Norden bombing system (NBS), along with the drift, airspeed, and true altitude data. Radar operator Buckley had his Q-13 radar in a 360 degree-scan sweep mode (technically called the PPI, or plan position indicator display) when he identified the briefed aiming point, the east-side docks. With that in hand, Buckley lined up the bearing marker on his scope and radioed the heading to Sweeney. He and Van Pelt calculated the winds and radioed the drift angle to Beahan, who inputted it into the NBS.

Captain Van Pelt, on the five-inch repeater scope, was technically in charge of a radar bomb run, with Sergeant Buckley his assistant. Course corrections to Sweeney were expressed as so many degrees left or right using "one-quarter needle-width turns," meaning very easy turning so as not to cause "spoking" on the radar or to aggravate the Norden's very delicate gyroscopes. Nagasaki's shipping docks were an excellent radar aiming point in that they offered the very best type of scope presentation—land/water contrast. When the aiming point reached a certain slant distance from the ship, Buckley reconfigured the Q-13 set into "sector scan" mode, which created a pie-shaped sweep presentation with the airplane at the point of the pie. This directed all the energy of the cavity magnetron into the sector sweep, magnifying the aiming point presentation. The largest drawback to the Q-13 radar scope was its small five-inch diameter—Buckley and Van Pelt practically had to squint to make out the returns on their tiny screens.

Along with the minor heading changes that Van Pelt was giving Sweeney, he and Buckley were giving Beahan periodic range calls to the aiming point:

"Thirty miles . . . Mark, now!"

"Twenty-five miles . . . Mark, now!"

With each call, Beahan entered the data into the NBS, which replaced the visual sighting angle information normally provided by the sighthead's rate and displacement knob. Meanwhile, like all bombardiers, Beahan kept a back-up stopwatch running, rehacking it after each mark call. Should the radar suddenly fail, a simple mathematical calculation using *Bockscar*'s ground speed would give him the number of elapsed seconds remaining before the dropping angle (release point) would be reached. One may think of this as a last-resort emergency procedure, a kind of dead-reckoning release.

In a handwritten summary prepared by Captain Beahan at the postmission debriefing, the bombardier stated that the Nagasaki bomb run lasted eight minutes. He reported that he momentarily saw the briefed aiming point (the east-side harbor docks) through a break in the clouds but realized if he took over at that point and then lost sight again he would have messed up what had so far been "a good job" by Van Pelt and Buckley on the radar bomb run. He therefore said nothing at that time to the crew.[28]

At about thirty seconds to go (records vary), the bombardier, so his report read, suddenly "spotted large hole in clouds—picked out race track—good to syn[chronize the Norden crosshairs] on."[29] Clearly, this was not the shipping docks, the briefed aiming point! However . . . as Beahan understood perfectly, it did offer the opportunity to bomb *visually*—assuming the city of Nagasaki generally was the de facto target—thereby not technically contravening General Groves' prime drop directive.

When Beahan acquired the racetrack (or stadium, it is never quite clear in the reports) through the Norden, he shouted, "I'll take it, I can see the target, there's a hole in the clouds." At that moment, radio operator Spitzer flipped on the radio tone to alert Bock the release was imminent.[30] All the critical release data had already been fed into the Norden and the automatic release system was functioning normally. Beahan clutched in the NBS, and it took control of the ship's heading. Everyone waited for the seconds to tick down.

"Bomb Away!" It was 11:01 a.m. Tinian time, August 9, 1945. Fat Man would impact nearly two miles from the briefed aiming point. Although this is only my speculation, it is possible Beahan made the release using a combination of stopwatch timing, radar bearings and range calls, and what he could see through the Norden bombsight. A bombardier in trouble will use every aid that is available to him, including his gut, expressed in bombardier-speak as "Kentucky windage."

Immediately after Fat Man left the airplane, Sweeney executed the violent breakaway maneuver. As at Hiroshima, after three-quarters of a minute the weapon detonated. And as with the first mission, the first shock wave arrived several seconds later. This time, however, due to the hills surrounding the blast site, there were four more shock waves that followed, each bouncing off the ground and the sides of hills.

After the aftershocks subsided, third pilot Fred Olivi remembered Jim Van Pelt joining him near the throttle pedestal, both men standing between Albury and Sweeney. Van Pelt kept saying over and over again how relieved he was that Beahan had taken the responsibility for dropping this terrifying weapon, and he had not been required to make a radar release. Jim Van Pelt later became a highly respected medical doctor, dedicated to saving lives.[31]

The crew very briefly circled the rapidly growing mushroom cloud, inadvertently getting dangerously close at one point, just as had the *Enola Gay*. Sgt. Raymond Gallagher alertly shouted a warning that the cloud was rapidly overtaking them. Sweeney did a sharp turn and fire-walled the engines, they only barely escaping—a closer call than Tibbets' crew had.

With *Bockscar*'s fuel situation having now gone critical, Sweeney pointed the ship toward their emergency airfield at Okinawa, instructing radio operator Abe Spitzer to tap out the bomb damage assessment report: "Nagasaki bombed. Results technically successful. Proceeding to Okinawa. Fuel problem." After two and one-half hours of deep suspense and uncertainty on Tinian, the brass was greatly relieved the weapon had been successfully delivered, though those concerns had been supplanted by news of Sweeney's fuel emergency.

The next several hours were, in Beahan's words, "really a sweat job."[32] Everyone on the crew was wondering if there would be enough fuel to get to Okinawa or if they would have to take a swim. Sweeney and Albury put the airplane "on the step," a fuel-saving technique involving normal power settings but trimming for a very gradual descent followed by a level off, then stepping down into another descent, and so on. If done properly, the procedure could also extract a little more speed, the only negative being the loss of altitude, which Sweeney had a good deal of, having started from 30,000 feet. Power was reduced from the recommended cruise rpm of 2,000 rpm to 1,600 rpm, to save a few more drops. There was little chatter in the cabin, each man lost in his own thoughts.

At long last the northern tip of Okinawa, the Ryukyu's largest island, slipped under *Bockscar*'s wings. It was still forty-five miles to Yontan Airfield and Kuharek's fuel gauges had settled on Empty. Sweeney had been hailing Yontan tower in order to request an emergency landing but could get no response; the field was extremely busy recovering their own Seventh Air Force bombers and escort fighters. After several more furious but futile attempts to make radio contact, and with *Bockscar* already in the landing pattern, Sweeney ordered Olivi to start shooting flares in hopes the other airplanes would clear out of the way. Olivi asked which color flares, and Sweeney shouted: "All of them!" Unfortunately for the crew's already strained nerves, the cockpit began filling with burned powder smoke from the discharged flares. The rear compartment crew was especially frightened. Strapped in on the other side of the long tunnel and seeing and smelling the smoke, they feared the aircraft had caught fire.[33]

At this point another discrepancy appears in the mission accounts. Sweeney said in his book that prior to ordering the flares, the right outboard engine (number four) quit from fuel starvation.[34] After feathering it, he ordered Albury to throttle up the right side inboard engine, number three, to compensate for lost power and asymmetrical thrust. This, he said, forced him to hold a much higher final approach speed in case another engine quit and the aircraft entered an approach stall due to low airspeed.[35] Indeed, Sweeney would come in very hot—Olivi tells us the B-29 normal best flare speed was about 120 mph and that Sweeney arrived at 150![36] (Sweeney said it was 140 mph.[37])

The primary problem with this scenario is that Olivi's first mention of an engine quitting occurs *after* the landing: "As we made the turn from the active runway, our inboard engine #2 twirled to a stop. No gas!"[38] He made no mention of an earlier loss of #4. Another version appeared in a 1984 handwritten memo by Kermit Beahan, which Olivi published in his own book, stating "as we taxied up to the airfield ramp both outboard engines (#1 and #4) sputtered to a stop."[39] Professional pilots reading this account may be tempted to conclude that Sweeney's discussion about an airborne engine loss and the need to hold a higher airspeed was intended to mask an excessively high approach speed on a relatively short and unfamiliar runway by a somewhat rattled aircraft commander. Once a pilot "has the airfield"—that is, once the airplane reaches a certain point and even if all power is lost—a safe "dead-stick landing" can still be conducted. There is more than one way to slow an aircraft down. One can simply chop power; if Sweeney did lose an engine on approach once he made the airfield, he could have pulled the throttles back on the left side rather than keep the power up on number three, allowing him to continue the approach at normal speeds. Another way to slow down is by sideslipping, which creates additional drag and reduces airspeed without loss of control. In *War's End*, Sweeney makes no mention of any attempt to slow the airplane down before touchdown.

The hot approach and landing was in fact extremely dangerous. For reasons one cannot explain, Sweeney matter-of-factly tells us he planned to land halfway down the seven-thousand-foot runway.[40] This would leave him with almost no room to stop. Even with the reversible (braking) propellers on the Silverplate Superforts, such a plan would still almost certainly have him running off into the weeds at the opposite end of the airport. As it was, according to Olivi, he landed hard and fast about one-third of the way down the pavement.[41] Predictably, the ship bounded about twenty-five feet back into the air. When the airplane arrived the second time, it was cocked to the left and began veering toward several parked B-24 Liberator bombers. Sweeney braked hard (no doubt hardest on the right pedal) and barely managed to get the ship straightened out, though by then they were rapidly running out of runway. He quickly reversed the props and stood on the brakes, and was just able to make a very tight right turn onto the last taxiway prior to the overrun—Olivi said that while it was almost a ground loop, "we were [at least] on the ground in one piece!"[42] With the entire crew still shaking, *Bockscar* limped into a hardstand to get refueled.

There is yet one more matter on the Okinawa approach and landing that needs addressing. During the penetration descent, Sweeney had passed by another American airfield that was three and a half to four minutes closer than Yontan, and apparently Sweeney never considered landing there instead. Located on the island of Ie Shima, the field had three runways compared to Yontan's two, its longest strip identical (7,000 feet long × 150 feet wide) to the one Sweeney eventually landed on. What is more, Sweeney had been in radio contact with the Ie Shima control tower, even asking them to patch him through to Yontan's tower. The question every pilot would ask—remember Sweeney was running on fumes and had an airport just off his starboard side that was some fourteen or fifteen miles closer than his destination field—is why did he not divert to Ie Shima?[43]

The answer can only lie in the overpowering imperative of the mission prebrief. In extremis, as Sweeney was, it is only natural to develop a certain tunnel vision and lose situational awareness. It apparently never occurred to the crew that in-flight circumstances had changed so drastically from the original plan that they should have reassessed their landing options—at that moment the United States was operating eleven separate Okinawan airfields that could be used in an emergency. It is also possible Sweeney was somehow influenced by the high-ranking Lt. Gen. Jimmy Doolittle's headquarters and presence on the Yontan field, but that is pure guesswork.

The balance of that incredible day was anticlimactic. Sweeney had trouble getting the brass to take him seriously enough to report his status back to Tinian. He finally got an audience with General Doolittle, who only weeks earlier had brought his Eighth Air Force from Europe to help with the expected land invasion of the Japanese homelands. Doolittle heard Sweeney's story and approved a radio report to Tibbets and Farrell. After about five hours on the island, fortified with a meal and full fuel tanks, Sweeney's crew—along with Bock and the long-lost Hopkins, both of whom had followed him in to Yontan—departed for Tinian and a full debriefing.

There were those in the 509th who seriously questioned Major Sweeney's selection as commander of the second atomic strike, perhaps most prominently then-commander Fred Ashworth.[44] He and others believed that aircraft commanders such as combat veteran and deputy group commander Lt. Col. Tom Classen, Capt. George Marquardt, Capt. Fred Bock, or even Lt. Don Albury were better qualified. One cannot help but suspect that Tibbets allowed friendship and his own bias to cloud his thinking—Chuck Sweeney and Bob Lewis had been his two personal aircraft commander picks for the Silverplate bombers; all the other aircraft commanders had been inherited when the 393rd Bomb Squadron was pulled out of the Pacific deployment schedule and assigned to the 509th Composite Group.

Long too proud to admit it, Tibbets clearly regretted his choice of Sweeney. In many interviews over the years, he gave hints, but it was only in 2005 that he made it clear. In a letter that retired U.S. Navy vice admiral Fred Ashworth wrote to Captain Beahan's daughter, Lisa Beahan Harrison, he said that Tibbets had been "asked recently if he would pick Sweeney again. 'Absolutely not,' Tibbets said. 'I would have given it to George Marquardt.' "[45]

In the third and final version (1998) of his autobiography, *Return of the Enola Gay*, released one year after Sweeney published *War's End*, Paul Tibbets created an entirely new chapter in which he turned on Sweeney, thoroughly excoriating him for his poor performance on August 9, 1945. In his book's two previous (1978 and 1989) editions, Tibbets had protected his squadron commander, saying the problems that occurred on the mission were "through no fault of Sweeney."[46] Tibbets completely reversed himself in 1998. "Even before Sweeney left the ground he revealed his indecisiveness [regarding the fuel problem. Later in the flight,] he was to proceed without delay to the target. He didn't."[47] Driving the point home, Tibbets emphasized, "He was in a jam of his own making. He was at fault."[48] Clearly the animosity had been smoldering below the surface for years, and Sweeney's book had at last kindled it into flames. This was further reinforced by another source (preferring anonymity) who wrote me: "At 509th reunions, the Nagasaki flight was a sore subject for Tibbets. His mission was always the focus."

The Three Musketeers had a number of private and public disagreements with certain other "facts" in Sweeney's book. For example, as the shock wave from the earlier Hiroshima bomb struck the three B-29s, Sweeney stated that "Kermit Beahan, a man familiar with taking fire, turned to me with panic on his face."[49] One wonders where the panic really was—with a bombardier who had thirty *real* combat missions against the Luftwaffe; who had crash-landed twice; and who would end the war with two Distinguished Flying Crosses, eight Air Medals, and a Purple Heart, or a first-combat mission pilot fearful of screwing up one of the most important raids of the war. Additionally, there were any number of instances where Sweeney related events in such a way so as to recast himself in a better light—the landing and related on Okinawa among them.

Tibbets was especially angry over the jacket of Sweeney's book, *War's End*, and the main reason for that reaction largely explains why, after fifty-three years, he turned so brutally on his old friend. Dutch Van Kirk told me that Tibbets had been furious when he saw the cover identifying the author as a "Major General, USAF (Ret.)."[50] In fact, Sweeney had retired as a part-time general in the Massachusetts Air National Guard and not from the active-duty U.S. Air Force. Tibbets himself had been black-balled from the two-star list because of long-lingering animosities over his fame and high-placed regular officers whom he had rubbed the wrong way. According to Van Kirk, Paul Tibbets had succumbed to jealousy. "Chuck had gotten two stars and he, Paul Tibbets, whom everyone expected to get at least two or three, received only one."[51]

In the end, by virtue of an incredible serendipity, Sweeney and crew came out smelling like a rose. Results from the Nagasaki mission exceeded expectations, with more military damage and fewer civilian casualties than had been forecasted. Beahan's bomb had impacted almost directly over a major Mitsubishi Arms/Akunora Engine manufacturing complex, with the hills of Nagasaki shielding a large portion of the civilian population from the blast effects. In his book, Dutch Van Kirk called it "a good miss."[52] According to a copy of a handwritten document supplied by Lisa Beahan Harrison, during the crew's mission debrief, General Farrell exclaimed at one point: "You guys picked a better aiming point in 20 seconds than we did in 20 weeks!"—to which Captain Beahan responded: "General, it was the only damned thing I could see."[53]

Tom Ferebee offered another perspective in his 1995 information-packed interview with Miami reporter Don Sider. Ferebee told Sider that Beahan would not go to the debriefing until they talked. Beahan had been worried about not having struck the briefed aiming point. He wanted to get assurances from

Ferebee that it was all right because Ferebee had made such an issue before takeoff "to make sure he knew it was the right place [to drop], or not let it go." Beahan need not have worried. According to Ferebee, after it was determined where the bomb hit and what it had done, "Admiral Purnell told Beahan, 'Captain, sometimes you have a horseshoe up your ass, and today you did. Now we can tell them we hit the industrial area.' Ol' Beahan became a real hero all of a sudden and here they were about to shoot him."[54]

Senior Allied leaders back in the Zone of the Interior, insulated from the August 9 sausage making, saw only that the tactical and strategic objectives of the strike had met or even exceeded expectations. One can appreciate the fact that no one in the AAF was inclined at that point to talk about any dirty linen. So it was that all the human mistakes made prior to and on the Nagasaki mission were quietly forgotten, and that is where matters rested until the 1990s and early 2000s when the aircrews' own stories began to be published and others started speaking out.

Following the Soviet declaration of war on August 8 and the Nagasaki bombing the next day—the second atomic strike in three days—the Japanese realized the end had come. As the Air Force Association's John Correll noted, Japan's influential war minister, General Korechika Anami, told his staff that the Americans could have one hundred bombs and that the next target might be Tokyo. That and the possibility the Japanese people faced extermination tipped the balance for Emperor Hirohito, who on August 15 forced the Imperial War Council to submit to the Potsdam Accords. World War II was finally and mercifully over.

## Acknowledgments

While it is not possible to mention everyone who made a contribution to this book, there are some who must be singled out. Retired U.S. Navy veteran Nelson Mears of the Sheridan, Arkansas, B-17 Memorial Park provided the basic drawing for the forward compartment cutaway view of the *Red Gremlin*. The military/aviation artist Sir Ernie Hamilton Boyette at (www.aviationartstore.com) graciously allowed us to reproduce his painting of that same Fortress. Kimberly Johnson of the Texas Women's University Library facilitated our securing a hard-to-find publishable image of WASP pilots Didi Johnson and Dora McKeown with Paul Tibbets and Dean Hudson. Chequita Wood of *Air Force Magazine* fast-tracked our request to use their enlightening Norden sighting angle/dropping angle schematic. Many thanks to the National Museum of the Air Force at Dayton, Ohio, and to William "Mickey" Russell of the Air Force Historical Research Agency at Maxwell Air Force Base, Alabama, for making available several of their images. And without the expert work of photo archival researcher Gina McNeely, most of the visuals in this book would have been that much the poorer.

A number of World War II–era pilots, bombardiers, and navigators provided "I-was-there" answers to many technical questions. I am especially grateful to near-centenarian and retired U.S. Air Force lieutenant colonel Russell Woinowsk, who in 1940 was among the initial 125 men to graduate from the nation's first formal bombardier school at Lowry Field, Colorado, and who later flew combat missions in B-24 Liberators. In addition to clarifying details on Norden bombsight operation, Russ kindly introduced me to the Kermit Beahan family. Also a tip of the hat to nonagenarian Ed Hyde, a B-29 navigator who flew combat missions out of Guam in the summer of 1945. Ed's detailed memory of those flights, the Superfortress, and surrounding events were very helpful.

Ron Barrett, president of the Air Force Navigator-Observer Association and as experienced a navigator/bombardier as this writer knows, provided a personally compiled thumb drive containing nearly every navigator and bombardier training manual and related material written from World War II through Vietnam—an extremely valuable resource unavailable anywhere else.

A prospecting trip through Tom Ferebee's home state of North Carolina unearthed a treasure at Raleigh. The good folks at the state's North Carolina History Museum rolled out the red carpet, giving me full access to their library's

Thomas Ferebee Papers Collection and the Ferebee museum exhibit. All was made possible by then–chief curator Dr. Joseph Porter, director Ken Howard, and museum registrars Camille Hunt and Katherine Beery. I am deeply grateful for their generous cooperation.

A stop at Charlotte, North Carolina, yielded a captivating interview with Tom Ferebee's youngest brother, Joe Ferebee. Still active in the family construction business he founded, Joe provided important details about what it was like growing up in the Flav and Zella Ferebee family before and during the Depression. Joe's older brother, Bill Ferebee, later supplied more insight in an extensive telephone interview. During this same period I entered into a fascinating correspondence with Florence Finnegan, a Ferebee cousin and unofficial family historian. From Florence I learned the most about Tom Ferebee's ancestors, and she also supplied the photo of Cadet Ferebee.

An intriguing email exchange with Captain Beahan's children, Lisa Beahan Harrison and retired U.S. Air Force lieutenant colonel Kermit K. Beahan Jr., was very helpful in fleshing out details about the 97th Bomb Group's European and North African combat experiences, plus both were utterly indispensable to my understanding of what really happened over Nagasaki. Getting acquainted with the highly personable Brig. Gen. Paul Tibbets IV has been a special treat, to say nothing of the remembrances he passed along about his grandfather. Vicki Van Kirk Triplett was a real trooper, handling loose ends after her father passed away, as well as very graciously giving permission to use his just-commissioned photo. Soft-spoken Mary Ann Ferebee, Tom Ferebee's widow, gave me an understanding of Tom's personal side as a devoted husband and father—who would have guessed that the outwardly rough and gruff bombardier loved to garden in his retirement, specializing in jalapeño peppers and his own hybrid "Florvidalia" onions!

I would be remiss if I did not recognize the outstanding publishing team at the Naval Institute Press. Senior acquisitions editor Susan Todd Brook led the editorial efforts in her usual professional manner, making important text revisions. Susan was ably supported by her hard-working assistant editor, Taylor Skord. Kudos also to senior production editor Emily Bakely, who did great work on the endnotes and keeping the book-making machinery running smoothly. Thank you also to artist/cartographer Chris Robinson for his fine B-17 and B-29 schematics, and Maryam Rostamian, who designed a terrific cover. A special mention goes to my eagle-eyed copy editor, Patti Bower, who truly went above and beyond the call of duty in making sure I got all the details right.

Three books were crucial to the telling of the Three Musketeers' story. Many thanks to Charlotte Meares, who allowed me to quote from *Fire of a Thousand Suns.* Written with George "Bob" Caron, this privately published, well-written book provided many previously unknown details about Tibbets and his crew. It is now out of print with limited availability. Paul Tibbets' own autobiography was published under three titles: *The Tibbets Story* (1978); *Flight of the Enola Gay* (1989); and *Return of the Enola Gay* (1998). I am enormously grateful to Brig. Gen. Paul Tibbets IV and Mrs. Andrea Tibbets for allowing me to liberally quote from those books. All three are out of print and, as with *Fire*, have limited availability. As mentioned in the introduction, I am greatly indebted to Suzanne Simon Dietz, along with Vicki Van Kirk Triplett, for allowing me to quote extensively from *My True Course*, Sue's 2012 authorized biography of Dutch Van Kirk. This delightful book tells Dutch's entire life story and is jam-packed with important facts and figures, along with many additional previously unpublished musketeer vignettes.

My largest debt goes to Dutch Van Kirk himself. His willingness to answer any and all questions during two full days of interviews plus a series of follow-up telephone calls made all the difference. Our conversations bore little resemblance to the "how did it feel to drop the bomb?" kind of question/answer sessions he usually encountered. We talked about Paul and Tom, and we talked shop—"Are your nav log airspeeds stated in knots or mph?" (knots); "How many star fixes did you take?" (no fixes, just two Polaris speed lines). Once I asked him how it was the three of them had gotten along so well. He didn't hesitate. "No one ever tried to tell the other guy how to do his job." It is Van Kirk's voice that is at the very core of this narrative, his contributions immeasurable.

Finally, it is important to recognize my wife, Dee Dee Harder. Her "Gal Friday" assistance and continual encouragement over the past several years has been pivotal, especially during that time when I was largely incapacitated by serious medical issues. Further, she has been instrumental in providing vital technical support, an indispensable skill in this age of computerized writing and publishing. It has become a writer's cliché, but in this case it is literally true—I could not have written this book without her.

# Notes

**Epigraph:** The phrase originated in this context in a 1942 *Life* magazine article, when the editors referred to the B-17's pilot, navigator, and bombardier as the "Three Musketeers of the Army Air Forces."

## Chapter 1. Tibbets

1. The profile of Tibbets was formed from characterizations provided by a score of writers, most importantly, Thomas and Morgan-Witt, *Enola Gay*; and Greene, *Duty*, plus interviews with Dutch Van Kirk and various Ferebee family members.
2. Marx, *Seven Hours to Zero*, 78.
3. Greene, *Duty*, 88.
4. Ibid., 84.
5. Tibbets, *The Tibbets Story*, 11–18.
6. Ibid., 14.
7. Ibid., 19–22.
8. Letson, "General Paul Tibbets."
9. Killian, "Two Pilots Log Their Memoirs."
10. Tibbets, *The Tibbets Story*, 24–31. Tibbets may be in error here. Blees operated only from 1899 to 1907 and was located in Macon, Missouri. Paul Sr. was born in 1890, so he was only seventeen when Blees closed. The Missouri Military Academy, located in Mexico, Missouri, has been in continuous operation since 1889. Perhaps Paul Sr. started at Macon and finished at Mexico.
11. Greene, *Duty*, 194. Tibbets told Greene that, despite the positives, those five years of military school had robbed him of his boyhood.
12. Tibbets, *The Tibbets Story*, 32–39.
13. Letson, "General Paul Tibbets."
14. Greene, *Duty*, 240. The episode was both serious and frightening. Paul Jr. and several fraternity brothers were hospitalized, and it was four days before Tibbets regained his eyesight. Tibbets, *The Tibbets Story*, 302.
15. Letson, "General Paul Tibbets."
16. Tibbets, *The Tibbets Story*, 37. Working part-time in a venereal disease clinic wielding an arsenic-loaded syringe and needle hadn't helped young Paul's motivation to become a physician.

17. Ibid., 40–48. The term "dodo" for fledgling pilot cadets had been used for years at Randolph. It referred to the extinct dodo bird, which had inhabited Mauritius Island in the Indian Ocean and had lived undisturbed for so long that it lost its need and ability to fly.
18. Letson, "General Paul Tibbets."
19. The aviator's version of the gosport speaking tube was invented in 1917 at the Royal Navy base at Gosport, England, by Robert Raymond Smith-Barry at his School of Special Flying. No doubt he had been influenced by similar "megaphone" communication tubes long used by ships of the Royal Navy.
20. Tibbets, *The Tibbets Story*, 43.
21. Ibid., 47. The writer's uncle, Orvis Nelson, graduated from Kelly Field in October 1934, and at that time they had a third course called Bombardment. Apparently the nation's growing isolationism had so negatively impacted the Air Corps' bomber inventories that by 1937–38 there was no longer a need for a formal Bombardment course at Kelly.
22. The tactical officer's reasoning appears questionable. General Headquarters Air Force (not Air Corps, as stated in Tibbets' book) was organized in 1935 as a special strategic strike unit, equal in status to the traditional ground-support Air Corps itself. The General Headquarters Air Force was intended to address the proper usage of the new long-range, multiengine bombers on the drawing boards. Whatever role single-engine pursuit ships were to play in the command could only have been of secondary importance. Ironically, the tactical officer's advice to go to Observation was in fact a better fit with Tibbets' own personal goals. Further, had Tibbets chosen Pursuit, he could easily have drawn duty he wouldn't have liked. There are many stories about the era's highly rated pursuit pilots being posted to places like Panama "guarding the canal" and bored out of their minds at the lowly work and few flying hours. Had Tibbets taken the post expected of a high-ranking cadet, we would likely have never heard of him.
23. Tibbets, *The Tibbets Story*, 48.
24. Letson, "General Paul Tibbets"; and Tibbets, *The Tibbets Story*. The B-10B was the nation's first "'modern'" all-metal, retractable-gear, multi-crewed, multi-engined bomber, though by 1938 the new B-17 had already made it obsolete. Because of the budgetary constraints during the late 1930s and until the Flying Fortresses arrived, there was a lapse of several years when the United States was equipped only with old B-10Bs and B-18s, another twin-engine bomber only marginally better than the B-10B.
25. Tibbets, *The Tibbets Story*, 52–53.
26. Most probably, Tibbets' airplanes were A-20A Havocs, equipped with two 2,200 HP engines. This model entered American service in the spring of

1941. The British bought many of this same, quite successful version, calling them Bostons.

27. Sakrison and Tennyson, "The Enola Gay: SuperFortress."
28. During World War II the American air forces used "mph" speed meters in their cockpits, rather than "knots" (nautical miles per hour), which came of age with jet engines and much faster airspeeds that required greater reliance on intercontinental celestial and LORAN (long-range navigation using radio pulses). Those latter navigation aids dealt in degrees, minutes, and seconds. One nautical mile equals one minute (sixty seconds) of longitude arc measured along any meridian, or 6,076 feet (a statute mile = 5,280 feet).
29. Tibbets, *The Tibbets Story*, 66–73.
30. On June 20, 1941, the U.S. Army Air Corps was renamed the U.S. Army Air Forces.
31. Tibbets, *The Tibbets Story*, 70–72. Readers of a certain age will recall the 1950s television series "Sky King" and the pilot's first *Songbird*, the civilian version of the UC-78 Bobcat. There were many variants of this aircraft, with just as many nicknames—Bamboo Bomber, the Wichita Wobbler, San Joaquin Beaufighter, Rhapsody in Glue, the list goes on.
32. Curtis LeMay, who was still a junior officer in the mid- to late 1930s, was among the very first pilots to earn navigator/observer and optical bombardier wings.
33. Tibbets, *The Tibbets Story*, 69–71.
34. Later in life Tibbets told his two sons, "Your mother got a bum deal." Greene, *Duty*, 105.
35. Thomas Ferebee Papers, 97th Bomb Group Orders, May 11, 1942.

## Chapter 2. Ferebee

1. Thomas Ferebee Papers (TFP), Sider interview.
2. Florence Finnegan, email interview, August 2013; Bill Ferebee, telephone interview, August 8, 2013.
3. TFP, *Mocksville Enterprise*, August 10, 1945.
4. Moore, *Growing Up in Davie County*, 15–24.
5. Ibid.
6. Joe Ferebee, personal interview, May 3, 2013.
7. *Mocksville Enterprise*, 1936 newspaper clipping, Tom Ferebee trip to Capitol Hill. Courtesy of his cousin Florence Finnegan.
8. TFP, David Perlmutt, *Charlotte Observer*, August 6, 1995.
9. Bill Ferebee, telephone interview, August 8, 2013; Van Kirk, personal interview, May 1–2, 2013.
10. TFP, *Mocksville Enterprise*, August 10, 1945.
11. TFP, Frank Tursi, *Winston-Salem Journal*, November 8, 1987.

12. TFP, Sider interview.
13. Bill Ferebee, telephone interview, August 8, 2013; Van Kirk, personal interviews, May 1–2, 2013. By the time Dutch and Tom met, Tom's hands were already misshapen from all the many breaks and dislocations in his knuckles and fingers.
14. Mary Ann Ferebee, personal interview, May 1–2, 2013. Mary Ann related a college incident that made a lasting impression on the young man. Tom was caught cheating on a test. The lady instructor said, "Tom, why did you do that? You know I would have passed you anyway."
15. TFP, Frank Tursi, *Winston-Salem Journal*, November 8, 1987.
16. TFP, AAF Officer Qualification Record, July 1, 1947.
17. TFP, David Perlmutt, *Charlotte Observer*, August 6, 1995.
18. Ibid.
19. Ferebee's AAF Officer's Qualification Record shows that in the summer of 1941 he played for Winston-Salem as a North Carolina Professional Class B League outfielder and was paid $150.00.
20. Humphreys, *Bombardier*, 17–33. This book was self-published by a group called Bombardier, Inc., an association of former World War II bombardiers. It's a prime source for the next several pages of text.
21. Callander, "Short Heyday." Callander states that there were also "many prewar enlisted gunners" also trained as bombardiers.
22. Humphreys, *Bombardier*, 16–18.
23. Ibid.
24. Ibid., 17–33; and Pardini, *Legendary Norden Bombsight* were prime sources for this segment.
25. Pardini, *Legendary Norden Bombsight*, 282–84.
26. By early 1944 the manning crisis had ended and the bombardier course was lengthened to eighteen weeks plus another six weeks of gunnery school. The latter was necessary because the G model B-17, the final and best version, was equipped with a .50-caliber chin turret in the nose manned only by the bombardier.
27. Pardini, *Legendary Norden Bombsight*, 146.
28. Ibid., 43–50.
29. Searle, "Bombsight War." The removable-sighthead portion of the Norden bombsight acquired nicknames. In Europe it was known as "The Football." In the Pacific it was more often referred to as "The Blue Ox." Interestingly, and in spite of official U.S. Army Air Forces histories, Van Kirk told me that Tom Ferebee never removed the Norden sightheads from his B-17s. Apparently that policy was applied unevenly—certainly by mid-1943 it was clear such measures were no longer necessary. Too many B-17s had been shot down over enemy territory not to believe a number of intact sights had been recovered.

30. Harder, *Flying from the Black Hole*, 48–52.
31. The fifteen Silverplate B-29 atomic bombers in the 509th Composite Group used only Norden sights.
32. This was *The Bombardier's Oath*: "Mindful of the secret trust about to be placed in me by my Commander-in-Chief, the President of the United States, by whose direction I have been chosen for bombardier training . . . and mindful of the fact that I am to become guardian of one of my country's most priceless military assets, the American bombsight. . . . I do here, in the presence of Almighty God, swear by the Bombardier's Code of Honor to keep inviolate the secrecy of any and all confidential information revealed to me, and further to uphold the honor and integrity of the Army Air Forces, if need by, with my life itself." Sweeting, "Not So Secret Weapon." All those precautions went for naught due to a spy. A Norden employee, Herman Lang, copied the plans and turned the whole program over to the Nazis in 1938. In an almost hilarious aside, the Germans were not impressed, preferring to press on with their own Lofte 7 bombsight design. In the end, American's super-secret bombsight was only a secret to Americans.
33. TFP, David Perlmutt, *Charlotte Observer*, August 6, 1995.
34. Pilot, bombardier, and navigator cadets received officer commissions upon winning their wings. Depending on the slots available at each flight school—something that apparently was not offered even-handedly throughout the training fields—a certain percentage of cadets with lower-class standings were designated "flight officers." In most cases, and once on the line, those men were soon promoted to second lieutenant.

## Chapter 3. Van Kirk

1. Dietz, *My True Course*, 12–16. This is also a prime source for the next several pages of text.
2. It is interesting to note that the mothers of all three men—Enola Gay Haggard, Zella Ward, and Grace Snyder—were all of Dutch heritage.
3. Dietz, *My True Course*, 13.
4. *Pennsylvania River Coal*, Robert Bickel Family History, pennsylvaniarivercoal.net/familyhistory.html.
5. This discussion of Van Kirk's early years is from Dietz, *My True Course*.
6. Dutch Van Kirk, personal interviews, May 1–2, 2013. In 1975 Van Kirk had x-rays for back trouble and was informed he had only one kidney, which came as a complete surprise to him. The doctor wondered how he could possibly have gotten into the service. Even more curious for a flying cadet, while telling this story to me, Van Kirk laughed, "I'm color-blind too!"
7. World War II trainers were much more demanding flying machines than similar small airplanes today. The technology was cruder, the airplanes less

stable, the maneuvers to be mastered more difficult. And instructors did not necessarily apply the same performance standards from one school to another. The same cadet might wash out at one field and pass through another. In Van Kirk's case, the Sikeston post commander told him he was "a marginal pilot" and the RAF likely meant a death sentence.

8. Sources for World War II navigator training were Harder, *Flying from the Black Hole*, chap. 5, "Early Bomb Aimers and Navigators"; Greer, "Individual Training of Flying Personnel"; and *Navigators Information File*, Hdqs, USAAF, October 1944.
9. Dietz, *My True Course*, 196.
10. Sarasota was the winter headquarters for the famed Ringling Bros. Barnum & Bailey Circus. John Ringling was a prominent member of that community and had been a prime mover in establishing the art school. The average enrollment was about seventy-five girls. It is today the accredited degree-granting Ringling College of Art and Design.

## Chapter 4. Sarasota

1. Thomas Ferebee Papers (TFP), Sider Interview.
2. Theodore Van Kirk, personal interviews, May 1–2, 2013. During our conversation Dutch chuckled, saying "Tom Ferebee talked like he had a mouthful of grits until the day he died."
3. Ibid.
4. TFP, Frank Tursi, *Winston-Salem Journal*, November 8, 1987.
5. Ibid.
6. Ibid.
7. Dietz, *My True Course*, 217.
8. Tibbets, *The Tibbets Story*, 71–72.
9. Ibid., 72.
10. Van Kirk, personal interviews, May 1–2, 2013.
11. Tibbets, *The Tibbets Story*, 71.
12. Ibid., 72.
13. Parton, *Air Force Spoken Here*, 160–61.
14. Both Bangor's Dow Field and nearby Presque Isle Field were heavily used by ferrying warplanes and transports. They were about 140 air miles apart.
15. Tibbets, *The Tibbets Story*, 74–79. Also helpful in recounting the trans-North Atlantic crossings is Ernest K. Gann's *Fate Is the Hunter*, 175–208.
16. Both Tibbets and Van Kirk stated in their books the destination was Goose Bay, Labrador, despite VIII Bomber Command HQ "Operation Bolero" orders dated May 22, 1942, showing Gander Lake as the first-leg destination. Again, as it was at Presque Isle and Dow Fields, Maine, both Goose Bay and Gander Lake, Newfoundland, were important ferry stops and

relatively close to one another. Whichever airfield was open and could accommodate ferry aircraft would have been used. Note: Readers should assume mileages in this book are expressed in statute rather than nautical miles unless otherwise noted.

17. The fields were established under very difficult conditions by USAAF captain (later colonel) Bernt Balchen, famed flier, Norwegian polar explorer, and naturalized U.S. citizen. During the Cold War, BW-8 was called Sondrestrom Air Base, operated by the United States. It reverted back to Denmark in 1992. "Bluie" was the code word for Greenland. "West" meant the western shore. "One" meant the farthest southern tip, "Eight" was about half up the coast.
18. On July 15, 1942, two 97th Group B-17s escorting six P-38s crashed near BW-8 due to weather complications. Fortunately, all twenty-five men were finally rescued—a grand adventure story in itself. Rockett's crew was on the field during the early stages of the rescue efforts and followed it closely. Fifty years later, under 260 feet of accumulated ice and snow, one of the P-38s was recovered in remarkably good condition. After years of restoration, the newly named *Glacier Girl* is an air show favorite and arguably the most famous P-38 Lightning in the world today. Dietz, *My True Course*, 243–52.
19. Ibid., 249. Jean Van Kirk said Grandpa Van Kirk was so proud of Ted that he jumped in his car and rushed the *Sunbury Daily Item* newspaper up to show Uncle Lee Van Kirk at his potato farm.
20. This section describing overwater navigation in early 1942 was supported by the author's personal navigation reference library, training, and experience.
21. Parton, *Air Force Spoken Here*, 154–55. A 10 percent loss rate had been expected moving the fighters and bombers across the North Atlantic during Bolero. The actual losses were 5.2 percent. Most crews were rescued, with only a few lost at sea. Because of their vulnerability, however, future fighter transits were mostly conducted via surface shipping.
22. In February 1944 the U.S. strategic air forces in England reorganized. The bomber, fighter, and air support command designations were dropped and all three organizations were folded directly into Eighth Air Force.

## Chapter 5. Fortress Europa

1. Freeman, *Airfields of the Eighth*.
2. Rickard, "Boeing B-17C Flying Fortress."
3. It is possible this condition was exacerbated by the high-level rancor between senior RAF and USAAF leadership over bomber tactics. The RAF wanted the Americans to join them in their night-area bomb campaign; the USAAF was determined to implement a daylight, precision-bombing plan. Van Kirk telephone interview, November 18, 2013.

4. Ashton Estate/OHL Limited website, East Northamptonshire, UK, www.ohllimited.co.uk/ashtonweb.
5. Tibbets, *The Tibbets Story*, 79.
6. Parton, *Air Force Spoken Here*, 169.
7. It is almost novelesque how Spaatz figures into this story. To begin with, he was raised in Boyertown, Pennsylvania, just sixty miles south of Van Kirk's Northumberland. We find him present at the beginning of the musketeers' odyssey when Tibbets took off on the August 17, 1942, Rouen strike. In September he would pin a Purple Heart on Tibbets. In October he would personally telephone Tibbets, appointing him the pilot of Gen. Mark Clark's secret mission; a few weeks later the crew would fly General Eisenhower into Operation Torch. Three years later, Spaatz was Tibbets's commanding general on Tinian, greeting the *Enola Gay* crew on their return from Hiroshima. Interestingly, Spaatz was not Dutch, as most think. In 1937 his wife convinced him to change the spelling of his German family name from Spatz to Spaatz (pronounced "Spots"), both for phonetic reasons and to suggest Dutch origin rather than German. His nickname, "Tooey," came from a resemblance to another red-haired West Point cadet named F. J. Toohey.
8. General Eaker ordered Armstrong to "complete the training of our new heavy bomber group and fight them in 16 days." Parton, *Air Force Spoken Here*, 160.
9. Dietz, *My True Course*, 255–57.
10. Parton, *Air Force Spoken Here*, 156.
11. Dietz, *My True Course*, 258.
12. Van Kirk telephone interview, August 14, 2013.
13. Parton, *Air Force Spoken Here*, 166–67. Technically, the first U.S. air action was conducted by six British Boston III "light" bombers (aka U.S. A-20 Havocs). Manned by American crews, they attacked Luftwaffe airfields in the Netherlands on the Fourth of July 1942. U.S. Army Air Forces headquarters, however, deemed the raid more a "political stunt" meant to bolster English and American civilian morale; the results were negligible.
14. Eighth Air Force military histories have Eaker leading the first American heavy bombing mission against the Axis. It is a military convention that the highest ranking officer in the attack is credited with being the leader. However, it was Major Tibbets flying as pilot-in-command of *Butcher Shop* and 97th Bomb Group commander Col. Frank Armstrong (flying as his copilot) that actually led the first attack. Tibbets, *The Tibbets Story*, 80–83. A little known fact: On August 14, 1945, then–brigadier general Frank Armstrong, commander of the 315th Bomb Wing, also led the very *last* World War II strategic bombing raid against a target in Honshu, Japan. Ottley, "The Long Haul."

15. Duffin and Matheis, *12 O'Clock High Logbook*; and Correll, "Real Twelve O'Clock High." In 2004 the U.S. Air Force Academy recognized the movie and honored the 306th Bomb Group by redesignating their airmanship operations the 306th Flying Training Group. As an aside, I am a proud alumnus of the 367th Bomb Squadron / 306th Bomb [Group] Wing.
16. Tibbets, *The Tibbets Story*, 90.
17. Caldwell, *JG 26: Top Guns*.
18. There is much discussion among aviation enthusiasts as to whether this fighter is an "Me-109" or a "Bf-109," so designated for the company that Willy Messerschmitt worked for at the time of its design, Bayerische Flugzeugwerks, or BFW. The experts tell us both designations are correct, depending on the model.
19. The term "flak," coined circa 1938, is an acronym for Fliegerabwehrkanone, literally "airplane defense cannon." Also called "ack-ack." During the Vietnam War era the same was dubbed "Triple A," for antiaircraft artillery.
20. Dietz, *My True Course*, 261.
21. Ibid., 277–78.
22. Parton, *Air Force Spoken Here*, 177; and Aitkin, *Dieppe 1942*.
23. Van Kirk personal interviews, May 1–2, 2013.
24. Tibbets, *The Tibbets Story*, 91. The American bomber force remained pathetically weak until late 1943, when General Eaker was finally able to send up several hundred bombers at a time. Parton, *Air Force Spoken Here*, 242.
25. Parton, *Air Force Spoken Here*, 178.
26. Freeman, *B-17 Flying Fortress*, 8, 29. One of the glaring weaknesses of the B-17 design was surfacing. In the mid-1930s the Air Corps believed the nation's air defense needs could be met with medium two-engine bombers, mostly for such tasks as coastal patrols against submarines. Few foresaw that in ten years, bombers would be intercontinental in nature. The B-17's initial design had a relatively small fuselage, despite being equipped with tremendous firepower. That translated into a modest payload capability. Technology was developing rapidly, however, and by 1937 it was realized longer-range bombers would be necessary. As a result, four engines were hung on the B-17 medium bomber prototype, and it was redesignated a "heavy bomber." What could not be changed was the useful load and the physical limitations of the Fort's basic airframe. Bottom line: the maximum bomb load Tibbets could physically carry in his B-17E was fourteen 300-lb. bombs (or 4,200 lbs.). The Avro Lancaster, on the other hand, the equivalent RAF four-engine heavy bomber in 1942, had the capability of carrying 14,000 lbs. of bombs, or three times as much. By 1945 improved power plants allowed the Lanc to carry the 22,000-lb. "Grand Slam," the equivalent weight of two five-ton "Little Boy" atomic bombs. The B-17G,

the last model built during World War II, had a max bomb load capability of only 8,000 lbs.

27. Tibbets, *The Tibbets Story*, 92.
28. This was before H2X mapping radar became available and the Gee/Oboe/Gee-H precision navigation radio beacon transmitter stations in England were fully up and running.
29. Dietz, *My True Course*, 284. Late 1942 survival packs were relatively primitive compared to later versions and were carried in a flight suit knee pocket. Contents included food rations, chocolate bars, fish lines, a silk map of France and the Low Countries, and two gold pieces.
30. Ibid., 227; and USAAF, *B-17 Flying Fortress Pilot Training Manual* (AN 01-20EF-1), 1943.
31. All performance data obtained from the *B-17 Flying Fortress Pilot Training Manual*. The B-17 was the last of the American tail-dragger bombers. All subsequent medium and heavy bombers used the modern tricycle gear.
32. Freeman, *Mighty Eighth War Manual*; and *B-17 Flying Fortress Pilot Training Manual*. By mid-1943 the famous "combat box" formation had fully matured. Its development is generally credited to then–colonel Curtis LeMay and consisted of any number of twelve-plane groupings in lead, high, low, and low-low elements spread out in all three dimensions.
33. For detailed explanations of headings and airspeeds, see my earlier work, *Flying from the Black Hole*. Note that the higher one flies, the greater the disparity between indicated air speed (IAS) and true airspeed (TAS). For example, 200 mph IAS at 10,000 feet at 0 degrees C = TAS 235 mph. A 200 mph IAS at 25,000 feet at -25 degrees C = TAS 305 mph. Airmen had constantly to guard against mixing centigrade (Celsius)/Fahrenheit and mph/knots.
34. Throat rather than boom mikes were used throughout the war, though by 1945 the "boom" technology had improved greatly and their use expanded. The throat mikes were strapped tight against the crewman's larynx and worked fine as long as one spoke in a normal voice; otherwise distortions occurred. Their chief advantage was to eliminate the terrific engine and slipstream noise feedback in unpressurized bombers. In the B-29, the first pressurized U.S. bomber, boom mikes were used more extensively.
35. Tibbets, *The Tibbets Story*, 93.
36. Thomas Ferebee Papers (TFP), *Charlotte Observer*.
37. Tibbets, *The Tibbets Story*, 93. Tibbets said he was proud no one on his crew had panicked.
38. Ibid., 94; and *B-17 Flying Fortress Pilot Training Manual*. The "turbos" refer to the four electrically driven turbo superchargers dedicated to each engine. They boosted the engine's manifold pressure, which sucked more oxygen (aka fuel) into the combustion chambers on takeoff and high-altitude flight.
39. TFP, Transcript of Don Sider interview.

40. Tibbets, *The Tibbets Story*, 95.
41. In both the book and movie *Twelve O'Clock High* authors Lay and Bartlett based the character of Brig. Gen. Frank Savage (Gregory Peck) on a composite of Col. Frank Armstrong and Brig. Gen. Newton Longfellow. By mid-1943 Longfellow had labored so hard on his combat missions and staff work, he had a breakdown similar to though not as dramatic as the one suffered by fictional Brig. Gen. Frank Savage in Lay and Bartlett's *Twelve O'Clock High*. Major General Eaker let his old friend and 1920s flying partner down gently, sending Longfellow back to the United States to head up a training command.
42. Tibbets, *The Tibbets Story*, 96. Tibbets had flown his Le Trait B-17E—sans instrument panel—back to England by the seat of his pants. The plane never flew again.
43. Dietz, *My True Course*, 274, 282–83.
44. Ibid., 276.
45. Parton, *Air Force Spoken Here*, 177–79.
46. Van Kirk interviews, May 1–2, 2013. During the war bombardiers used several bombing techniques. There was of course the standard "each man" drop his own load using the Norden optical bombing system. Another was the "drop on lead bombardier" method, in which all bombardiers would release when the lead bombardier released. Also RAF "Pathfinder" Mosquitoes were later used as lead bombers specially equipped with pinpoint Gee/Oboe/Gee H radio aids that refined the "drop-on-lead" technique. Tom Ferebee, in the ETO and North Africa of 1942–43, was almost always a leader and used only the Norden system.
47. Dietz, *My True Course*, 276–77.
48. Original PRU poem is taken from Hughes, *History of Air Navigation*, 7–8, citing the *RAF Journal*, April 18, 1942. Splitt's modification is from Dietz, *My True Course*, 287–88. Gamboge is a strong yellow color. There seems to be general agreement the concept of aerial "gremlins" as RAF slang originated in Malta, the Middle East, and India, with the earliest recorded poem appearing in the journal *Aeroplane* in Malta on April 10, 1929. It's unclear why red gremlins were considered "good."
49. Freeman, *B-17 Flying Fortress*, 23. With the many different B-17D, E, F, and G models used during World War II, there was a great deal of enlisted aircrew fluidity. Their number fluctuated according to how many machine guns were on the aircraft. In all models, however, the officer crew remained the same—pilot, copilot, bombardier, and navigator. When radar "blind" bombing became feasible later in the water, enlisted radar operators were added. These men worked with the navigator and bombardier to conduct what was called "through the cloud bombing." The main obstacle to a regularly scheduled high-altitude precision bombing campaign in Europe was the weather.

50. TFP, *Charlotte Observer.*
51. Dietz, *My True Course*, 289–90.
52. Ibid., 289.
53. Tibbets, *The Tibbets Story*, 96–97. Inelegant, hard to fly, and unpopular with most crews, the B-24 Liberator could fly faster and carry over a ton more bombs than the B-17. With a tip of the hat to my B-52 Stratofortress comrades, I believe the Liberator was the original BUFF or "big ugly fat fellow."
54. Parton, *Air Force Spoken Here*, chap. 11; and Hess, *B-17 Flying Fortress*. The early model B-24s had a poor ventral station gunnery system. As a result, the Sperry Ball Turret used in the B-17E, F, and G models was very quickly adapted to the Libs. Regarding deeper missions into Germany, American bombers would not be properly protected until early 1944 when the P-51 Mustang escort fighter became available.

## Chapter 6. The Generals and North Africa

1. The Clark mission events are outlined in Tibbets, *The Tibbets Story*, 101–6.
2. Dietz, *My True Course*, 295. This procedure of interpreting ocean waves to determine wind speed and direction would later be incorporated in the USAAF *Navigators Information File* (NIF 2-22-2), April 1944.
3. Parton, *Air Force Spoken Here*, 183.
4. Today it is known as Tipaza, Algeria.
5. The Abwehr (meaning "defense") was the German intelligence-gathering organization, counterpart to the American Office of Strategic Services, later the Central Intelligence Agency.
6. Tibbets, *The Tibbets Story*, 105–6. It is difficult to imagine the always image-conscious Clark in this predicament. Tibbets tells us that King George VI was greatly amused when General Clark related the story.
7. Dietz, *My True Course*, 296.
8. C. Peter Chen, *World War II DataBase*. "Cherchell Conference, 21 Oct. 1942–22 Oct. 1942," http://ww2db.com/battle_spec.php?battle_id=194.
9. Dietz, *My True Course*, 295; Tibbets, *The Tibbets Story*, 102–6; and Theodore Van Kirk interviews, May 1–2, 2013.
10. "Drivers" and "bubble chasers" are Air Force slang for pilots and aerial navigators. Aircraft sextants use an enclosed "bubble" to establish an artificial (celestial) horizon. Ocean ship sextants measure altitude above the visible horizon and do not require a bubble.
11. Dialogue and narrative between Tibbets and Van Kirk on the Gibraltar return from Dietz, *My True Course*, 296–97; and Van Kirk interviews, May 1–2, 2013.
12. Nelson and Haggerty, *45 Seconds to Hiroshima*, 43–44.
13. Van Kirk interviews, May 1–2, 2013.

14. Dietz, *My True Course*, 295.
15. Thomas Ferebee Papers (TFP), Frank Tursi, *Winston-Salem Journal*, November 8, 1987.
16. TFP, David Perlmutt, *Charlotte Observer*, August 6, 1995.
17. Van Kirk had by this time gotten close enough to Tibbets to feel comfortable playing jokes on him. On one occasion after takeoff, the colonel asked for a departure heading. Van Kirk radioed up, "380 degrees." Tibbets had gotten nearly all the way around when he suddenly piped up, "What the hell did you say?" Grinning to himself at having "gotten" the boss—there are only 360 degrees on a compass—Van Kirk responded, "Heading is 20 degrees!" Dietz, *My True Course*, 291.
18. Doolittle was promoted to major general twelve days later, November 20, 1942. Due to so many rapid changes during this period, many reference works are in error regarding the ranks of U.S. senior colonels and generals at this time.
19. Dietz, *My True Course*, 304.
20. Parton, *Air Force Spoken Here*, 185.
21. Doolittle, *I Could Never Be So Lucky Again*, 310–11.
22. Major Knox would return to Hurn to participate in a second airlift of general staff officers led by General Spaatz. Tragically, with Eisenhower's chief of air staff, Brig. Gen. Asa Duncan on board, Knox's B-17 was lost over the eastern Atlantic on November 17, most likely due to a runaway engine fire. All on board perished. Parton, *Air Force Spoken Here*, 200; "Gen. A.N. Duncan Missing in Plane," *New York Times*, November 26, 1942; USAAF 1942–47 Missing Air Crew Reports (MACR), 15097, NARA. Both Tibbets and Doolittle are in error in their autobiographies when they imply that the Knox-Duncan incident occurred on the November 5 flight.
23. Tibbets, *The Tibbets Story*, 108; Dietz, *My True Course*, 305–6.
24. Doolittle, *I Could Never Be So Lucky Again*, 310–11.
25. Takeoff dialogue and narrative from "8th Air Force Historical Society of Georgia, Dutch Van Kirk, guest speaker," *YouTube*, August 10, 2013, https://www.youtube.com/watch?v=hoCsruPtmL4.
26. In January 1943 Lt. Gen. Dwight Eisenhower had been relieved by Lt. Gen. Frank Andrews as commander of U.S. forces in the ETO to become supreme commander of the North African campaign. It is possible that, had Andrews lived (he perished in a B-24 crash in May 1943), he might have been selected to lead the Normandy invasion instead of Eisenhower. Joint Base Andrews (formerly Andrews Air Force Base) in Washington, D.C., was named in his honor.
27. Tibbets, *The Tibbets Story*, 109.
28. That was not the case for the delayed Doolittle B-17. After takeoff, as per the plan, they headed out into the Atlantic to stay clear of German radar

and coastal patrols. Bad luck came their way when four Junkers Ju 88s, twin-engine all-purpose light bomber/heavy fighters, stumbled over them on a return leg to France. A desperate four-against-one battle ensued. The B-17 had no trained gunners on board, that space taken by the VIP passengers. At length, tracer bullets ripped into the airplane, wounding copilot Thomas Lohr and damaging an engine. Summers called for the only other pilot onboard, General Doolittle, to come forward and take his place. Meanwhile, General Lemnitzer had manned one of the waist guns and was blasting away at the Ju 88s like a twenty-one-year-old (Doolittle believed he damaged one of them). Just at the moment when it looked like curtains, the Junkers broke off and headed for home. After the war it was learned the Germans had been desperately short of fuel and only just made it back to their field at Biarritz, France—another very close call for Allied general staff. Doolittle, *I Could Never Be So Lucky Again*, 310–13.

29. Dietz, *My True Course*, 307.
30. Maison Blanche is "White House" in French, perhaps referring to the first main terminal building constructed in 1924.
31. Tibbets, *The Tibbets Story*, 112.
32. Dialogue and narrative from Dietz, *My True Course*, 308; Van Kirk, Theodore, "My True Course."
33. Dietz, *My True Course*, 312–13.
34. Tibbets, *The Tibbets Story*, 115. During our personal interviews Van Kirk questioned Tibbets' memory of this attack, saying he did not recall any whistles or even if the colonel was present on the field. Such discrepancies in recollections is not unusual; after a half-century or more, one's mind can play tricks. A plausible explanation in this case and what I surmised in the narrative is that Tibbets had been in another hangar and remained separated from Van Kirk and Ferebee for some time.
35. It was likely during this attack that Van Kirk first noticed the lack of propeller synchronization on the German two-engine planes. With rare exceptions, the Germans did not use four-engine attack aircraft. Allied pilots could not tolerate the annoying, unsettling sounds and additional vibration caused by unsynchronized propellers on their own larger, four-engine aircraft. Van Kirk, telephone interview, October 2, 2013.
36. Dialogue and narrative from Tibbets, *The Tibbets Story*, 115–16.
37. The usual maximum fuel load for a B-17F was about 2,500 U.S. gallons, and about 3,600 gallons if fitted with "Tokyo Tanks."
38. Dietz, *My True Course*, 310.
39. Eighth Air Force Historical Society records indicate the 97th Bomb Group officially began North African combat operations on November 13, the Friday before this weekend.
40. Tibbets, *The Tibbets Story*, 117–18.

41. Ibid.
42. Dietz, *My True Course*, 314.
43. Tibbets, *The Tibbets Story*, 120. President Roosevelt had heard about the 97th Bomb Group's devastating raids in North Africa and ordered a promotion for the commander. Atkinson was embarrassed to reap the reward earned by Tibbets, telling him "[my promotion to brigadier general] belongs to you." Ibid., 128.
44. Dietz, *My True Course*, 315–17.
45. Tibbets, *The Tibbets Story*, 117.
46. Dietz, *My True Course*, 352.
47. Van Kirk interviews, May 1–2, 2013.
48. Dietz, *My True Course*, 286. It was also during this period that General Spaatz told Tibbets he considered him the most combat-experienced bomber pilot in the Air Force. Tibbets, *The Tibbets Story*, 127.
49. Greene, *Duty*, 246.
50. Van Kirk interviews, May 1–2, 2013. "Craps" was first known as *crapaud*, French for "toad," in reference to the original style of play with people crouched over a sidewalk. During World War II the street-style "craps" became very popular with U.S. soldiers, who often used an Army blanket as a method of dice control.
51. Ibid.
52. By this time General Eisenhower had consolidated his confusing command structure by appointing Major General Spaatz commander of all North African air forces.
53. Dietz, *My True Course*, 327. In the 1995 interview with Sider, Ferebee denied the eggs-for-B-17 story. Van Kirk always insisted it was true.
54. Dietz, *My True Course*, 323–24. During January the *Red Gremlin* crew also conducted ferry flights for RAF Air Chief Marshall Sir Arthur Tedder and General Spaatz.
55. Doolittle, *I Could Never Be So Lucky Again*, 328.
56. These two awards can be given either for heroism or for extraordinary achievement. Here they tended more to the latter category.
57. TFP, AAF Officer Qualification Record, July 1, 1947.

## Chapter 7. Interregnum

1. In years to come Tibbets would use the phrase "shot in the ass" many times in print and video to describe the abundance of confidence he had in himself during the war.
2. The narrative and dialogue of the Norstad altercation is from Tibbets, *The Tibbets Story*, 127–36.
3. Ibid, 130–31. In his autobiography, Tibbets relates a truly ironic tale. After dropping General Clark off at Algiers after the base had been secured, he

was on a return leg westbound, and as he passed by the Oran airfield, he got a call from its tower with an emergency. A German fighter had two senior U.S. Army officers pinned down on the opposite end of the field. Tibbets came in low with the *Red Gremlin*'s machine guns bristling, chasing the German pilot away and landing near the stranded men. Van Kirk and Ferebee jumped out of the airplane and helped the two in. Tibbets quickly taxied the B-17 to the safe side of the field and dropped the two officers on the ground without seeing their faces, then promptly took off. Only later would he learn the fellows he'd rescued were Colonel Norstad and Colonel Vandenberg. Ibid., 134–35.

4. Ibid, 133.
5. Dietz, *My True Course*, 330–33.
6. Ibid., 346.
7. For details on Van Kirk's return, see ibid., 348–53.
8. In the new reorganizations, it was decided that several bomb groups would make up a wing, with the 97th Bomb Group absorbed into the Fifth Bomb Wing.
9. Thomas Ferebee Papers (TFP), Frank Tursi, *Winston-Salem Journal*, November 8, 1987.
10. TFP, Citation for Distinguished Flying Cross, May 19, 1943. This one was for heroism.
11. The first attack (on Ploesti) was conducted on August 1, 1943. It is considered the single most-costly American bomber raid of World War II, with nearly sixty B-24 Liberators and crew lost. Tom Ferebee said later in life more than half seriously and after watching a cable TV special on the mission, "If I had known [those Ploesti missions] were like that, I wouldn't have gone!" He was always in the lead and did not see that many bombers shot down. TFP, Sider interview, May 12, 1995.
12. TFP, AAF Officer Qualification Record, July 1, 1947.
13. TFP, Whom-It-May-Concern, BG Atkinson, HQ5thBW, January 10, 1944.
14. TFP, David Perlmutt, *Charlotte Observer*, August 6, 1995. Regarding pilot training, both Ferebee and Van Kirk were given assurances each would have another chance. Nothing ever became of those promises. For the record, Ferebee's AAF file shows that sometime before the summer of 1947 he took fifty hours of private pilot training in a Piper Cub.
15. Ibid.
16. TFP, Sider interview.
17. Ibid.
18. Dietz, *My True Course*, 366.
19. Ibid., 367.
20. Van Kirk telephone interview, June 16, 2013; and Dietz, *My True Course*, 371.

21. Dietz, *My True Course*, 376.
22. According to a photo at the National Archives and Records Administration, "Outstanding B-17s" No. 203-JM-NASHF-5W, the *Red Gremlin*, flown by Capt. C. R. "Dick" Wiley, arrived in the United States on July 13, 1943. It and *Superman* were singled out by the newspapers upon their return. After the war, the musketeers learned the *Gremlin* had been sold as surplus, winding up in somewhat reduced circumstances hauling chickens and freight in South America.
23. Dietz, *My True Course*, 384.
24. Ibid.
25. Per Van Kirk: "Until the day Tibbets died, we argued about whether I volunteered for the job." Van Kirk telephone interview, June 16, 2013.
26. Tibbets, *The Tibbets Story*, 140. In another "small world" aside, I went through navigator and bombardier schools with Lt. Bill Eubank, General Eubank's son.
27. Doyle, *B-29 Superfortress in Action*, 5. The Manhattan Project was not the most expensive program of the war. The atom bomb effort came in at $2 billion; the plagued B-29 project ended up costing the United States an astounding $3 billion. There was no choice but to make the B-29 work; the Superfortress was the *only* U.S. vehicle, either operationally or on the drawing boards, capable of delivering the oversized, five-ton atomic bombs. Boyne, "The B-29's Battle of Kansas," 94–97.
28. Skiles, "Pretty Baby."
29. Tibbets, *The Tibbets Story*, 140–41. In the interest of keeping the narrative moving along, Tibbets' wide-ranging duties between the spring of 1943 and September of 1944 have been abbreviated.
30. Ibid., 144.
31. Ibid., 147.
32. Performance data derived mostly from Bowers, *Boeing B-29 Superfortress*; Doyle, *B-29 Superfortress in Action*; and Savage, *B-29 Walk Around*.
33. Details on this episode and Tibbets' role came from Boyne, *B-29's Battle of Kansas*, 94–97, and Caron and Meares, *Fire of a Thousand Suns*.
34. Tibbets, *The Tibbets Story*, 149–50.
35. Tibbets, *Return of Enola Gay*, 151–56; and Letson, "General Paul Tibbets." Tibbets told the Dora/Didi story in especially great detail in the Letson interview.
36. Building on the growing legend about the mythical creatures who plague aviators, RAF pilot and budding children's book author Roald Dahl wrote a story published in 1943 called "The Gremlins." One of the book's female gremlins was named Fifinella, after a famous British race horse, the "flying filly." Walt Disney planned a film based on the best-selling book, but copyright issues prevented the picture from ever being made.

37. Tibbets, *Return of the Enola Gay*, 155. For seventy years, Dora Dougherty Strother McKeown and Dorothea "Didi" Johnson Moorman were the only certificated female B-29 pilots. In 2013 the Commemorative Air Force, a Texas-based nonprofit organization dedicated to preserving and showing historical aircraft, checked out Debbie Travis King as a qualified copilot on "Fifi," the only airworthy B-29 in the world today (the name has no association with Fifinella). Dora Dougherty, who went on to become a highly accomplished and honored pilot, remains the only woman ever certificated as a B-29 Superfortress aircraft commander. Once again, the "Tibbets luck" had held; purely by chance, two of the most capable pilots in the WASPs had been among the eight candidates he had interviewed at Eglin Airfield. Paine, "Now There Are Three," 54–58; and Correll, "The Feeder Force," 69–70.
38. The B-4 was the standard-issue luggage for the on-the-fly airman during the war and decades afterward. It was essentially a canvas cloth case with handy zippered side pockets, sized roughly between a standard suitcase and what we today call an airline "carry-on."
39. In yet another "small world" encounter, Gen. Uzal G. Ent was born and raised in the tiny community of Northumberland, Pennsylvania, Dutch Van Kirk's hometown. Ent had led the first Ploesti raid in August 1943 and had been brought home to train the new B-29 crews. Only weeks following the meeting with Paul Tibbets, General Ent was gravely injured in a B-25 crash when a replacement copilot misunderstood a hand signal on takeoff and retracted the gear prematurely. Paralyzed from the waist down, he died in 1948 due to complications from his injuries. He is buried near the Fred and Grace Van Kirk monument, Riverside Cemetery, Northumberland, Pennsylvania. Dietz, *My True Course*, 378.
40. The other two candidates were Brig. Gen. Frank Armstrong and Col. Roscoe "Bim" Wilson, both of whom outranked Tibbets. Both rose to multi-starred flag rank. Tibbets, *The Tibbets Story*, 159.
41. Tibbets said he "was floored" when Ent told him he could not speak of his new work even with his own family. Lucy, along with sons Paul III and baby Gene, were living at Grand Island Army Air Field, Nebraska, where Paul Tibbets called home during the first half of 1944.
42. In the spring of 1945, Tibbets airmen were told Captain Parsons would be joining their organization but at first did not take him or his ordnance unit seriously. The young men did not know that a Navy captain was equivalent in rank to a U.S. Army, Air Force, or Marine full colonel.
43. General Ent's instructions have been reconstructed primarily from accounts in Tibbets, *The Tibbets Story*, 152–57; Letson, "General Paul Tibbets"; and "National Press Club (NPC) Lunch w/Paul Tibbets," Washington, D.C., 1995. Published on YouTube, August 14, 2012.

44. The only other World War II aircraft that was technically capable of delivering atomic bombs was the RAF's four-engine Avro Lancaster heavy bomber. The term "longhairs" was the universal pejorative used by American World War II military men when speaking of scientists and intellectuals.
45. Tibbets, *The Tibbets Story*, 156–57.
46. The dialogue and narrative in General Ent's office has been reconstructed from the following sources: Tibbets, *The Tibbets Story*, 151–57; and Letson, "General Paul Tibbets"; and Terkel, "One Hell of a Big Bang."

## Chapter 8. Wendover

1. One ate dinner on the Utah side, then walked through a door to the Nevada side for gambling and slot machines at the State Line Casino/Hotel. Krauss and Krauss, *509th Remembered*, 216.
2. Hope's crack was mentioned in scores of Wendover Field reminisces.
3. Tibbets, *The Tibbets Story*, 162.
4. Terkel, "One Hell of a Big Bang." Tibbets never bothered to visit the bases at Mountain Home in Boise, Idaho, and at Great Bend, Kansas, the other two airfields that General Ent offered Tibbets for the assignment.
5. Thomas Ferebee Papers (TFP), Sider interview, May 12, 1995.
6. Capt. Kermit Beahan had seen more heavy action than even the Three Musketeers. On September 7, 1942, his bomber was damaged beyond repair and returned to England with wounded and killed on board, crashing on landing; on October 2 his airplane was severely damaged by flak and returned with wounded on board; on December 14 a one-thousand-pound bomb tore loose from its supports, causing the ship to go out of control and the pilot narrowly able to avoid crashing; on December 18 his aircraft was severely damaged by flak and crashed in North Africa barely within friendly Allied lines; on January 29, 1943, flak and fighters severely wounded the pilots and his airplane crashed again. On February 3, 1943, Beahan's squadron commander recommended he "be relieved from further combat . . . due to combat strain and returned to the U.S." Courtesy Lt. Col. Kermit K. Beahan Jr. (USAF ret.), Secret Orders, 342 Bomb Squadron/97BG-A-JAT-1, "Evacuation of Officer," Joseph A. Thomas, Major Air Corps, Commanding Officer, February 3, 1943.
7. Dietz, *My True Course*, 386–88.
8. Scores of Wendover accounts mention this ubiquitous warning. Similar signs appeared at Los Alamos and other atomic installations.
9. Kuznick, "Defending the Indefensible."
10. The apartment description was largely derived from a drawing in Krauss and Krauss, *509th Remembered*, 98.
11. Letson, "General Paul Tibbets."

12. Dietz, *My True Course*, 389. Van Kirk told a story on himself: During a 509th reunion in the 1960s, Van Kirk and Ferebee came marching in to register. Fred Bock's wife—he, the aircraft commander of the B-29 *Bockscar*—was manning the desk. She took one look at them and said, "Why, you two guys [still] think you can do anything, don't you?" Van Kirk said: "She was still giving us hell twenty years later."
13. Quoted in Stone, "For Aircrews, A-Bombings a Matter of Duty."
14. Dietz, *My True Course*, 385.
15. Details on the 509th organization are from Campbell, *The Silverplate Bombers*, 97–99.
16. Quote and narrative from Tibbets, *The Tibbets Story*, 162. On February 9, 1943, Captain Classen was awarded the Distinguished Service Cross for saving every man on his B-17 crew, in spite of their being adrift at sea for fifteen days and given up for dead. The transport squadron was named after a popular radio program of the day. Tibbets, *The Tibbets Story*, 176.
17. Nearly all other written accounts show Uanna to be a major. According to an AAF memo to General Farrell generated on Tinian, he was still a captain as late as July 26, 1945. After graduating with a BS degree in engineering and an MS degree in education from Tufts University (and later a PhD in public administration from American University in Washington, D.C.), Uanna became involved with Army Counter Intelligence. After Pearl Harbor he advanced rapidly, commanding large numbers of men in the Army's Corps of Intelligence Police. Later General Groves tapped him to head up the security for Tibbets' group. In the 1950s, he was involved with the CIA and other government agencies requiring specialized security. According to official records, Uanna died of a heart attack in 1961 in Addis Ababa, Ethiopia. His son, Steven Uanna, however, believes his father was murdered, ostensibly to prevent his knowledge of various government conspiracies from becoming known. No solid evidence as to the veracity of those charges has surfaced. Biographical information and documents archived in William Lewis Uanna Collection, Manhattan Project Heritage Preservation, *Atomic Heritage Foundation*, http://mphpa.org/profile/william-l-bud-uanna; and "Uanna, Security Expert: Officer of U.S. Embassy in Addis Ababa," *New York Times*, December 23, 1962.
18. Tibbets' first speech was recorded in many individual memoirs and books, including Krauss and Krauss, *509th Remembered*, 214; Beser, *Hiroshima and Nagasaki Revisited*, 33–34; and Thomas and Morgan-Witts, *Enola Gay*, 25. The text here was reconstructed from the listed sources.
19. Van Kirk said that the former 504th Bombardment Group aircrews were even more "pissed off" after the briefing than before, despite the two-week furlough. They knew they were a top outfit that should have already been deployed against the Japanese, and here they were screwing around out in

the middle of nowhere with some kind of a hairbrained project that Tibbets would not even explain. Dietz, *My True Course*, 398.

20. Tibbets, *The Tibbets Story*, 163–66. In his book, Tibbets described in some detail how he and Uanna handled this episode.
21. During the several decades following the atomic bombings, Tibbets did many interviews on the subject of how many men he sent into the wilderness. The most probable number is only three, with one of them a lieutenant colonel in his own headquarters organization who, for personal reasons and without permission, borrowed a B-29 to fly home. Letson, "General Paul Tibbets"; and Krauss and Krauss, *509th Remembered*, 86.
22. Caron and Meares, *Fire of a Thousand Suns*, 158.
23. Thomas and Morgan-Witts, *Enola Gay*, 59.
24. Caron and Meares, *Fire of a Thousand Suns*, 157. Caron described Tom Ferebee as someone who "could have been cast in a film as a dashing riverboat gambler."
25. Dietz, *My True Course*, 436.
26. Thomas and Morgan-Witts, *Enola Gay*, 48.
27. In the interest of narrative clarity, much of the technical details on those modifications has been omitted. See Campbell, *The Silverplate Bombers*, for more information.
28. Terkel, "One Hell of a Big Bang."
29. Tibbets, *The Tibbets Story*, 170; and Terkel, "One Hell of a Big Bang."
30. The procedure and phrase "breakaway turn" was used in the Cold War's Strategic Air Command whenever delivering what are today referred to as gravity-propelled "dumb" bombs, both conventional and nuclear.
31. Caron and Meares, *Fire of a Thousand Suns*, 164.
32. Tibbets, *The Tibbets Story*, 170–71; and "National Press Club (NPC) Lunch w/Paul Tibbets," Washington, D.C., 1995. Published on YouTube, August 14, 2012.
33. The airfield was named after Cuba's longtime dictator Fulgencio Batista, whom Fidel Castro overthrew in January 1959. The exercises brought out another side to what some perceived as the arrogance of the musketeers. The three made the first trip down to Batista in a C-54 to get things organized and install a unit of their own military police (MP). It was about three o'clock in the morning when the plane landed and the MPs had not eaten in some time. Always thoughtful of his men, Tibbets looked at Van Kirk and Ferebee and said, "You two make sure the men are fed before they get bedded down." Ferebee and Van Kirk awakened the mess sergeant, who refused to get up. An enraged Ferebee pulled his .45 pistol, pointed it at the sergeant, and said, "These [enlisted MPs] haven't had breakfast yet and by God they are going to get it." Van Kirk tells us "the officers helped make the men's beds too." Dietz, *My True Course*, 395.

34. Ibid., 389–90; and Christman, *Target Hiroshima*, 166–67. According to Christman, Deak Parsons' biographer, the naval officer had also voiced his concerns to Groves about Van Kirk's navigators, likely making it easier for Van Kirk and Tibbets to gain approval from the usually hard-to-convince general. In any event, the Manhattan Project leader was pleased with the result, Groves later remarking, "Our navigators were all top-notch."
35. Krauss and Krauss, *509th Remembered*, 234. In subsequent reunions years later, everyone who made it down to Cuba remembered their visits to Old Havana's "Sloppy Joe's." Famous since the early 1930s, this celebrity hang-out (think Ernest Hemingway) was on the "must visit" list for 509th personnel. Owner Jose Garcia had years earlier concocted a sandwich made from *ropa vieja*, loosely translated as "old clothes" and, at least in Cuba, based on a dish made of shredded meat in sauce. Postwar, it became the foundation of an American staple—the sloppy joe sandwich.
36. TFP, Sider interview, May 12, 1995.
37. Prime resources for the technical discussion about the bombs came from Rhodes, *The Making of the Atomic Bombs*; and Christman, *Target Hiroshima*.
38. Bomb specifications came from Coster-Mullen, *Atom Bombs*; Glasstone and Dolan, *Effects of Nuclear Weapons*; and Sublette, "The First Nuclear Weapons." Interestingly, of the 140 pounds of U-235 in Little Boy, only *two pounds* created the explosion. The other 138 pounds contributed zero energy yield. It was soon learned that plutonium was ten times more efficient than U-235. Glasstone and Dolan, *Effects of Nuclear Weapons*, 5–6.
39. Olivi, *Decision at Nagasaki*, 179. The plutonium bomb would lead to thermonuclear or hydrogen bombs in 1953. Briefly, it takes the high temperatures of an atomic (fission) bomb to set off a secondary hydrogen (fusion reaction) bomb. The fusion bomb derives its explosive energy from fusing (feeding on) the nuclei of the atmosphere's hydrogen isotopes and turning them into helium nuclei, the same process that powers our sun.
40. TFP, Mark Andrews, *Orlando Sentinel*, August 4, 1985. This testing was not without its own dangers. In 1995 Ferebee spoke of one example: "The first 'fat man' was too big to go in the airplane. Two of us almost got killed. We were standing in the pit [while they were loading the 10,000-lb. test bomb]. After they finally got it up to the bomb bay [the B-29 moved a bit and the cable broke]. That thing came down . . . and whipped the gun turrets two feet forward [just missing us]. They had to send the airplane back to Wright Field [in Ohio] to modify the bomb bay." TFP, Sider interview, May 12, 1995.
41. Dr. Robert Serber, a member of Capt. Deak Parson's team (introduced in the appendix), has been credited with creating the code names for the first three early atomic bomb designs. The uranium "Thin Man" was very long

and slim and required both B-29 bomb bays, which Serber named after Dashiell Hammett's detective novel *The Thin Man*. The plutonium bomb was designated *Fat Man* due to its rotund shape and was so named in a nod to Sydney Greenstreet's character in the film *The Maltese Falcon*. It was later discovered the uranium bomb could be reduced in length sufficiently to fit into a single bomb bay and so was redesignated *Little Boy*, after the diminutive actor Elisha Cook Jr., who was manhandled by the Humphrey Bogart character in that same film. Serber and Crease, *Peace & War.*

42. An old-fashioned general, Groves knew little of aviation and its technology. Indeed, when reading the memoirs of those who worked with him during the war, one gets the impression he had a personal phobia against, and perhaps even a fear of, flying. Until 1944, when time pressures and personnel complaints reached a crescendo, General Groves forbade Project Manhattan scientists to travel by air.
43. Tibbets, *The Tibbets Story*, 224.
44. Ibid.
45. In September 1944 General Ent had instructed Tibbets to be prepared to drop bombs in both Europe and Japan. By the spring of 1945, however, it was clear Germany was near collapse and atomic weapons would not be necessary there. In response to later charges that the United States would never have dropped bombs on Caucasians, Tibbets issued vigorous denials. Aside from his unambiguous orders regarding both theaters, he had been wounded by the Germans and was personally ready for some payback. Letson, "General Paul Tibbets."
46. One humorous event amid all the family anguish: Tibbets had told Lucy those strange civilians running around Wendover were "sanitation engineers." One day, frustrated over a stopped-up bathtub drain, she made a telephone call. One of the "plumbers," as Lucy thought of them, dutifully came over and cleaned the drain without making a fuss. The Manhattan Project physicist later informed Tibbets, and they both had a good laugh—the joke was on them. Tibbets, *The Tibbets Story*, 167.
47. Narrative and quotes on the C-54 trips from Dietz, *My True Course*, 390–91.
48. Christman, *Target Hiroshima*, 162–68.
49. Ibid., 180–81.
50. Unfortunately, the same would not hold true between Maj. Charles Sweeney and U.S. Navy commander Fred Ashworth, their counterparts on the Nagasaki mission. Those difficulties are examined in detail in the appendix.
51. Christman, *Target Hiroshima*, 166; and Van Kirk telephone interview, August 14, 2013. Parsons was quoted as saying he thought Tibbets had a "very progressive attitude" regarding their relationship and the project. The Three Musketeers always considered Deak Parsons "a real gentleman and a first-class officer."

52. A story, probably apocryphal, began circulating that during a subsequent meeting at the Pentagon, Arnold greeted the obstructive general with a "Good morning, major."
53. Letson, "General Paul Tibbets"; and Caron and Meares, *Fire of a Thousand Suns*, 159.
54. Campbell, *The Silverplate Bombers*, 14.
55. The *Enola Gay* and the other Silverplate bombers were modified stock B-29s. The later B-29A and B versions included many of the Silverplate improvements. The B models moved the radar operator to the forward compartment just behind the navigator to enhance crew coordination. An order for five thousand B-29Cs was cancelled when the war ended. In a bit of sleight of hand in the late 1940s, the new U.S. Air Force redesignated the upcoming B-29D as the B-50 in an attempt to make it appear completely new. Doyle, *B-29 Superfortress in Action*, 52; "Boeing B-29," *Skytamer Archive*, http://www.skytamer.com/1.2.htm; and Ottley, "The Long Haul."
56. Caron and Meares, *Fire of a Thousand Suns*, 181.
57. Tibbets, *The Tibbets Story*, 179.
58. Thomas and Morgan-Witts, *Enola Gay*, 131.
59. Tibbets, *The Tibbets Story*, 180.

## Chapter 9. Tinian

1. Grant, "Growth at Guam."
2. Krauss and Krauss, *509th Remembered*, 18–19. Ashworth had worn the letter around his waist in a money belt, and it had become so sweat-soaked in the tropical climate that he had to read it to Admiral Nimitz.
3. The account of the Tinian deployment is from Tibbets, *The Tibbets Story*, p. 181; and Caron and Meares, *Fire of a Thousand Suns*, 184–85.
4. Dietz, *My True Course*, 416.
5. Postwar USAF bomber nose numbers would be matched up with the last several digits of their serial numbers.
6. Nelson and Haggerty, *45 Seconds to Hiroshima*, 129–30. John Rodgers Field is known today as Honolulu International Airport.
7. Those smelly, open ditches made a big impression and are mentioned in many accounts.
8. Thomas Ferebee Papers (TFP), *Seabee Map of Tinian*, "As if It Were New York City," June 15, 1945; and Tibbets, *The Tibbets Story*, 181. While both islands cover roughly thirty-six to thirty-eight square miles, Manhattan from north to south is longer and narrower.
9. Krauss and Krauss, *509th Remembered*, 316.
10. From various accounts in ibid.
11. Tibbets, *The Tibbets Story*, 183–84.
12. Caron and Meares, *Fire of a Thousand Suns*, 191.

13. Groves, *Now It Can Be Told*, 267, 283; and Rhodes, *The Making of the Atomic Bomb*, 626–27. LeMay was not happy that General Groves, through Farrell and Purnell, was able to retain control of the atomic bombs; he believed the time and method of delivery was the province of the theater commander.
14. Christman, *Target Hiroshima*, 104. The head of the Military Policy Committee was famed scientist Vannevar Bush, a prime mover in the establishment of the Manhattan Project. He reported directly to President Roosevelt.
15. Campbell, *The Silverplate Bombers*, 119. Because their air defenses were negligible, sorties to Marcus and Rota were not eligible for combat mission credit.
16. Dietz, *My True Course*, 429.
17. Military historians record that from early March to mid-August 1945, more than 2,200 B-29s made emergency landings on Iwo Jima, saving the lives of over 22,000 American airmen. There was poetic justice in this—U.S. Marine Corps casualties in taking the island were 26,000 (6,800 killed in action).
18. Caron and Meares, *Fire of a Thousand Suns*, 190. The author of the poem has never been identified, despite it having appeared in a score or more books. The various versions differ slightly.
19. Ibid., 194–95.
20. Tibbets, *The Tibbets Story*, 194. Van Kirk later said that "Tibbets was the [beach prank] ringleader. . . . Occasionally on the ground [he] would cut loose on things like that, but when you got into an airplane with Paul Tibbets you were all business. You better be anyhow." Van Kirk telephone interview, October 2, 2013; and Dietz, *My True Course*, 419.
21. Tibbets, *The Tibbets Story*, 194. The 1844 Alexander Dumas novel tells of the seventeenth-century adventures of a young man called d'Artagnan who joins three friends in the French Guard named Athos, Porthos, and Aramis. The four rejoiced in their motto "all for one, one for all."
22. The baseball game narrative and dialogue is from Dietz, *My True Course*, 421.
23. Blanchard's attempts to co-opt the 509th and the checkout ride narrative are described in Letson, "General Paul Tibbets"; TFP, Sider interview, May 12, 1995; Tibbets, *The Tibbets Story*, 185–88; and Dietz, *My True Course*, 435.
24. In 1965, Blanchard succeeded in seeing "four stars" when he became USAF vice chief of staff. It was fleeting; a year later, at age fifty, he was dead from a massive heart attack.
25. TFP, Sider interview, May 12, 1995.
26. Tibbets owned up to his North African mistakes in Tibbets, *The Tibbets Story*, 186–88. He said that LeMay was actually pleased with the way the B-29 check ride turned out, explaining his subsequent relations with the general were always good. In his 1997 interview with Letson, Tibbets

related an interesting postscript regarding Blanchard's attempt to retry the case: "'I still think [Blanchard said] we should [use] one of our own crews.' LeMay looked at him and said, 'That's great. Let's suppose we do that and they fuck it up. Are you going to take responsibility?' Blanchard wouldn't take responsibility for anything. That ended that."

27. Van Kirk had welcomed the check ride; he had become privately concerned because the three of them had not practiced the "big one" together as a crew and because he personally had so little time in a B-29. Dietz, *My True Course*, 427.
28. In their best-selling book, *Enola Gay*, Thomas and Witt (the authors published a similar book in the UK in 1977 under the title *Ruin from the Air*) sometimes succumbed to the kind of hyperbole that often infects nonpilot writers. When describing the breakaway turn during the check ride with Blanchard (218–19), they state, "Tibbets yanked back the control columns, sending the bomber into a sickening stall. It hovered momentarily on its tail, then slid back, turned, and spun toward the ground." Even if the aircraft had structurally survived such a suicidal maneuver, that would have ended any B-29 pilot's career. I asked Dutch Van Kirk about this specific incident, if it could possibly have happened as Thomas and Witt described. He said, "Absolutely not!" Van Kirk telephone interview, November 18, 2013. The B-29 operating manuals specifically prohibited the following maneuvers: "loop, dive, spin, Immelman turns, inverted flight, roll, and vertical bank."
29. The Eatherly episode is drawn from Tibbets, *The Tibbets Story*, 192–93.
30. "General Spaatz Order to Drop Atomic Bombs," War Department, Office of the Chief of Staff, General Handy, Washington, D.C., July 25, 1945. General Handy was acting chief of staff due to General Marshall's absence, the latter with President Truman at the Potsdam Conference.
31. Four days after leaving Tinian, the *Indianapolis* was torpedoed by a Japanese submarine. Out of 1,200 crewmen only 317 survived, the U.S. Navy's greatest loss of life in a single sinking in its history.
32. The events described in this paragraph came from Christman, *Target Hiroshima*, 178–79.
33. Ibid.

## Chapter 10. The Big One

1. Tibbets asked: "What time do you want to drop that bomb, Dutch?" Van Kirk: "Well, you better damn well drop it in the morning; we don't have lights [on North Field, meaning they couldn't recover the aircraft back at Tinian after dark]." Tibbets: "OK, work it backward from there to a takeoff time." Van Kirk, "My True Course."

2. Author Al Christman recorded Deak Parsons' recollections of the various events and timelines in Christman, *Target Hiroshima*, 180–85. Previous works have not always gotten the details correct regarding this prebrief and the mission brief the next day. This text reflects the correct sequence of events based on Van Kirk personal interviews, May 1–2, 2013; Caron and Meares, *Fire of a Thousand Suns*, 228–29; and Christman, *Target Hiroshima*, 182–83.
3. Thomas and Morgan-Witts, *Enola Gay*, 271.
4. Van Kirk and a few others had figured it out on their own. Dutch put two and two together after recognizing several of the nuclear physicists at Wendover from prewar *Life Magazine* photos. However, so ruthless was the Tibbets and Uanna security program that it is doubtful he shared his thoughts with anyone, perhaps not even best friend, Tom Ferebee. Van Kirk personal interviews, May 1–2, 2013.
5. The aircraft commander and flight crews' military ranks indicated are as of August 6, 1945. *Jabit III* was based on the pilot's name, John Abbot Wilson. Krauss and Krauss, *509th Remembered*, 94.
6. Nineteen-year-old Nelson had been a late crew replacement when the original radio operator was reassigned for unknown reasons. He had been a whiz at radio school but was left unassigned for so long that he had only just been promoted from private first class to corporal. He was among the lowest-ranking aircrew members in the 393rd Bombardment Squadron. Nelson and Haggerty, *45 Seconds to Hiroshima*.
7. Sweeney, *War's End*, 146–47. In Krauss and Krauss, *509th Remembered*, 188, Jim Van Pelt and Don Albury related how their plane got its name. One day at Wendover, the crew had a four o'clock get-up for an early flight. When Van Pelt woke up Beahan, the bombardier was grouchy and not feeling well. Beahan said, "A great artiste like me doesn't have to get up this early. He lets the other boys take care of that." From that point forward, Beahan was both "Honey Bee" and "the great artiste." Some believed the true origins of both nicknames referred more to Beahan's winning ways with the ladies. When the crew arrived on Tinian, the vote was unanimous on what to name their B-29.
8. In most reference works *Necessary Evil* is referred to by its Victor number, "No. 91." The airplane was "owned" by aircraft commander Norman Ray (Crew C-14); Marquardt had been assigned it for the Hiroshima mission. His usual B-29 was No. 88, later given the name and nose art, *Up An' Atom*. Krauss and Krauss, *509th Remembered*, 263, 267.
9. McKnight's assigned airplane was *Top Secret*. Due to maintenance or operational issues, aircrews often flew in B-29s other than their "own." Again, before August 6, none of these aircraft bore nose art. Krauss and Krauss,

*509th Remembered*, 261. Thomas and Morgan-Witts erred when they said McKnight was flying *Top Secret*, and this mistake has been repeated in countless books and articles. While their book *Enola Gay* was often exciting and insightful, it contains a number of technical errors and, frankly, a few scenes that cannot be substantiated by other accounts.

10. The passages critical of the Iwo contingency plan are my personal conclusions.
11. Thomas Ferebee Papers (TFP), Sider interview, May 12, 1995.
12. Dietz, *My True Course*, 442.
13. Van Kirk personal interviews, May 1–2, 2013; and Dietz, *My True Course*, 441.
14. Manning, "Enola Gay Bombardier."
15. Tibbets, *The Tibbets Story*, 38–39.
16. Nelson and Haggerty, *45 Seconds to Hiroshima*, 144. In 2002 Studs Terkel asked Tibbets how his mother felt about having her name on the airplane. Tibbets said he only knew what his dad told him later. "My mother," Tibbets told Terkel, "never changed her expression very much about anything, whether it was serious or light, but when she'd get tickled, her stomach would jiggle . . . [When the atomic bomb drop] was announced on the radio, [Dad] said, 'You should have seen the old gal's belly jiggle!'" Terkel, "One Hell of a Big Bang."
17. Captain Lewis flew many more sorties in No. 82 than did Tibbets, and, to some degree, one can sympathize with the idea he thought it was *his* airplane. When the non-musketeer version of the crew picked up No. 82 at the Martin plant at Omaha, they, like all enterprising airmen, managed to find a mechanical problem with the aircraft requiring a layover (Junior Nelson was chosen to discover something wrong with the radios). After doing the town for a couple of days, the boys were inspired to name No. 82 and found someone to paint *Omaha One More Time* on the fuselage. That lasted one day; the moment Tibbets saw the artwork, he ordered it removed. Nelson and Haggerty, *45 Seconds to Hiroshima*, 126.
18. Tibbets, *The Tibbets Story*, 197.
19. For the record, there were several forgotten fellows in No. 82 / *Enola Gay*. When Capt. Bob Lewis flew as aircraft commander of Crew B-9, his copilot was Lt. Richard McNamara; the bombardier was Lt. Stewart Williams; and the navigator was Lt. Harold Rider. The enlisted crew remained the same as when Tibbets commanded the aircraft with Van Kirk and Ferebee on board. Krauss and Krauss, *509th Remembered*, 262.
20. Tibbets had ordered the painter to also replace the 509th arrow and circle symbol on the vertical stabilizer (tail) with a large black letter "R." This was intended to make No. 82 appear to be in the same outfit as hundreds

of other B-29s in order to fool close approaching enemy planes. Tibbets tells us this was "probably an unnecessary precaution." Tibbets, *The Tibbets Story*, 200.

21. Thomas and Morgan-Witts, *Enola Gay*, 277. The authors were quoting Sgt. Bob Caron quoting Captain Lewis.
22. The narrative and chronology of the Sunday afternoon events are taken from Christman, *Target Hiroshima*, 184; and Tibbets, *The Tibbets Story*, 198–206.
23. Laurence, *Dawn over Zero*, 205–6.
24. Christman, *Target Hiroshima*, 144, 187. This safety system was developed by Captain Parsons' ordnance deputy, Lt. Cdr. Francis A. Birch. The U.S. Navy's role in developing an operational atomic bomb was vital, a story woefully undertold in nearly all nuclear weapon histories.
25. Tibbets, *The Tibbets Story*, 199–201.
26. Thomas and Morgan-Witts, *Enola Gay*, 278.
27. Terkel, "One Hell of a Big Bang."
28. Thomas and Morgan-Witts, *Enola Gay*, 260–261. Other contributions to this scene came from Terkel, "One Hell of a Big Bang"; and TFP, Sider interview, May 12, 1995.
29. It was only when the AAF began flying in the stratosphere over Japan's Home Islands that the upper atmospheric jet stream was discovered. It was one of the reasons LeMay had to resort to low-level bombing; B-29s and the Norden bombing system could not deal with 100-mph-plus winds.
30. Thomas and Morgan-Witts, *Enola Gay*, 261.
31. Difficult for English speakers to pronounce correctly, the name "Aioi" is usually rendered "A-EE, Oh-EE."
32. Laurence, *Dawn over Zero*, 212. A highly respected reporter, Laurence had been singled out in April 1945 by Gen. Leslie Groves to serve as the official historian of the Manhattan Project. Evans, *War Stories*.
33. Caron and Meares, *Fire of a Thousand Suns*, 233. The 1,000-round ammunition restriction was due solely to gross weight concerns.
34. This was more than enough fuel for the Hiroshima mission; the full 640-gallon tank welded into the rear bomb bay was in fact more crucial to center of gravity issues because of the 9,700-pound Little Boy bomb in the forward bay.
35. Thomas and Morgan-Witts, *Enola Gay*, 282. The call sign change was another manifestation of security worries. Groups of Japanese soldiers were still hiding in the hills and caves of Tinian overlooking North Field, and they were in radio contact with Tokyo. Shortly after arriving, Tibbets' men were startled to hear Tokyo Rose greet the "new unit with the black-arrow-in-a-circle tail insignia." Krauss and Krauss, *509th Remembered*.
36. Van Kirk personal interviews, May 1–2, 2013.

37. Caron and Meares, *Fire of a Thousand Suns*, 232.
38. Ibid., 232, 241.
39. The fritters were made from pineapples, flour, sugar, and milk, prepared in a deep-fried batter of bite-sized portions. Van Kirk did not care for them but admitted that on the August 6 flight he ate them anyway—they did provide an energy boost. Dietz, *My True Course*, 452; and Van Kirk telephone interview, November 18, 2013.
40. Tibbets, *The Tibbets Story*, 204. How Tibbets planned to distribute the cyanide is unknown. To have waited until an emergency arose would have been absurd. There would have been no time to explain about the pills, pass them out, and let the men digest the information while simultaneously attempting to save the airplane and men. The only conclusion one can make is that the colonel thought it was an overly dramatic gesture by Groves and the other leaders, and he simply decided not to upset the crew by shielding them from the entire subject. Besides, only he and Parsons had any real knowledge of the Manhattan Project, and they quietly carried one pill each.
41. Sweeney, *War's End*, 162.
42. A lifelong Dodger fan, Caron had written to Bob Finch, Branch Rickey's assistant manager, for an official cap. Initially rebuffed, Caron was so persistent that Finch finally sent him the cap, with a letter stating, "Anyone who can write that kind of letter in the midst of disappointment . . . deserves everything in the world. I hope . . . you wear it down the main street of Tokyo." Caron and Meares, *Fire of a Thousand Suns*, 176.
43. "Interview with Crew of Enola Gay," U.S. National Archives, August 1945. *YouTube*, uploaded on June 30, 2007. https://www.youtube.com/watch?v=X7Pt215DLio.
44. The bulk of the technical narrative on the B-29 is from *The B-29: Airplane Commander Training Manual*, AAF Manual 50-9, February 1945; and *B-29 Flight Operating Instructions*, USAAF Manual 50-9, March 1945.
45. Tibbets had enormous faith in the tender loving care that his group maintenance officer, Lt. Col. John Porter, and crew chief, Sergeant McCaleb, regularly gave the *Enola Gay*.
46. Lewis' crew had been flying combat missions in No. 82; knowing that the ship would be subject to a lot of attention, Van Kirk and Ferebee took it upon themselves to inspect the airplane and "clean it out." On this occasion, one of the "unauthorized items" they removed was a pair of "trophy" panties still preserved from Crew B-9's Omaha escapade. Dietz, *My True Course*, 453.
47. Ibid.
48. The timelines for the August 6 mission come from Christman, *Target Hiroshima*; Tibbets, *The Tibbets Story*; Dietz, *My True Course*; and *Navigator's*

*Log of the Enola Gay*, facsimile of Captain Van Kirk's original Hiroshima mission log, August 6, 1945. Author's copy courtesy Dutch Van Kirk.

49. Caron and Meares, *Fire of a Thousand Suns*, 235.
50. Ibid., 234.
51. With the arrival of jet bombers, putt-putts were replaced by wheeled external power carts with a special receptacle that ground crews could plug into a port on the side of a bomber's fuselage.
52. The engine start, takeoff checklist items, and performance specifications came from *B-29 Airplane Commander*, AAF Manual 50-9, February 1945; *B-29 Pilot's Flight Operating Instructions*, USAAF Manual 50-9, March 1945; Skiles, "B-29 Pilot Report"; and Krauss and Krauss, *509th Remembered*, 38.
53. Dramatic advances in airborne mapping radar had been made since the British introduced their revolutionary H2S system early in the war. The United States was given access to the technology, leading to the American H2X radar used in leader B-17 and B-24 bombers. Early B-29s were fitted with the externally mounted APQ-7 "Eagle" radar but it proved too cumbersome and caused too much aerodynamic drag. By 1945 the internally mounted APQ-13 mapping/bombing radar system was ready, offering greatly improved resolution, lighter weight, and a full bombing as well as navigation capability. Harder, *Flying from the Black Hole*, 53, 55, 72.
54. Due to their troubled history, B-29 mechanics and ground crewmen sometimes referred to the Wright R-3350 Cyclones as "Wrong" engines.
55. The electro-magnetic flux-gate allowed magnetic readings to be displayed in an electronic form that could be passed on to repeater indicators and the autopilot. It also provided a directional reference that was stable over the long term, while the directional gyro was more stable and accurate over the short term, especially when the airplane was in a turn. The directional gyro was periodically corrected en route via the flux-gate compass.
56. Krauss and Krauss, *509th Remembered*, 178.
57. Sweeney, *War's End*, 166.
58. Tibbets, *The Tibbets Story*, 209.
59. Ibid., 210.
60. This passage is my own analysis.
61. TFP, David Perlmutt, *Charlotte Observer*, August 6, 1995; and National Press Club, Lunch w/Paul Tibbets, Washington D.C., 1995. YouTube, August 14, 2012. According to Thomas and Morgan-Witts, *Enola Gay*, 290, Lewis said, "She's too heavy. Pull her off—now!" When Lewis reached for the yoke, Tibbets said, "No! Leave it!" Over the years, Tibbets himself related other versions of their takeoff dialogue. The gist of the exchange, however, never varied. I asked Dutch Van Kirk about the colonel's occasional judgment lapses. He said, with a touch of exasperation, "You know,

Paul Tibbets wasn't always right in his decisions!" Tibbets appears to have been most vulnerable when it came time to stand behind someone who had earned his personal loyalty, even if their conduct was questionable. Van Kirk personal interviews, May 1–2, 2013.

62. Skiles, "Pretty Baby."
63. Sweeney, *War's End*, 166. Thomas and Morgan-Witts, *Enola Gay*, 284, state that McKnight left for Iwo Jima at 1:51 a.m., several minutes after the weather planes had launched. In Tibbets, *The Tibbets Story*, 214, however, Tibbets is very clear that McKnight took off just after the three strike airplanes departed at 2:45 a.m. We are using the Tibbets version here.
64. *Navigator's Log of the Enola Gay*, facsimile. Magnetic variation—the difference in degrees between the magnetic and geographic north poles—was only one to three degrees between Tinian and Japan. Van Kirk's master flux-gate compass had a feature that allowed him to set the applicable variation for each leg. The pilots' repeater compasses automatically showed this corrected heading.
65. Tibbets, *The Tibbets Story*, 219. Tibbets had become addicted to Old Bond Street pipe tobacco while at Polebrook in 1942. Sgt. Ray Gallagher, who would fly as Major Sweeney's assistant flight engineer / scanner in *Bockscar* on the Nagasaki mission, worked with Tibbets in 1944 on the B-29 test program at Eglin Field, Florida. When Tibbets and crew were checking out the WASPs in *Ladybird*, Gallagher gave Dora Dougherty some sage advice: "If you want to ask Paul Tibbets a question, wait till he is smoking his pipe. Don't ask a question when he's smoking a cigarette." Krauss and Krauss, *509th Remembered*, 212.

## Chapter 11. Hiroshima

1. Christman, *Target Hiroshima*, 186–87; Thomas and Morgan-Witts, *Enola Gay*, 293; and Groves, *Now It Can Be Told*, 318. Van Kirk made the astute observation that the two men, who were not wearing parachutes, were in a physically dangerous position. Should either of them have slipped off the narrow catwalk—a bit of turbulence could have done it—they would have tumbled onto the comparatively flimsy bomb bay doors, which likely would not have held their weight. Dietz, *My True Course*, 462.
2. Dietz, *My True Course*, 462.
3. Thomas and Morgan-Witts, *Enola Gay*, 293; and Groves, *Now It Can Be Told*, 318. Van Kirk later said that "carrying the bomb did not bother me, but the fact they were fooling around [in the bomb bay] with black powder did." Dietz, *My True Course*, 466. Joseph Marx in *Seven Hours to Zero* makes an egregious error on page 76 when he states that Parsons' "first steps were the installation of the *uranium slug* [author italics]."

4. Tibbets, *The Tibbets Story*, 211.
5. Beser, *Hiroshima and Nagasaki Revisited*, 5. Beser was the only man to fly both the Hiroshima and Nagasaki missions.
6. Nelson and Haggerty, *45 Seconds to Hiroshima*, 149; Caron and Meares, *Fire of a Thousand Suns*, 241; and Van Kirk personal interviews, May 1–2, 2013.
7. Caron and Meares, *Fire of a Thousand Suns*, 242; and Tibbets, *The Tibbets Story*, 213.
8. As uncomfortable as the bombardier's no-back little seat was, Ferebee could deal with it. "They always said I could sleep anywhere, and at that time, I guess I could." Thomas Ferebee Papers (TFP), Sider interview, May 12, 1995.
9. Van Kirk, "My True Course."
10. Tibbets, *The Tibbets Story*, 215.
11. "Robert Lewis, "The Notebook: The History of Robert Lewis's Enola Gay Log," September 10, 2010, *Conelrad Adjacent*. http://conelrad.blogspot.com/2010/09/notebook-history-of-enola-gay-flight.html, posted by Bill Geerhart. Van Kirk was essentially using the radar as a driftmeter. The speed and direction of the wind, aided by E6-B circular slide rule calculations, could be determined by observing the ship's drift angle on radar when on at least two significantly different magnetic headings. Navigators call this a "double-drift" procedure. *Air Navigation*, AF Manual 51-40, vol. 1. USAF, August 1, 1968.
12. Van Kirk personal interviews, May 1–2, 2013.
13. From the *Navigators Information File*, Headquarters, USAAF, October 1944.
14. For his celestial computations, Van Kirk had to convert the local time into Greenwich Mean Time (GMT), the internationally accepted standard upon which all star tables are based.
15. *Navigator's Log of the Enola Gay*, facsimile of Capt. Van Kirk's original Hiroshima mission log, August 6, 1945. Celestial navigators had to work in nautical miles because the globe is divided into arcs of degrees, minutes, and seconds. One minute of arc along a meridian (longitude line) is equal to one nautical mile. Part of Van Kirk's computations involved converting those figures in his log from knots to miles per hour for pilot use. World War II navigators tried not to confuse their pilots with nautical miles, knots, or other related terms as it could lead to very serious problems. Eventually the old English statute mile system had to be abandoned as the risks and confusion became too great. Today all American military aircraft airspeed meters are registered in knots.
16. Van Kirk personal interviews, May 1–2, 2013.

17. Tibbets, *The Tibbets Story*, 217. Mt. Suribachi was the scene of the famous flag-raising photograph idealized in the U.S. Marine Corps Memorial sculpture at Arlington National Cemetery, Washington D.C.
18. *Navigator's Log of the Enola Gay.*
19. Krauss and Krauss, *509th Remembered*, 103.
20. Christman, *Target Hiroshima*, 189.
21. Like civilian jet airliners, the cabin was kept at about 8,000-feet pressure altitude. To keep sea-level pressure would run the risk of an explosive decompression in the event of a fuselage breach.
22. Nelson and Haggerty, *45 Seconds to Hiroshima*, 150.
23. Ibid., 151.
24. Lewis "The Notebook."
25. Dietz, *My True Course*, 469.
26. Pardini, *The Legendary Norden Bombsight*, 344; and Dietz, *My True Course*, 471.
27. Dietz, *My True Course*, 469.
28. Tibbets, *The Tibbets Story*, 222.
29. Harder, *Flying from the Black Hole*, 52. Visitors to the Smithsonian Institution's Udvar-Hazy Center at Washington Dulles International Airport may view Ferebee's bomb sight through the *Enola Gay*'s nose plexiglass, still mounted in its original location on the restored B-29. Bruce Callander, a World War II bombardier and former editor of the *Air Force Times*, has described this bombsight synchronizing process as "roughly equivalent to tuning a radio and adjusting the temperature in a shower at the same time." Ibid., 51.
30. Christman, *Target Hiroshima*, 191.
31. The less majestic discussion and Van Kirk's 2012 comments came from "8th Air Force Historical Society of Georgia, Dutch Van Kirk, guest speaker," *YouTube*, August 10, 2013, https://www.youtube.com/watch?v=hoCsruPtmL4; Van Kirk, "My True Course"; and Van Kirk personal interviews, May 1–2, 2013.
32. The APQ-13's retractable radome was blistered in the fuselage belly between the two sets of bomb bay doors. Stiborik's actions are from *Navigators Information File*, Hdqs, USAAF, October 1944; and my own radar navigator experience.
33. Tibbets, *The Tibbets Story*, 223.
34. TFP, David Perlmutt, *Charlotte Observer*, August 6, 1995.
35. The electronic tone concept would later be used by the Strategic Air Command to score circular error on simulated nuclear bomb drops.
36. Terkel, "One Hell of a Big Bang."
37. TFP, Frank Tursi, *Winston-Salem Journal*, November 8, 1987. A brief word on Little Boy's triggering systems: Like *all* subsequent nuclear weapons,

the bomb had multiple fusing and safety devices. Each one had to fire sequentially in order for the weapon to detonate. First the anchored arming wires had to properly withdraw when it left the bomb bay, activating the fifteen-second safe separation timers. Then six barometric sensing devices had to all close at the correct altitude. The final sequence in the series circuitry was the radar proximity fuse that signaled arrival at the preselected detonation altitude above the earth. Campbell, *The Silverplate Bombers*, 83; and Krauss and Krauss, *509th Remembered*, 19.

38. Tibbets, *The Tibbets Story*, 224–25.
39. Van Kirk personal interviews, May 1–2, 2013.
40. Krauss and Krauss, *509th Remembered*, 83.
41. TFP, Frank Tursi, *Winston-Salem Journal*, November 8, 1987.
42. Harder, *Flying from the Black Hole*, 52, 269.
43. For the record, some scientific journals state the elapsed time was 44.4 seconds, and detonation above target occurred at 1,968 feet.
44. It had long been understood that an air burst would generate a wider radius of destruction—too much of the energy would be absorbed by the earth with a ground detonation. Also, the United States sincerely desired the destructive forces to be heat and blast and *not* long-term radiation effects. By exploding the bomb one-third of a mile above the city, perhaps as much as one-half of the long-term radiation was mitigated. All the same, the effects of fallout were poorly understood at the time, and nearly all those within a half mile of ground zero suffered a fatal dose of radiation. Still, Hiroshima and Nagasaki were not left dangerously radioactive. Indeed, as early as mid-September 1945, American scientists and other personnel (including several *Enola Gay* and *Bockscar* crewmen) researching the effects of the blasts were able to walk through Nagasaki without protection and did not suffer any ill effects. Surprisingly, on-site instruments showed that lingering radioactivity, even at the ground zeroes, was at relatively low levels. Tibbets, *The Tibbets Story*; and Marx, 183–85.
45. A "shack" is bombardier slang for a bull's eye; during the interwar years the practice aiming point was, in fact, a small building. Regarding radar bombing, despite General Groves' deep suspicions about its accuracy, that would be the future. Not only could successful bombing be conducted at night or "through the clouds," but improvements in technology would also make radar consistently more accurate than optical aiming. Nevertheless, optical bombsights would continue to be installed in U.S. strategic bombers all the way through the B-52F Model Stratofortress. They were employed extensively in the Vietnam-era B-52D to assess immediate post-strike bomb damage. The Norden sight was last used to drop weapons in the B-26/A-26 medium bomber during that same war. Harder, *Flying from the Black Hole*, 267.

46. Knebel and Bailey, *No High Ground*, 131.
47. Caron and Meares, *Fire of a Thousand Suns*, 249.
48. Malnic, "Paul Tibbets, Pilot Who Bombed Hiroshima."
49. Tibbets, *The Tibbets Story*, 226.
50. Nelson and Haggerty, *45 Seconds to Hiroshima*, 152.
51. Dietz, *My True Course*, 472; and Christman, *Target Hiroshima*, 192. Ferebee later owned up to also yielding to instinct when he shouted at the same time, "They're shooting at us!"
52. Christman, *Target Hiroshima*, 192.
53. Marx, *Seven Hours to Zero*, 191.
54. Caron and Meares, *Fire of a Thousand Suns*, 249. Unfortunately, most of the photos taken by the photo ship did not turn out due to technical difficulties. Neither did most of Caron's, except for a half-dozen exposures at the very end of the roll. One of those frames became the iconic Hiroshima mushroom cloud image.
55. Tibbets, *The Tibbets Story*, 225.
56. "Interview with Crew of Enola Gay," U.S. National Archives, August 1945. *YouTube*, uploaded on June 30, 2007, https://www.youtube.com/watch?v=X7Pt215DLio; Tibbets, *The Tibbets Story*, 227–28; and Nelson and Haggerty, *45 Seconds to Hiroshima*, 153.
57. Most published estimates of the Hiroshima uranium bomb state that it yielded about 15 kilotons (15,000 tons) of TNT. The Trinity and Nagasaki plutonium bombs yielded 18 and 21 kilotons, respectively.
58. Lieutenant Beser heard Lewis say, "Look at that sonofabitch blow!" Beser, *Hiroshima and Nagasaki Revisited*, 112.
59. Tibbets, *The Tibbets Story*, 228.
60. Caron and Meares, *Fire of a Thousand Suns*, 250.
61. Tibbets, *The Tibbets Story*, 228; and Christman, *Target Hiroshima*, 193.
62. Caron and Meares, *Fire of a Thousand Suns*, 251–52.
63. Ibid.
64. Van Kirk telephone interview, October 2, 2013.
65. Beser, *Hiroshima and Nagasaki Revisited*, 112. Beser strained his credibility in other accounts as well. Perhaps the most notorious example was a story that he likely supplied to writers Thomas and Morgan-Witts. Beser claimed to have stumbled into Mrs. J. Robert Oppenheimer's home at Los Alamos and discovered her naked on a couch, drinking a cocktail. Seemingly a libertine, she then casually waved him through the living room and into the bedroom he had been assigned in the house. In his interview with Letson, Paul Tibbets declared this anecdote "complete BS." Thomas and Morgan-Witts, *Enola Gay*, 39–40.
66. Dietz, *My True Course*, 478.

67. Nelson and Haggerty, *45 Seconds to Hiroshima*, 154; Knebel and Bailey, *No High Ground*, 163. Although the mushroom cloud had risen above 50,000 feet, Caron lost sight of it due both to clouds and the curvature of the earth. It is unclear whether this number was statute or nautical miles.
68. Lewis's journal entry was cited in Tibbets, *The Tibbets Story*, 229.

## Chapter 12. The Rest of the Story

1. Tibbets, *The Tibbets Story*, 230.
2. Before landing procedures and crew action items taken from *The B-29 Training Manual*, AAF 50–9, February 1945; and Skiles, "B-29 Pilot Report."
3. Nelson and Haggerty, *45 Seconds to Hiroshima*, 155.
4. *Navigator's Log of the Enola Gay*, facsimile of Captain Van Kirk's original Hiroshima mission log, August 6, 1945, courtesy Dutch Van Kirk.
5. Sakrison and Tennyson, "The Enola Gay"; and Tibbets, *The Tibbets Story*, 231.
6. *Navigator's Log of the Enola Gay*.
7. Caron and Meares, *Fire of a Thousand Suns*, 253.
8. Tibbets, *The Tibbets Story*, 232.
9. Dietz, *My True Course*, 481–82.
10. Ibid., 483.
11. Nearly everyone—crewmen and historians alike—gets this aircraft's name wrong, including Tibbets and Sweeney in their own books! It is *not* Fred "Bock's Car" or "Boxcar." It is *Bockscar*, a play on Fred's name and the old railroad general freight boxcar. Visitors to the National Museum of the Air Force at Dayton, Ohio, can see for themselves the correct name on the side of the airplane's fuselage along with the image of a boxcar sprouting wings.
12. LeMay meeting and dialogue from Dietz, *My True Course*, 491; and Tibbets, *Return of the Enola Gay*, 250.
13. Lt. Col. Tom Classen and his crew A-5 were immediately dispatched to the States in "No. 94." Before they could bring the third plutonium bomb back to Tinian (the first two were the "Trinity" test bomb and "Fat Man"), the war ended. A fifth atomic bomb could not have been made ready for several more weeks.
14. Another important event also happened on August 15, at least as far as Capt. Dutch Van Kirk was concerned. Special orders had been cut promoting him to temporary major. Dietz, *My True Course*, 494.
15. Ibid., 498.
16. Krauss and Krauss, *509th Remembered*, 308–13.
17. Dietz, *My True Course*, 500.
18. Ibid., 511.
19. Ibid.

20. Tibbets, *The Tibbets Story*, 245–53.
21. Four days after the first atomic bomb test, a French engineer and amateur clothing designer named Louis Réard (who was running his mother's lingerie shop near the Folies Bergère in Paris) called his new "explosive," two-piece "atom-sized" swimsuit "*le bikini.*" "A Brief History of the Bikini," *Reminisce Magazine*, http://www.reminisce.com/1960s/a-brief-history-of-the-bikini/.
22. The seldom-used rank of U.S. Navy commodore is equivalent to an Army, Air Force, or Marine Corps brigadier general. *Target Hiroshima* by Al Christman is an outstanding biography of Deak Parsons, a man who would later become known as the "atomic admiral." He was nicknamed "Deacon" at the Naval Academy, a play on his last name, which was later shortened to "Deak." He died of a heart attack at age fifty-two the morning after learning that his good friend Dr. J. Robert Oppenheimer had lost his security clearance over what were later found to be untrue charges he was a communist. Parsons was deeply respected by everyone and the unsung hero of the 509th.
23. Tibbets, *The Tibbets Story*, 248. Although three Trinity-type tests were originally scheduled, only Able (air burst) and Baker (underwater detonation) were conducted.
24. The observer was professor Simon Alexandrov, the Soviet Union's delegate to the new UN Atomic Energy Commission. Christman, *Target Hiroshima*, 224.
25. Tibbets, *The Tibbets Story*, 252; and Dietz, *My True Course*, 516–18.
26. Postwar Van Kirk biographic information is from 8th Air Force Historical Society of Georgia, Dutch Van Kirk, guest speaker, *YouTube*, August 10, 2013, https://www.youtube.com/watch?v=hoCsruPtmL4; and Dietz, *My True Course.*
27. The GI Bill is officially titled the "Servicemen's Readjustment Act." By the late 1950s it had enabled over 9 million veterans to receive advanced professional training or a college education.
28. Van Kirk gave me a crystal-clear example of what he was often up against in educating young people about the war. At one school gathering, the host introduced him thus: "Students, this is Mr. Theodore Van Kirk, who is here to tell us about World War Eleven." Van Kirk interviews, May 1–2, 2013.
29. I was deeply saddened that Dutch Van Kirk, who had supported this book and approved of the concept and title, did not live to see a late draft of the manuscript. Ironically, it arrived at his home on the very day he died.
30. Postwar Ferebee biographic details are from Dietz, *My True Course*, and the Thomas Ferebee Papers (TFP).
31. Tom Ferebee was one of the few USAF officers—junior or senior—who did not take any of LeMay's guff if he disagreed with him. Ferebee was also among the even *fewer* who successfully got away with it.

32. It was extremely rare for a nonpilot flying officer to become a full colonel and get this job in that era. Despite his self-admitted articulation difficulties, Ferebee proved an extraordinarily competent senior officer who was greatly admired by nearly everyone that ever worked for or with him. Mary Ann Conrad Ferebee, Personal interviews, May 1–2, 2013.
33. TFP, Sider interview, May 12, 1995. Each of those B-47s carried a punch three hundred times more powerful than either Little Boy or Fat Man.
34. Operation Arc Light is the code name for the eight years of B-52 operations in Vietnam and South East Asia, 1965–73.
35. TFP, Mark Andrews, *Orlando Sentinel*, August 4, 1985.
36. Ferebee and Van Kirk remained true to form to the end. After informing Dutch he had only six months to live, Tom asked, "Will you say something nice at my funeral?" Van Kirk replied, "I will if I can think of anything." Dietz, *My True Course*, 535.
37. Postwar Tibbets biographic details from Tibbets, *The Tibbets Story*; Harden, "Pilot Didn't Regret A-Bomb"; "Paul Tibbets, Jr." *National Aviation Hall of Fame*, http://nationalaviation.org/tibbets-jr-paul/; Associated Press, "Enola Gay Pilot Tibbets Dead at 92"; and Paul Tibbets IV, Email interviews, 2014.
38. Credited with 22.5 World War 2 air victories, the heavily decorated Colonel Schilling was instrumental in making aerial refueling operational. Tragically, he was killed in a car crash in England in 1956.
39. Scene with Truman is in Terkel, "One Hell of a Big Bang."
40. Tibbets, *The Tibbets Story*, 273.
41. Ibid., 280–81. Tibbets was turned down three times for promotion to major general. He asked a well-connected civilian friend to surreptitiously check out his Pentagon file. His suspicions were confirmed when the friend uncovered extremely damaging comments inserted by Gen. Lauris Norstad.
42. Tibbets, *The Tibbets Story*, 291.
43. Paul Tibbets IV, Email interviews, 2014.
44. Battle casualties from Lacey, "Battle of Okinawa"; and Gallagher, "The Enola Gay Controversy."
45. "Paul Tibbets, Jr." National Aviation Hall of Fame (NAHF), www.nationalaviation.org/tibbets-jr-paul/.
46. Dietz, *My True Course*, 556.
47. Harden, "Pilot Didn't Regret A-Bomb," *Columbus Dispatch*, November 2, 2007.
48. Paul Tibbets IV, Email interviews, 2014. In the interview with Mike Harden of the *Columbus Dispatch* the day after Tibbets passed, Tibbets' granddaughter, Kia Tibbets (who grew up in his house), was quoted as saying, "He always told me that he loved me. It's not a side of him that other people saw." Ibid.

## Appendix

1. Sweeney, *War's End*, 176–77.
2. Dietz, *My True Çourse*, 488–89.
3. Sweeney, *War's End*, 197–99.
4. Tibbets, *Return of the Enola Gay*, 247; and Sweeney, *War's End*, 203.
5. Sweeney, *War's End*, 204–5.
6. Ibid., 208; Krauss and Krauss, *The 509th Remembered*, 175–76.
7. Olivi, *Decision at Nagasaki*, 127.
8. Sweeney, *War's End*, 203–4.
9. Olivi, *Decision at Nagasaki*, 96.
10. Krauss and Krauss, *The 509th Remembered*, 20; and Admiral Fred Ashworth private letter to Lisa Beahan Harrison, November 7, 2005.
11. Krauss and Krauss, *The 509th Remembered*, 37.
12. Ibid., 19–20.
13. Tibbets, *Return of the Enola Gay*, 248.
14. Nagasaki: "The Commander's Voice," *YouTube*, Part 2 of 3 parts, featuring Charles Sweeney, uploaded January 5, 2010, https://www.youtube.com/watch?v=A56-OD8dVu8.
15. Olivi, *Decision at Nagasaki*, 119. Admiral Ashworth said that at the preflight briefing the instructions were to wait no more than twenty minutes. Krauss and Krauss, *The 509th Remembered*, 20.
16. Correll, "Near Failure at Nagasaki."
17. Olivi, *Decision at Nagasaki*, 121.
18. Sweeney, *War's End*, 211–12.
19. Olivi, *Decision at Nagasaki*, 119.
20. Van Kirk interviews, May 1–2, 2013.
21. Sweeney, *War's End*, 199.
22. Olivi, *Decision at Nagasaki*, 121.
23. Ibid., 121, 128.
24. Admiral Fred Ashworth private letter to Lisa Beahan Harrison, November 7, 2005.
25. Sweeney, *War's End*, 216.
26. Olivi, *Decision at Nagasaki*, 122.
27. Van Kirk interviews, May 1–2, 2013.
28. Capt. Kermit Beahan, one-page, handwritten Nagasaki post-mission summary, copy courtesy Lisa Beahan Harrison.
29. Ibid.
30. Ibid.; and Dietz, *My True Course*, 489.
31. Olivi, *Decision at Nagasaki*, 125–26.
32. Krauss and Krauss, *The 509th Remembered*, 31.
33. Olivi, *Decision at Nagasaki*, 133–34.
34. Sweeney, *War's End*, 224.

35. Ibid.
36. Olivi, *Decision at Nagasaki*, 134.
37. Sweeney, *War's End*, 225.
38. Olivi, *Decision at Nagasaki*, 134.
39. Ibid., 130.
40. Sweeney, *War's End*, 224.
41. Olivi, *Decision at Nagasaki*, 134.
42. Ibid.
43. Map of airfields on Okinawa, 1945. Original archived at USAF Historical Research Agency, Maxwell AFB, Alabama, http://en.wikipedia.org/wiki/Yontan_Airfield#/media/File:Okinawa_airfields_1945.jpg.
44. Krauss and Krauss, *509th Remembered*, 20.
45. Admiral Fred Ashworth private letter to Lisa Beahan Harrison, November 7, 2005.
46. Tibbets, *The Tibbets Story*, 238.
47. Tibbets, *Return of the Enola Gay*, 248.
48. Ibid.
49. Sweeney, *War's End*, 169.
50. Van Kirk personal interviews, May 1–2, 2013.
51. Ibid.
52. Dietz, *My True Course*, 489.
53. Capt. Kermit Beahan one-page, handwritten Nagasaki post-mission summary, copy courtesy Lisa Beahan Harrison.
54. TFP, Sider interview, May 12, 1995.

# Bibliography


## Thomas Ferebee Papers (TFP) North Carolina History Museum Raleigh, North Carolina

*The reference number precedes the document title.*

2006.112.13. 97th Bomb Group Orders, May 11, 1942

2006.112.38. Whom-It-May-Concern, BG Atkinson, HQ5thBW, January 10, 1944

2006.112.174. Citation for Distinguished Flying Cross, May 19, 1943

2006.112.93. *Mocksville Enterprise*, "Davie Boy Is War Hero," August 10, 1945

2006.112.139A-C. Frank Tursi, "Tom Ferebee: Davie Native Nailed Down a Spot in History," *Winston-Salem Journal*, November 8, 1987

L.2007.1.138A-C. David Perlmutt, "'This can't happen again,'" *Charlotte Observer*, August 6, 1995

L.2007.1.299. *Seabee Map of Tinian*, "As if It Were New York City," June 15, 1945

L.2007.1.3, A-D. Mark Andrews, "The Sunday Q&A," *Orlando Sentinel*, August 4, 1985

L.2007.1.46. Transcript of Don Sider interview (Miami stringer), May 12, 1995

226.112.124. AAF Officer Qualification Record, July 1, 1947

## Publications

Aitkin, Ronald. *Dieppe 1942: The Jubilee Disaster.* London: Book Club Associates, 1980.

Associated Press. "Enola Gay Pilot Tibbets Dead at 92," *Air Force Times*, November 1, 2007. http://www.airforcetimes.com/article/20071101/NEWS/711010319/Enola-Gay-pilot-Tibbets-dead-92.

Beser, Jacob. *Hiroshima and Nagasaki Revisited.* Memphis: Global Press, 1988.

Bowers, Peter M. *Boeing B-29 Superfortress, Warbird Tech Series.* North Branch, Minn.: Specialty Press, 1999.

Boyne. Walter J. "The B-29's Battle of Kansas," *Air Force Magazine*, February 2012.

Caldwell, Donald L. *JG 26: Top Guns of the Luftwaffe.* New York: Ballantine Books, 1993.

Callander, Bruce D. "Bombardier," *Air Force Magazine*, December 1990.

———. "The Short Heyday of the Bombardier," *Air Force Times*, April 9, 1984.

Campbell, Richard H. *The Silverplate Bombers.* Jefferson, N.C.: McFarland, 2005.

Caron, George R., and Charlotte Meares. *Fire of a Thousand Suns.* Westminster, Colo.: Web Publishing Company, 1995.

Christman, Al. *Target Hiroshima: Deak Parsons and the Creation of the Atomic Bomb.* Annapolis, Md.: Naval Institute Press, 1998.

Correll, John T. "The Feeder Force," *Air Force Magazine*, January 2014.

———. "Near Failure at Nagasaki," *Air Force Magazine*, July 2011.

———. "The Real Twelve O'clock High," *Air Force Magazine*, January 2011.

Coster-Mullen, John. *Atom Bombs: The Top Secret Inside Story of Little Boy and Fat Man.* Waukesha, Wisc.: J. Coster-Mullen, spiral bound, 2012.

Cragon, Harvey G. *How the Norden Bombsight Works.* Dallas: Cragon Books, 2010.

Dietz, Suzanne Simon. *My True Course: Dutch Van Kirk: Northumberland to Hiroshima.* Lawrenceville, Ga.: Red Gremlin Press, 2012.

Doolittle, James A. *I Could Never Be So Lucky Again.* With Carroll V. Glines. New York: Bantam Books, 1991.

Dorr, Robert F. *B-29 Units of World War II.* Oxford, U.K.: Osprey Publishing, 2002.

Doyle, David. *B-29 Superfortress in Action.* Carrollton, Tex.: Squadron Signal Publications, 2011.

Duffin, Alan, and Paul Matheis. *The 12 O'Clock High Logbook.* Albany, Ga.: BearManor Media, 2005.

Evans, Harold. *War Stories: Reporting in the Time of Conflict from the Crimea to Iraq.* Pierpont, N.H.: Bunker Hill, 2003.

Freeman, Roger A. *Airfields of the Eighth—Then and Now.* London: Battle of Britain International, 2001.

———. *B-17 Flying Fortress.* New York: Crown, 1983.

———. *Mighty Eighth War Manual.* Minneapolis: Motorbooks International, 1991.

Gallagher. Edward J. *The Enola Gay Controversy.* Lehigh University Digital Library, http://digital.lib.lehigh.edu/trial/enola/.

Gann, Ernest K. *Fate Is The Hunter.* New York: Simon and Schuster, 1961.

Gibson, Michael L. *Aviation in Northamptonshire: An Illustrated Guide.* Northampton, U.K.: Northampton Libraries, 1981.

Glasstone, Samuel, and Philip J. Dolan. *The Effects of Nuclear Weapons*, 3rd ed. Washington, D.C.: U.S. Department of Defense and U.S. Department of Energy, 1977.

Grant, Rebecca. "The Growth at Guam," *Air Force Magazine*, December 2013.

Greene, Bob. *Duty: A Father, His Son, and the Man Who Won the War.* New York: Harper Collins, 2000.

Greer, Thomas H. "Individual Training of Flying Personnel." In *The Army Air Forces in World War II*, Vol. VI, *Men and Planes*, edited by W. F. Craven and J. L. Cate (Chicago: University of Chicago, 1955), http://www.ibiblio.org/hyperwar/AAF/VI/AAF-VI-17.html.

Griffith, Hubert. "The Gremlin Question." *Royal Air Force Journal*, no. 13, April 18, 1943. http://www.angelfire.com/id/100sqn/gremlins.html.

Groves, Leslie M. *Now It Can Be Told*. New York: Da Capo Press, 1983.

Harden, Mike. "Pilot Didn't Regret A-Bomb," *Columbus Dispatch*, November 2, 2007.

Harder, Robert O. *Flying from the Black Hole: The B-52 Navigator-Bombardiers of Vietnam*. Annapolis, Md.: Naval Institute Press, 2009.

Hess, William. *B-17 Flying Fortress: Weapons Book No. 40*. New York: Ballantine, 1974.

Hughes, Arthur J. *History of Air Navigation*. London: George Allen & Unwin, 1946.

Humphreys, Edwin C., ed. *Bombardier: A History*. Paducah, Ky.: Turner Publishing Company, 1993.

Johnsen, Frederick A. *Boeing B-17 Flying Fortress*. Warbird Tech Series. North Branch, Minn.: Specialty Press, 2001.

Kieft, Lester. *Joseph Priestley and the Priestley House*, 2nd ed. Northumberland, Pa.: Friends of the Joseph Priestley House, 2006.

Killian, Michael. "Two Pilots Log Their Memoirs," *Chicago Tribune*, November 5, 1978.

Knebel, Fletcher, and Charles W. Bailey II. *No High Ground*. New York: Bantam Books/Harper & Brothers, 1961.

Krauss, Robert, and Amelia Krauss, eds. *The 509th Remembered, A History . . . Told by the Veterans That Dropped the Atomic Bombs . . .* Buchanan, Mich.: 509th Press, 2005.

Kuznick. Peter J. "Defending the Indefensible: A Meditation on the Life of Hiroshima Pilot Paul Tibbets, Jr.," *Asia-Pacific Journal: Japan Focus*, November 2007. http://japanfocus.org/-Peter_J_-Kuznick/2642.

Lacey, Laura. "Battle of Okinawa." MilitaryHistoryOnline.com, April 13, 2003. http://www.militaryhistoryonline.com/wwii/okinawa/default.aspx/.

Laurence, William L. *Dawn over Zero: The Story of the Atomic Bomb*. New York: Alfred A. Knopf, 1946.

Lay, Beirne, Jr., and Sy Bartlett. *12 O'Clock High*. New York: Harper & Brothers, 1948.

Letson, Dawn. "General Paul Tibbets: An Oral History." Women Air Service Pilots Oral History Project, Interviewed by Dawn Letson, February 24, 1997. Denton: Texas Woman's University, 2002. http://cdm16283.contentdm.oclc.org/cdm/ref/collection/p214coll2/id/4798.

Malnic, Eric. "Paul Tibbets, Pilot Who Bombed Hiroshima, Dies at 92," *Los Angeles Times*, November 2, 2007.

Manning, Brad. "Enola Gay Bombardier Was Quite Cool; Man Slept On Way to Drop A-Bomb," *Charlotte Observer*, August 5, 1990.

Marx, Joseph L. *Seven Hours to Zero*. New York: G. P. Putnam's Sons, 1967.

McCullough, David. *Truman*. New York: Simon & Schuster, 1992.

Moore, Jamie W., ed. *Growing Up in Davie County*. Charleston, S.C.: History Press, 2005.

Nelson, Richard H., and Forrest S. Haggerty. *45 Seconds to Hiroshima*. Bloomington, Ind.: Author House, 2005.

Nisos, Michael. "Bombardier and His Bombsight," *Air Force Magazine*, September 1981.

Olivi, Fred J. *Decision at Nagasaki: The Mission That Almost Failed*. With William R. Watson Jr. Printed by author, 1999.

O'Reilly, Charles T., and William A. Rooney. *The Enola Gay and the Smithsonian Institution*. Jefferson, N.C.: McFarland, 2005.

Ottley, John, Jr. "The Long Haul." *Aviation History Magazine*, September 2014.

Paine, Lauran, Jr. "And Now There Are Three." *Sport Aviation Magazine*, August 2013.

Pardini, Albert L. *The Legendary Norden Bombsight*. Algen, Pa.: Schiffer Military History, 1999.

Parton, James. *Air Force Spoken Here: General Ira Eaker and the Command of the Air*. Bethesda, Md.: Adler & Adler, in Cooperation with the Air Force Historical Foundation, 1986.

Polmar, Norman. *The Enola Gay: The B-29 That Dropped the Atomic Bomb on Hiroshima*. Washington, D.C.: Brassey's and Smithsonian Institution, 2004.

Rhodes, Richard. *The Making of the Atomic Bomb*. New York: Simon & Schuster, 2012.

Rickard, J. "Boeing B-17C Flying Fortress," December 1, 2007. http://www.historyofwar.org/articles/weapons_B-17C.html.

Sakrison, David, and Jon Tennyson. "The Enola Gay: SuperFortress." Season 2, episode 1 of *Missions That Changed the War*, Military Channel TV series. Narrated by Gary Sinise, Sleepingdog Productions, Inc., 2012.

Savage, Dennis M. *B-29 Superfortress Walk Around*. Carrollton, Tex.: Squadron Signal Publications, 2011.

Searle, Loyd. "The Bombsight War: Norden vs. Sperry," *Spectrum IEEE* 26, no. 9 (September 1989): 60–64.

Serber, Robert, and Robert P. Crease. *Peace & War: Reminiscences of a Life on the Frontiers of Science*. New York: Columbia University Press, 1998.

Skiles, Jeff. "B-29 Pilot Report: Superfortress," *Sport Aviation Magazine*, February, 2014.

———. "Pretty Baby," *Sport Aviation Magazine*, July 2014.

St. John, Philip (author), and Mark Thompson (producer). *Bombardier: A History.* Paducah, Ky.: Assembled by Turner Publishing, 1993.

Stone, Andrea. "For Aircrews, A-Bombings a Matter of Duty," *USA Today*, April 17, 1995.

Sublette, Carey. "The First Nuclear Weapons." *Nuclear Weapons Frequently Asked Questions.* Version 2.18, July 3, 2007. http://nuclearweaponarchive.org/Nwfaq/Nfaq8.html.

Sweeney, Charles W. *War's End: An Eyewitness Account of America's Last Atomic Mission.* With James A. Antonucci and Marion K. Antonucci. New York: Avon Books, 1997.

Sweeting, C. G. "Not So Secret Weapon," *Aviation History Magazine*, March 2014.

Terkel, Studs. "One Hell of a Big Bang" (interview with Paul Tibbets), *Guardian*, August 6, 2002. http://www.theguardian.com/world/2002/aug/06/nuclear.japan.

Thomas, Gordon, and Max Morgan-Witts. *Enola Gay: Mission to Hiroshima.* New York: Pocket Books, Simon & Schuster, 1978.

Tibbets, Paul W. *The Tibbets Story.* With Clair Stebbins and Harry Franken. New York: Stein and Day, 1978.

———. *Return of the Enola Gay.* New Hope, Pa.: Enola Gay Remembered, Inc., 1998.

U.S. Army. "Patterns and Predictability: Soviet Evaluation of Linebacker II." *Foreign Military Studies Office.* http://fmso.leavenworth.army.mil/.

Van Kirk, Theodore. "My True Course," Lecture Series (transcript), National Museum of the United States Air Force, Dayton, Ohio (2012), http://www.nationalmuseum.af.mil/shared/media/document/AFD-140131-009.pdf.

Zed Merill & Associates, "The Last Heroes: Nagasaki: The Mission That Came Close to Failing," DVD, 45 minutes, 2010.

# Index

# About the Author

**Robert O. Harder** was an Air Force Reserve Officer Training Corps (ROTC) Distinguished Military Graduate, commissioned in 1966 at the University of Minnesota, Duluth, as a regular Air Force second lieutenant. A set of slightly myopic eyes set him on a course to Mather AFB, California, where he won his navigator wings. He was subsequently assigned to navigator-bombardier (radar) training, which included a four-week special weapons (hydrogen bombs) school. During the Cold War, he served in the 306th Bomb Wing of the Strategic Air Command, flying nuclear training sorties and standing Pad Alert, ready on a moment's notice to launch against the Soviets. Harder flew 145 combat missions as a B-52D Stratofortress navigator-bombardier in the Vietnam/Southeast Asian War.

Although a generation younger, the author has much in common with his subjects. Like young Ferebee and Van Kirk, farming played a strong role in his early life. Similar to then-colonel Tibbets, he is a multi-engine (piston/propeller) instrument-rated commercial pilot as well as an FAA-certificated flight instructor. As with then-major Ferebee and Captain Van Kirk, he was an Air Force bombardier and navigator. Like all three, he has flown heavy bomber combat missions from the Marianas, made his way across the Western Pacific using dead reckoning and celestial navigation (sextant), and dropped bombs on enemy Asian targets.

A retired chain retail executive and real estate investor, Harder is a freelance writer. He and his wife, Dee Dee, live in Chicago and at their summer cabin on Big Sandy Lake, Minnesota.